Translating the Jewish Freud

Stanford Studies in Jewish History and Culture
Edited by David Biale and Sarah Abrevaya Stein

Translating the Jewish Freud

Psychoanalysis in Hebrew and Yiddish

Naomi Seidman

Stanford University Press
Stanford, California

Stanford University Press
Stanford, California

© 2024 by Naomi Seidman. All rights reserved.

No part of this book may be reproduced or transmitted in any form or by any means, electronic or mechanical, including photocopying and recording, or in any information storage or retrieval system without the prior written permission of Stanford University Press.

Printed in the United States of America on acid-free, archival-quality paper

Library of Congress Cataloging-in-Publication Data

Names: Seidman, Naomi, author.
Title: Translating the Jewish Freud : psychoanalysis in Hebrew and Yiddish / Naomi Seidman.
Other titles: Stanford studies in Jewish history and culture.
Description: Stanford, California : Stanford University Press, 2024. | Series: Stanford studies in Jewish history and culture | Includes bibliographical references and index.
Identifiers: LCCN 2023040063 (print) | LCCN 2023040064 (ebook) | ISBN 9781503638563 (cloth) | ISBN 9781503639263 (paperback) | ISBN 9781503639270 (ebook)
Subjects: LCSH: Freud, Sigmund, 1856-1939—Religion. | Freud, Sigmund, 1856-1939—Translations into Hebrew. | Freud, Sigmund, 1856-1939—Translations into Yiddish. | Judaism and psychoanalysis—History.
Classification: LCC BF109.F74 S425 2024 (print) | LCC BF109.F74 (ebook) | DDC 150.19/52092 [B]—dc23/eng/20240130
LC record available at https://lccn.loc.gov/2023040063
LC ebook record available at https://lccn.loc.gov/2023040064

Cover design: Michele Wetherbee
Cover Photograph: Portrait of Sigmund Freud courtesy of Marcel Sternberger Archive © 2016 Stephan Loewentheil. Image concept by Nancy Rosenblum, Frisco Graphics.

Contents

Acknowledgments	vii
Introduction: In the Freud Closet	1
1. Crypto-Jews	17
2. A Jewish Rosetta	45
3. Surfaces	61
4. The Jewish Freud in an Age of Black Lives Matter	85
5. Touching, Feeling, Translating Freud	104
6. Psychoanalysis for Diabetics	134
7. The Yiddish (Un)Conscious	182
8. A Godless Jew in the Holy Tongue	209
9. Jews, Dogs, and Other Animals	248
Out of the Closet, an Epilogue	275
Notes	281
Index	331

Acknowledgments

This book is the product of a network of institutions, friends, family, students, and colleagues. But if I had to name a start, a lecture I presented in 2013 as a Shoshana Shier Visiting Professor of Jewish Studies at the University of Toronto might serve that function. Since 2018, I have benefited from the support of the Chancellor Jackman Chair in the Department for the Study of Religion (DSR) and the Centre for Diaspora and Transnational Studies and their directors and acting directors: John Kloppenborg, Pamela Klassen, Robert Gibbs, Kevin O'Neill, and Kamari Clarke. In DSR, Marsha Hewitt has been an enthusiast for the project and a font of knowledge of all things psychoanalytic. The Anne Tanenbaum Centre for Jewish Studies (ATCJS) provided a welcoming home, and its director, Anna Shternshis, was the best sort of colleague-friend. I send a shout-out to Michael Twamley in DSR and Galina Vaisman, Natasha Richichi-Fried, and Constance Chan at ATCJS for their warmth and patience as I found my sea legs. In Toronto, I was blessed with brilliant and knowledgeable student research assistants: In 2013, that was Noam Sienna, who opened the world of the Jewish press to me. More recently, Jacob Hermant, Eli Jany, Ido Moses, Miriam Schwartz, Cliel Shdaimah, Vered Shimshi, and Dikla Yogev supplied me with archival sources, searched for interesting images, and helped secure permission to use this material. Emily Pascoe twice reviewed and commented on every page of the manuscript, checking my sources, pointing me to the website "Hey Alma," and finding relevant passages in Freud I had overlooked.

In 2016, I was fortunate to receive two fellowships to support this research with the gift of time, a John Simon Guggenheim Memorial Award and a National Endowment for the Humanities Senior Research Fellowship at the Center for Jewish History in New York. In 2020–21, I spent a research year at the Frankel Center for Judaic Studies Seminar on "Translating Jewish Cultures," ably led by the brilliant Maya Barzilai and Adriana X. Jacobs. In both the Center for Jewish History and the Frankel Center I was surrounded by talented and passionate colleagues and friends, whose suggestions and comments propelled my work forward. There and elsewhere, I was aided by generous archivists and librarians, including Bryony Davies at the Freud Museum in London, Amanda Seigel and Lyudmila Sholokhova at the Dorot Jewish Division of the New York Public Library, David Mazower at the Yiddish Book Center, Ilya Slavutskiy and Vital Zajka at the YIVO Institute for Jewish Research, Dovid Braun at the Max Weinreich Center for Jewish Studies (the YIVO Education Department), and Gabriel Mordoch at the University of Michigan Library. These archivists, librarians, and educators, far from being zealous gatekeepers who barred my path, always opened doors to me that were otherwise barred, before, during, and after the pandemic.

I am grateful to the institutions that invited me to present this work at all stages and to the attentive and curious audiences who responded to it. These include Boston University; Centre Culturel International de Cerisy (Colloque Le Yiddish, l'inconscient, les langues); Chulent; Duke University/University of North Carolina; Graduate Theological Union; Harvard University; Johns Hopkins University; KlezCalifornia; Limmud UK; New York University (Mellon Translation Seminar); Oxford Summer Institute on Modern and Contemporary Judaism; Syracuse University; University of California, Davis; University of Chicago; University of Michigan, Ann Arbor (Frankel Center for Judaic Studies); University of Minnesota; University of Pennsylvania (Herbert D. Katz Center for Advanced Judaic Studies); University of Toronto; University of Virginia; University of Wrocław; YIVO Institute for Jewish Research; and YIVO Chicago. My research group on "Race, Politics, and the American Jewish Experience" at the Kogod Research Center at the Shalom Hartman Institute of North America, led by Rivka Press Schwartz, discussed my chapter "The Jewish Freud in an Age of Black Lives Matter." At these conferences, research seminars, and lectures, and over coffee and Indian food, a number of colleagues and participants provided me particularly valuable feedback (with apologies to anyone I have forgotten): Emily Apter, Zachary Baker, Maya Balakirsky-Katz, Kate Barush, Jonah Boyarin, Jonathan Boyarin, Zac Braiterman, John Efron,

Lucia Finotto, Rena Fischer, Ken Frieden, Kata Gellen, Abigail Gillman, Amelia Glaser, Miki Gluzman, Bluma Goldstein (of blessed memory), Alessandro Guetta, Liora Halperin, Dagmar Herzog, Martin Kavka, Max Kohn, Chana Kronfeld, Cecile Kuznitz, Ben Lerman, Shaul Magid, Roni Masel, Françoise Meltzer, Leslie Morris, Elly Moseson, Alex Moshkin, Ken Moss, Anita Norich, Stephen Portuges, Alyssa Quint, Arnold Richards, Malka Scheinock, Yael Sela, Mark Shell, Dina Stein, Karolina Szymaniak, Anna Elena Torres, Karen Underhill, Zohar Weiman-Kelman, and Kalman Weiser. The participants in the manuscript review in Toronto, supported by the Anne Tanenbaum Centre for Jewish Studies and the Department for the Study of Religion, helped me understand what I was trying to say. For that, thanks go to Elena Basile, Doris Bergen, Ronald Charles, Rebecca Comay, Michael Lambert, Ido Moses, Emily Pascoe, Robin Rogers, Vered Shimshi, Anna Shternshis, and Sherry Simon. The two knowledgeable and astute anonymous readers for the press guided me in the final stages. Deena Aranoff, my brilliant and treasured colleague at the Graduate Theological Union, was a pillar of friendship and support throughout this process.

What really kick-started the book were the three lectures that Daniel Boyarin invited me to deliver in April 2019 at the University of California, Berkeley, as part of the Taubman Lecture series. I am enormously grateful to Daniel for goading me to expand a project long stuck at around twenty pages into three lectures. The lecture series, held at the Magnes Collection of Jewish Life and Art, included a reception, catered by Janice MacMillan, with a delicious, bounteous, and witty buffet table of Viennese and Eastern European Jewish food. It was at the last of these lectures that Rachel Biale (who ably publicized the event and filled the room) presented me with the crown jewel of my Freudiana collection—a Seidman-Freud mug with the image, designed by Nancy Rosenblum of Frisco Graphics, that also appeared on the lecture poster.

At Stanford University Press, David Biale and Sarah Abravaya Stein helped me find a place for the manuscript, and Margo Irvin, Cindy Lim, Cynthia Lindlof, and Tim Roberts ably guided the manuscript into print. At home, the love and company of John Schott, Ezra Schott, Bungie, Vanessa, and Mooch (short for Moochkala) kept me going.

This book is dedicated, with *derekh erets* and love, to David Biale, a generous, wise, and *mentshlikh* friend, who has been my guiding light for decades.

Translating the Jewish Freud

Introduction
In the Freud Closet

An introduction is often the occasion for authors to recount how they came up with the idea for a book. My first book, on the sexual dimension of the Hebrew-Yiddish language divide (a theme also touched on in this book), emerged from a class Aaron Lansky offered during the long-ago summer I worked as a college intern at the Yiddish Book Center. The seed for my most recent book, about the Orthodox girls' school network Bais Yaakov, was planted one Friday afternoon in 2010, when I happened to meet a group of Bais Yaakov students in the courtyard of a synagogue in Krakow. Alas, for this book, I have no memory at all of an initial flash that sparked the project. In the ten years or so (but who remembers?) that this project has been marinating and simmering before finally—during the past year or two—coming to a boil, writing a book about Freud and Jewish languages meant mostly that those around me had go-to gifts for birthdays and other occasions: I am now in possession of a broad if still incomplete range of Freudiana, including Freudian refrigerator magnets (both the Freud Magnetic Poetry Kit and the dress-up Freud doll, with couch), a Freud finger puppet (with bespectacled eyes tragically chewed off by our dog), Freudian Post-its, Freudian slippers, a Pink Freud T-shirt, a Freud planter pot, a Freud pen with sliding couch (acquired from the Freud Museum in London), and a bespoke mug (courtesy of Rachel Biale) with the image that graces the cover of this book. The closet off our living room that became a pandemic home office, in which I stored much of this collection and wrote most of this book, is known to the members of my household as "the Freud closet." In a memorial poem, W. H. Auden wrote that after his death Freud had gone from being a person to becoming "a climate of opinion." But even Auden might not have guessed that Freud would also go on to become a subgenre of tchotchke. As a rough gauge of the popularity of Freud within this genre, the Unemployed Philosophers Guild lists only six Jesus items (for instance, the "Jesus Shaves" mug, which "when you pour in hot liquid, a miracle transpires—His beard gradually vanishes before your very eyes!") to Freud's twenty-one.[1] For those alert to the Freudian resonances of everything and anything, it will not have escaped attention that assembled in my closet is a low-budget, kitsch, secular version of the "gods and idols" that crowded the surfaces of Freud's own office and treatment room.

As do these rooms, the Freud closet also has a few hundred books, either by or about Freud—far from any kind of complete selection. The rarest and most prized of these books are the long-out-of-print Hebrew and Yiddish translations of Freud's work that constitute a prime focus of the present research project. These, like Freud's antiquities, arrived at their destination from far afield. Itzik Gottesman, a Yiddish folklorist at the University of Texas, generously mailed me a copy of the first edition of Sarah Lerman's 1928 Yiddish translation of *Group Psychology and the Analysis of the Ego* that had sat for decades in the family cabin in the Catskills; the pages, after the first fifteen or so, were uncut—no surprise, really. Miriam Borden, a doctoral student at the University of Toronto, was kind enough to send me a copy of the second edition (also issued in 1928) that she found in one of the boxes housing the contents of a defunct Jewish socialist library in Toronto; as the borrowers' card attests, the book had last been due on February 19, 1948. I paid thirty-five shekels, a steal, for my first acquisition in this area, a tattered copy of Yehudah Dwossis's Hebrew *Totem and Taboo* (1939), at the Book Gallery, a used bookstore in Jerusalem. The boxed set of M. Brachyahu's 1959 Hebrew translation of *The Interpretation of Dreams* in two volumes (with a third volume devoted to Brachyahu's explication of psychoanalysis), beautiful blue-green dust jackets intact, turned up a few years later in a Tel Aviv bookstore; the staff of the Naomi Prawdar Yiddish Program at Tel Aviv University generously offered to mail the set—too bulky for carry-on—to California, and then, after it was lost in transit for six months (during which I grievously mourned it) and then miraculously returned to sender, mailed it again. A few others, no less precious for that, came from eBay. The biggest treasure, Max Weinreich's Yiddish *Introductory Lectures on Psychoanalysis*, I have only in PDF form, though I have laid eyes and (careful) hands on physical copies in the Reading Room of the Center for Jewish History in New York and at the Jewish Historical Institute in Warsaw. But I do own a pristine copy, acquired from the Yiddish Book Center, of Weinreich's 1935 *The Path to Our Youth*, the most interesting and important of the Hebrew and Yiddish psychoanalytically inflected works published during Freud's lifetime. These books constitute the core of the research collection I acquired in order to write my book. Unless it is the case that I wrote this book as justification for acquiring such a collection.

Walter Benjamin might have thought so. In his essay "Unpacking My Library," he touched on the bliss of the book collector, asserting that "no one has had a greater sense of wellbeing than the man who carries on his disreputable existence in the mask of Spitzweg's 'Bookworm.'"[2] As do Benjamin's books, my books hold the pleasurable memories of "the cities where I found so many things," which include, for Benjamin, "a musty book cellar in North Berlin" and the "student den in Munich" where he immersed himself in some of the books.[3] But the pleasure of collection, Benjamin acknowledges, hardly depends on reading. A collector has "a relationship to objects which does not emphasize their functional, utilitarian value—that is, their usefulness—but studies and loves them as the scene, the stage, of their fate."[4] I did eventually put these books to use, but the title of this Introduction is designed to signal also "the scene, the stage, of their fate," their place in the world, in my world.

I am well aware, of course, that the phrase "the closet" in the title of this Introduction may well be taken more metaphorically than I intend, conjuring a host of academic assumptions that all suggest that this book, like so many that preceded it, will demonstrate that Freud inhabited a "Jewish closet," which is to say, that he hid his Jewishness in the interest of promoting psychoanalysis as free from the taint of Jewish associations or because he felt ambivalent about his own Jewishness. This has been the central insight in a range of Jewish studies scholarly monographs on Freud, whether or not they used the term "closet" (many did). In the 1990s, under the influence of postcolonial studies and queer theory, this became a major interpretive principle for understanding Freud. In the view of such scholars as Daniel Boyarin, Jay Geller, Sander Gilman, and Ann Pellegrini, psychoanalysis emerged not from the center of European thought (despite its Viennese birthplace) but from its (internal) colonial margins; accordingly, Freud's "decentering" of the human psyche emerged from the double consciousness that is a primary effect of colonialism, in which the subjectivity of the colonized is alienated and split by the colonial gaze (a psychological insight associated most strongly with Frantz Fanon in *Black Skin, White Masks*). As Boyarin puts it,

> Before Fanon, Freud seemed to realize that the "colonized as constructed by colonialist ideology is the very figure of the divided subject [that] psychoanalytic theory [posits] to refute humanism's myth of the unified self" (Parry 29). In a profound sense, "humanism's myth" is a colonial myth. It follows that psychoanalysis is *au fond* not so much a Jewish science as a science of the doubled colonized subject—more perhaps than its practitioners have realized or conceded.[5]

Queer theory plays an important role in conceptualizing the position of the Jewish "doubled colonized subject," given that the colonial perspective on Jewish difference (particularly circumcision and Jewish gender roles) feminized and sexually stigmatized Jewish men. It was in this context that Eve Kosofsky Sedgwick's *Epistemology of the Closet* (1990), which itself explores the salience of the analogies between the homosexual and Jewish closets, contributed valuable tools for understanding the intersubjective and unstable terrain of Jewish visibility, concealment, avowal, recognition, and negation in Freud's work.[6] Gilman, working through this complicated knot of sex and Jewishness, argues in a number of works that Freud's most distinctive theories about sexuality and gender differences, for instance, the role of penis envy in constructing female identity, by "recoding race as gender" serve as a universalizing cover for the sexual anxieties of Jewish men within a culture that feminized them: "Thus for Freud every move concerning the articulation of human sexuality responds to his desire to resist the charges of his own specificity by either projecting the sense of his own sexual difference onto other groups, such as women, or by universalizing the attack on Jewish particularism, mirrored in the particularism of the Jew's body."[7] Even when Freud talked about circumcision without "recoding" it to refer to women, these references are sometimes so indirect that Boyarin can claim that Freud "discursively hid or closeted his circumcision," for instance, in the little Hans case study, by speaking of it as if it were not his own body being described by the term. Nor could Freud's apparently direct assertions of his own Jewishness fully release him from the Jewish closet, since

> uncloseting this identity would not result in an automatic dissolving of the toxic energy of the anti-Semitic, misogynistic, and homophobic

imagery (Dean). Rather, "coming out" is perhaps a prophylactic, a way of defending oneself from full participation in the most noxious forms of that discourse. In this respect, Freud hides in, and sometimes emerges from, the queer and Jewish closets of his time.[8]

By now, the "Jewish closet" is so ubiquitous a concept that a reader would be forgiven for assuming that this book, too, aims to explore these familiar themes.[9] To take up residence in a closet stocked with Freud's writings, writings about "the Jewish Freud," and translations of his work into Jewish languages may be to invite the production of a book that is structured more or less as a metaphorical Jewish closet and that does the work of "outing" the Jewish Freud (again). So I will say at the outset that although I find much of the literature on the "Jewish closet" illuminating and compelling, early on in my thinking about this book I resolved to try a different path. My Freud closet holds precious translations of his work into Hebrew and Yiddish, works concealed only in the sense that few in the world of psychoanalysis (including Freud) can read them. But this does not make it a closet where Jewishness is concealed—quite the contrary. These translations, with their different script and greater age than most of the books with which they rub shoulders, despite being *in* a closet are not themselves a closet, unless they are a different sort of closet; and I do not claim that they supply a key by which to read the concealed Jewishness of Freud's work. These books instead allow me to avoid the almost too attractive and powerful framing of the Jewish closet, given that their Jewishness hardly needs hunting down. Rather than hidden depths, the object of my study is accordingly surfaces, affects, and touch: surfaces that hold material objects marked as Jewish, affects that traverse these objects, and the touch that brings these domains together. This approach, as it turns out, also owes something to Kosofsky Sedgwick, not as an explorer of the Jewish and queer closets but in this case as a pioneer of "surface reading" and affect theory. Surface reading—exploring "what is *beside* rather than what is *beneath* or *behind*"—allows her to find "some ways around the topos of depth or hiddenness, typically followed by a drama of exposure, that has been such a staple of critical work of the past four decades."[10] Nowhere is this more true, it could be argued, than in studies of Freud's Jewishness, which in this way are archetypes of the "drama of exposure." In keeping with its avoidance of academic argumentation, attention to objects, touch, and affect is not meant to challenge or displace "paranoid" or "symptomatic" readings. Rather, the surface functions as a supplement, building on an awareness that our well-established, disciplinarily inculcated suspicious habits about how texts mean and what texts conceal occasionally blind us to what they convey, for instance, as books that can be touched rather than as texts that must be "interrogated."

In Chapter 3, I discuss the surface-reading approach to Freud in detail—what it entails, and the peculiarity of applying it to Freud, who is generally credited with forging (along with Marx) the "symptomatic" hermeneutic style that surface readings avoid. So I will just say here that Freud himself had what could be described as a surface relationship with a few of the books in my closet, writing prefaces for Dwossis's Hebrew translations of *Introduction to Psychoanalysis* and *Totem and Taboo*, and a letter that served as a preface for Weinreich's Yiddish *Introduction to Psychoanalysis*. In each case, Freud made clear that he was unable to read or understand the Hebrew or Yiddish. The much-quoted prefaces to the two Hebrew translations appear in the *Standard Edition* (SE) and indeed are the only such prefaces to achieve this canonical status. The preface for *Totem and Taboo* begins with Freud's acknowledgment that he is someone who is "ignorant of the language of the holy writ, who is completely estranged from the religion of his fathers . . . and who cannot take a share in nationalist ideals, but who has yet never repudiated his people, who feels that he is in his essential nature a Jew and who has no desire to alter that nature."[11] Ignorance of the language in which it is written does not make Freud's relationship with Dwossis's translation any less meaningful: "It is an experience of a quite special kind for such an author when a book of his is translated into the Hebrew language and put into the hands of readers for whom that historic idiom is a living tongue: a book, moreover, which deals with the origin of religion and morality, though it adopts no Jewish standpoint and makes no exceptions in favor of Jewry." This passage, like so many of Freud's others, has been subject to symptomatic analysis, turning Freud's own hermeneutical key of "negation" against him.[12] Freud, in these readings, is attempting to hide the true extent of his Hebrew knowledge, as part of a more general strategy of concealing the depth and breadth of his Jewishness. Yosef Hayim Yerushalmi notes that Freud approaches the question of his Jewishness in this passage "*via negationis*, by a series of reductions" that reveal his ambivalence.[13] More generally, Yerushalmi believes that "the very violence of Freud's recoil against Jewish belief or ritual must arouse our deepest suspicion."[14] As evidence that Freud did indeed know Hebrew, Yerushalmi notes his insistence in a letter to Arnold Zweig on the correct pronunciation of his beloved dog's name,

Jofie—"Jo wie Jud." Reflecting on the meaning of this name, Yerushalmi continues: "Of all the languages Freud knew or could have known there is only one that makes sense. In Hebrew, Yofi means—Beauty."[15]

But to view Freud's preface to *Totem and Taboo* as a ruse to throw readers off the suspicion that he can understand the Hebrew letters he claims not to be able to make out is to miss what happens when we take Freud at his word. As with Poe's purloined letter, what we are looking for might be right in front of our noses, on the surface of the text and *only* on the surface, since it is the visible fact that Dwossis's work is in Hebrew, a script Freud can recognize but not read, that excites Freud's response. Even if Dwossis's translation is opaque to him—or rather, *because* Dwossis's reading is opaque to him—Freud's relationship with the book he is introducing is far from devoid of content or affect, and only the narrowest understanding of how books signify or how languages work would suggest that it is. It is the barest minimum of comprehension Freud claims: that the book is in Hebrew, that it contains his own German words clothed in Hebrew garb, and that there are readers who unlike him can understand this language, by virtue of their participation in the modern transformation of Hebrew from "holy writ" to "living language." The book Freud holds in his mind's eye, in the case of *Totem and Taboo*, or the page of (the proofs of?) the Yiddish *Introduction to Psychoanalysis*, sent by Weinreich, that "I held in my hand with great respect," is thus a book or page rather than a "text," and the feelings Freud describes in holding it are rendered not clearer but more puzzling if we suppose, with Yerushalmi, that Freud is only pretending not to be able to read its contents.

In this sense, the books in my closet, some of which were also in Freud's library, might be thought of as fetishes, not so different from those beautiful, fascinating, inscrutable objects in Freud's antiquity collection.[16] As objects rather than "texts," they signify in their appearance, in their visible and material reality. Writing about what goes missing in translations of Yiddish texts, Anita Norich points to their Hebrew script, "the physical and spatial relations of the text on the page."[17] These Hebrew and Yiddish books are fetishes also in the Freudian sense, defined by the way they combine lack and presence. This is the case for Freud, who could not read these languages but nevertheless thought and wrote about these books. But it is also the case, differently, for contemporary Yiddish and Yiddishists (including myself), in this post-Holocaust, post-vernacular moment. This is true, in Norich's view, for Yiddish translators, who are now responsible for making readers "feel *heymish* (at home, but also intimate, familiar), for giving them (back?) the home many of them have never known."[18] Zohar Weiman-Kelman similarly describes the losses "tied to the turbulent history of Yiddish [that] bind the language itself to a traumatic encounter with lack." Despite the risk of *fetishizing* Yiddish, the fetish, "as a figure holding both absence and presence," enables "an interaction with Yiddish content as a way of feeling lack rather than disavowing it."[19]

The powerful affects that stir Freud's words about Dwossis's Hebrew book and the ones palpable in Norich and Weiman-Kelman reflect very different historical contexts. My own feelings about the books in my closet are certainly not identical with what Freud felt about them: Freud was seeing his own thought, which he had expressed in German (a Viennese German crossed by and suffused with other languages), rendered in a Hebrew and Yiddish that I am willing to believe (contra Yerushalmi) he could recognize but not really read. The translations are old-fashioned, dense, and often clunky, but what I feel for them is hardly limited to what they say or how they say it. If Freud was moved at his own words in a foreign-but-familiar tongue, I am moved by what are in some complicated sense my "own" languages (one a half-lost "mother tongue," the other learned in school as a child) speaking Freud's words, a different but not entirely unrelated constellation of relationships. It is not the Jewish words but the psychoanalytic content that registers as the more foreign element to me, culturally if not intellectually. I wasn't raised on the Upper West Side of Manhattan among professors and professionals who spoke psychoanalysis as something of a native tongue. I grew up in a Yiddish-speaking ultra-Orthodox family in a Brooklyn neighborhood that I am guessing housed not a single psychoanalyst or analysand. Karl Kraus wrote that "psychoanalysis was the disease of assimilated Jews; Eastern European Jews made do with diabetes."[20] Despite my father being an Orthodox Yiddish journalist and an intellectual, it would be fair to say that my upbringing was among Jews who made do with diabetes, a background that contributed to my feeling an outsider to the field even as I plunged into writing this book. In other words, in some stratum of my psychic development I share something of the attitude toward Freud of his Hebrew and Yiddish readers in the 1920s and 1930s, and maybe even of some of his translators, who were generally untrained in psychoanalysis and had little connection to its formal structures (although Weinreich spent the autumn of 1933 studying with the child psychologist

Charlotte Bühler in Vienna, where he also established a friendship with the psychoanalyst Siegfried Bernfeld).

Freud was well aware of the resistance, dismissal, and outright hostility aroused by his thought among so many of his potential readers. He knew that many reduced his complex ideas to absurd and "wild" caricature.[21] He was also aware of all the people (Jewish and not) for whom psychoanalysis was less a threatening or daring set of ideas than a famous, fascinating, and fancy thing that was basically for other people: a famous and fascinating field, however, discovered or invented by a Jew. This, of course, is an absurdly superficial relation to the complex, brilliant, groundbreaking, rich insights that make up Freud's thought, and Freud can hardly be blamed for trying to resist such reductive readings of his work (even if they occasionally worked in his favor). But these efforts were entirely unsuccessful, in his own day and into ours, in which the fascination with Freud's Jewishness persists in both popular and academic circles, superficial and "deep" variations. This is certainly part of why I am moved by these particular material objects, the Hebrew and Yiddish translations of his work, and moved that Freud was moved by them as well.

I have no doubt that Freud's Jewishness contributed to my interest in the Hebrew and Yiddish translations of his work, giving the translations surplus meaning beyond the odd and fusty words on the brittle pages. But actually opening up and reading these books produced a whole new affective dimension to the work. It was true that I have never been analyzed and never troubled myself to purchase a complete *Standard Edition* (I make do with a conveniently searchable PDF). Nevertheless, I am in possession of a little collection of Freud books that almost no one else in the field has read, despite whatever store of Freudian knowledge they acquired that no doubt far exceeds my own. What I have, in other words, is not only a closet but also a niche, a little piece of valuable real estate more appealing for its location at the peaceful outer margins of the teeming centers of the dauntingly vast field of psychoanalysis. Like my closet, my niche is small, manageable, and cozy, combining *hygge* with historical pathos and a touch of humor. Having a niche (and what a niche!) reverses certain structures of exclusion: I, who even at the moment of completing this book still feel myself to be essentially an outsider to the field, had somehow found an unexpected and neglected corridor—a royal road—straight into the heart of the psychoanalytic enterprise. Only this feeling (or fantasy), embodied for me in a shelf of hard-to-find books I painstakingly, pleasurably procured, could have persuaded me to plant a flag in this particular terrain.

The translations also helped reassure me that I wasn't writing what one colleague of mine called "another Jewish Freud book." If indeed the Hebrew and Yiddish books on my shelf helped me escape this fate (the reader will have to judge that), the reason is that they offered a new frame for understanding the Jewish Freud. Taking as my research subject not Freud and his Jewishness but the Jewish frame around Freud's work constructed by others (especially his early translators in Hebrew and Yiddish) allowed me what I hope is a greater measure of self-consciousness about the Jewish framings of Freud and psychoanalysis than practitioners in the field have sometimes shown. Focusing on the Jewish interpellation-as-recognition of Freud calls attention to the desires and habits of thought of researchers, rather than (yet again) the purported Jewish anxieties and ambivalences of their research subject. By tracing the history of the ways scholars and translators have engaged with and constructed Freud's Jewishness, I am exploring the Jewish Freud at one remove rather than throwing myself directly into a game of detection and discovery. What I am studying is thus not so much Freud's Jewishness as the persistent desire to discover and engage with Freud's Jewishness, a feature that propels much of the Hebrew and Yiddish translation and reception of Freud's work and one I readily acknowledge as a motivation in my own work. Freud's Jewishness in this sense set loose what Gilles Deleuze and Felix Guattari call, as their revisionary (and surface-oriented) term for what Freud called the unconscious, a "desiring-machine," which does not so much "mean" as produce and *work*.[22] What the Jewish-Freud desiring-machine desires, obviously enough, is the Jewish Freud, a more Jewish Freud, a Freud who will speak his Jewishness; what the desiring-machine produces is translations and works of scholarship (my own and others) in which Freud's Jewishness is discovered, "exposed," explored, played with, and touched. This game, when played by academics, has a built-in source of pleasure (beyond the sheer pleasure of touch) that helps explain its "stickiness," its ability to retain players, which is that it places the Jewish studies scholar in the pleasurable and rewarding position vis-à-vis Freud as the "subject supposed to know" (to use Jacques Lacan's phrase for the typically American misunderstanding of what a psychoanalyst is). This desire is certainly a major component of the engine that drives my research (I can read those languages that Freud couldn't!), but it is also the subject of the research, given that along with riding I also explore this engine of Jewishness, this Jewish desire to make Jewish connections, to find Jewish "secrets," to touch the Jewishness of famous Jews, to signal one's own Jewishness to others, to recognize Jewishness in a stranger—desires that may be nearly coextensive with Jewishness itself in its social, intersubjective, and transferential dimension.

Translating the Jewish Freud traces the affective pathways, surface associations, and networks of relationship that connect Freud and Jewish languages, Freud's work and their translations into Hebrew and Yiddish, and readers of Jewish languages (a category in which I include myself). The phrase "Jewish languages" is awkward shorthand in this context, given that what constituted a "language" shifted over the periods I am studying, and given that the concept of a "Jewish language" is no neutral descriptor but carries with it a set of Jewish nationalist or ethnocentric assumptions I hope to avoid reifying. But these concepts of Hebrew and Yiddish as tightly associated with Jews and Jewishness, even Jews who could not speak or read those languages, are also an important part of the story I am investigating. Freud's lifetime spanned major shifts in the historical phenomena and ideological conceptions of Hebrew and Yiddish and in understanding the Jewishness of Jewish languages. The prefaces he wrote for Dwossis's and Weinreich's translations remind us that exploring Freud's relationship to Hebrew and Yiddish should not end, as it sometimes does, with references to his early childhood and youth, his father's Hasidism or Haskalah, his mother's Galician Yiddish, his family's Eastern European ancestry—the buried sites typically mined for evidence of Freud's authentic-because-concealed attitudes toward or knowledge of Hebrew and Yiddish. Nor is the only relevant context for discussions of his attitude toward Yiddish the views prevalent in Jewish and non-Jewish circles that characterized Yiddish as a grotesque and deformed jargon. Freud wrote this preface in 1930, during the last decade of his life, and in the period in which he was first being translated into Hebrew and Yiddish as part of a lively, mutual, and openly acknowledged engagement between Freud and the Hebrew and Yiddish cultural scenes. Hebrew, as reflected in the preface, is in some more-or-less remote but still meaningful sense his ancestral language as well as, more collectively and religiously, the "holy writ." But Freud makes clear that he is fully aware of the modern secular revival of Hebrew, a revival whose secularity and modernity are indeed signified by its capacity to speak Freud's words and express thoughts unbound (in his view) by any "Jewish standpoint."

These translations allow us another point of entry to the persistent questions of whether Freud's findings in books such as *Totem and Taboo* derived in any way from Jewish experience, either Freud's own or a broader cultural inheritance. Whatever arguments can be made on that score, and in particular about this book, however free it was of a Jewish standpoint, Freud had no doubt that its translation into what he recognized as a Jewish language had profound Jewish meaning. Freud's son Ernst reported that his father "always had a genuine love for Hebrew and Yiddish" and "refused to accept royalties" when his works were translated into either of those languages.[23] The "always" may be referring to Ernst's perspective, as witness to the later decades of his father's life. Nevertheless, it is fair to guess that the feelings stirred by the appearance of his words in an openly Jewish script involved not only the deep-rooted shame and denial that are a staple of the discourse on Freud's "Jewish closet," even if these, too, may have played a part. This shame, part of a broader spectrum of the shame of being Jewish in a culture that denigrated Jewishness, by the 1930s also evidently included the shame of not being Jewish enough, in the sense of not being able to read Hebrew or Yiddish. But shame, of whatever variety, is not the whole story: Freud also participated in and no doubt benefited from the culturally therapeutic attempts to transvalue Jewish languages. The Hebrew revival and the resurgence of Yiddishist nationalism are often studied through the writings of participants or ideologues associated with the revolutionary shifts in these languages. Freud's words stand as evidence that these language revolutions could also affect those further afield whose access to Hebrew and Yiddish was largely limited to their meaningful, opaque surfaces.

These affects, specific, contingent, and historically rooted as they are, are also contagious, collective, and thus intergenerational. Among "the hands of readers" that have touched a copy Dwossis's *Totem and Taboo*, with Freud's preface in Hebrew garb, are my own, though I avoid handling it, since the loose pages rain brittle brown fragments. I confess that I also long avoided reading it, for many years considering mere ownership satisfying enough. All three of the Hebrew translations of Freud's works by Yehuda Dwossis and two of the three completed volumes of Max Weinreich's (unfinished) Yiddish *Introductory Lectures on Psychoanalysis* are in Freud's library in London and so are among the small portion of his library he transported to that city (others went to friends or booksellers).[24]

My research begins from these books, but it extends to three distinct but interconnected areas: The first is Freud's Jewish languages, by which I mean the fragments of Hebrew and Yiddish within Freud's writings, his attitudes toward these languages as expressed in the preface to the Hebrew *Totem and Taboo* and elsewhere, and so on. The second focus is the Hebrew and Yiddish translations of his work and the reception of psychoanalysis among Hebrew and Yiddish readers. Finally, I explore the role that psychoanalysis played in Max Weinreich's Yiddish research on Jewish childhood and youth in Vilna in the 1930s, bringing this research into dialogue with Freud's own thinking about Jewishness. These are related not in the familiar structure of Yiddish and Hebrew being behind or beneath Freud's German but as languages and cultures beside one another that partly overlapped. The scholarly discovery and exposure of Freud's Jewish closet often entailed an argument about Freud's relations with Jewish languages, as in Yerushalmi's argument that Freud must have known more Hebrew and Yiddish than he acknowledged. My own approach to Freud's relationship with these languages relies on no such skepticism, beginning from the assumption that Freud described his knowledge of Hebrew and Yiddish accurately—both in regard to how well he knew these languages and in regard to how he felt about them. A focus on the surface of what Freud is saying allows us to move beyond a strictly referential approach to languages—that they are primarily ways of referring to the world—to other ways of understanding what and how languages mean.

    Most important for me, in this connection, is the "phatic" dimension of language, by which languages serve as means of establishing and maintaining connections within a collective, whether or not any individual "knows" these languages.[25] These connections, in my reading, involve not only the exemplary case of speakers in embodied conversation but also readers and translators and scholars who follow the phatic paths laid out through and by Jewish languages. Freud may also provide guidelines for conceptualizing language in this way, in using the term "the navel of the dream" in a footnote to explain why a dream (in this case, his famous Irma dream) could never be exhaustively analyzed, since a dream has a point of connection with all that lies before or beyond it, an "unplumbable" point of contact. For all the apparent mystical lyricism of the phrase, Freud was referring not to the inchoate pre-linguistic realms of an individual psyche but to the network of experiences, memories, thoughts, and wishes that at some point that can never be determined segues from the psyche and history of an individual dreamer to the world that lies before and beyond her. Language is a primary network or web that crosses and erases the boundary between the dreamer and the world that stretches out around her. By training my gaze at both the fragments of Hebrew and Yiddish in Freud and the languages as they appear, "whole" but "translational," in the translations of Freud's work, I find myself working within just this kind of relationship between a dreamer and a cultural world, an individual and a collective—a relationship that involves and negotiates both points of contact and zones of opacity. Freud's work is contiguous with the translations in my closet as a dream is with the language and culture in which it is dreamed, as individuals are bound together by a myriad of shared or half-shared points of contact. In this case, the point of contact that is Jewish languages.

Translation is clearly such a point of contact, involving deep entanglement and immersion. Translation, moreover, is never a mere epiphenomenon in Freud studies, marginal to the more central project of understanding, conceptualizing, contextualizing, and developing Freud's thought. Translations form part of the network of agents and relationships, in Bruno Latour's sense of Actor-Network-Theory (ANT), that together constitute the meaning, the reception, the phenomenon of Freud and of psychoanalysis. Drawing from ANT, Rita Felski pushes back against the largely unconscious assumptions that privilege original over translation, which is seen as a lesser text than the original, a distortion or betrayal of it. Felski writes:

> Mediation does not subtract from the object but adds to the object. That I discuss *Mrs. Dalloway* with my fellow students, read articles about it, buy a mug emblazoned with a Virginia Woolf quote, has the effect of making the novel more real, not less real. Art's power and presence are not attenuated by its relations, but made possible by its relations, which help bring it into view.[26]

From this perspective, the Hebrew and Yiddish Freud translations, my collection of Freud mugs and T-shirts, and finally this book constitute a network of relations, linguistic but also affective and material, that help "bring [(a certain) Freud] into view."

The nine chapters of this book follow a rough arc from a focus on the Hebrew and Yiddish in Freud to a focus on Freud in Yiddish and Hebrew. The first three chapters make a single complicated argument: Chapter 1 explores the general understanding of what could be called a pervasive ideology of modern Jewish languages, in which Jewish languages are viewed as lying "beneath" European tongues. As I discuss, this landscape has striking parallels with Freud's topographical model of the psyche as similarly layered, mutually reinforcing parallels that help explain the compelling ideological force of both models. Chapter 2 asks whether these might be interconnected rather than parallel structures, given that Freud's topographical model includes references to buried languages and given how heavily this model rests on the case of Anna O., who as a hysteric spoke a decomposed German "jargon" and as Bertha Pappenheim translated Yiddish into German. Acknowledging the seductiveness of the conceptualization of Jewish languages as inhabiting a stratum "deeper" in the psyche than European languages, Chapter 3 nevertheless asks what the notion of Jewish languages as "buried" might miss about their existence on the surface, whether the surface of Freud's texts or in the global dispersion of Yiddish.

Chapters 4 and 5 comprise a kind of theoretical bridge between the two major portions of the book, with the first focusing on the frame of Jewishness in the study of psychoanalysis and the second focusing on translation as a form of (Jewish) touch. Chapter 4 situates my book within the cultural and political context in which it was written, reckoning with the question of what kind of "Jewish Freud" might or should guide a researcher in an era of racial reckoning, in which understandings of (Ashkenazic) Jewish "whiteness" and privilege intersect in dynamic ways with questions about the meaning and value of Jewish difference, collectivity, and languages. Chapter 5 traces a lineage of psychoanalytic translation theory as a foundation for constructing a translation theory adequate to the study of translations of Freud into Jewish languages, a theory that recognizes translation as a form of intimate entanglement and affectively charged (Jewish) connection.

Chapters 6 through 9 are case studies of the problematic of the translation and reception of Freud in Hebrew and Yiddish, with a particular focus on the sorts of Jewish connections they embody. These chapters are perfectly suitable as stand-alone readings for those mostly interested in this part of the story and disinclined to swallow the book whole. Chapter 6, whose title is a reference to Kraus's witticism, surveys Freud's reception in the Jewish popular press in the decades in which his fame was growing. Chapter 7 focuses on the translation of Freud's work into Yiddish and the intersections between this translation project and the transformations Yiddish was undergoing during these same years. Chapter 8 explores the ways that Freud's work was "ingathered" and "salvaged" in the course of its Hebrew translation in Zionist Palestine during the years that Freud and his books were in grave danger in Europe. Chapter 9 explores a different kind of connection between Freud and Jewish languages, staging an encounter (that never transpired) between Freud and Max Weinreich, his authorized Yiddish translator, on the subject of animal phobias, which Weinreich considers a Jewish trait and Freud sees as an effect of the Oedipal complex. This chapter traces what psychoanalysis looked like when it openly took the form of a "Jewish science," as it did at YIVO, the "Jewish Scientific Organization." The Epilogue returns to the material space of the closet with which this book begins, taking pilgrimage theory and museum studies as approaches to explore the closet as an offshoot or replica of more "sacred" or "original" Freudian sites, with which my closet is connected through what could be called translation, or a "transfer of spirit."

In imagining Dwossis's Hebrew translation of his work in the hands of readers, Freud participated in a network of linguistic, social, and material Jewish connections that also traverses my Freud closet. These entanglements with another language sprang from but exceeded his own German words. In these translations, Freud was in touch with a navel that connected the Hebrew he had forgotten or never knew with the world of Hebrew letters and with the city that would preserve the translation composed in it for long enough for me to stumble on a copy in a bookstore. If a writer is alive to witness the "afterlife" of a text, as Freud was for these translations, translation reaches into a future the writer can dimly see, however opaque the letters might remain. Scholarship on translation, like translation (and indeed all research), reaches backward, but what it encounters in this case is a gesture that reaches forward to grasp the hand that reaches back. My own book is no *Totem and Taboo*, but its launching is yet another turn in these still spiraling, often interrupted, pendulum swings and daisy chains of words and hands and languages and dreams, which traveled and continue to travel across oceans and historical chasms, between Vienna and Vilna and Jerusalem and Toronto and Berkeley, where this book began without my realizing it was already under way.

1

Crypto-Jews

"You know nothing about me—you can know nothing about me."

"Be not sure of that, my friend; I am acquainted with many things of which you have little idea."

"*Por exemplo*," said the figure.

"For example," said I, "You speak two languages."

The figure moved on, seemed to consider a moment and then said slowly, "Bueno."

"You have two names," I continued; "one for the house and the other for the street; both are good, but the one by which you are called at home is the one which you like best."

The man walked on about ten paces, in the same manner as he had previously done; all of a sudden he turned, and taking the bridle of the burra gently in his hand, stopped her. I had now a full view of his face and figure, and those huge features and Herculean form still occasionally revisit me in my dreams. I see him standing in the moonshine, staring me in the face with his deep calm eyes. At last he said—

"Are you then *one of us*?"

—George Borrow, *The Bible in Spain: or the Journey, Adventures, and Imprisonment of an Englishman in an Attempt to Circulate the Scriptures in the Peninsula* (1843)

The colonized's mother tongue, that which is sustained by his feelings, emotions and dreams, that in which his tenderness and wonder are expressed, thus that which holds the greatest emotional impact, is precisely the one which is the least valued. . . . He himself discards this infirm language, hiding it from the sight of strangers. In short, colonial bilingualism is neither a purely bilingual situation in which an indigenous tongue coexists with a purist's language (both belonging to the same world of feeling), nor a simple polyglot richness benefiting from an extra but a relatively neutral alphabet; it is a linguistic drama.

—Albert Memmi, *The Colonizer and the Colonized* (1965)

So how much Yiddish did Freud know? How much Hebrew? Evidence of at least some knowledge lies buried in footnotes and private correspondence or parades in plain sight: an odd neologism in a dream; Yiddish curses in the posthumously published case notes for the Rat Man; references to recondite Jewish customs in personal letters; the *shnorrers* and *shadkhonim* that populate Freud's book on jokes; a set of the four-volume 1928 Berlin edition of the Babylonian Talmud (in the original Aramaic) in his library; a biographical report that Freud's mother spoke only Yiddish to the end of her days; a Hebrew poem addressed to Freud by his father.[1] This well-thumbed pack of cards has by now yielded a scholarly consensus: Freud knew more Hebrew or Yiddish than he cared to admit.[2]

It isn't just we, poking around after Freud's death, who are asking the question. Freud himself was beset by the curious. In February 1930, the American Yiddishist and psychologist A. A. Roback initiated a correspondence with Freud by sending him a copy of his recently published book *Jewish Influence in Modern Thought*, which included a substantial chapter titled "Is Psychoanalysis a Jewish Movement?" along with another titled "Jewish Founders of New Psychological Movement [sic]."[3] Roback inscribed a Yiddish dedication in the book, as the Freud Library catalogue attests (Roback also sent him five other books and two offprints of articles he authored over the next decade, including *Curiosities of Yiddish Literature* and *I. L. Peretz: Psychologist of Literature*).[4] Freud responded to Roback's overture by writing that he normally avoided engaging with reviewers and critics but was making an exception for Roback, who had struck in him "a chord of Jewishness." Whatever had driven Roback to write such a book and then send it to Freud, with a dedication "in Hebrew characters," Freud felt something like it, too. He said as much to the delegates from the local YIVO chapter who visited him in London in 1938, saying that he shared with them "a community of interests and emotions."[5] He told his Bnai Brith brothers at an event in honor of his seventieth birthday in 1926 how comfortable he felt in that circle and, more generally, among Jews. What explained "the attraction of Jews and Jewry," he wrote in the remarks delivered on his behalf (he was too ill to attend), were "many obscure emotional forces which were the more powerful the less they could be expressed in words, as well as a clear consciousness of inner identity, the safe privacy of a common mental construction."[6] What the *Standard Edition* has as "safe privacy" is, in Freud's German, *Heimlichkeit*.[7] Commenting on this rendering, Diane Jonte-Pace writes that "to bring Freud's terminology to the surface, a better translation of the phrase might be 'the canniness [or familiarity] of a common psychic structure,' which will also evoke the uncanny, since Freud sees *heimlich* as a word . . . which develops toward an ambivalence until it coincides with its opposite, *unheimlich*."[8] For Jonte-Pace, Freud's use of the term *Heimlichkeit* resonates with such other uncanny psychic phenomena as "fears of being castrated and being buried alive, death, the mother, and immortality."[9] Without denying the power of this symptomatic reading, I would add that what I hear in Freud's *heimlich* is the echo of Yiddish, the very language of (Ashkenazic) Jewish intimacy. For me, another way to translate or "bring Freud's terminology to the surface" is to say that Freud found Bnai Brith *heymish*.

Roback's book, with its Yiddish dedication, demonstrates his familiarity with the workings of psychoanalysis, remarks (as many did) on the preponderance of Jews in its ranks, and suggests various ways that psychoanalysis might derive from philosophical, psychological, or literary strands of the Jewish tradition. In a section on "Freud, Chassid (or Humanist)," Roback acknowledges that he is "not sure that Freud was reared in a Chassidic atmosphere or that much of the Chassidic lore so prevalent in Austrian Jewry permeated his psychological system," but he nevertheless suggests that Freud was Hasidic both in the "etymological sense" of being a kind person and in "the mystic halo surrounding his doctrines [that] brings it into line with Chassidism in its philosophical and historical aspects."[10] Those who assume that Freud was passionately invested in safeguarding psychoanalysis from the taint of Jewish particularism might be surprised to learn that Freud reacted rather temperately to this argument, perhaps because in this case it was coming from a position of Jewish pride. Responding to that section of Roback's book, Freud mildly objected to Roback's ascription to him of "mystical leanings," a charge he wryly remarked "no one has as yet reproached me with." But Roback was not entirely wrong, he added, since

> you will be interested to learn that my father actually came from a Hasidic milieu. He was 41 when I was born, and had been estranged from his home-town associations for almost 20 years. I had such a non-Jewish upbringing that today I am not even able to read your dedication which is evidently in Hebrew characters. In later years I have often regretted this gap in my education.[11]

As if to soften Roback's anticipated disappointment that he was unable to read Yiddish, Freud signed off, "With an expression of that sympathy which your valiant championing of our people commands." Presumably Freud was not clear enough in relaying to Roback how little Yiddish he knew (or how annoyed he may have been feeling about Roback's persistence), because in his next letter, a month later, Roback appended a postscript (quoted here in its entirety) noting Freud's presence on the Presidium (honorary board) of YIVO and taking the opportunity to press Freud again on his knowledge of Yiddish:

> P.S.—I was glad to see that both you and Professor Einstein have consented to serve on the presidium of the Yiddish Scientific Institute, to which I have given up a good deal of my time. It would please me to know that you speak, read, or at least understand Yiddish. Personally, I think the nation cannot exist without its own language, and besides, the treasures of our fine literature are worth preserving.
>
> If you looked into a little book compiled by I. Bernstein called *Proverbia Judaeorum Pudica et Erotica* you would probably be able to infer that anal eroticism is quite frequent among the Jews as a class.[12]

Roback's reference is to the folklorist Ignatz Bernstein's 1908 booklet, which compiled, transliterated, and translated into German 227 erotic and "coarse" Yiddish proverbs, an addendum to the much larger collection of Yiddish proverbs that was Bernstein's life's work.[13] Roback, having missed the mark in suggesting that psychoanalysis might be influenced by Jewish mysticism, swung rather lower in his second attempt at implicating Freud in Jewish culture, suggesting that the founder of psychoanalysis would find both fascinating "treasures of our fine literature" and ample confirmation of his own ideas about sexuality in the vulgar Yiddish proverbs that express Jewish anal-erotic inclinations. He was not wrong in thinking he might interest Freud in this material. Although Roback had no way of knowing it, in 1909 Freud had begun a collaboration with the classicist and folklorist D. E. Oppenheim on an article titled "Dreams in Folklore." Despite the general and anodyne title, the paper as it stands has only two sections, "Penis Symbolism in Dreams Occurring in Folklore" and (the significantly longer) "Feces Symbolism and Related Dream Actions." Shortly after Freud turned his first draft over to him in 1911, Oppenheim broke with Freud along with Alfred Adler and five others, and the manuscript was discovered only when Oppenheim's daughter put it on the market in 1956.[14] Although Freud was familiar with Bernstein's collection, he and Oppenheim took their material primarily from F. S. Krauss's *Anthropophyteia*, a scholarly periodical that collected scatological folklore from Central and Eastern Europe, with Jewish folklore from these regions appearing alongside the lore of various non-Jewish, mostly peasant populations. Beyond the long-lost cowritten manuscript, Krauss is frequently cited in Freud's other writing. In fact, Roback's suggestion that psychoanalysis might take a particular interest in scatological folklore came up in a 1910 exchange between Krauss and Freud, who responded to Krauss's question about the usefulness of his folkloric findings for psychoanalysis by writing that they lent support to the psychoanalytic discovery of anal eroticism, which had subjected the movement to ridicule "by showing how universally people dwell with pleasure on this part of the body, its performances and indeed the product of its function."[15] Roback, in other words, was right to believe that Freud might be interested in scatological folklore, taking it as more direct evidence for his discoveries than politer cultural artifacts. But while Roback sought to direct Freud specifically to Jewish scatology, Freud characteristically was inclined to view anal pleasures as a universal feature of human psychology (or at least prevalent in non-Jewish as well as Jewish Central and Eastern Europe).

On the question of how much Yiddish he knew, in his response to Roback's letter Freud had to disappoint his correspondent yet again, since "Yiddish—habe ich nie gelernt oder gesprochen."[16] Unlike many who put similar questions to Freud in the decades that followed, Roback took Freud at his word, adding a note to the published correspondence that Freud's use of the term *Chuzba* in the same letter, appearances to the contrary, was actually a sign of how *little* Yiddish he knew, since according to Roback he misspelled it: "Freud apparently had not seen this very common Jewish expression in print, or he would have written *Chuzpa*."[17] Despite apparently accepting that Freud did not know (much if any) Yiddish (although Freud does not deny that he understands it), two years later Roback appealed to him again on a related matter, asking him to contribute to a compilation of statements testifying to "the importance of Yiddish and its right to exist [*Existenzberechtigung*]" for a collection Roback was assembling in hope of breaking "the icy contempt for Yiddish among the Americanized Jews." Once again, Freud regretfully begged off the project on the grounds that "I hardly know anything about" the language.[18] Roback's urge to forge a connection with Freud through Jewish languages remained a driving force in their decade-long correspondence: In his last, unanswered letter to Freud, dated August 17, 1939, Roback confessed that "I have always wondered what your given name would be in Hebrew. You have surely been named after a relative. Would it be Samuel or Solomon (Sholom) by any chance?"[19]

My aim here is not to echo Roback's persistent questions about Freud's knowledge of Jewish languages or provide again Freud's responses or those that have emerged since his death. What interests me is the question itself: Why is Roback so hungry to know Freud's Hebrew name or how much Yiddish Freud knew, and why are so many others (myself included) still probing Freud on these matters? What is it that Roback wanted when he wanted to know Freud's Hebrew name? What did Roback stand to gain by learning that Freud spoke some Yiddish? What do these questions already assume? What is the *shape* of these questions? Why does Roback ask them so delicately? How can we account for the complicated choreography of his approach, the propulsive energy of this desiring-machine, its clumsiness, indirection, obsequiousness, persistence, pride, the chords plucked, the pleasures sought and denied and sought again?

Roback's book and the Roback-Freud correspondence are early expressions of what has become a familiar discourse—an academic cottage industry—revolving around, as in the title of Roback's book, "Jewish influence" on psychoanalysis or the more pointed question of his chapter title, "Is Psychoanalysis a Jewish Movement?" Roback's approach and that of the much more substantial body of scholarship that arose after Freud's death differ in two major points: Roback lacked access to nearly all the details about Freud's background and personal life that have become available since Freud's death; and Roback asked Freud these questions directly, while scholars now ask these questions about rather than to Freud. The correspondence that began when Roback struck "a chord of Jewishness" in Freud functioned on both the social and scholarly levels and thus stands as an early example of the academic engagement with psychoanalysis that seeks patterns of Jewishness, however constructed, in Freud's thought. The antisemitic denigration of psychoanalysis as "a Jewish national affair" and Freud's resistance to that claim are well-known.[20] What I am exploring here is rather the Jewish countercurrent to both these claims, driven by a desire to frame Freud through a Jewish lens and connect with him through shared Jewish languages. This is a desire that Freud sometimes welcomes (until he doesn't) and that he is not immune from sharing. The desire for Jewish connection, as Roback also shows, has a distinctly aggressive component, as if it were a Jewish right to know that were being expressed, a right to know that is resisted not only because of Jewish shame or "ambivalence" but also on the implicit grounds of a right to privacy and peace against Jewish assault. It is not only Freud's relationship with his Jewishness that is at issue in any of these exchanges and research projects. The narrative that posits that Freud is hiding his Jewishness is itself a narrative that has escaped critical attention, a scholarly desire to expose Freud as Jewish, or more Jewish than he will admit.

Freud is not, of course, the only target of this desire to discover, or sniff out, or unmask the (linguistic, social, cultural, philosophical, religious, "racial") Jewishness of acculturated Jews, the more famous, the better, just as Jews and antisemites are not the only ones who feel this curiosity. In 1988, *Saturday Night Live* brilliantly parodied this familiar and irrepressible curiosity with a sketch about a game show called "Jew, Not a Jew," introduced by an announcer as "the game all Americans love to play!" Tom Hanks, in the role of host, explains how the game is played:

> Now, let's take a minute to review the rules for "Jew, Not a Jew"! According to Jewish law, anyone whose mother is a Jew, *is a Jew*, so if an individual's father is a Gentile, and his mother is Jewish, that person is considered a Jew. However, reverse the bloodlines, and that person is NOT a Jew! But, for the purposes of our game, anyone with any Jewish lineage at all will be considered a Jew. Okay, now let's get back to our game! Hands on the buzzers now! Hands on the buzzers! . . . Writer/Producer/Star Michael Landon: Jew or Not a Jew?[21]

When the Johnsons guess "Jew," the host responds, "He was born Eugene Horowitz in Brooklyn, New York! Michael Landon is Jewish! Good, Johnsons! Ten points! Ten points."

Roback, of course, is not playing the SNL game "Jew, Not a Jew" about Freud, whose Jewishness, unlike Michael Landon's, is hardly in question. The game he is playing is a more internally Jewish variation on the one the SNL writers parody, which might be called "Just *How* Jewish?" This game, too, reveals its patterns in popular folklore and serious scholarship, shaping the Roback-Freud correspondence and, more broadly, social engagement between more and less acculturated Jews—"visible" ("Jew-y") and "invisible" or converted Jews, "valiant champions" of the Jewish people and those less inclined to publicly supply their Jewish bona fides. This game, as opposed to its variant in "Jew, Not a Jew," aims not to discover the bare fact of Jewishness but to find thicker and more satisfying signs of it, to put meat on Jewish bones by learning someone's Hebrew name or the extent of the person's knowledge of a Jewish language. Freud's willingness to respond to Roback shows that he was not entirely averse to Roback's probing, even as he consistently parries at least some of his questions. However much or little Yiddish knowledge Freud had or was willing to show Roback, no reader of the Jewish jokes in *Jokes and Their Relation to the Unconscious* (1905) could miss that Freud was well acquainted with the various pre-SNL incarnations of the games "Jew, Not a Jew" and "Just *How* Jewish?" and no doubt was called on to play those games on more occasions than the one described here.

The game I have been discussing has its primary location in conversation, gossip, or jokes, although it leaves textual traces in personal correspondence and social satire. The scholarly inquiries into the Jewish origins of psychoanalysis or the possible influence of Hasidism or Kabbalah on Freud's thinking take shape at a critical distance from these social engagements and their satirical echoes, transforming Jewish curiosity into academic inquiry and critique (critique in which the *scholar*'s Jewishness is neutralized and Freud's "neutrality" exposed as Jewish). But Roback, who participated in both the scholarly ("Jewish influence") and personal (the correspondence) dimensions of this engagement, might demonstrate how close this game in its scholarly form is with the game as played socially. The affective, psychosexual, and aggressive currents that roil the surface of jokes about German and Eastern European Jews sharing a train car might also help illuminate the Jewish studies scholarship that similarly brings together (academically) visible Jews (who may nevertheless hide Jewish "standpoints" behind more "neutral" scholarly agendas) with those whose work flies a more universal flag. In both cases, Jewish cultural capital and the ambivalent power of Jewish visibility are mobilized to discover and demonstrate the latent, indirect, unstated, denied Jewishness of a less openly Jewish writer, thinker, or public figure.

Among the most sophisticated and interesting academic engagements with Freud in this vein is Yosef Hayim Yerushalmi's 1991 *Freud's Moses: Judaism Terminable and Interminable*, which focuses even more persistently than Roback did on the question of how much Hebrew and Yiddish Freud knew. Yerushalmi, less old-fashioned and delicate than Roback and in possession of a trove of evidence to which Roback had no access, scoffs at Freud's demurral to Roback that his upbringing was too "un-Jewish" to provide him with the ability to make out Roback's Yiddish dedication:

> His education was "so un-Jewish"? After being tutored by his father he studied Bible, Jewish history and religion, as well as Hebrew throughout

his Gymnasium years with Samuel Hammerschlag, whom he hails as a wonderful teacher and to whom he remained almost filially devoted to for the rest of his life.[22]

As evidence that Freud's claim to be illiterate in Jewish languages is hardly credible, Yerushalmi takes a different dedication to Freud than the one Roback appended to his gift, the Hebrew poem that Jakob Freud inscribed in the family Bible, which he had rebound as a gift for the thirty-fifth birthday of his son Sigmund (called Shlomo in the dedication). Yerushalmi argues that it is plausible to assume "that one writes important dedications in languages the recipient is expected to understand, in this case even if it involved a little help along the way."[23] Nor is Yerushalmi prepared to accept that Freud was unable to read Roback's Yiddish dedication, presumably also inscribed with every expectation that it could and would be read: "Even granting that German was spoken in the home that Freud did not leave until he was twenty-seven, is it not reasonable to suppose that Yiddish was a lingua franca alongside it and that he could speak or at least understand it as well?"[24]

Roback was able to question Freud directly about whether he knew Yiddish; Yerushalmi clearly regrets that he lacked a similar opportunity. The "Monologue with Freud" that ends his book is driven by a "compulsion" to bring back the ghost of Freud in order to ask him about matters "that relate to your Jewish identity and some of which I believe you suppressed." What Yerushalmi particularly hopes Freud will finally concede is the character of psychoanalysis as "a Jewish science": "I think you believed that just as you are a godless Jew, psychoanalysis is a godless Judaism. But I don't think you wanted us to know this. Absurd. Possibly. But *tomer doch*—perhaps, after all."[25] Yerushalmi's turn to Yiddish at the end of this thought is a pointed flourish: the phrase *tomer doch* is among the "thirteen Yiddish words in the portions of Freud's correspondence published to date," and in Yerushalmi's view a particularly significant phrase, since unlike words like *chutzpah* it is "known only to Yiddish speakers."[26] *Tomer doch*, which Yerushalmi translates for his English reader (since of course Freud himself would hardly need such a translation) as "perhaps, after all," does double work: in its semantic meaning, it reopens a possibility Freud foreclosed, that psychoanalysis is "after all" (which is to say, Freud's protestations to the contrary) a Jewish science. Expressing this lingering possibility in Freud's own Yiddish substantially strengthens Yerushalmi's case. Echoing Freud's Yiddish words back at him makes it harder for Freud (or his ghost) to feign ignorance of Jewish languages. Although Yerushalmi never precisely spells this out, Freud's knowledge of Jewish languages lends substance to the possibility that psychoanalysis is in fact a "godless Judaism." If the scholarly engagement with the Jewish Freud is a sublimated expression of the social game I have been describing here, then Yerushalmi is a master player, an elegant strategist who amasses points by turning Freud's own (Yiddish) words against him.

The distinctive social rituals and academic engagements between more and less visible, literate, and acculturated Jews make an appearance in psychoanalytic literature, most directly in Freud's retelling of Jewish jokes of that type. As many have before and since, Freud takes Jewish jokes as expressions of a Jewish "character," asserting that "I do not know whether there are many other instances of a people making fun to such a degree of its own character."[27] By contrast, Theodor Reik's 1962 book, *Jewish Wit*, views Jewish jokes as expressions of the desire to restore a Jewish intimacy corroded by modernity, to "tighten again the bonds that begin to loosen" among Jews, and particularly between "visible" Jews and those who have been "fully assimilated to Western civilization."[28] As Reik sees it, more openly affiliated Jews mourn the threat to communal bonds they feel in the presence of assimilated Jews and try to rectify this loss by reestablishing a frayed Jewish intimacy, both within the world of the Jewish joke and through its telling. The phatic function of language described by Bronislaw Malinowski and Roman Jakobson, which establishes and maintains social connections, here demonstrates how Jewish languages might work to establish particularly Jewish connections—however fraught these might be. Dan Ben-Amos sheds light on how this aim is accomplished, describing orally delivered jokes as "communicative events" that, in the case of Jewish jokes, create a shared Jewish encounter between the teller of the joke and those who get the joke.[29] In Ben-Amos's view, which is closer to Reik than to Freud, Jewish jokes achieve their aims of temporary solidarity not by expressing a Jewish essence or relying on structures of Jewish social cohesion but in fact precisely by exposing the fragility of Jewish collectivity:

> Joke-telling is a verbal expression which manifests social differentiation. The fact that Jews tell jokes about each other demonstrates not so much self-hatred as perhaps the internal segmentation of their society. Recurrent themes of these anecdotes are indicative of areas of tension within the Jewish society itself, rather than the relations with outside groups. Apparently the proverbial social cohesion of Jewish family and society

generates a great deal of internal friction and reciprocal criticism, much of which is expressed through humor.³⁰

Reik's primary illustration for how jokes express both Jewish "social differentiation" and the aim of bridging social gaps (an aim achieved within the joke and achieved again by its retelling) is one that Freud also analyzed, the famous joke about the Galician Jew sharing a train compartment with "an unknown gentleman" who takes his feet off the bench opposite when the gentleman enters the compartment. A while later, the gentleman pulls out a calendar and politely asks him when Yom Kippur falls. The Galician Jew puts his feet up back on the bench, saying (in Reik's transliteration), "Asoi!" (*azoy*, Aha!).³¹ While Reik acknowledges that "there is certainly an aggressive tendency in the joke," he considers it misleading to overemphasize the aggression, since "the impudent behavior has as its aim not injury nor insult to the partner, but his lowering in the sense of equalization, in putting him on the same level as oneself. . . . The Polish Jew tries to make the other like himself, to treat him as an Alter Ego." Such "lowering" of a German Jew to one's own (Polish) level, Reik hypothesizes, may be akin to the sexual degradation by which some men treat women in order to render them "sexually approachable."³² Of course, what constitutes the lower and higher ranks is more ambiguous than Reik assumes: while the German Jew might have more class and social status in European society, from an internal Jewish perspective the passenger who needs no calendar to know when Yom Kippur falls might retain some Jewish status, if only in his own mind. While Reik focuses on what the joke exposes about the psychology of the Galician Jew, who behaves differently among non-Jews and those he recognizes (though not immediately) as fellow Jews, the German Jew is not as flat a foil for the more visible Jew as Reik's analysis assumes: He, too, may have complicated psychosocial aims to achieve beyond his expressed (vestigial-religious) aim of learning the (non-Jewish) date of Yom Kippur. He, too, might have Jewish "chords" a Galician Jew might pull. The gentleman may in fact be *bageling* his compartment mate, to mobilize a contemporary term defined by the *Jewish American Lexicon* as "1. Either trying to guess whether someone in your presence is Jewish or letting someone in your presence who appears to be Jewish know that you are too in such a way that will avoid embarrassment if you're wrong; 2. Inserting a Jewish phrase or concept into a conversation in order to indicate that one is Jewish or to determine whether the other person is Jewish."³³ Less-visible Jews, as whoever coined this term knows, have their own reasons for occasionally wishing to signal their Jewishness, at least to other Jews. A generation of Jewish studies scholarship, schooled to find *hidden* Jewishness, has regularly missed the way this game is played differently from the other direction.

I am not the first to focus on what drives Jewish studies scholarship to seek out the hidden or disavowed Jewishness of its research subjects. In a discussion of *Freud's Moses*, Jacques Derrida begins by praising Yerushalmi's "masterly decipherment" of Jakob Freud's Hebrew inscription, but the praise is ironized and qualified by Derrida's attention to the aggression submerged in Yerushalmi's insistence that Freud knew more Hebrew than he acknowledged:

> This true scholar wants also to give back to Freud his own competence, his own capacity to receive and thus to read the Hebrew inscription [by his father in the family Bible]. He wants above all to make him confess it. . . . Like Freud's father, the scholar seeks to call Sigmund Shelomoh back to the covenant by establishing, that is to say, by restoring, the covenant. The scholar repeats, in a way, the gesture of the father. He recalls or he repeats the circumcision, even if the one and the other can only do it, of course, *by figure*.[34]

Yerushalmi, in wanting to "give back to Freud his own [Hebrew and Yiddish] competence," is not seeking to denigrate Freud by bringing him down to his (more Jewish) level, as in the Jewish jokes Reik analyzes. He instead hopes to "raise him up" to a level that approaches Yerushalmi's own considerable Jewish intellectual capital. But what this nevertheless adds up to is that Yerushalmi feels justified in calling Freud back to the Jewish fold that (in Yerushalmi's view) he has attempted to escape by forcing on him a confession of his Jewishness—which Derrida views as a kind of circumcision. What I think Derrida means by reading confession alongside circumcision (as he does elsewhere), a circumcision that is committed and repeated "by figure," is that both acts—one the words wrenched from Freud and the other imposed on his body—inscribe Freud as Jewish through acts of symbolic violence (and in the case of circumcision, both symbolic and physical violence). In Derrida's view, Yerushalmi's attempt to "restore" Freud's Jewishness is another turn in a sacrificial cycle that began when his father brought him "into the covenant" by circumcising him, an event recorded in the family Bible that holds the Hebrew inscription. Yerushalmi thus joins Freud's father in performing a "circumcision" that imposes Jewishness on a dead man, "calling Sigmund Shelomoh back" to his Jewishness, an act against which he can defend himself no better than an eight-day-old boy.

It may be a symptom of this (sexual?) aggression that the game of "Jew, Not a Jew," in its social and scholarly variations, is so "sticky," retaining players from one generation to the next and encouraging repetition to the point of exhaustion. The question persists past the moment in which Michael Landon is unmasked as Eugene Horowitz of Brooklyn and retains its force past the point at which the answers to these questions—Jewish or not, just how Jewish—are supplied. Jews who play this game want to know what they already know, even if and because what it is they thereby know remains unclear. It is not only Chabad Hasidim on New York street corners who want to know if passersby are Jewish. A whole range of Jews, and not only Jews, seem to have an insatiable curiosity in this regard, as Eliza Slavet writes in *Racial Fever: Freud and the Jewish Question*. More-Jewish Jews (the Galicianer, the yarmulked) call out straying Jews, Jews in hiding. Jewish studies scholars, if my bookshelves stand as evidence, take similarly persistent pleasures in bringing Proust and Kafka and Benjamin and Freud "home," back to the Jewish fold, to the point of rooting them out and making them speak about who they really are. More hidden Jews understand the game and find their own ways through it. The pocket calendar and Yom Kippur, in the joke, are red herrings—mere mechanisms to establish that Jewish connection, to call on the calendar that once connected, that might still connect, Jews with one another.[35] Scholars who establish Jewish connections or expose Jewish secrets are already fully enmeshed in its logic. In this sense, the discovery of Jewishness is not a research finding but a playground for a range of Jewish practices and pleasures, a knot that cannot be untangled once and for all. No doubt some of the *grip* of this game is the pleasure it provides whatever the outcome, since it is the very probing that constitutes the pleasurable connection. For the prying researcher, there might also be another sort of pleasure in the permanent advantage it grants the scholar, the kind psychoanalysis has also been charged with wielding, of being a game in which only one outcome is truly possible, since negation is only another (necessary, symptomatic) stage in the inevitable emergence of the denied or unconsciously known truth.[36]

What is at stake in the question of how much Hebrew or Yiddish Freud happened to know is not exhausted by the contingent dimensions of Freud's biography, as an individual of whose earliest-known forebears were from the Galician town of Buczacz; whose parents moved from the town of Freiburg (Czech, Příbor) in the Moravian region of Czechoslovakia, where, according to Ernest Jones, "the Jews would speak German (or Yiddish) among themselves"; who had retained some or forgotten most of the Hebrew he learned as a youth; who could recognize Hebrew script but may not have been able to read Yiddish; who could exchange a few Yiddish words with his friends or converse more or less easily in the language with his mother; who concealed this knowledge or chose not to reveal it or revealed it only selectively or was forthright in acknowledging it or acknowledged it in misleading ways—whatever the case might be.[37] The question of Freud's knowledge of Jewish languages awakens and calls into play a much broader set of assumptions, desires, mythologies, and ideologies about what could be called the psycho-linguistic experience of Jewish acculturation. I have suggested that the question about Freud and Jewish languages has a *shape*. This shape is the language landscape that acculturated Jews are understood to collectively inhabit, in which Jewish languages lie "buried" underneath or persist within European tongues, however this encryption or persistence might be conceived. In his famous "Introductory Talk on the Yiddish Language" (1912) Franz Kafka reminded the audience:

> It is, to say the least of it, not so very long ago that the familiar colloquial language of German Jews, according to whether they lived in town or in the country, more in the East or in the West, seemed to be a remoter or a closer approximation to Yiddish, and many nuances remain to this day. For this reason the historical development of Yiddish could have been followed just as well on the surface of the present day as in the depths of history.[38]

The question of how Jewish languages lie beneath European tongues even as they are woven into their surfaces was of interest not only to Ashkenazic Jews, and not only in relation to Yiddish. Elias Canetti (1905–94), whose family took a similar path to Freud's from East to West, reflected on the peculiar relations among his own many languages; Canetti spoke two languages in earliest childhood—Ladino and Bulgarian—but he retained knowledge of only one of these languages after he learned first English and then German, the language of his adult life and literary production. Canetti writes that he heard many fairy tales first in Bulgarian, perhaps from the "peasant girls" who worked in his home, "but I know them in German; this mysterious translation is perhaps the oddest thing I have to tell about my youth." By contrast, the Ladino Canetti continued to occasionally hear in family circles after leaving Bulgaria was not similarly "translated" into German; the most "dramatic events, murder and manslaughter, so to speak, and the worst terrors have been retained by me in their Ladino wording, and very precisely and indestructibly at that. Everything else, that is, most things, and especially anything Bulgarian, like the fairy tales, I carry around in German."[39]

George Steiner (1929–2020), younger and more distant from a Jewish vernacular than Canetti, also provides a map of the many Jewish and European languages that formed the spectrum of his language consciousness, with Jewish languages taking a fragmented and peripheral place in and as the oldest stratum of this landscape:

> I have no recollection whatever of a first language. So far as I am aware, I possess equal currency in English, French, and German. What I can speak, write, or read of other languages has come later and retains a "feel" of conscious acquisition. . . . Even these three "mother tongues" were only a part of the linguistic spectrum in my early life. Strong particles of Czech and Austrian-Yiddish continued active in my father's idiom. And beyond these, like a familiar echo of a voice just out of hearing, lay Hebrew.[40]

It is hardly surprising that psychoanalysts, too, have taken an interest in the role of Jewish multilingualism in their own psyches and others'. The French psychoanalyst Robert Samacher, born in 1940 in Paris, distinguishes between Yiddish as "the language of my mother" and French, which he calls his "maternal language" (*la langue maternelle*):

> The language my mother spoke to me and rocked me in was Yiddish. This language was reserved solely for my mother while the language in which I chose to express myself with the rest of the world was French. . . . Yiddish, which characterized the particular bond with my mother, was repressed: I forgot it except in her presence, it was reserved for her. This allowed me to continue to associate its words and expressions with a certain sensuality, combined with a bodily presence. Yiddish, my mother's language, made me close to her, attracted me and was refused in the same movement. . . . Yiddish introduced an intimacy and a proximity against which I had to defend myself. I defended myself by answering in French, a language that allowed me to introduce a break between body and letter (being) [*et lettre*, (*l'être*)], between body of language and signifier.[41]

Eva Hoffman, born in 1945 in Poland, describes how her father would occasionally disappear for a few days and then return, "bringing into the apartment the invigorating aroma of cigarettes, his capacious leather coat, and the great wide world. Usually, my mother and he fall into an earnest conversation in Yiddish—the language of money and secrets."[42] Exploring the place of a Yiddish accent in the Hebrew and English testimonies of Holocaust survivors, Hannah Pollin-Galay argues that the "tonal" persistence of Yiddish in the Hebrew and English testimonies of Holocaust survivors casts Yiddish as a "shadow language" that marks the survivor as foreign in her present context, establishes the authenticity of her narrative, and functions as a potential "tool for enacting a verbal excavation process."[43]

These various psycho-linguistic portraits and self-portraits, to which many more could be added, confirm the rough outlines of a broadly shared modern European Jewish language landscape that might allow us to add nuance to the question of how much Yiddish Freud knew and to Freud's answer that he never learned or spoke Yiddish. Knowledge of a language is not susceptible to precise measurement; nor do languages have clear boundaries that distinguish one from another. The association of languages with national territories and borders spatializes and reifies them in ways that cannot do justice to the diasporic, shifting language worlds described by the writers I have cited. Rainer Guldin writes that languages should be viewed "not as radically differing self-contained cultural continents existing on separate shores or riverbanks facing each other, but as moving and constantly intermingling currents and heterogeneous interlinked archipelagos."[44] This insight, illuminating as it is, goes unnoticed because of what Yasemin Yildiz calls the "highly consequential political linkage between language and nation," which "relegated linguistic practices without proper names to the status of deviation, hodgepodge, or simply invisibility."[45] The link between language and nation that now seems so natural, Yildiz argues, is of relatively recent vintage, emerging in eighteenth-century German philosophical, political, and hermeneutic contexts. The contact zones that connect all languages through "constantly intermingling currents" are of course particularly fluid between the *Nahsprachen* German and Yiddish; it is partly this fluidity that led Kafka to remind his audience of "how much more Yiddish you understand than you think."[46] So, too, is Yiddish an excellent example of how linguistic practices might be "relegated to the status of deviation."

It is not only as speech or accent or lexical meanings that Jewish languages signify but also through their visual representation, that aspect of Roback's inscription that Freud did not fail to register and—to some extent—accurately decode. David Damrosch calls this kind of visually distinctive alphabet a "scriptworld," writing that "alphabets and other scripts continue to this day to serve as key indices of cultural identity, often as battlegrounds of independence and interdependence."[47] Yiddish and German grammar and speech might supply evidence of the interdependence of these languages, but the Hebrew script in which Yiddish is written declares its difference, "deviation," or even "independence" from German; and it did so long before this independence was officially declared by Jewish nationalists. Despite the very specific and even idiosyncratic linguistic conditions of their own psychic development, both Canetti and Steiner gesture to the larger social language worlds they inhabit, for the languages of an individual are of course never the individual's alone—they come from elsewhere, whether this elsewhere is the Jewish family or the gentile street, and are shared as part of the intersubjective and sociocultural character of language itself. As Steiner writes, "the "polyglot matrix" in which he was raised "was far more than a hazard of private condition. It organized, it imprinted on my grasp of personal identity, the formidably complex, resourceful cast of feeling of Central European and Judaic humanism."[48]

I would suggest that what reverberates in the question of Freud's knowledge of Jewish languages is itself a distinguishing feature of modern Jewish linguistic consciousness, a myth or ideology about Jewish tongues and their meaning, structure, and interconnections with non-Jewish languages. This myth is what we know when we seek an answer to the question of how much Yiddish Freud knew, and which is shared by serious academics and jokesters, scholarly inquiry and popular culture. To summarize this assumption: Jewish languages persist within or behind non-Jewish languages acquired later—as a past that continues to reverberate on the surface of the present or as an interior or secret concealed beneath or within these other tongues. This is how the Yiddish sociolinguist Max Weinreich describes the survival of elements of Yiddish in the German of German-speaking Jews, despite many forces that worked to eradicate the language:

> But even after the [German Jewish] vernacular, instead of Yiddish, became the language of the home of Jews in western and central Europe, a remnant of Jewish idioms and Jewish intonations remained in practically every family.... What is the source of the endurance of a language that for nearly two hundred years was presumably no longer extant? This phenomenon can seemingly be explained in only one way: Despite the

administrative pressure of the authorities and the cultural pressure of the coterritorial majority, despite the domineering thrust of the Jewish leaders, Yiddish apparently remained dear to the hearts of western Jews. . . . The Yiddish language was still strong enough to transmit certain of its elements from generation to generation for six generations.[49]

What Weinreich does not add here is that the endurance of Yiddish in lexicon, speech patterns, and intonation is not only sociolinguistic datum but also cultural mythology, a feature of how German-speaking Jews understood themselves and were understood by others. In the 1850 essay "Judaism in Music," Richard Wagner formulated Jewish linguistic foreignness and difference as persisting for millennia: "Culture has not succeeded in breaking the remarkable stubbornness of the Jewish naturel as regards the peculiarities of Semitic pronunciation. . . . The Jew speaks the language of the nation in whose midst he dwells from generation to generation, but he speaks it always as an alien. . . . The general circumstance that the Jew talks the modern European languages merely as learnt, and not as mother tongues, must necessarily debar him from all capability of therein expressing himself idiomatically, independently and conformably to his nature."[50] Myths about connection between Jews and Jewish languages fueled antisemitic conceptions of Jewish foreignness to European languages, but they also invited reflections on Jewish attachments to "dear" Jewish languages and expressed themselves in Jewish and non-Jewish literature, sociolinguistic analyses and antisemitic screeds, jokes and folklore. This myth about a deep connection between Jews and "their" languages, according to John Murray Cuddihy, also expresses itself in psychoanalysis, as in Freud's discussion of jokes and "slips" in which Jewish languages feature or "break through." The myth or trope is not limited to Freud. A Jewish American joke Cuddihy retells captures the idea of a language that "slips through" an assimilated facade:

> A *nouveau riche* Jewish couple moved to a non-Jewish neighborhood, changed their name from Cohen to Cowles, and sought admission to a country club that frowned on Jews. Finally admitted, they show up at the Sunday night club dinner, Mrs. Cowles, née Cohen, decked out in all her jewels and a brand new gown. The waiter serving soup slips and it lands in Mrs. Cowles's lap. She lets out a shriek: "*Oy Gevalt*, whatever that means."[51]

This joke and its variations no doubt circulated more widely in earlier generations, but the fact that they are still readily understood today is testimony that the ideological assumptions they rely on are not entirely dead, even if the sociocultural fantasies, offensive stereotypes, or unfortunate realities they record (name changes, country clubs, shrieking nouveau riche Jewesses) are dated or obsolete: A Jewish tongue lies buried beneath the crust of languages acquired later, and Jewish words are liable to spring out at moments of stress, "exposing" the speaker as a Jew. This notion of a "primal" Jewish tongue is not unique to Jewish culture—it rests on more general understandings of how languages work, with distinctions between "mother tongues" (itself a profoundly ideological term), native tongues, childhood tongues, ancestral or heritage languages understood to be operating in a psychic "core," from languages learned later or associated with "outsiders" remaining on the "surface."[52] It is just such a general assumption that leads Steiner to wonder which of his three native languages is the most "fundamental," even as he allows himself to doubt the existence of a "bedrock" speech:

> In the course of a road accident, while my car was being hurled across oncoming traffic, I apparently shouted a phrase or sentence of some length. My wife does not remember in what language. But even such a shock-test of linguistic primacy may prove nothing. The hypothesis that extreme stress will trigger one's fundamental or bedrock speech assumes, in the multilingual case, that such a speech exists.[53]

The topographical metaphor of a bedrock language at the very bottom of a stratified multilingualism is a feature not only of the popular imagination or "folk linguistics." This same ideology implicitly underlies scholarly investigations, as in the geological metaphor that underlies the linguistic terms "strata" and "substrate," defined as "the persistent remainder of one tongue within another, the forgotten element secretly retained in the apparently seamless passage from one language to the next."[54]

The linguistic metaphor of languages as stratified, with substrates that persist below or within later-acquired languages, no doubt informs the more specific structure Weinreich developed in studying Jewish multilingualism, which distinguishes between "internal" and "external" bilingualism, which is to say, the two languages used by Jews (the sacred tongue and a Jewish vernacular) and the Jewish language alongside the one shared with "the coterritorial majority."[55] The implicit spatial metaphor Weinreich mobilizes is so familiar as to seem obvious or inevitable, but other conceptions are (at least remotely) possible: Polish, as one example of a language Jews shared with their non-Jewish neighbors, might be seen as inside the borders of Poland (itself, of course, a contingent, imagined, and shifting space) with Yiddish correspondingly outside both in its marginality at the edges of Polish society and in its international and diasporic reach beyond Poland. Different spatial maps are indeed occasionally proffered: Ber Borochov, in "The Task of Yiddish Philology" (1913), a manifesto frequently cited as the founding document of Yiddish studies, views the components of Yiddish (German, Hebrew, and Slavic) as arranged according to a slightly different topography:

> Ideas and relations pertaining to everyday life are expressed in words from German. The phenomena that arose from inner Jewish life are usually expressed in Hebrew. Forms and feelings of everyday life within the narrow family circle, as well as slurs and denotations of negative properties, are expressed in words derived from Slavic.[56]

While everyday life is expressed in Yiddish's German component, inner Jewish life is, not surprisingly, expressed in Hebrew. But strikingly, there are experiences Borochov considers more "interior" than that: in the "narrow family circle," Slavic reigns. God, Borochov points out, is not only named differently in each of these component languages, but he also has a different character in each "concentric circle": *Got* (from German) refers to the universal deity; *Reboyne shel oylem* (Lord of the Universe, from Hebrew) refers to the God of Israel; and *Gotenyu-tatenyu* (beloved God, beloved Father, with a Slavic affectionate ending) "expresses an intimate, childlike relationship to the almighty power."[57] Freud taught us to recognize the contours of a human father in the "almighty power" of God, the Hebrew God above all. Yiddish conveys the additional lesson that God takes many shapes, and at least some of these forms are tinged with the intimacy of family, an intimacy signaled by mobilizing the Slavic capacity to convey domestic warmth (and perhaps also borrowing from the Slavic Christian God). In contrast with Borochov's mapping of the three major components of Yiddish, which is trained on traditional or religious Yiddish, metaphors for post-traditional Jewish multilingualism generally rely on a simpler (if not impoverished) spatio-temporal topography, which places both ancestral and native Jewish languages within or beneath European tongues or those learned later. This implicit or explicit map, for all its apparent neutrality, is laid out on a field riven by charged hierarchies and value-laden binaries: Jewish/non-Jew, self/other, inside/out, deep/shallow, authentic/superficial, truth/falsehood. Jewish languages are those that express and embody the interior of collective Jewish life and the interior of each Jewish individual. Languages shared with non-Jews are correspondingly exterior or on the surface—with all that topography implies.

For all its currency across many cultural lines, this conception of Yiddish or other Jewish languages as constituting the interior of the Jewish self is of relatively recent vintage. A more traditional Jewish linguistic map places not European languages but Hebrew, or more precisely, *loshn-Koydesh* (rabbinic Hebrew, interlaced with Aramaic) as the prestigious "acrolect" over Yiddish, the "basilect." This structure manifests itself quite literally and visually in the published *Tales of Rabbi Nakhmen* (1816), in which the Hebrew translation by his scribe appears at the top of the page, with the Yiddish, the language in which Rabbi Nakhmen recounted the tales, below it. The hierarchy that normally assumes the primacy of the original over translation is here trumped by the more powerful hierarchy that rates Hebrew higher than Yiddish. What changes is not the relative position of Yiddish on the traditional or modern map, since it occupies the lower position in both formations. What matters is rather which language Yiddish is below and the quality of the "lowness"—what being on the bottom *means*. The modern map that places Yiddish below European languages (rather than below Hebrew) itself has at least two successive stages: In the one that reigned first, Yiddish was "low" as a despised jargon, as the language of the Eastern European unwashed masses, as a language suppressed in Western European acculturation, as a women's tongue.[58] But in its turn-of-the-twentieth-century nationalist recuperation, this lowness was transvalued—remembered and repeated in a different key. As the language of the "folk," Yiddish was viewed as the medium for Jewish distinctiveness, intimacy, and at-homeness; Jewish interiority came to be understood as the authentic site of Jewishness, with Yiddish signifying the marrow, the *mameloshn, dos pintele yid*. Christopher Hutton traces the "quasi-Freudian" reverberations of this discourse:

> The "language question" which confronted European Jewry under the impact of the Jewish Enlightenment has often been cast in the quasi-Freudian terms of parental imagery. It is a commonplace of Jewish metalinguistics that Yiddish is the language of maternity, of the "mother" (*mamelošn*, a "kitchen" language), whereas Hebrew is associated with the father, with male solidarity and learning, with God and therefore authority. Pre-Modern Hebrew has the authority of the written word,

Yiddish traditionally—and still today in widespread "lay" perceptions of the language—is associated with talk, with transience and with the everyday, the vernacular, the informal, the intimate. Clearly the rise of secular Jewish organizations, of Yiddishism as an ideology, the development of a modern Yiddish literature, the establishment of the State of Israel and Hebrew within it, has altered the structural relations between these languages. However, the essence of the ideology of Yiddish has survived untouched through to post-War America.[59]

The persisting ideologies about the "maternity" of Yiddish emerged from the historically gendered and quasi-familial relationship between Yiddish and Hebrew. The ideology of Yiddish, born within an internally Jewish family drama, persists "untouched" within a different structure, as an outsider or deviation within the map of national European tongues. To quote Albert Memmi, "colonial bilingualism is . . . a linguistic drama."[60]

Given the mutual entanglement of the national and the familial in such terms as "mother tongue," it is no surprise that ideological and sociopolitical dimensions of language should find psychological expression. The Paris-based psychoanalyst Max Kohn begins his (French) book on Freud and Yiddish by asserting, "My unconscious speaks Yiddish; that is certain"; but he explicates this apparently individual and contingent circumstance by noting its broader ideological resonances: "For many, Yiddish signifies the primacy of Jewish identity."[61] The place of modern Yiddish within the modern European Jewish psyche maps onto the place of the unconscious within the self, according to the topographical model of the psychoanalytic psyche, Freud's earlier formulation. But this is no mere analogy; Kohn's assertion emerges from a process whereby Yiddish lowness, in its various significations, is internalized, psychologized, and allotted a role in a Jewish-Freudian family drama. The language strata within an individual and the layered psyche are related not through formal correspondence, which requires distinctions, but in their overlap. Despite normally avoiding psychoanalytic terms "like the plague," Elias Canetti feels compelled to evoke the *unconscious* in reflecting on how his childhood languages have been "translated" into German (the language of his adult self, his exterior reality, and his writing) by some part of his psyche to which he lacks direct access:

> The events of those years are present to my mind in all their strength and freshness (I've fed on them for over sixty years), but the vast majority are tied to words that I did not know at that time. It seems natural to me

to write them down now; I don't have the feeling that I am changing or warping anything. It is not like the literary translation of a book from one language to another. It is a translation that happened of its own accord in my unconscious, and since I ordinarily avoid this word like the plague, a word that has become meaningless from overuse, I apologize for employing it in this one and only case.[62]

The unconscious, in this striking formulation, is an invisible translator, known only by the fruits of its fluent, effortless work, its skill at substituting for and thus erasing an original tongue. And indeed, translation, in its usual sense, is a process that suggests the workings of the unconscious, insofar as its operations are often enigmatic and invisible. To view the unconscious as the translator of a language that has been lost may be to view it as well as the encrypted repository of words that abide within it silently, as it were. Indeed, Canetti claims that although he forgot every word he ever knew of Bulgarian, some essence or aura of the language persisted for decades after he left Bulgaria as a child and was reawakened by a 1937 visit to Prague, where he felt an uncanny familiarity with Czech without being able to understand the language, and despite the fact that Czech and the Bulgarian he had forgotten are not mutually comprehensible. Walking around the city, he writes,

> As though enchanted, I went from courtyard to courtyard, what sounded to me like defiance was perhaps mere communication, but if so, it was more highly charged and contained more of the speaker than we tend to reveal in our communications. Possibly the force with which Czech words hit me might be traced back to my childhood memories of Bulgarian. But those memories had vanished, I had completely forgotten Bulgarian, and how much of a forgotten language stays with us I have no way of knowing. It was certain that in those Prague days various impressions made on me by widely separate periods of my life converged. I absorbed Slavic sounds as parts of a language which touched me in some inexplicable way.[63]

The affinity of Bulgarian and Czech for one another, embodied in Canetti's relationship to the two (distantly related) Slavic languages—one forgotten and one unknown—manifests itself on a psychic level deeper than the particulars of grammar or vocabulary, a realm governed by sound and feeling ("defiance"), phonology and affect. As Daniel Heller-Roazen describes this experience, "In Prague, Canetti heard not a language but an echo: the sound within one tongue of another that had been forgotten."⁶⁴ How different was that from what Kafka was hearing in Yiddish, in the same city that Canetti was later to visit? For Kafka, Andrea Kilcher writes, hearing Yiddish evoked "the unconscious and the forgotten of the established [*geordnete*] languages of the West European Jews." Yiddish not only "shadowed" the European tongues spoken by Jews; it also defamiliarized them, in serving as a reminder that all languages are composed of "*Fremdwörter*" (foreign words).⁶⁵ The connection between Yiddish and the unconscious is overdetermined: Yiddish functions as the "forgotten" language that haunts and shadows the other languages spoken by modern European (or American) Jews; as the principle of foreignness that unsettles and dislocates more "established" languages; as the intimate and "interior" language of European Jews; as the language of mothers over fathers; as the language of Jewish intimacy; as the psycholinguistic "bedrock" of modern Jewish individuals.

The psychic architecture that views the self as constituted by an inside versus an outside, a hidden private realm and a more public face, precedes and exceeds psychoanalysis as a mode of conceiving subjectivity: Gaston Bachelard, in the *Poetics of Space*, explores the isomorphism of self, body, and house, reading the anxieties of everyday life as emerging from an inevitable tension and overlap in (and as) every psyche between claustrophobia and agoraphobia.⁶⁶ Jacques Lacan, in his essay "The Mirror Stage," speaks of "fantasies that proceed from a fragmented image of the body to what I will call an 'orthopedic' form of its totality—and to the finally donned armor of an alienating identity that will mark his entire mental development with its rigid structure." This structure of the self "is symbolized in dreams by a fortified camp, or even a stadium—distributing, between the arena within its walls and its outer border of gravel-pits and marshes, two opposed fields of battle where the subject bogs down in his quest for the proud, remote, inner castle."⁶⁷

The ubiquitous trope that figures the self as distributed between a "house" or fortified castle (the body, clothing, character "armor") and what these fortifications enclose or house (the soul, the authentic person, the fragmented self) has specifically Jewish expressions. The distinction between inner and outer, naked and clothed, secret and revealed, is already deeply embedded in rabbinic hermeneutics and anthropology; Jewish mysticism, like other varieties of mysticism and esotericism, can hardly be imagined without this distinction. But the inside-outside dichotomy survives secularization, becoming a linchpin for the modern Jewish self-understanding encoded in the famous Haskalah (Jewish Enlightenment) slogan "Be a man in the streets and a Jew at home." That this imperative is also linguistic is clear enough from the 1866 Hebrew poem in which it first appears, Yehuda Leib Gordon's "Awake, My People!" The poem exhorts Jewish readers to learn and speak the language of their European neighbors (*bi-leshonam siha*) "who have erased from their hearts hatred and folly, and stretch out their hands to you in peace."[68] Whatever Gordon may have meant by recommending in this poem that his readers speak Jewish languages only at home, more fiery Jewish nationalists such as Moshe Leib Lilienblum (1843–1910) took it as unwelcome advice to "hide the 'Jew' in us (that is, our being Jewish), this contraband merchandise, in the secrecy of our tent, as if it were a disgrace for a man in the nineteenth century to be known as a Jew."[69]

The concept of a Jewish self hidden behind a European facade may also emerge from earlier and more traumatic historical experience. Yirmiyahu Yovel traces modern conceptions of the interior, isolated, and alienated self to the phenomenon of converso identity, in which the suspicion that New Christians were Judaizing exposed, if it did not actually construct, a Jew hidden within an apparent Christian, with the Christian functioning as a deceptive cover or protective facade for an authentic self. Yovel finds it not at all surprising that it was Saint Teresa of Avila (1515–82), daughter and granddaughter of New Christians humiliated by the Inquisition for allegedly Judaizing, who "more than any Westerner since Augustine, and before Freud (and Pessoa)—discovered and explored the inner mind . . . and she passed it on to rest of Europe. Her several faces and masks were linked by her attempt to penetrate into 'The Interior Castle' (the title of her major book)."[70] The line Yovel draws from the phenomenology of converso experience to the more widespread alienation and fissures of modern Western subjectivity may lend religious specificity and historical substance to Michel Foucault's related genealogy in *The History of Sexuality, Volume 1*, which traces a similar trajectory from the tribunals of the Spanish Inquisition and, more generally, the Christian confessional to Freud's consulting room in Vienna. Foucault argues that, contrary to popular understandings, Freud was not liberating prudish Europeans from the demand to conceal sexual matters but inheriting and reviving the religious demand of full confession, particularly of sexual sins:

> Paradoxically, the *scientia sexualis* that emerged in the nineteenth century kept as its nucleus the singular ritual of obligatory and exhaustive confes-

sion, which in the Christian West was the first technique for producing the truth about sex. Beginning in the sixteenth century, this rite gradually detached itself from the sacrament of penance, and via the guidance of souls and the direction of conscience—the *ars artium*—emigrated toward pedagogy, relationships between adults and children, family relations, medicine, and psychiatry.[71]

Although Foucault makes no note of it, confessional practices with deep Christian roots crossed over not merely into secular territory but more particularly into secular Jewish territory. If there is an unacknowledged gap in Foucault's genealogy, the figure of the converso may help bridge it, connecting psychoanalysis not only to the Inquisition but also to the objects of its most persistent interest and most intimidating scrutiny: Judaizers among the New Christians. These crypto-Jews ferreted out (or invented) by the Inquisition may thus be the spiritual ancestors of neurotic moderns on the psychoanalytic couch, compelled to speak their most profound (sexual and/or Jewish) truths.

As it turns out, Foucault was not the first to notice the resemblance between psychoanalysis and confession. Among the published aphorisms of Bertha Pappenheim is one that draws a similarly pointed connection, rendered more intriguing by what we know of her own place in psychoanalytic history: "Psychoanalysis is, in the hands of the doctor, like confession in the hands of a Catholic priest—whether it is a valuable tool or a double-edged sword depends on who is using it, and for what."[72] In contrast with Pappenheim and Foucault, who locate the echoes of the confessional or the Inquisition in the practices of psychoanalysis, Nancy Hartevelt Kobrin views the theory and practice of psychoanalysis as emerging instead from the realm of the victims of the Inquisition. For Hartevelt Kobrin, psychoanalysis reflects and expresses the phenomenology of the converso experience and its associated traumas, which produced a "reaction so delayed that when a scientific inquiry of mental trauma took place in the mid-nineteenth century, two of its most important founding fathers were Jews: J. M. da Costa, M.D. and Sigmund Freud, M.D."[73]

Da Costa, an American physician who served in the Civil War and studied the effects of war on "the irritable heart of the soldier," was indeed a descendant of Spanish exiles. Freud—who cites da Costa in *Studies in Hysteria*—was an Ashkenazic Jew who took an interest in Sephardic history, in common with many of his contemporaries. Jonathan Skolnik has recorded the fascination in nineteenth-century German literature and culture (Jewish and non-Jewish alike) with such figures as Spinoza and Uriel Acosta, whose resistance to religious dogma, *Innerlichkeit*, and ambiguous social experiences resounded in the modern era. For German Jews, these figures foreshadowed contemporary experience, in which "incomplete secularization that exacts conversion as the price for acceptance is tainted by the memory of the Inquisition."[74] As evidence of Freud's interest in the converso experience, Hartevelt Kobrin cites the correspondence Freud carried on in his student years with Eduard Silberstein in a self-taught Castilian punctuated with Sephardic references, as in an 1873 letter that complained of an unpleasant encounter with a Sephardic "ass of a bureaucrat . . . who can bray in his kind of Castilian as well as *Spaniolish*," which Freud glossed as Judeo-Spanish. While this descendant of Spanish exiles was no hero to Freud, he certainly respected the most famous of them, Spinoza, his *Unglaubengenossen* (fellow unbeliever).[75] Hartevelt Kobrin concludes that "Freud would merely pick up where the Marranos left off. His theory of the unconscious resonated with the idea of a 'hidden,' vulnerable self."[76] If for Foucault Freud is a belated priest-confessor in secular-scientific disguise, or worse, a Torquemada, for Hartevelt Kobrin he is the New Christian suspected of secret Judaizing who created a new form of thought from the trauma of self-concealment (and whose confession is sought by a range of inquisitive Jewish studies scholars).

The Freudian unconscious, Freud readily acknowledged, has many literary and historical sources that precede and inform its psychoanalytic conceptualization.[77] But among these must be counted the long and overdetermined fascination with a secret, "vulnerable" Jewish self, to be rooted out by the Inquisition, kept from public view by assimilationists, concealed within "private" correspondence while being excluded from discourses that aspire to universalism, or nurtured as the intimate seat of one's deepest being. John Murray Cuddihy, who relates the Jewish drama of acculturation to both the stratified psyche and the relationship between ego and id (a later development in Freud's thought), suggests that the distinctive structures and operations of the Freudian psyche reflect the social structures inhibiting and governing Jewish entry into Central European civil society, with the id and ego reenacting the Jewish desire to "pass" into gentile society:

> [A] classical genre of the Jewish joke, the inner structure of Freud's theory of dreams, and the public discussion in nineteenth-century Europe of the eligibility of the Eastern European shtetl Jew for admission to civil society—the so-called Jewish Emancipation problematic—all have the same structure: there is (a) the latent "dark" id or "Yid" pressing for

admission to consciousness or civil society; (b) there is the social-moral authority—the censor (external or internalized)—insisting that to "pass" properly into Western awareness or Western society the coarse id-"Yid" should first disguise itself (assimilate) or refine itself (sublimate)—in a word, civilize itself, at whatever price in discontent; and finally, (c) there is the id-"Yid" in the very act of "passing," its public behavior in Western public places carefully impression-managed by an ego vigilant against the dangers of "slips."[78]

Daniel Boyarin, reflecting on Cuddihy's "brilliant and highly influential (if disturbing) book," suggests that Cuddihy's views on Jewish moderns striving to pass within Western society emerge "from a position that fully accepts the mystifying European notion that there is only one civilization and only one civility, that of Protestant Europe. Knowing nothing of eastern European Jewish literature or 'high' culture, of *Edelkayt* [Yiddish, nobility of soul] or the *mentsh*, he imagines an *Ostjude* constructed more or less in the image known from the Borsht Belt."[79] The structure Cuddihy describes, Boyarin makes clear, must be expanded to include conceptions of Yiddish that associate it not with murky "darkness" but with the ethical sublime and to take other opportunities to recognize the world of *Ostjuden* from their own perspective. Not all these descendants felt the imperative of "passing into civil society" or of "loosening" collective bonds. The lowness of Yiddish has multiple connotations, reflecting but exceeding shifting cultural conditions; but, as Boyarin rightly points out, Yiddish also has its own heights, its own high cultures (and the high culture of Yiddish-language psychoanalysis is a primary focus of this book). The specifically Jewish tensions that Cuddihy sees reverberating, unspoken and unnamed, within Freud's stratified psyche might illuminate the development of psychoanalysis. But Cuddihy's analysis, and not only his, tends to view Hebrew and Yiddish from the viewpoint of German, as language fragments buried within the European tongue rather than as languages in their own right. If it is true, as Cuddihy argues, that psychoanalysis derives some portion of its structure from the linguistic landscape of European Jewish modernity, in which Jewish languages lie buried beneath European tongues, then psychoanalysis must take a different form in Hebrew and Yiddish translation, in a language that renders Freud from right to left, with the Hebrew alphabet determining the direction of the gaze.

2

A Jewish Rosetta

> Among the wonders of the joke is that it exists in a space between the "I," the sociocultural order, and the rest of society; it proves just how true it is that the unconscious is not a solitary resident in the individual psyche.
> —Itzhak Benyamini, "Jokework" (2007)

The previous chapter explored the parallels and overlaps between a certain ideology about European Jewish linguistic modernity and the stratified psyche that is among Freud's main conceptual metaphors. It is important to acknowledge, then, that Freud's conception of a stratified psyche is ostensibly drawn not from modern Jewish experience but from his lifelong passion for archaeology. Egyptian, Greek, Roman, and Chinese antiquities—displaced gods, fetishes, and idols—crowded the surfaces of his consulting rooms, with the exception of two kiddush cups spotted in a photo by an eagle-eyed graduate student in Jewish studies.[1] Lynn Gamwell traces the role played by archaeology in the topographical model of the psyche to Freud's boyhood fascination with the field, and in particular with Heinrich Schliemann's excavation of Troy; in this, Freud was participating in a much broader craze. As Gamwell writes,

> Freud's life spans the development of modern archaeology. When he was born in 1856, Troy was a myth, and looting ancient treasures was a profitable business. At the end of his life, in 1939, archaeology was a science, and national archaeological museums had been built in many cities, including Cairo and Athens. Earlier in the nineteenth century, geologists had begun to employ stratigraphy as a dating method, and Darwin's publication of *Origin of Species*, in 1859, permitted the assumption that man has a long history.[2]

As many (including Freud himself) have pointed out, it is inaccurate to say that Freud "discovered" the unconscious, which was implied, alluded to, or conceptualized in literature, philosophy, psychology, and folklore before him; but Freud's "topographical" and archaeological metaphors for the psyche are particularly rich and illuminating. The archaeological metaphor, which spatializes temporal phenomena, and the antiquities, which further reified and potentially fetishized the findings of the archaeologist, played a role in psychoanalysis from the very start to the end of Freud's long career, appearing in letters, case histories, and works of cultural critique and apparently playing an active part in clinical sessions as well.[3] In a beautiful and poetic book-length account of what it was like to be analyzed by Freud, the poet H.D. (Hilda Doolittle) remembers Freud repeatedly calling her attention to the antiquities on his imposing desk, "almost like a high altar, a Holy of Holies," as if he were attempting to find out "how deeply I felt the dynamic idea still implicit in them in spite of the fact that ages or aeons of time had flown over many of them" or to suggest by these "tangible shapes . . . the intangible and vastly more fascinating treasures of his own mind."[4] The notion of psychoanalysis as a kind of archaeological excavation, according to Donald Kuspit, "is not simply a dramatic device to enliven and adorn the discourse of psychoanalysis—a way of disseminating and even popularizing its approach to the psyche—but the major instrument of its self-understanding."[5]

The metaphor appears in one of the first case studies Freud wrote up, of Fräulein Elisabeth R., who was treated by Freud and Breuer for hysteria in 1892. In this treatment, according to Freud, Breuer "arrived at a procedure which I later developed into a regular method. This procedure was one of clearing away the pathogenic psychical material layer by layer, and we liked to compare it to excavating a buried city."[6] Freud elaborated in quite extraordinary detail on the similarities between the psyche of a suffering neurotic and "a buried city" in the famous paper he delivered in April 1896 to the Viennese Society for Psychiatry and Neurology, "The Aetiology of Hysteria," in which he hypothesized that hysteria was a response to the trauma of a half-forgotten childhood sexual assault or "seduction" (a theory he was soon to withdraw). The passage is worth reading in full:

> Imagine that an explorer arrives in a little-known region where his interest is aroused by an expanse of ruins, with remains of walls, fragments of columns, and tablets with half-effaced and unreadable inscriptions. He may content himself with inspecting what lies exposed to view, with questioning the inhabitants—perhaps semi-barbaric people—who live in the vicinity, about what tradition tells them of the history and meaning

of these archaeological remains, and with noting down what they tell him—and he may then proceed on his journey. But he may act differently. He may have brought picks, shovels and spades with him, and he may set the inhabitants to work with these implements. Together with them he may start upon the ruins, clear away the rubbish, and, beginning from the visible remains, uncover what is buried. If his work is crowned with success, the discoveries are self-explanatory: the ruined walls are parts of the ramparts of a palace or a treasure house; the fragments of columns can be filled out into a temple; the numerous inscriptions, which, by good luck, may be bilingual, reveal an alphabet and a language, and when they have been deciphered and translated [*und deren Entzifferung und Übersetzung*], yield undreamed-of information about the events of the remote past, to commemorate which the monuments were built. *Saxa loquuntur* [Stones talk]![17]

By now, psychoanalysis and archaeology are so mutually entangled that Freud's analogy is not merely transparent but nearly inevitable: the psyche is a site in which "events of the remote past" lie buried under layers of sediment; the psychoanalyst is a traveler with a shovel, rejecting the tall tales of present-day "perhaps semi-barbaric" inhabitants (which Alan Bass calls "an obvious reference to the descriptive psychiatry that catalogued symptoms without attempting to understand them,"[8] though perhaps the reference is also to the explanations of the semi-barbaric patient or her family) in favor of digging deeper; the visible remains are the symptoms that might with luck come to be recognized as the surface manifestations of a buried trauma; having enlisted "local inhabitants" to do the grunt work, the psychoanalyst takes on the task of decoding the encrypted language inscribed on these buried monuments to discover the historical events they commemorate. Sabine Hake identifies three distinct dimensions of the metaphor: Freud's "dependence on a model of stratification that obliges the analytic method to a strictly temporal-historical perspective; his emphasis on the continuing presence of the past, either in the form of repressed childhood memories or the legacies of antiquity; and his identification with the role of the archaeologist, who makes possible the return of what is forgotten or assumed to be dead."[9]

Hake also focuses on the curious detail of the multilingual inscriptions that pave the way for the archaeologist's interpretations of the events of the past, if he is lucky enough to find such monuments. Freud was clearly referring here to the Rosetta Stone, the most famous of the polyglot monuments deciphered in the course of the nineteenth century. The Rosetta Stone, a black stele discovered near the Egyptian town of Rosetta in 1799 that was covered in three different scripts (Greek, demotic, and hieroglyphic), enabled the French Egyptologist Jean-François Champollion to unravel what had been the persistent riddle of hieroglyphics, once he recognized that the same praise of King Ptolemy V was recorded in each language. In Freud's view, the psyche presents us with a similarly obscure pictorial script in the form of dreams, slips of the tongue, and illnesses, which encode traumatic memories or unspeakable desires in the "hieroglyphics" of dream imagery or bodily symptoms. The method for using transparent languages to decode unfamiliar scripts is laid out in Freud's case study of Katharina, an innkeeper's daughter who approached Freud during his 1893 summer holiday. Katharina's case elicited Freud's comment that he and Breuer "often compared the symptomatology of hysteria with a pictographic script which has become intelligible after the discovery of a few bilingual inscriptions. In that alphabet, being sick means [sexual] disgust."[10] Freud makes it clear that the bilingual scripts of an individual psyche follow their own unique and particular logic (it is for Katharina in particular that "being sick means disgust'). Despite the idiosyncrasies of these scripts, not only hysterical symptoms but also dream images are essentially writing systems, with discernible grammatical patterns and more-or-less-fixed equivalents building bridges between the less intelligible and more intelligible language. For Freud, "the interpretation of dreams is completely analogous to the decipherment of an ancient pictographic script such as Egyptian hieroglyphs."[11] If a symptom or dream image encodes and thus encrypts a buried trauma or childhood wish, psychoanalysis involves the decoding of opaque dream images or corporeal signs with the help of the more accessible or transparent equivalents with which they are linked.

If Moses was an Egyptian, perhaps the repeated references in these discussions to hieroglyphics signal that Freud is speaking here of Jews and their writing systems. If so, then the polyglot monument buried within Freud's topographical model of the psyche is a different kind of Rosetta Stone, one more indigenous to the Viennese Jewish bourgeoisie than the Egyptian stele housed since 1802 in the British Museum. This Rosetta Stone was the multilingual patient whose illness provided Breuer and Freud the initial impetus for their study of hysteria: "Anna O.," a name we now know was an alias for Bertha Pappenheim, was treated by Breuer from December 1880 to June 1882. It is a sign of the close-knit Jewish milieu of this treatment that Freud's fiancée (later wife) Martha Bernays was Pappenheim's friend and later also a relative by marriage.[12] Anna O.'s multilingualism, which played a role in her hysteria, was broadly representative of the Viennese Jewish milieu she shared with her doctor—the "polyglot matrix" Steiner associates with Central European Jews, in recognizing it as "far more than a hazard of private condition."[13] Freud was kept apprised of Anna O.'s treatment by Breuer and mined the case for the theory of hysteria he and Breuer were co-constructing.[14] Hysteria, rather than being an organic ailment (whether of the uterus, some other organ, or the nervous system) or the product of hypochondria or an overactive imagination, should be understood as a kind of signifying system in which trauma, desire, and memory are translated or "converted" into bodily symptoms; the "period illness" of hysteria is now in fact referred to as conversion disorder, adopting Freud's neologism.[15] While these translations connected events and bodies, they also involved language: Among the signs that a paralysis is psychogenic rather than organic is that it afflicts parts of the body distinguished and named in ordinary language, for instance, a hand; neurological ailments travel along different, less linguistically shaped pathways. Language is thus critical in the psychogenesis of these illnesses, as it is for the practitioners attempting to understand the (linguistic) logic they embody in the hopes of (linguistically) reversing their effects.

To review: Anna's hysterical illness began when she was twenty-one and nursing her dying father and manifested itself in a range of worrisome symptoms: a nervous cough, the alternation between "two entirely distinct states of consciousness," a squint, anorexia, hydrophobia, violent outbursts, terrifying hallucinations of snakes, contracture and paralysis first of the right hand and arm and then of her entire body, and profound disturbances in her ability to speak. The case study describes it in this way:

> In the afternoons she would fall into a somewhat somnolent state which lasted till about an hour after sunset. She would then wake up and complain that something was tormenting her—or rather, she would keep repeating in the impersonal form "tormenting, tormenting" [*klagte sie, es quäle sie etwas, oder vielmehr sie wiederholte immer den Infinitiv: Quälen, quälen*]. For alongside of the development of the contractures there appeared a deep-going functional disorganization of her speech. It first became noticeable that she was at a loss to find words, and this difficulty gradually increased. Later she lost her command of grammar and syntax; she no longer conjugated verbs, and eventually she used

only infinitives, for the most part incorrectly formed from weak past participles; and she omitted both the definite and indefinite article. In the process of time she became almost completely deprived of words. She put them together laboriously out of four or five languages and became almost unintelligible. When she tried to write (until her contractures entirely prevented her from doing so) she employed the same jargon [*Bei Versuchen zu schreiben . . . schrieb sie denselben Jargon*].[16]

Anna O.'s language disturbances, which affected her ability to speak German, also manifested themselves as a retention of or even increase in her fluency in other languages. As her jumbled German speech disappeared, "she spoke only in English—apparently, however, without knowing that she was doing so. . . . When she was at her very best and most free, she talked French and Italian." After her father's death, Anna O.'s condition deteriorated further, and she lost touch with reality to the point that she perceived the people around her as "wax figures."[17] At this point she spoke only English and could no longer understand German. "She was, however, able to read French and Italian. If she had to read one of these aloud, what she produced, with extraordinary fluency, was an admirable extempore English translation." Anna O. eventually recovered her ability to write, "but in a peculiar fashion. She wrote with her left hand, the less stiff one, and she used Roman printed letters, copying the alphabet from her edition of Shakespeare."[18]

Given how linguistic and "grammatical" Anna O.'s symptoms are, perhaps it is no surprise that their remedy also involved language. It was in the midst of this illness that Anna discovered and coined the term for—in the English that was her sole medium of communication at the time—"the talking cure" (which Breuer misleadingly allows his readers to believe healed her; in fact, Bertha Pappenheim's severe mental illness persisted for years after this "cure"). Breuer writes: "It happened then—to begin with accidentally but later intentionally—that someone near her repeated one of these phrases of hers while she was complaining about the 'tormenting.' She at once joined in and began to paint some situation or tell some story, hesitatingly at first and in her paraphasic jargon; but the longer she went on the more fluent she became, till at last she was speaking quite correct German."[19] It was in this halting speech that began with an echo that Anna O. found her way back to the origins of her illness, finally arriving at the very moment her fluency in German vanished and her paralysis took hold. She was sitting at her father's bedside and saw a black snake approaching.

She tried to ward it off with her right arm, which was draped over the back of the chair, but her arm had fallen asleep. In her terror, "she tried to pray. But language failed her: she could find no tongue in which to speak, till at last she thought of some children's verses in English and then found herself able to think and pray in that language."[20]

If Anna O. is the Rosetta Stone buried within the founding metaphor of psychoanalysis, there might be other languages concealed beneath the German, English, Italian, and French named and given their proper status in the case study, signifying or obscuring the "events of the ancient past." While Breuer does not identify the language in which Anna was trying to pray when language "failed her," Sander Gilman draws attention to the Jewish languages that Breuer does not quite name in describing her multiple speech impairments:

> Breuer, the provincial Jew as Viennese doctor, heard her German collapse into *mauscheln*. The syntax wavered, the conjugation of the verbs began to disappear, until finally she used only incorrect past tenses created from the past participle. This is, of course, a fantastic form of Yiddish, the language of the Jew that is neither German (the language of the assimilated Jew) nor Hebrew (the language of liturgy). Breuer sees this decay of German into Yiddish, labeling it as Jargon, the pejorative term that German speakers used when referring to Yiddish.[21]

Matthew Johnson reminds us that the term "Yiddish" or its conception as a full-fledged language, distinct from German rather than a dialect or garbled version of it, was hardly available to Breuer in this period. "It seems unlikely that Breuer intended specifically to invoke Yiddish when writing these sentences, but there is a strong affinity between his descriptions of Anna O.'s language and regnant understandings (or caricatures) of Yiddish at the time: e.g. that Yiddish is a 'jargon' without grammar and an unintelligible 'mixture' of different languages."[22]

Whatever languages Anna O. might have known and been able to call by their names, there is no question that Bertha Pappenheim knew Yiddish, as well as some Hebrew. Decades after the hysterical disintegration of Anna's German into "Jargon," Bertha Pappenheim became a social worker, feminist activist, and translator—from English and Yiddish into German. After translating, under the pseudonym P. Berthold, Mary Wollstonecraft's *A Vindication of the Rights of Woman,* Pappenheim turned to such early modern Yiddish sources as the *Memoirs of Glikl of Hamln* (a distant ancestor); the collection of rabbinic and folk tales *Mayse Bukh*; and the *Tsenerene*, the Jewish "women's Bible."[23] These were interrelated projects in which activism on behalf of contemporary Jewish women dovetailed with her translations of early modern Yiddish literature: Pappenheim's translation of Wollstonecraft expressed her commitment to the rights of women, and her translations of the *Memoirs of Glikl* and the *Tsenerene* were aimed at recovering German Jewish women's history for a new era and lending the denigrated Yiddish tongue the dignity of respectful translation. Through the attention to Jewish women and the practice of Yiddish-German translation, Pappenheim made a contribution to the German "Jüdische Renaissance," in which intellectuals mined tradition for resources that might explain their Jewishness to themselves and help their generation heal the alienations of Jewish modernity.[24] As Michael Brenner describes the Jewish Renaissance,

> In a new context and used for different purposes, traditional texts, artifacts, and even songs attained a new meaning and thus became new traditions in themselves. Multivolume encyclopedias redefined Jewish knowledge, modern translations represented classical Jewish texts in new garb, Jewish museums displayed ceremonial artifacts in a secular framework, arrangements of Jewish music transformed traditional folk songs and synagogue liturgy for a concert audience, and popular novels recalled selected aspects of the Jewish past.[25]

Pappenheim, who had moved in 1888 from Vienna to Frankfurt, the center of these activities, participated in this Renaissance not only through her translations but also by lecturing to adult audiences about Yiddish literature and Jewish women's history at the famous Freie Jüdische Lehrhaus. In Brenner's view, Pappenheim was "well aware of the original spirit of this women's Bible, which was part of the tradition excluding women from traditional Hebrew studies." Nevertheless, her 1930 translation of the *Tsenerene* "tried to turn the initially degrading character of the book into its opposite" by making "emancipated women conscious of their heritage as women and as Jews."[26]

Less formally, Pappenheim was also capable of converting German into Yiddish, a rather more difficult endeavor that constitutes surer evidence for Elizabeth Loentz that "Bertha Pappenheim had a strong command of the Yiddish language." In a June 1912 letter to her colleagues, Pappenheim reported that she had translated six pages of a German report on the Jewish sex traffic in Galicia for the Hasidic rebbe of Aleksandrow, who had requested the translation. She complained that it was exhausting "holding the fountain pen the wrong way round," but the translation work itself apparently posed no difficulty she felt the need to mention.²⁷ The stiffness of her hand and her writing "the wrong way round" are among the reverberations of her early illness in this episode, either in parallel or reverse form. Perhaps there is an echo, in her report on the visit to the Alexander Hasidic court, of another of her symptoms—her speaking "four or five languages" at once. Pappenheim records in remarkable detail a conversation with the Grand Rabbi's sister, "a true Glückel" who fully understood the issues and who spoke what Pappenheim considered a charming mélange of biblical quotation, rabbinic idiom, and Yiddish proverb:

> She grasped, with incredible speed, when I explained what I wanted to achieve. She looked at me with skeptical eyebrows, and said, *"Eine Schwalbe, die das Jam ausschöpfen will?*—da kann nur **Rebaun schel aulom** helfen, aber as es in grosser Reinigkeit zu **Rebaun schel aulom**'s Ehre geschieht wird er helfen, und der **Rebbe**, mein Bruder—er soll leben—wird Sie **mazliach** sein." [*A swallow that wants to dry up the sea*, only **God** can help, but since this is done with great purity for **God**'s honor, **God** will help, and my brother, the **Rebbe**, may he live, will also help and you will **be successful**; Hebrew or Hebrew-derived Yiddish phrasing in bold, Yiddish proverb in italics]."²⁸

Pappenheim's praise for, attunement to, and perfect comprehension of this characteristically multilingual Hasidic speech expresses itself not only in her reports. Her appreciation for Yiddish habits of speech also leads Pappenheim to forge a "foreignizing" style in translating old Yiddish into German, a style in which the multilingual character of her source texts continued to reverberate in the German and that deviates from the "purer" German by which her predecessors in the field domesticated their Yiddish sources.²⁹ As Pappenheim, if not as Anna O., she also found words to pray, composing German prayers in which Hebrew intermingled with German; a selection of these prayers was published after her 1936 death as *Gebete*.³⁰ However one understands Breuer's report that in the course of her illness Anna O. lapsed into a disorganized, ungrammatical, pathological jargon, Bertha Pappenheim clearly saw the recuperation of Yiddish for emancipated women as a different kind of talking cure, in which the denigrated language lurking beneath, promiscuously mixing with, and distorting the European tongue was given a respectable name and allowed to have its say.

From this perspective, Breuer's failure to cure Anna O. and his erasure of this failure in the case study are inextricable from his failure to name the language of her mongrel speech or of the prayer she cannot utter. These multiple failures and amnesias, on Breuer's part and on Anna O.'s, may be an old Jewish story. Psalm 137 is very nearly a proleptic paraphrase of Anna O.'s major hysterical symptoms, paralysis and aphasia: "If I forget you, Jerusalem, may my right hand forget its skill. May my tongue cling to the roof of my mouth" (Ps 137:5).[31]

This same psalm also stirred Freud's sleep, appearing in a famous dream Freud recounted and interpreted in the section on "Absurd Dreams" in *The Interpretation of Dreams*, which he called "My Son, the Myops . . ." Freud tells us that this dream emerged from "a tangle of thoughts" that occupied his mind on the evening of January 5, 1898, after he had seen a performance of Theodor Herzl's play *Das neue Ghetto*.[32] The nocturnal thoughts circled around "the Jewish problem, concern about the future of one's children, to whom one cannot give a country of their own, concern about educating them in such a way that they can move freely across frontiers." Freud's dream is set at a fountain in Siena, on whose edge he sits, "greatly depressed and almost in tears"; free-associating on this image leads him to another verse in the biblical psalm just mentioned, "By the waters of Babylon, we sat down and wept" (Ps 137:1).[33] As with Anna O.'s symptoms, and as if to remember that Babylon is also Babel, Freud's dream speaks a mélange of languages, sometimes in a single phrase. The main scene Freud remembers from this dream involves a boy who may or may not be his son saying something incomprehensible as he is being handed over to Freud by "a female attendant—an attendant or nun": "The boy refused to kiss her, but, holding out his hand in farewell, said 'AUF GESERES' to her, and then 'AUF UNGESERES' to the two of us (or to one of us). I had a notion that this last phrase denoted a preference."[34] Freud's interpretation focuses closely on these mysterious utterances:

> Our interest is aroused by the phrase "*Auf Geseres*" (at a point at which the situation in the dream would have led one to expect "*Auf Wiedersehen*") as well as its quite meaningless opposite "*Auf Ungeseres*." According to information I have received from philologists [*Schriftgelehrenten*], "*Geseres*" is a genuine Hebrew word derived from a verb "*goiser*," and is best translated by "imposed sufferings" or "doom." The use of the word in slang would incline one to suppose that it meant "weeping and

wailing" [*Nach der Verwendung des Wortes im Jargon sollte man meinen, es bedeute "Klagen und Jammern"*].³⁵

In contrast with Breuer's failure to name the language of Anna O.'s prayer and the ambiguity of his reference to the jargon into which her German speech deteriorates, Freud names and draws attention to the Jewish and Hebrew fragments within the multilingual script of his dream. Having consulted with "biblical scholars" (Strachey translates the term as "philologists"), Freud explains to us that the mysterious phrase uttered by the boy is derived from *ein echt hebräisches Wort*. A number of critics have suggested that Freud mentions taking recourse to the expertise of others in this interpretation as a way of distancing himself from the implication that he understands the Jewish languages of his own dreams. Ken Frieden describes this aside as a strategy in which "Freud simultaneously claims and disavows the knowledge of Hebrew and Yiddish his dream employs" as part of a general pattern of disavowing his own Jewishness; elsewhere in this dream analysis, for instance, Freud refers to Passover as *Osterzeit*, Eastertime.³⁶ This avoidance, as Frieden sees it, hinders Freud's ability to truly explicate the meaning of his dream. Taking fuller stock of the range of Jewish associations of *Auf Geseres* than Freud himself does, Frieden suggests that the boy is wishing evil decrees on the non-Jewish attendant who delivers him to his father, while wishing his father, understood to be Freud, the (beneficial) release from such decrees.

Adam Lipszyc similarly focuses on "the enigmatic slogan *Auf Ungeseres*" in describing Freud's ambiguous Jewish self-presentation in this dream, echoing Frieden's skepticism that Freud needed to consult a scholar about its meaning and, like Frieden, pursuing the meaning of these words further than Freud had:

> For whoever the *Schriftgelehrte* were that Freud consulted concerning the meaning of the word *Geseres*—there are good reasons to believe that he consulted none and he knew all that himself—my own *Schriftgelehrte* has provided me with quite fascinating data concerning the semantic field defined by the Hebrew root *gzr*. It seems that the meanings belonging to this field can be grouped into two distinct and conflicting series. On the one hand, the root would refer to the meanings connected with the persecutions of the Jews, beginning with the paradigmatic Egypt. On the other hand, however, it would refer to the strict injunctions of the law springing from God himself or from the religious authority, down

to the specific and emblematic law of circumcision. Now, it would be most temping to link this bundle of contradictory meanings to the later development of Freud's thinking. First, it will be remembered that Freud came to understand both blinding and circumcision as symbolic substitutes for castration. Second, it will be remembered that the figure of Moses and the story of the exodus from Egypt became a virtual obsession for the father of psychoanalysis. Thus, it is rather hard to accept the fact that the Jewish thread of analysis of that particular dream should break so quickly.[37]

While Frieden and Lipszyc focus on the Hebrew meanings of these words, Freud's interpretation of the dream also associates the word with the meanings it accrues—"weeping and wailing"—in "Jargon." Using the same German term Breuer uses to describe the hysterical deterioration of Anna O.'s speech, Freud is only slightly less ambiguous about its meaning. The ambiguity resolves itself one way in Brill's translation, "from its employment in the Jewish jargon," and another in the Strachey translation quoted earlier: "the use of the word in slang." Freud's analysis of his dream similarly leaves ambiguous whether he consulted with a scholar on the full range of meanings of the Hebrew/Yiddish *Geseres* or only on its biblical and/or Hebrew meaning, while being aware of what it meant in slang without the help of experts. This ambiguity is only partially resolved when, in the course of his free associations on the word *Geseres*, Freud recalls that he encountered the word in an anecdote he heard about the son of a colleague who suffered from an eye ailment; after one eye healed, the other became inflamed, and the boy's mother called the doctor, who rebuked her: "'Why are you making such a *Geseres*?' he shouted at the mother. 'If *one* side has got well, so will the *other*.'"[38] Does the association of the word *Geseres* with this anecdote mean that Freud heard the word just that one time, and if so, did he understand it? Are these ambiguities also an effect of Freud's attempt to distance himself from a denigrated Jewish language or dialect? Was the Galician-born Brill, Freud's first English translator, making Freud's intent clearer by rendering *im Jargon* as "in the Jewish jargon," or was he imposing a more explicit Jewishness onto Freud's German than Freud intended or was inclined to acknowledge? Should Strachey's translation of *Jargon* as "slang" be read as his attempt to smooth away Freud's (or Brill's) embarrassing Jewish edges, or might he have been unaware that the German word can mean both "slang" and the particular slang of Jews, which we might call Yiddish? Perhaps the delicate matter of Brill's Galician origins and nonnative English, which Freud's English followers saw in his "conscientious but inelegant" translation style, is relevant here: one psychoanalytic memoir describes "the lingering traces of a mother tongue in [Brill's] 'almost vaudeville-stage German-Yiddish accent,' which he has never completely lost."[39] As Lydia Marinelli and Andreas Mayer put it, "His European origins had brought Brill close to Freud but put him at a disadvantage in his activity as English translator."[40] Brill's awkward translation style was not necessarily evidence of an embarrassing Yiddish accent. On the contrary, what Gilman sees in Brill's awkward style is the attempt to erase all traces of Jewishness from the English, both his own and Freud's (although it is also true that Brill occasionally made Jewish content more explicit than either Freud or later translators did).[41] The ambiguities threaded through these questions about Freud, his translators, and his interpreters may be unavoidable, given that they inhere in the word/term/name *Jargon*, which only in retrospect and through a specific historical, cultural, and ideological lens is understood as a pejorative term for (what we now call, as if "neutrally") Yiddish.

So is poking around with a shovel and pick among the ruins of Freud's Jewish multilingualism participating in the game Derrida charges Yerushalmi with playing at a dead man's expense, of "discovering"—which is to say, imposing—a Jewishness he is in no position to deny, stripping him in the process of the shreds of German by which he attempted to cover his (Jewish) nakedness? Yerushalmi, Derrida claimed, was performing a second circumcision in attempting to show that Freud knew more Hebrew than he cared to admit. But associating him with Yiddish—or with jargon—might inflict a greater and even more clearly sexual form of symbolic violence, a castration rather than a circumcision, given the associations of Yiddish and femininity, Yiddish the *mameloshn* and Yiddish the language of Freud's mother.[42] Reik, we may recall, sees just such aggression in the Jewish "impudence" that "lowers" a more assimilated Jew to the ranks of the Polish Jew (as his "Alter Ego") through, for instance, discovering in this Jew a secret store of Yiddish (as men degrade women they find unapproachable). Does Jewish studies scholarship, in its own forms of aggressive approach, similarly aim to bring Freud over to the Jewish camp, and so to "own" Freud and his discoveries?

It is no real defense against Derrida's charge to point out that Freud not only analyzed this game; he also participated in it. The joke that appears in Freud's book on wit immediately follows the one about the Galician Jew with the outstretched feet in the train, but this joke takes the situation of

Jewish modernity by the opposite end of the stick, as it were. If the Galician Jew making himself too comfortable is the butt of the train joke, this joke targets the hyperassimilated Jewish woman, whose Jewishness is expressed not at the moment she begins to feel more comfortable but only under great pressure:⁴³

> The doctor who has been asked to look after the Baroness at her confinement pronounced that the moment had not come, and suggested to the Baron that in the meantime they should have a game of cards in the next room. After a while a cry of pain from the Baroness struck the ears of the two men: "Ah, mon Dieu, que je souffre!" Her husband sprang up, but the doctor signed to him to sit down: "It's nothing. Let's go on with the game!" A little later there were again sounds from the pregnant woman: "Mein Gott, mein Gott, what terrible pains!" "Aren't you going in, Professor?" asked the Baron.—"No, no. It's not time yet." At last there came from next door an unmistakable cry of "Aa—ee, aa-ee, aa-ee!" [*Endlich hört man aus den Nebenzimmer ein unverkennbares*: "Ai, waih, waih geschrien."] The doctor threw down his cards and exclaimed: "*Now* it's time."⁴⁴

As in his dream analysis (which involves a different mother shrieking in Yiddish), Freud's joke about the Baroness very nearly allows the Yiddish language to break through his German prose. For the Baroness, this eruption is a response to the pressure of painful labor. For the teller of the joke, the eruption is justified by the implicit permission granted to aggression by its framing as jest and by the projection of this shameful eruption onto an affected and "exalted" Jewish woman whose degradation will restore a certain intimacy among those who tell and hear the joke. I say that Freud "very nearly" allows the Yiddish language to break through because here, as in Anna O.'s hysteria and his *Auf Geseres* dream and despite the "unmistakable" character of the cry, a certain ambiguity persists: In what language (or dialect or nonlanguage) is the woman crying out? Freud does not entirely clear the matter up in his analysis of the joke, explaining the outburst without naming the Baroness or her language as Jewish. Rather, the joke shows *Wie der Schmerz durch alle Schichtungen der Erziehung die ursprüngliche Natur durchbrechen läßt*, which Strachey renders as "how pain causes her primitive nature to break through all layers of education."⁴⁵ Are we to understand, in this retelling, that the Baroness is shrieking in a "decomposed" German? In Viennese *mauscheln*? In Yiddish? Or is this unmistakable cry an outcry of her "original nature," a primal grunt? Do these possibilities add up, in the world of the joke, to the same thing—the assumption that Yiddish is the pure expression of primitive (Jewish) nature? If we are meant to understand this as *distorted* Yiddish, then what distorts it? The "animal" pain of a protracted labor? Or the Baroness's assimilation, which buries her Yiddish under "civilized" languages until she can retrieve only distorted fragments? Or Freud's awkward attempt to cover up his own knowledge of this primitive language?

Cuddihy takes this last stance, arguing that Freud "launders the Jewish component" of the joke, just as he makes no mention "of the baroness's Jewishness, but merely speaks of the cries of pain uttered by 'an aristocratic lady in child-birth.'" In Cuddihy's view, psychology stands in here for sociology: this is a joke about "passing," in which "the French layer is peeled away, then the German layer, finally laying bare the *mama-loshen* of primary socialization 'underneath,'" which masquerades—"passes"—as a joke about women, pain, and culture.[46] (It is also a literalization of "the long tradition in which translation and childbirth come to figure each other.")[47] Reik, who retells the joke, makes the character of the outburst clearer than Freud had, speaking of "the transition from the French to the Yiddish cries." But in describing this "return to the mother-tongue or to the jargon once spoken" as restoring "the emotional atmosphere of childhood," Reik also keeps some cards close to his chest, failing to register the sexual and misogynist aggression that is the engine of this joke (and that displaces the discomforts of assimilation onto Jewish women) by treating this pointed exposure as if it were a touching anecdote. Brill and Strachey's renderings either miss Freud's allusions to Yiddish or faithfully reproduce (knowingly or not) his (possibly intentional) ambiguity.

But that era is over: Reik's retelling of the joke, Cuddihy's reading of it, and the scholarship that has followed in their wake have produced a near consensus not only on how the joke should be read but also on how it should be translated. Hence the new Penguin translation: "Finally, from the next room they hear an unmistakable cry of 'Ai, waih, waih' [equivs: 'O weh,' 'Oy vay']."[48] As in the joke, Yiddish gradually, partially, and with increasing clarity "unmistakably" breaks into the world of Freud-in-English, finally appearing in familiar form in the third of the three "equivalents" for the woman's cry, as if the translator, Joyce Crick, were herself compelled to repeat the woman's triple exclamation. Crick, it is true, hedges her bets by reproducing Freud's "unmistakable" cry of "Ai, waih, waih" and only adding in brackets "[equivs: 'O weh,' 'Oy vay']"; she also appends a footnote to the line citing Leo Rosten's account of an identical story about "the apocryphal Countess Misette de Rothschild," in which the final cry is rendered less ambiguously as the Yiddish "Oy Ge-valt," with the translator commenting that the Baroness reverts "not only to the universal nature Freud ascribes to a woman in labor, also to her social origins."[49] This is the "joke," she wryly adds, that Freud "later describes as an 'unmasking.'"[50] Crick's is a remarkable translation performance, mobilizing doublets (equivs.), transliteration brackets, and a footnote that pulls the reader down from the body of the text to its bottom margin, where the case is made that what we are looking at in Freud is a Jewish language.

The questions that arise about what exactly the woman is crying out in the joke Freud recounts is of course also the question of what Freud is trying to say in recounting the joke: about the woman in childbirth, about how jokes function, and about himself. In this sense, as the one who obscures the joke's meaning even as he analyzes it, it is Freud who is the half-buried artifact whose multilingual monuments invite our own deciphering. But given that we are using the tools he taught us to wield, Freud is also a/the doctor here, who has learned to convert the inarticulate symptoms of a suffering body into language, who understands how to translate incomprehensible utterances into the dilations of a cervix, which are also the stirrings of a troubled past. As always, Freud is also an archaeologist with the pick, not only interpreting obscure hieroglyphics but also extracting fragments of a half-buried culture (which is to say, collecting Jewish jokes) and displaying them as artifacts (or publishing them in a scholarly book). The effects of this joke, as a desiring-machine that produces babies and translations and interpretations and (Jewish or scholarly) connections, and as an engine of gynophobia, misogyny, and (internalized) antisemitism, do not stop at Freud. The question of whom the joke is on, and who can effectively wield it, may never be effectively settled.

3

Surfaces

> Sometimes a cigar is just a cigar.
>
> —Sigmund Freud (but only in the popular imagination)

The previous chapters laid out the structural parallels and historical resonances that connect Freud's topographical model of the psyche and the modern ideology of a layered Jewish linguistic consciousness. These twin ideologies reveal their interconnections in a range of texts, including the joke Freud relates about the Baroness progressing from French and German to (what may be) Yiddish in the throes of labor while her husband and doctor play cards outside the door. But I have already begun to lay my own cards on the table. It seems to me that the assumptions about Jewish language consciousness that drove Roback's questions to Freud, fueled the scholarly pursuit of the Jewish Freud, and shaped the Penguin translation of the joke about the Baroness have finally begun to slacken. This ideological shift might be discerned in the telling differences between the SNL episode "Jew, Not a Jew" that I discussed earlier and a more recent Instagram version of the game called "Jew or Not Jew" that has been a popular weekly feature on the Hey Alma Instagram site since 2018.[1] Like the SNL sketch, the Hey Alma game is described as "a game where you guess if celebrities are Jewish or not"; on one Tuesday in 2022, for instance, 65 percent of followers correctly guessed that Rachel Brosnahan is a non-Jew, while 59 percent incorrectly believed Tony Shalhoub to be Jewish.

Despite the evident similarities between the games, they have entirely different aims: SNL trafficked in and parodied both stereotypes about "hidden" Jews in Hollywood and the eagerness of the American public to sniff them out. By contrast, Hey Alma announced its goal this way: "to show that you can't tell if someone is Jewish based only on their appearance or name. We want it to be fun but also enlightening—to show that Jewish celebs (and Jews in general!!) do not look a certain way." Where the SNL sketch relied on deeply held tropes of the hidden assimilated Jew, the Hey Alma game explicitly aims to catch out its followers on the biases or assumptions that might lead them to believe that a celebrity is or isn't Jewish. In other words, the light SNL trained on celebrities like Michael Landon, exposing him as "born Eugene Horowitz," is aimed by Hey Alma at its own followers, the mostly Ashkenazi Jewish feminists who are its target audience. It is these readers who are asked to check their assumptions as part of a broader push in progressive Jewish circles to take cognizance of the range of practices (the game of "Jewish geography") and cultural presuppositions (Ashkenormativity) that functionally and painfully exclude Jews of color, converts, or other Jews who fail to meet classic assumptions about what marks a Jew as Jewish.[2] Where Derrida called attention to the barely suppressed aggression in Yerushalmi's attempt to impose Jewishness on Freud, Hey Alma wants us to notice that the social game of "recognizing" other Jews hurts those Jews *not* recognized as Jews, who fail to register as Jews at all in Ashkenazi-dominated North American social scenes. The Hey Alma version of the game and the ideology it expresses may be relatively novel, but the problem is hardly new. For Primo Levi, the difficulties of making his circuitous way home from Auschwitz were compounded not only by the persistent antisemitism of the non-Jews he encountered on the road but also by the failure of Jews he met to see him as one of their own, given the odd way he pronounced Hebrew and his mystifying ignorance of Yiddish, the universal Jewish language. After Levi and a group of his friends meet two girls in the Soviet Union in 1945, he asks them if they are Jewish, trying to Yiddishize his German: "The girls (they were perhaps sixteen or eighteen years old) burst out laughing. 'Ihr sprecht keyn Jiddisch; ihr seyd ja keyne Jiden!' [If you don't speak Yiddish, you're not a Jew]."[3] Levi tries to explain that they are Italian Jews who don't happen to speak Yiddish, but he is unable to break through their "rigorous logic." These old assumptions are indeed eroding, not only because Ashkenazic Jews are taking better notice of the diversity of the Jewish world but also because the primal link between Yiddish and Jewishness is revealing itself as a fiction, in an era in which (secular) Yiddish speakers are as liable to be made in the classroom as in the bedroom.[4] The category of "Jewish languages" no longer seems as self-evident as it did for many of the figures discussed here and must now be understood not as a neutral description of the essence of a language but as a marker of its ideological framing and the product of a particular "proprietary perspective" that views languages as "a group's property."[5]

In this new ideological climate, it is no surprise that the game of Jewish hide-and-seek described (and occasionally played) in the first two chapters is also beginning to lose its long grip. We are now well past the era of Central European Jewish multilingualism that George Steiner describes, and most Jews do not live in a context in which a Jewish emancipatory program meets obstacles to social integration through strategic practices of disavowal and "passing." This is the background that gives form to the questions about how much Yiddish Freud knew and helps explain the Jewish jokes about the eruption of Yiddish, but it is not ours. It is also true that a certain academic style and set of tropes have begun to reveal its limits. From this perspective, the narratives that insist on the persistence of Jewishness after assimilation, whether as unfortunate inheritance or secret prize, may express the paranoid fantasies or hopeful desires of the observer as much as the reality of German-speaking Jews. To hear the echo of Yiddish in German speech may testify not to the stubbornness of Jewish languages but to the nostalgia that accompanies their loss, whether it is the nostalgia of those German-speaking Jews or their contemporary or belated interpreters.

We should not be misled by the apparent neutrality of Max Weinreich's terminology of external versus internal bilingualism, nor be taken in by the familiarity of the maskilic (Jewish Enlightenment) architecture that places Jewish languages inside and European languages as the surface or exterior of the self. While Yehuda Leib Gordon called for such an arrangement in his 1866 poem, by 1870, in his poem "For Whom Do I Toil?" he was lamenting the rush of his generation of modernizing Jews to European languages, leaving him without a readership for his Hebrew work. Nor should we be drawn in by the post-maskilic nostalgia that views Yiddish as not contingently but rather archetypically the mother tongue, with all others being covers for the authentic, shameful, primal Jewish "interior." Even before the present "postvernacular" wave of Yiddish speakers who learned the language in classrooms, many of those who championed Yiddish as the *mameloshn* or "the soul of the people" were not, in fact, native speakers. Kalman Weiser reminds us that a number of champions of a range of other Eastern European national tongues were also not native speakers of those languages, as was the case for such Yiddishists as "the chief convener of the Czernowitz Conference, Nathan Birnbaum—a native German speaker—and the founder of the socialist Zionist party, Poale Zion, Ber Borochov

[1881–1917], whose native tongue was Russian," because his parents wanted to distance him from their own native Yiddish.[6] Weinreich learned Yiddish as an adolescent in his youth movement, while Borochov began to study the language only at the age of twenty-six.

The joke type about Mrs. Cowles and the Baroness von Feilchenfeld that still circulates in some form or another thus indirectly expresses, it could be argued, the *dream* of an intimate Jewish language and the *hope* that a Jewish language might heal the alienations of modernity and smash the facade of alienating and alienated social conditions. Against the notion that jokes such as these expose the "authentic Jewishness that has been left behind," Christopher Hutton argues that they mobilize scraps of Yiddish "as the vehicle for the controlled regression to an Eastern European self, . . . with roots in past mythologies but arising at a transition point in Jewish history." It is thus not "static 'authenticity'" that drives or is discovered in these jokes but "an interplay between the identity of the 'little Jew' and the intellectual or 'outsider' Jew."[7] The Jewish joke emerges not from a fullness that can no longer be contained or submerged but from a perceived lack that seeks a missing object, the "little Jew" (*pintele yid*). Describing his early life as an Algerian Jew, Derrida echoes something of Freud's expressed regret that he lacked a Jewish language in the striking phrase: "I have only one tongue, and it is not my own." The missing other tongues do not cease to signify in their absence: Derrida writes of his regret that he was raised to speak only French, since "we could not even resort to some familiar substitute, some idiom internal to the Jewish community, to any sort of language of refuge that, like Yiddish, would have ensured an element of intimacy, the protection of a 'home-of-one's-own' [*un chez-soi*] against the language of official culture."[8] Kata Gellen, commenting on those who, like Derrida, lack access to a "an organic language of community, family, and home," suggests that *Muttersprache* and *mame-loshn* are not roughly equivalent expressions but "actually inverse phenomena. . . . Monolanguage is a major language suffering the pain of an absent *mame-loshn*."[9]

Reflecting on his privileged upbringing, Georges Perec similarly spoke of "the continuity of a tradition, a language, a belonging" as the only thing that was "specifically forbidden to me":

> I don't know exactly what it is to be a Jew, what it is that makes me a Jew. It is a fact, if you like, but a mediocre fact, a mark, but a mark that doesn't bind me to anything precise, to anything concrete: it is not a sign of belonging, it is not tied to a belief, a religion, a practice, a culture, a

folklore, a history, a destiny, a language. It would be instead an absence, a question, a raising of a question, a hesitation, an anxiety: a certain anxiety behind which is silhouetted a different certainty, abstract, heavy, insufferable: that of having been designated a Jew, and because a Jew a victim, and of owing one's life to nothing but chance and exile. My grandparents or parents could have emigrated to Argentina, the United States, Palestine, Australia; I could have been born, like various close or distant cousins, in Haifa, Baltimore, Vancouver, but among the nearly limitless range of these possibilities, only one thing was specifically forbidden to me, to be born in the country of my ancestors, in Poland, in Lubartów, Puławy, or Warsaw, and to grow up there in the continuity of a tradition, a language, a belonging.[10]

The lack of a Jewish language was a feature of Jewish culture during Freud's lifetime as well, as a linguistic condition or dimension of the Jewish linguistic psyche that was not a language stratum but the memory or ruins of one. In a section of his memoir titled "The Bookcase," Osip Mandelshtam (1891–1938) writes of "the bookshelf of [his] early childhood" as having been "deposited, like a geological bed, over several decades," with discrete "paternal and maternal elements" and an "inoculation" of "alien blood." On the chaotic lowest shelf,

> the books were not standing upright side by side but lay like ruins: reddish five-volume works with ragged covers, a Russian history of the Jews written in the clumsy, shy language of a Russian-speaking Talmudist. This was the Judaic chaos thrown in the dust. . . . This was the level to which my Hebrew primer, which I never mastered, quickly fell.[11]

So, too, for Mandelshtam, does "the spiky script of the unread books of Genesis, thrown into the dust one shelf lower than Goethe and Schiller," occupy the bottom shelf in the bookcase. Mandelshtam begins this chapter with the assertion that "just as a little bit of musk fills an entire house, so the least influence of Judaism overflows all of one's life" and describes the "Judaic chaos" underlying the "brilliant covering" of Petersburg life as "the unknown womb world whence I had issued."[12] Nevertheless, Hebrew does not count as that cultural matrix from which Mandelshtam continues to draw; it is perhaps the absence of Hebrew knowledge that is the more influential factor. But absence, too, can influence. In a chapter titled "On Not Knowing Hebrew," Robert Alter argues that Hebrew could play a powerful role in the modernist creativity even of thinkers with little access to the language.¹³ I do not mean to replace Yerushalmi's suspicion that Freud knew Hebrew or Yiddish with a certitude that he did not, a certitude that carves out an exception but otherwise leaves intact both Yerushalmi's assumptions and the privilege accorded the one asking those questions. Derrida and Alter should alert us that knowing or not knowing a language is not and never was a simple dichotomy. Gellen writes, on Canetti's complicated linguistic journey, "that it reveals an array of mother tongues suspended between mastery and mythology, host and home, yours and ours, German and Jewish."¹⁴ We have yet to map the range of hybrid or paradoxical positions lost within the surety that there is a language called Yiddish that one might be said to know or not know, or recognize the way that asking these questions already constitutes something of an answer. Max Kohn, having provocatively asserted that his unconscious speaks Yiddish, continues: "It has no message, it is addressed to no one in particular, and no one can claim to be the recipient of it, not even me. It is neither a presence nor an interlocutor. For I think in French."¹⁵ As for Freud's Yiddish, rather than identify the language with the unconscious, Kohn makes the case that it is the absence of Yiddish from Freud's German rather than its hidden presence that "free[s] a place for the unconscious."¹⁶ For Freud, the legacy of Yiddish is as a language "that he no longer speaks even if he understands it," in which "one language, German, has come in place of another, Yiddish."¹⁷ It is the relationship between these two related/heterogeneous languages that for Kohn opens a gap that is (also) the unconscious, precisely because Freud does *not* speak Yiddish.

Recognizing the absence of Yiddish from Freud's German reopens the question already posed of why scholars are so eager to find in Freud a Jewish language, alive and well (or even, as for Kohn, influential in its absence). Given the way that Yiddish is seen as a language buried within non-Jewish tongues, this question might benefit from developments in the field of crypto-Jewishness, which has been wrestling with whether buried Judaism is a reality or fantasy. Writing in 1931, Cecil Roth makes it clear that his *History of the Marranos* is driven by enthrallment, romance, and emotion, desires from which even serious scholarship cannot protect him:

> I have the great honor to present to the Reader, in the following pages, what may fairly be described as the most romantic episode in all history.... The submerged life which blossomed out at intervals into such exotic flowers; the unique devotion which could transmit the ancestral ideas unsullied, from generation to generation, despite the Inquisition

and its horrors; the figures of rare heroism which every now and again emerged to burst upon the world; the extraordinary climax in our own days—all combine to make a story unparalleled in history for sheer dramatic appeal.[18]

The ideology of Jewish languages hidden beneath European ways and of Jews hidden "within" Christians are not only parallel in structure: Jewish languages also play a significant part in this "most romantic episode." In an epilogue describing the survival of Marranos until his own day, Roth recounts the story of a Polish Jewish businessman who visited Portugal in 1919 and met with a family rumored by their neighbors to be Jewish; while these "Jews" had never heard of Hebrew despite it being "the universal language of Jewish prayer," when the businessman recited the Shema to them, one of them covered her eyes and asserted, "He is indeed a Jew . . . for he knows the name of Adonai." (Freud, as it happens, also knew the name of Adonai, a topic of sustained discussion in his final book.) Roth concludes, "Thus this solitary survival of the old Hebrew tongue, which had been preserved orally through the long generations of subterfuge and persecution, at last brought the remnants of the Marranos into touch with a representative of the outside Jewish world."[19]

Roth was not the last to wax poetic about crypto-Jews and crypto-Jewish communities. Stories of Catholics in New Mexico in the 1970s and 1980s "tending the dying embers of their ancient faith" in secret for generations, as Barbara Ferry and Debbie Nathan put it in a story in the *Atlantic*, "held enormous appeal for Jews elsewhere in the United States, still grappling with the legacy of the Holocaust and eager for stories of Jewish survival against all odds."[20] Contemporary observers noted that crypto-Jewish narratives spoke not only of the traumas of the Jewish past but also of the conditions of the present, and not only for the descendants of Spanish conversos. Michael P. Carroll suggests that "the explosion of new identity claims, of all sorts, in the three to four decades following the Civil Rights Movement of the 1960s created a cultural climate in the US that would have made claims to a crypto-Jewish identity seem more plausible, both to audiences in New Mexico and to the general public, than would otherwise have been the case."[21] Dalia Kandiyoti, in a recent study of the literary "return" of the figure of the converso, similarly writes: "Stories that stage the quest for largely undocumented pasts that may have survived residually or in a ghostly fashion speak to our fascination with extinction and survival. In Jewish and related traditions there is a long-standing rejection of extinction and quests for recovery and return."[22]

Despite the continuing appeal of such narratives, contemporary historians are far less likely to view crypto-Jews as sentimentally as Roth did or believe as firmly in the historical reality of crypto-Judaism. Along with ongoing debates about the veracity of at least some claims to Sephardic New Christian descent, a scholarly consensus suggests that the Inquisition did not so much root out "secret Jews" as manufacture them from New Christians as a consequence of its own sociopolitical interests rather than the secret practices of its hapless targets.[23] Kandiyoti suggests that the growing body of narratives of converso return may work in similar ways:

> We think of a remnant as what has survived. Yet in many imaginative acts of return, remnants of the past are not found but produced. . . . What is not "found" and lacks widely accepted physical, documentary, or genetic evidence is produced in narrative, such as in scenes of return to ancient sites, the representation of embodied, symptomatic responses, and the insertion of the "missing" converso element into the historical imaginary.[24]

In the absence of a reliable archive, the genealogical impulse that constitutes as it discovers crypto-Jewish filiation and kinship is often compelled to proceed through a chain of absences rather than "physical, documentary, or genetic evidence." In place of the Jew who has survived "intact" behind a Christian facade, writers provide us with a not-quite-lineage of not-quite-Jews, who nevertheless succeed, through a repeated pattern of estrangement and alienation from all traditions, in constituting something of an imagined community. Thus, in *The Marrano as Metaphor* Elaine Marks takes Freud, Jacques Derrida, Hélène Cixous, and others as the exemplary modern "crypto-Jews" who establish the pattern of her own secular Jewish identity.[25] Erin Graff Zivin similarly writes that "the marrano enters Derrida's work to name an anti-identitarian category with which he can, paradoxically, express a certain identification."[26] In Safaa Fathy's 1999 documentary *D'ailleurs, Derrida*, Derrida describes his "obsession" with the figure of the Marrano as revolving around the structure of a secrecy devoid of content:

> What is an absolute secret? I was obsessed with this question quite as much as that of my supposed Judeo-Spanish origins. These obsessions met in the figure of the Marrano. I gradually began to identify with

someone who carries a secret that is bigger than himself and to which he does not have access. As if I were a Marrano's Marrano . . . a lay Marrano, a Marrano who has lost the Jewish and Spanish origins of his Marranism, a kind of universal Marrano.²⁷

The notion of a Marrano empty of Jewish interiority or content was available in Freud's lifetime as well. Speaking in 1936 of the increasing numbers of German Jews who were "returning" to Judaism in the face of Nazi pressure, but in forms he considered devoid of religious or spiritual substance, Abraham Joshua Heschel diagnosed them as "Marranos metamorphosed in a new form," in which an external identification with Judaism, developed in reaction to how others view Jews, covers an internal Jewish void.²⁸ It was Jewishness, in these cases, that was the outward shell, a crypt that enclosed not Jewish intimacy or substance but its loss and absence.

Without denying the historical persistence of Jewish practices in fragmentary or syncretistic form among descendants of Iberian conversos, it is possible to read crypto-Judaism more broadly as a cultural hermeneutic that addresses not the unrecoverable distant past but the alienations of modernity, gaps in the archives, the fragmentation of history, the "archive fever" of historians, and the search for indelible traces of the past within the present, by Freud among others. Taking well-established academic discussions of crypto-Judaism as models for how to understand conceptions of "crypto-Jewish" languages, the ideology that posits that Jewish languages underlie a European cover can be read anew as either paranoid production (in its Inquisitorial mode) or wish fulfillment (for those seeking to find ostensibly lost "remnants"). If Freud participates in constructing Jewish genealogies from a fragmented literary record, his work can also help illuminate the notion of inheritance without content, drawing attention to the ways genealogical narratives conform to present desires as much as the pressures of the past. In "Family Romances," Freud writes about how "the child's imagination becomes engaged in the task of getting free from the parents of whom he now has a low opinion and of replacing them by others, who, as a rule, are of higher social standing. He will make use in this connection of any opportune coincidences from his actual experience, such as his becoming acquainted with the Lord of the Manor."²⁹ It is not only children that become engaged in the task of (re)imagining their "real" origins. The first section of *Moses and Monotheism* demonstrates that the "family romance" may also shape national myths about "the birth of the hero," by which a leader is supplied with an appropriately aristocratic lineage. Freud points out that in the case of the birth of Moses, this pattern seems to be reversed, with the national myth describing a son of humble origins rescued and raised among the most powerful family in the land:

> As a rule the humble family is the real one and the aristocratic family the fabricated one. The situation in the case of Moses seemed somehow different. . . . In every instance which it has been possible to test, the first family, the one from which the child was exposed, was the invented one, and the second one, in which he was received and grew up, was the real one. If we have the courage to recognize this assertion as universally true and as applying also to the legend of Moses, then all at once we see things clearly: Moses was an Egyptian—probably an aristocrat—whom the legend was designed to turn into a Jew.[30]

Much has been made of Freud's long and complex identification with Moses, an identification that spoke, according to some interpreters, to his desire to distance himself from his Jewish roots.[31] *Moses and Monotheism* gives warrant to those seeking to account for the persistence of Jewishness over many generations; but it also supplies the tools to recognize the role of wish fulfillment in the construction of genealogical narratives, whether those imaginary "bloodlines" are Jewish or not.

If the search for the Jewish Freud reflects the assumptions, fantasies, and desires of those on the hunt as much as Freud's own Jewishness, then it is time to reread the scholarship on "the Jewish Freud" as an artifact of a historically contingent reading process in which Freud's Jewishness constitutes a hermeneutic frame that conditions what will be discovered by peering through this frame. Gershon Shaked makes a similar point about critical attempts to frame Kafka as a Jewish writer: "He is not a 'Jewish' writer because of his ancestry or his cultural tradition—despite artificial attempts to establish intertextual connections between Kafka and Kabbalah—but rather because Jewish readers perceived an interconnection between the subtexts of his texts and 'Jewish' mentality, destiny, and theology."[32] Benjamin Schreier has recently sharpened this insight in relationship to Philip Roth and the field of Jewish American literature, which in his view constitutes its identitarian subject even as it imagines itself merely studying it. Rather than assume "that Jews call out from the texts of history to be recognized," Schreier argues, "we must consider the categorically disruptive possibility that such identification is conditioned by our critical practices."[33] In a section of a longer essay titled "Mistake II:

A Time I Mistook a Jew for a Jew," Lila Corwin Berman similarly invites historians to reflect on "the kinds of claims we make and those we wish to make when we assign Jewishness to our subjects." Rather than "identifying the bodies, objects, and territories of the Jewish people," scholars might move to "interpreting the ideas, politics, and material resources that structured bodies, objects, and territories as operating in Jewish frames."[34] The "Jewish frame" by which Freud was read, in his lifetime and after his death, may also have mistaken a Jew for a Jew, whether this mistake was propelled by a search for Jewish connections or perpetrated in service of denigrating Freud's discoveries. With Corwin Berman as our guide, we can subject these frames themselves, rather than the Jewish Freud they deliver, to historical contextualization and critical scrutiny.

Turning attention to the scholarly project of "the Jewish Freud" rather than to Freud himself has the merit of alerting us to the potential violence of the Jewish hermeneutic frame, from the Inquisition to Yerushalmi's attempts (in Derrida's critique) to expose Freud's secrets and draw Freud "back to the covenant." Such attention also accords with a recent turn in literary criticism, in which the reign of "symptomatic" (suspicious, "critical") readings has given way to other reading practices that aim to supplement or supplant symptomatic approaches: In the introduction to a special issue of the journal *Representations* devoted to "The Way We Read Now," Stephen Best and Sharon Marcus summarize the practice of "surface reading," a practice that emerged as a response to an era dominated by the "metalanguages" of Marxism and psychoanalysis, which "took meaning to be hidden, repressed, deep, and in need of detection and disclosure by an interpreter."[35] As Rita Felski puts it, literary theory in the twentieth century "cast its lot with the spirit of ceaseless skepticism and incessant interrogation," as if the task of the critic were something like that of an Inquisitor, rooting out what the text (the secret Jew) is hoping to keep hidden; under the sway of this "combative spirit," any other reading stance or affect becomes simply unthinkable.[36] But after decades of these pursuits, Felski asks, "What virtue remains in the act of unmasking when we know full well what lies beneath the mask?"[37] Foucault already drew attention to the risk that, in the fascination with what "hides," the surface might be "invisible only because it is too much on the surface of things."[38] Yerushalmi, in "The Purloined Kiddush Cups: Reopening the Case of Freud's Jewish Identity," in fact alludes to the Edgar Allan Poe story, writing that the two kiddush cups in the very front row in the photo of Freud's crowded desk were missed by scholars for the same reason Prefect of Police could not find Poe's purloined letter: "because it was staring him in the face."[39]

Perhaps the major way the Jewishness on the surface of Freud's desk (or work) goes missing is through the powerful ideological assumption that this Jewishness must be hiding, that it represents Freud's deepest, darkest secret, in line with the pathologies of other secular, acculturated Jews. The poet Shin Shalom (pen name of Shalom Joseph Shapira) gave particularly sharp expression to this assumption in a 1942 review of Zvi Woyslawski's Hebrew translation of *The Psychopathology of Everyday Life*. According to Shin Shalom, Freud asserts that the suppressed content of the unconscious is always sexual in nature. But was it a coincidence, Shin Shalom asked, "that the man who forged this great teaching was a Viennese Jew, a member of that generation of assimilating Jews who sought redemption in forgetting their Jewish essence, in being absorbed by or 'integrating with' the West? . . . Was there not a fundamental experience that was even more hidden, more suppressed, less amenable to analysis and thus more painful, which found expression in Freud's theory of exposure and confession, the cornerstone and foundation of his thought?"[40] The key to understanding Freud's work is to recognize that the *most* suppressed content is not and cannot be fully acknowledged or discussed. It is not Freud but Herzl, a member of the same generation and milieu, who provides the surer cure for their shared predicament, given that he is capable of facing the issue squarely, as Freud is not. Shin Shalom sees the starkest evidence of Freud's suppressed Jewish trauma in *The Psychopathology* and in *Moses and Monotheism*, that is, in one of Freud's early books and his last, since a man is "most naked in his youth and old age." Shin Shalom points to such relatively "naked" Jewishness in this passage at the beginning of the second chapter of *Psychopathology*, about the young man who forgets a line in Virgil's *Aeneid* as he is trying to recite it to Freud:

> Last summer—it was once again on a holiday trip—I renewed my acquaintance with a certain young man of academic background. I soon found that he was familiar with some of my psychological publications. We had fallen into conversation—how I have now forgotten—about the social situation of the race to which we both belong; and ambitious feelings prompted him to give vent to a regret that his generation was doomed (as he expressed it) to atrophy and could not develop its talents or satisfy its needs.[41]

About this exchange, Shin Shalom writes that "Freud's soul appears in a flash—this is the suppressed, revealing content that is the ultimate reason for the forgetting of a Latin word in the conversation that follows."[42] The conversation he is referring to involves Freud's attempts to help the young man he is speaking with come up with an explanation for forgetting a line of Virgil, and more particularly the word *aliquis*. After the young man associates the word *aliquis* with Simon of Trent and the blood libel, Freud responds with a guess that the stream of thoughts "is not entirely unrelated to the theme we were discussing before the Latin word slipped your memory."[43] In other words, Freud believes that both the overt topic of conversation and the unconscious forgetting of the Latin word might be explained by recourse to Jewish anxieties about antisemitism. Continuing to free-associate, the young man rapidly moves through a series of thoughts that connect blood, various saints, miracles, and martyrs, when he suddenly loses his fluency. "Something has come into my mind . . . but it's too intimate to pass on. . . . Besides, I don't see any connection or any necessity for saying it."[44] After Freud gently presses, he confesses that "I suddenly thought of a woman from whom I could easily get a message that would be very annoying to us both."[45] Freud correctly guesses that the message is "that her periods have stopped."[46] In other words, in this remarkably direct dialogue, full of literary detail, Freud presents a conversation that begins with an intimate exchange about antisemitism, stymied Jewish ambitions, and regret and moves on to a chain of religious associations that include topics of Jewish-Christian tension and that Freud assumes are related to the earlier discussion. What the young man can only haltingly express to his older friend is the more private matter of his sexual troubles.

Shin Shalom mentions another, similar conversation Freud relates that involved a different young man who also had trouble remembering a line of poetry, this time from Goethe's poem "Die Braut von Korinth." Freud notices that the line refers to heathens and "baptized Christians" and guesses that the young man's forgetting of this line might be caused by religious differences with a woman he has been thinking about: "Is yours perhaps a case that involves differences in religious belief?" Freud asks.[47] Shin Shalom paraphrastically expands and comments on this elliptical exchange:

> Which is to say, in our language [*beleshonenu*], were you a "Marrano," concealing your religion, "repressing" it? This is a "casual" question, and anyone who has read Freud knows the significance of such questions and can read in them, as in an open book, the secret of Freud's life and

work, the secret of the creative production of those "Marranos" that confess throughout the generations, from the Marranos in Spain and Portugal to the assimilated Jews of Berlin and Vienna, "the Germans of the Mosaic persuasion" and all those who lead foreign lives and write in a foreign tongue.[48]

Shin Shalom reads the exchange as connecting the secrets of the assimilated Jews of Berlin and Vienna with those that complicated and endangered the lives of their Marrano ancestors in Spain or Portugal. Writing in German requires Freud to conceal his Jewishness, but the genealogy becomes visible—"an open book"—in Hebrew, "our language," the language in which the implied and suppressed meaning of Freud's German question might be stated openly. Once again, Shin Shalom glosses over the overt (if anxious) role that Jewishness plays in this conversation, and in Freud's retrospective analysis of it, as both the *manifest* topic and as Freud's *first* assumption about the *latent* content of what was troubling the young man. Freud's German and Strachey's English, it seems, can also give voice to Jewishness and its vicissitudes. And yet: "My guess was wrong," Freud acknowledges, although "it was curious to see how a single well-aimed question gave him a sudden perspicacity, so that he was able to bring me as an answer something of which he had certainly been unaware up to that time," which was not a difference in religious affiliations but rather an age disparity between them.[49] What do we make of this apparent tension in Shin Shalom (and so many others after him) between "secret" and "suppressed" Jewish anxieties and their appearance on the pages of a published German book, on the very *surface* of Freud's conversation and discourse? Is Jewishness, expressed in German, necessarily hidden even when spoken, while Jewishness, expressed in Jewish languages, inevitably lies on the surface of these languages without coyness or indirection? And if so, is that because of the language spoken or the type of Jew who speaks it?

There is in fact an even closer example of what could be called Marrano speech, a more direct discussion and exposure of Jewishness, in *The Psychopathology of Everyday Life* than the ones Shin Shalom cites.[50] Freud included in the 1919 edition of the *Psychopathology* a telling anecdote about a slip of the tongue that constituted a "self-betrayal" of hidden Jewish identity, citing a 1916 publication by Victor Tausk.[51] The anecdote, which Tausk titled "The Faith of the Fathers," involves Herr A., a Jew who converted to Christianity to marry but who has been open about his Jewish past to his children. He finds himself at a summer guest home where the landlady is launching "sharp attacks on the Jews," apparently unaware that she is in the presence of a born Jew. The man, unwilling to speak up and spoil his family's holiday, is worried that his sons, "in their candid and ingenuous way, would betray the truth if they heard any more of the conversation." Calling to the boys,

> I said, "Go into the garden, *Juden* (Jews)," quickly correcting it to "*Jungen* (boys)." In this way I enabled "the courage of my convictions" to be expressed in a parapraxis. The others did not draw any conclusions from my slip of the tongue, but I was obliged to learn the lesson that "the faith of the fathers" cannot be disavowed with impunity if one is a son or has sons of one's own.[52]

In the two episodes of the *Psychopathology* Shin Shalom cites, Jewishness is the overt frame that ostensibly (but for Shin Shalom, hardly believably) covers a sexual worry; his own suspicion is that the *primary* secret in Freud's work is hidden Jewishness, which only in Freud's youth and old age is more nakedly presented. Tausk's "The Faith of the Fathers" differs from the cases Shin Shalom cites, since this story is Jewish through and through, in both the social situation it describes and the hidden content that threatens to erupt from beneath its facade. It is true that Herr A. is only able to express "the courage of [his] convictions" in a parapraxis, but surely Freud's citation of Tausk's anecdote in the context of his theoretical discussion of parapraxes qualifies Freud as a full-fledged theorist of the Jewish closet, who understood it well and felt just as free as Yerushalmi and Boyarin to (occasionally) fling open its door (even when not in his "naked" youth). It is true that, as Paul Roazen writes in his introduction to Tausk's collected writings, "The Faith of Our Fathers" is an autobiographical vignette;[53] Herr A. was none other than Tausk himself, who apparently lacked the courage of his convictions not only in failing to confront an antisemite but also in failing to publicly identify himself as the hidden Jew. Freud's failure to "out" Tausk, from the perspective of Derrida's critique of such aggressive Jewish hermeneutics, might be read as tact, but even so, it can hardly be read as a symptom of Freud's own self-closeting. As for Tausk's deception, his alter ego Herr A. rather cheerfully acknowledges that attempts at deception are of no use at all, given the difficulty of hiding the truth that one has a Jewish father when one also has sons. The anecdote here moves from analysis to prophecy, since it was Tausk's son—one of the very *Jungen/Juden* whose potential indiscretion so worried his father—who many years later confirmed what everyone suspected, that Herr A. was indeed a disguise for Victor Tausk.[54]

As discussed in the Introduction, scholars who see Freud as inhabiting a Jewish closet sometimes interpret his direct assertions of Jewishness as further iterations of the stubborn and unstable logic of the closet. And indeed the Herr A. episode of the *Psychopathology* demonstrates how difficult it is to disentangle avowal from disavowal, the Jewishness avowed on the surface of the anecdote in Freud's book, expressed but disguised by a pseudonym in Tausk's article, framed as an open secret in the introduction to Tausk's collected writing, concealed by Herr A. for fear that his sons will reveal the truth, a truth that is in fact brought to the surface again in the article by Tausk's son. It is hard to know whether all of this adds up, despite the apparent avowals, to yet another, even trickier Jewish closet. But it seems important to resist the Jewish studies version of what Lacan warns psychoanalysts against—taking the position of "the subject presumed to know," of placing ourselves in the role of those who stand outside and thus understand the closet, while Freud is doomed only to inhabit it. It was, after all, Freud himself who theorized the Jewish closet in 1919, as Tausk had done a few years earlier.

If the psychoanalytic concept of negation provides us a lens for reading Jewish disavowal as avowal, Jewish avowal as disavowal, then Freud's joke book helps us see the comedy of this ostensibly tragic hermeneutic oscillation, giving us the means of reading this structure anew. The vertiginous logic of the Jewish closet finds some parallels in the joke Freud relates of two Jews who meet at a train station in Galicia. "'Where are you going?' asked one. 'To Cracow,' was the answer. 'What a liar you are!' broke out the other. 'If you say you're going to Cracow, you want me to believe you're going to Lemberg. But I know that in fact you're going to Cracow. So why are you lying to me?'"[55] The joke demonstrates one way that Jewishness can be simultaneously avowed and disavowed, since the logic of negation demands that an open avowal be discounted as an evident lie. But unlike many symptomatic readings of Freud's Jewishness, which arrive triumphantly at some bottom-line Jewish truth, this joke exposes the arbitrary and circular character of avowal and disavowal and the absence of a bottom line, since Cracow and Lemberg are both Jewish cities and thus roughly interchangeable—either or both represent a Jewish "truth"; either and both can represent a Jewish "lie." What Freud provides us here is a Jewish closet without depths, without a knowable secret or intimate confines. This is the mere surface of a Jewish closet, a Jewish closet spread out as a railroad map of all of Jewish Eastern Europe, which is to say, the place where the closet, being everywhere, is also nowhere at all. Freud describes the convoluted performance of the search for truth in this joke as a "jesuitical [*jesuitische*]" exercise. But surely what he meant to say, if he were not too shy or afraid to say it, was that it was Talmudic. In calling for a reading of surfaces against "the hermeneutics of suspicion," Felski warns that "the hermeneutics of suspicion seems exceptionally resilient and impervious to direct attack, . . . sprouting new heads as quickly as we lop them off."[56]

The oddity or irony of my project has not escaped me: recommending a surface reading of the writings of Freud, the major source (alongside Marx and Nietzsche) of the drive for "depth" or "symptomatic" readings, and doing so through the pathway of Jewish languages, which so often have come to signify those very depths. It is in the wake of psychoanalysis that "apparent meaning and actual meaning fail to coincide; words disguise rather than disclose."[57] As Yael Segalovitz puts it, Freud has been read by a host of critics as "a hyperobservant (or, as Eve Kosofsky Sedgwick would claim, paranoid) *archeologist* or *detective*: a reader whom no detail escapes, who ties all elements of the text together with perfection, and who is able to demonstrate how the most trivial of features is in fact crucial."[58] But Freud provides us an ethics of avoiding imposing interpretation on those who do not invite it (mentioning his unconscious "penance" for psychoanalyzing a friend who had not invited him to).[59] In psychoanalytic practice, Freud also supplies a technique for not missing what is staring us in the face, in the recommendation that psychoanalysts listen to their patients with "evenly suspended attention," avoiding a danger "which is inseparable from the exercise of deliberate attention," which is the risk "of never finding anything but what he already knows."[60] This method applies equally to analysts and analysands, in the sense that free association enjoins patients to transmit, without selection or editing (insofar as that is possible), whatever words or thoughts pass through their minds. As Freud puts it,

> The treatment is begun by the patient being required to put himself in the position of the attentive and dispassionate self-observer, merely to read off all the time the surface of his consciousness, and on the one

hand to make duty of the most complete honesty while on the other not to hold back any idea from communication, even if (1) he feels that it is too disagreeable or if (2) he judges that it is nonsensical or (3) too unimportant or (4) irrelevant to what is being looked for.[61]

Freud's "evenly suspended attention" and the parallel instructions to patients to resist engaging in selectivity or editing their verbal associations—to "*read off* . . . the surface of his consciousness"—constitute an alternative interpretive method to the one so long marked as psychoanalytic in literary studies. For Segalovitz, this just-as Freudian or perhaps more truly Freudian method opens new avenues to an otherwise baffling text like *Moses and Monotheism*, once one recognizes that, like Freud's free-associating patients, the narrator appears to "not 'hold back any idea from communication,' notwithstanding its potential distastefulness, nonsensicality, or unimportance. The reader of *Moses*, as well, seems to have an affinity with Freud's patient relating his thoughts in a state of mobile attention."[62] Beyond *Moses and Monotheism*, Segalovitz suggests that "a wide corpus of works, from Freud to the Brazilian Clarice Lispector and the Israeli Yehuda Amichai, awaits a reading practice of evenly suspended attention."[63]

Alongside his metaphor of the psyche as a stratified ruin, with a monument buried deep within it, Freud thus also conceived of psychoanalytic interpretation as traveling more lateral routes, as in the famous passage from *The Interpretation of Dreams* quoted earlier:

> There is often a passage in even the most thoroughly interpreted dream which has to be left obscure; this is because we become aware during the work of interpretation that at that point there is a tangle of the dream-thoughts [*eine Knäuel von Traumgedanken*] which cannot be unraveled and which moreover adds nothing to our knowledge of the content of the dream. This is the dream's navel, the spot where it reaches down into the unknown. The dream-thoughts to which we are led by interpretation cannot, from the nature of things, have any definite endings; they are bound to branch out in every direction into the intricate network of our world of thought. It is at some point where this meshwork is particularly close that the dream-wish grows up, like a mushroom out of its mycelium.[64]

"The unknown" is not, Freud makes clear, something hidden that might become known, an event or trauma or desire that temporarily eludes our grasp. The tangle of dream-thoughts that presents an obstacle to the interpreter reaches into the unknown because these thoughts branch out in all directions "into the intricate network of our world of thought." The "navel of the dream" is that (non)site where an individual dreamer passes over into the first-person plural and a world where there are no clear distinctions between my thought and yours, my words and the words of all those who speak or have forgotten the same language or inhabit the same world of thought or whatever lies beyond it. The structure Freud depicts in this passage is not stratified but rhizomic, shooting out lateral roots that have no clear beginning or end, a structure that can be equally described as an entangled surface and an interconnected depth. It is the translator of Freud's German who takes up residence in that border zone that, like the dream's navel, connects Freud's German thought with the translations that carry it beyond where Freud might follow. It is not only Freud who cannot locate the point where his consciousness ends and another arises, intimately connected and yet distinct. Translators of Freud—translators in general—ply this particular territory between a dream and its navel, my thought and someone else's. John Forrester, English translator and explicator of Jacques Lacan, views such entanglements as integral to translation: "The problems of being Lacan's translator over the past few years have led to a singular intellectual phenomenon for me: an incapacity to remember whether certain ideas, when expressed in English, are 'mine,' my version of Lacan's ideas, or my translation of Lacan's French."[65] Elena Basile, reflecting on "the translator's craft as involving a form of unique *intimacy* with the other," sees translation as invariably touching "that sphere of intersubjective communication that is directly connected to affect and the unconscious: the sphere of sexuality."[66]

Speaking more specifically about what it means to have "an erotic relationship *in* and *with* Yiddish," Zohar Weiman-Kelman turns to "the figure of the fetish to explore the interplay of lack, pain, and pleasure in order to generate a new way to encounter the Yiddish past and feel its present."[67] In an essay on Yiddish, sexology, and "eroto-philology," Weiman-Kelman writes of the ways that reading Mordkhe Schaechter's unfinished Yiddish archive of "Libe" (love), his notes for a lexicon of Yiddish terms for love and sex, opens "the potential of an erotic encounter across time, queerly allowing past and present to 'pleasurably touch.'"[68] Like Forrester, like Basile, like Weiman-Kelman, in exploring the translations of Freud into Hebrew and Yiddish, I inhabit a *contact* zone in which opacity and transparency, displacement and equivalence, presence and absence, intellect and feeling and sexuality can hardly be distinguished. These relations between Freud's thought and their translational transfer (or transference) are contiguous and multidirectional, erotic and philological. The Jewish studies scholar can claim no point "above" the desiring-machine or outside the tangled knot of avowal and concealment. As language, Freud's work participates in and meets that of other languages, the most evidently shared and intersubjective component of the psyche, indeed, for Lacan, its very structure. These languages, "native" or not, whether we know them or only of them, languages or not-quite-languages, are both "ours" and "foreign." Reik presents his most extended meditation on Yiddish in a section of his book titled "The Voices of Others in You," describing the reappearance of certain "long forgotten" jokes and proverbs as "messages from an alien territory, but it is not alien, only alienated."[69] One such proverb returned "one evening I felt unappreciated and hurt by my daughters, then in their teens," when Reik caught himself murmuring "Kleine Kinder, kleine Sorgen—grosse Kinder, grosse Sorgen" (Yiddish, "small children, small worries—big children, big worries"). Reik continues: "I was taken aback by what I had said. Was it I who had said or thought this or was it another's voice? Suddenly I had a very vivid image of my father as if seen in the center of a Rembrandtesque illumination. . . . The image lasted not more than a moment, but I distinctly heard the voice that had resounded in me."[70] Reik in this moment occupies the position of his own father in relation to his daughters, taking up his father's position (as Tausk the converted Jew had done, and his child was to do) in a chain of kinship and/as signification. Trying to determine whether the voice of the other from the depths (as internalized father) or surface (language as a set of lateral connections that come from and proceed elsewhere) may be as pointless and undecidable as knowing whether the Galicianer Jew is taking the train to Cracow or Lemberg.

If the joke about the Baroness von Feilchenfeld is useful in showing how closely Freud's stratified psyche maps onto the psycho-linguistic architecture of the modern Jewish self, it may also be helpful for dislodging the implicit depth structure that both formations assume. Focusing on the social situation in which the joke circulates rather than the situation it describes is a curious reversal of the scenario of archaeological discovery, calling attention not to the unearthed inscription or to the deft interpreter who decodes it but to the "inhabitants living in the vicinity" whose understanding of the mysterious ruins they live beside is as useless as the hapless husband who takes his suffering wife at her (French or German) word. To focus on the multilingual Jewish performance *of* the joke rather than the Jewish multilingual *in* the joke is to begin to notice the difference between the archaeological site Freud visits by analogy and the artifacts actually assembled in his rooms. That Freud's work on jokes began with a scrapbook reminds us that his archaeological interests found their fulfillment not in digging but in collecting, and in this collecting the artifact is taken from its historical context and placed within a new "world of thought." In this sense, Freud's joke might be read not as the exposure of an authentic interior self or a token of a buried Jewish past but as a fetish or commodity that signifies the bourgeois economy in which the joke circulates and the scholarly economy in which it continues to do new varieties of work. Freud's Jewishness, read through the telling of this joke, can be read as a by-product and within the framing of acculturation, in which Yiddish appears not at birth but within a joke about birth, embedded in non-Jewish languages and within a discourse whose Jewishness is signaled as much by French and German as by the Yiddish or primal scream. This is a German (per Max Kohn) that is missing Yiddish and knows (as the fetish does) that it is missing it. Nevertheless, the multilingualism of Freud's joke, vibrating with what it conceals as it exposes, by what it has forgotten or cannot express as by what it fluently delivers, by what it defers and then performs, is no more or less Jewish a site than the bedrock of Yiddish or any other Jewish language.

If Freud's recitation of the joke about the Baroness can be read as an expression of estrangement from Jewish languages and intimacy, it can also be read as the establishment of such intimacy through the desiring-machine, the Jewish joke machine that works to forge Jewish connections. Exploring the persistence of Jewish jokes in the digital era, Simon Bronner suggests that "Jewish jokes display the paradoxical features of allo-Semitism," the practice Zygmunt Bauman describes as "setting the Jews apart as people radically different from all others."[71] Allo-Semitism may function within some circles as an engine of bigoted stereotypes, but it also operates within Jewish culture through a constructed ethnic difference that forges social ties in a medium hostile to intimacy by allowing, for instance, solitary and anonymous individuals sitting before computers "to access membership of a group in a commercial mass culture . . . to address the trade-offs of assimilation and social success."[72] Freud's social circle, for all the difference in these scenes, might similarly have used these jokes to reinforce endangered Jewish forms of sociality, to bagel themselves into connection. Reik analyzes the joke about the Galician Jew on the train (another "new technology" of the modern age) in just this way, as expressing the Eastern European Jewish desire to bring assimilated Jews "down to their level" in order to kindle the kinship bonds of a lost *Gemeinschaft*.

A (strategic, heuristic, noncombative) suspension of the hermeneutics of suspicion might similarly open up new readings of Freud's explicit citations of Jewish languages in *The Interpretation of Dreams*, for instance in the passage in which he mentions that he consulted *Schriftgelehrte* to understand the Hebrew/Yiddish word *Geseres* that he dreamed. In Ken Frieden's view, in this passage "Freud simultaneously claims and disavows the knowledge of Hebrew and Yiddish his dream employs."[73] Adam Lipszyc is more openly skeptical, focusing less on Freud's implicit claim that he knows Hebrew and Yiddish (given that he has dreamed in those languages) than on Freud's disavowal that he knows what the word means: "For whoever the *Schriftgelehrte* were that Freud consulted concerning the meaning of the word *Geseres*—there are good reasons to believe that he consulted none and he knew all that himself."[74] The ruse is a strangely transparent one, since no reader could fail to notice that it is Freud's own dreaming mind that produced this particular phrase, even if he claims not to understand it. But why scoff at that? Is it not possible to dream or even speak a word one doesn't understand? Freud believed that dreamers in fact generally fail to understand the common symbols that appear in dreams "unless an analyst interprets them to him, and even then he is reluctant to believe the translation."[75] If people dream in common symbols whose meaning eludes us, perhaps we might use (dream, think, speak, write) words we have in common with others that are nevertheless opaque to us. If this is so, philologists and biblical scholars might be precisely the interpreters we should turn to to illuminate the meaning of words we don't know or don't know that we know.

Beyond the possibility that language scholars might know something that (the waking) Freud does not is a further possibility, that neither Freud nor the philologist fully understands the meaning of the words they dream, even if both seek in their own way to plumb this meaning. Speaking of the difficulty of understanding a word in a foreign language, Slavoj Žižek cautions us against the assumption that the enigma derives solely from its status as a foreign word rather from emerging from the foreignness of language as language, and the foreignness of ourselves to ourselves. Citing

Hegel—"The enigmas of the ancient Egyptians were also enigmas for the Egyptians themselves"—Žižek writes:

> Our effort to determine exhaustively its meaning fails not only because of the lack of our understanding but because the meaning of this word is incomplete already "in itself" (in the Other language). Every language, by definition, contains an aspect of openness to enigma, to what eludes its grasp, to the dimension where "words fail." This minimal openness of the meaning of its words and propositions is what makes a language "alive."[76]

The interpretation of a dream, Freud tells us forthrightly, cannot be left only to the psychoanalyst with his pick and shovel; philologists must be consulted, along with the local inhabitants who may still have some knowledge of the languages inscribed on the buried monument, whose traces might still persist in their speech. The later chapters of this book introduce translators of Freud's work into Jewish languages, those who know—or think they know—the meaning of the Hebrew and Yiddish embedded within or absent from Freud's prose and animating his dreams. Freud was right, perhaps, to think that Bible scholars (as so many of his Hebrew translators actually were) had access to something in Freud's dreams that he himself could not recognize. It is thus Freud who teaches that a mysterious dream might call not (only) for psychoanalysis but (also) for translation. Or perhaps he is teaching us that these two bodies of knowledge, these two arts of interpretation, are less distinct than they may seem.

The languages of Freud's dreams do not end at the mind of the dreamer but move into a larger "world of thought," if they do not find themselves, with Freud, at a place where meaning fails. This book follows a few of the channels that connect Freud with those Hebrew and Yiddish philologists who translated his words into languages that touched his German, who made Freud's enigmatic Hebrew and Yiddish known, although not to him. These translators and philologists and biblical scholars themselves struggled with the question of what these Jewish languages meant and where they came from. Did they express the very interior of the Jewish psyche, or were they, like all languages, imposed and inscribed from elsewhere? In *Moses and Monotheism*, Freud makes the rather startling suggestion that the description of Moses as "slow of speech" might indicate, in "slightly distorted" form, "the fact that Moses spoke another language and could not communicate with his Semitic neo-Egyptians without an interpreter, at all events at the beginning of their relations."[77] But native speakers also stutter, also find themselves at a loss for words. Even a "native tongue," Jacques Lacan reminds us, expresses the interruptive externality of language to the self it constitutes. Which is to say that even Yiddish, the *mameloshn*, is yet another language that speaks (in) "the Name of the Father."

I have been arguing that Freud's work and its translation into Jewish languages might be productively explored through a surface reading, one happy to take Freud at his word and resist the temptation to read him through what he might be presumed to be hiding. But "symptomatic" and "surface" readings are often difficult to distinguish from each other. Depth is an effect produced by the play of surfaces, and surfaces are messages that may suggest depths. We look for precious artifacts "buried" in the archives, whether we descend to a basement or scroll through digitized files. As a Jewish studies scholar, I have been taught to keep digging, searching for a monument that by some lucky chance will be bilingual, which will allow me to decipher the long-ago events it commemorates. My chapter on the Yiddish translations of Freud describes a notebook that Max Weinreich called his "Freud Laboratory," which contains a multilingual glossary in which he worked out Yiddish equivalents for Freud's terminology. The document is in the YIVO Archives in New York, the very site that Weinreich reportedly called "the collective unconscious of American Jewry."[78] As in the joke about the Baroness, as in the hidden languages of Anna O., this archive presents itself as the rungs of a ladder that reach down to a primary source, a primal past. As with the joke, I can hardly ignore that Weinreich's notebook is a fragment of a much larger archive whose boundaries I cannot fathom, wrenched from its living context and made to speak the words I need it to speak. And yet, with Weinreich in hand I feel myself in the company of another of those scholars of Jewish languages that Freud consulted, who touch and were touched by Freud's dream with the long tentacles of their, "our" shared tongue (but who is this "our" and where does it end?). As philologists, tellers of Jewish jokes, and archaeologists of Jewish artifacts, we can hardly escape the lure of the buried self, the monument that promises to unlock the secrets of the past. So, too, do the surfaces over which we pore repeatedly invite us to discover what they insist that they hide and name this open secret the very Jewishness of the Jewish self.

4

The Jewish Freud in an Age of Black Lives Matter

> Robeson says the Berdichev Kaddish,
> angrily demanding
> with a Berdichever's voice. And I say
> Leyvi-Yitskhok's Kaddish, accusing
> Europe and my country, accusing
> God himself . . .
> Yisgadal
> Veyiskodash; great and holy may your
> name be forever, Booker T. Washington, Fred Douglass, and
> Jack Brown.
>
> —Aaron Kurtz, "Kaddish" (1966), trans. Amelia Glaser

George Floyd was murdered on May 25, 2020, in the spring that preceded the year of research leave in which I hoped to finally finish this book. Our house in Berkeley is just off Martin Luther King Jr. Way, a major route for the parades, protest marches, and mass bicycle rallies that regularly make their way from Oakland to Berkeley City Hall. In the weeks and months in which the country was waking up to the videotaped horror of the Floyd murder and learning to "say his name" (and that of Breonna Taylor, Ahmaud Arbery, and so many others), I would sometimes be at work in the Freud closet and, hearing chanting and drumming outside, close my laptop, feel for my shoes, and go out of the closet and into the street to join whatever band of people was marching down MLK.

I have spoken about the pleasure I take in that closet, and leaving it was also a (minor) renunciation or sacrifice, an acknowledgment that there were other things—lives—that mattered more than my treasured privacy or the thoughts about Freud I was struggling to clarify. In Nietzsche's *Gay Science*, Zarathustra writes of the sheer relief of closing "a very decent scholarly book," one written "while sitting in front of an inkwell, with a pinched belly, his head bowed low over the paper." In such a book, "cramped intestines betray themselves—you can bet on that—no less than closet air, closet ceilings, closet narrowness."[1] And it was a relief to close that laptop, breathe something different than my closet air, take a break from the narrowness and tedium and agony of writing. Elspeth Probyn explores academic writing as an act that "affects bodies. Writing takes its toll on the body that writes and the bodies that read or listen."[2] What she sees in the bodily posture of the scholar is, more particularly, shame: for adding yet another tome to the too many in the world; for participating in a form of writing excoriated for its elitism, turgid prose, absurd preoccupations, and inconsequential concerns; for being inadequate to the tasks scholars set themselves; for turning our backs on our families and friends and a world with urgent needs. Because writing and affect are both modes of contagion, writing about shame, even in an attempt at inoculating oneself against it, inevitably produces new, more stubborn variants of the shame virus, which then go on to infect readers. Probyn takes Primo Levi as the virtuoso interpreter of shame, in his heroic attempts (fighting shame) to chart "the gray zone, or the plurality and shades of shame," which includes the shame of the victim, the bystander, the witness, the writer, the reader—all who find themselves touched by and thus included in the horrific and shameful events Levi describes.[3] For Levi, shame overflows the boundaries between perpetrator, victim, and witness, blurring the distinction between an individual and the world and traversing the realms of society, politics, and scholarship. Shame, Probyn writes, arises "from a collision of bodies, ideas, history, and place."[4] As broadly shared as this affect might be, Probyn calls for affect theorists to be as concrete as Levi is about shame, to avoid flattening the specific shape of affects as experienced by this or that embodied individual into generalities and abstract theory.

To the lugubrious, ashamed, constipated scholar in his closet, Nietzsche counterposes a new kind of *Wissenschaft* that takes shape "in the open air," a teaching that emerges from a moving body on a mountain hike. I left my closet not to hike or dance alone in a meadow but to march in a crowd down a city street; the new *Wissenschaft* being constructed in those marches was no sublime and free meditation on nature but a communal political expression of rage against the murderous violence and injustice inflicted on Black and brown bodies on the hard pavements of American streets. I have described this as marching, but let me be more specific, since the word stands in for a host of gestures: the threshold moment at the first march I joined when I stepped down from sidewalk to street after a slight hesitation and thereby went from the bystander I intended to be to the participant I became; taking up a sign that someone handed me; feeling my normally fast ("New Yorker") walking pace slowed down by the sluggish crawl of the "marching" crowds; and finally synched with the mood, taking up the chant, saying the names of George Floyd and Breonna Taylor and Eric Garner, propelled by a raggedy drum beat and call and responses that came from various sides, surging and overlapping like waves. The sea of mostly masked marchers included, in Berkeley at least (and elsewhere, too, as everyone could see, as the media did not fail to note), mostly white faces. White faces in which I saw a reflection of my own, feeling what I myself was feeling.

There was a powerful pride in these body postures, signs, affects, objects, but joining the march did not entirely allow me to escape the scholar's shame of devoting time to "ivory tower" scholarship at such a moment; or the white person's shame of having benefited from the systems of racial violence that had killed George Floyd; or the bystander's shame of having witnessed, and witnessing now on repeat, that shameful act. And maybe there was also a Jewish shame in this brew, for me in particular, of having wrapped myself with lovingly cultivated and satisfyingly cozy Jewish objects and projects and connections, of having participated in what Elin Diamond calls "the Violence of 'We.'" Diamond is referring to the ways scholarship works through "normative rules of inclusion and exclusion" that fail to account for the power of its own framing, making ostensibly neutral intellectual judgments that in fact derive from an unconscious and unacknowledged set of identifications.[5] Joining the march, in this sense, meant not only giving up an uninterrupted afternoon of work but also, in another sense, of relinquishing for the moment my own "identificatory investments" in a charmed circle of Jewishness, the intimate nest of Jewish connections and languages and books and characters I was weaving around myself in my closet. Leaving the closet and joining a march, I was facing, along with millions of other Americans, the more unsettling and certainly less cozy truth that I was a white person in racist America.

George Floyd's murder came not long after the devastating attack at the Tree of Life synagogue in Pittsburgh (October 27, 2018), an attack that, along with the Charlottesville Unite the Right rally (August 11–12, 2017) at which white supremacist marchers notoriously chanted, "Jews will not replace us," struck many as the return of a long-repressed American antisemitism. In this context, it was not unreasonable to seek alliances across religious, racial, and ethnic lines. Black Lives Matter (BLM) certainly invited and attracted white allyship, but it was laser-focused on the specific violence and aggression that was a daily feature of life for Blacks and other people of color (including Jewish people of color) in America. And this was a lesson that required that white Jews become allies as whites. This stance was different, it seems to me, from the cultural-political position taken by liberal and progressive Jews a generation ago, in which being seen as *not* white ostensibly served a broadly progressive agenda, marking Jewishness as countercultural, presenting Jews as natural allies of other marginalized minorities, and combating bourgeois Jewish assimilationism (and, in some formulations, Zionism, read as mimicry of European colonialism).[6] The insistence that white-passing Jews are not really white has nearly the opposite effect today, signaling a reactionary unwillingness to acknowledge the white privilege of white Jews. Subjecting the term "white-passing" to scrutiny in the *Forward*, Nylah Burton acknowledged that if the Jewishness of white Jews was unmasked, they might be subject to prejudice or worse, but passing as white nevertheless came with a host of benefits even if the Jewishness of "white-passing" Jews were known, including that "their loan rates would stay the same and the police won't be more likely to pull the trigger." Burton concludes that, because of their ability to avoid the daily microaggressions and outright discrimination accorded to Black people, "white Jews aren't passing. White Jews are functionally white."[7] The British-Ghanaian philosopher Kwame Anthony Appiah laid out a similar argument in a *New York Times* "Ethicist" column that appeared in October 2020 in response to the rather plaintive question by a reader: "I'm Jewish and Don't Identify as White. Why Must I Check That Box?" Here is the complete question:

> I realize that with everything going on in the world, this is a small issue, but it's bothered me for some time: Forms of all kinds often ask for a person's race. I strongly support affirmative action for historically disadvantaged groups. I'm Jewish, a category almost always lumped with white. I'm fair-skinned and have an Anglicized last name, which my paternal grandfather adopted on his arrival in this country. In other words, I can easily "pass" as white and am unlikely to personally suffer any anti-Semitism. Nevertheless, I bristle at being considered or listing myself as white. My father did suffer from anti-Semitism as a young man, and I have relatives who perished in the Holocaust, some

in concentration camps.

I do not believe Jews in the United States need affirmative action. It's more of a moral question for me. I don't identify as white. Why should I list myself that way?[8]

Naming one's Jewishness, for the questioner, involves the "moral" principles of accuracy and integrity and makes it clear that such naming should not be taken as special pleading, as making a case for Jewish "affirmative action." The Ethicist (Appiah), taking the position that Ashkenazic Jews should check the "white" box, writes: "Like Jacob and Esau, the racial designations 'white' and 'Black' were born twins." Whiteness may be an inaccurate umbrella term for a group that includes European Christians and (some European) Jews, but so is Blackness a homogenizing reduction of the diverse individuals, with distinct origins, that fall within the category. If Blacks cannot escape the category they inhabit because of the "intellectual error" of reductive racial thinking, neither should whites, since racial reductivity is not merely an "intellectual error"; it also entails the "moral error" of racial hierarchy; it is the moral error that makes it imperative for white-appearing people (including white-appearing Jews) to affirm their own position within a racial system that they benefit from even if it misreads them. Appiah expressed sympathy for the historical and political reasons white-appearing Jews might resist being consigned to the category of white, but these attitudes aim to rectify only the intellectual error while doing nothing to correct the moral errors of the racial hierarchy of the United States. Appiah does not take this further, but it seems to me there is another step to take, which is that naming one's Jewishness, in at least certain contexts, may be a strategy for white-appearing Jews to *evade* recognizing their place within this hierarchy. The ethical act for such Jews is to "check the box" of whiteness, since

> being white is not just a matter of identifying as white; it involves being treated as white, and that isn't up to you. So, however you think of yourself, your whiteness is doing work in social life. In the current conjuncture, what's more, there's something to be said for accepting that you are, willy-nilly, white, because you can use your whiteness as an anti-racist instrument.

It is worth noting that Appiah did not take the opportunity in this exchange to compare antisemitism and anti-Black racism, maintaining a sharp focus on the American racial order.[9] But this comparison has certainly shaped the discourse on Jews and race. Frantz Fanon, for instance, discusses the whiteness of (European) Jews by comparing the admittedly horrific experience of the Jews in the Holocaust with the daily, normalized, inescapable indignities inflicted on Blacks:

> The Jew can be unknown in his Jewishness. . . . He is a white man, and apart from some rather debatable characteristics, he can sometimes go unnoticed. . . . Granted, the Jews are harassed—what am I thinking of? They are hunted down, exterminated, cremated. But these are little family quarrels. The Jew is disliked from the moment he is tracked down, as soon as he has been detected. But in my case everything takes on a *new* guise. I am given no chance. I am overdetermined from without. I am the slave not of the "idea" that others have of me, but of my own appearance.[10]

Bracketing for the purpose of this discussion Fanon's still-shocking description of the Holocaust as a "little family quarrel," it is worth contrasting his understanding of Jewish whiteness with Appiah's, expressed within a different political and geographic context. For Fanon, whiteness is that aspect of Jewish reality that allows (some) Jews to "go unnoticed"; Jewishness, as compared to Blackness, has the all-important advantage of being able to "hide," as it were, beneath a deceptive whiteness, the deceptiveness signaled by the qualifier in "white-appearing." For Fanon, being white makes Jews no less Jewish, even if this Jewishness may remain concealed from those who dislike the Jew "from the moment he has been tracked down." A very different conception of Jewish whiteness is at play for Appiah: white-appearing Jews do not hide their Jewishness behind the masks of their white skin. They are not even white-appearing: they simply *are white*, in the all-important sense that they are "treated as white" by a society that sees only that, and as white people escape the violence inflicted on Black or brown bodies. White Jews who have problems checking the box of whiteness are hiding not their Jewishness (as in the old formulation of Jewish assimilation) but their whiteness, perhaps to avoid participating in the painful business of white racial reckoning. Fanon had taken for granted that white skin was a deceptive screen over Jewish bodies; Appiah and many others were asserting that white skin was a sociological truth, full stop.

The set of Jewish identifications and political stances called for by the moment, coherent as they were within the focus of Black Lives Matter, intersected in complicated ways with my research project on the Jewish Freud. The renewed focus on what Fanon calls the "epidermal racial scheme" shared something with the surface theory at play in this book, the attempt to view Jewishness through other frames than the hermeneutic of suspicion. To translate Appiah into surface theory, surfaces might be deceptive, might constitute "intellectual errors"; even so, they matter—they could hardly matter more. I was looking for Freud's Jewishness as a surface phenomenon, one that I could touch in ways that didn't recapitulate the old distinctions between visible and "hidden" Jews, heroic discoverers of secret Jews and their cowering, exposed subjects. The project was not only about Freud's Jewishness and his place in a racial context different from the one in which the book was being written; given my approach, it was also about mine. If what Jewishness could mean was changing on my end, it was changing things on Freud's end, too. Appiah's cogent argument for why Jews should check that box (and how to think about it) did not lay out clearly whether checking the box was limited to filling out forms or required a more metaphorical box-checking in other contexts, for instance, in joining a BLM march as a white person (whatever that might look or feel like) or perhaps even in writing an academic monograph on the subject I was immersed in as a white person, and thus presumably keeping one's Jewishness unstated, unfelt, suspended. And this I was certainly not doing. Was my closet a way to keep my own Jewishness private, when in public I appeared—I was required, by the moral dictates of the moment, to appear—as a white person, the white person I in fact am? What happens to Jewishness in such cases, through such acts of renunciation and disciplining of the self? Did the necessity of checking the white box introduce a new variety of hidden Jewishness into the psychic landscape of Jewish modernity? The scholarship on the Jewish Freud relies on the assumption that Jewishness might remain unmentioned because mentioning it might make life inconvenient or worse or because Jewishness was shameful or painful or private. Jewishness might now be unmentioned because the imperative for Jews to check the white box went far beyond the filling out of forms, shaping a new kind of writing in which Jewishness was withheld as part of the BLM moment (and the white backlash that followed). This new kind of hidden Jew was making its presence apparent to a variety of writers, not all of whom resisted pointing it out. In an article in *Tablet*, Eddy Portnoy remarked on what he saw as the mysterious failure of "obit after obit" to mention that the comedian Richard Belzer was Jewish, despite just how Jewish a comic Belzer actually was; Portnoy cites as evidence Belzer's droll practice of intoning the opening words of the kaddish in a club whenever a fellow comic's joke died.[11]

The political currents of the moment were reverberating in the world of psychoanalysis, too, and in the intimate, public spaces of *Couples Therapy*, the Showtime series with the psychoanalyst Orna Guralnik. In a 2023 article in the *New York Times Magazine*, Guralnik spoke of the ways that couples were coming to realize that they "were talking about forces larger than themselves." While Freud had focused on "early family dramas," Guralnik herself was part of a generation of psychoanalysts who see "the social contract, our relationship to the collectives we belong to, as nested in the deepest corners of our unconscious." What was changing now was that patients themselves were understanding psychic experience similarly, finding new impetus and new discourses to talk about the class resentments or "white fragility" that troubled their relationships. As Guralnik put it, "My patients' repressed experiences with the ghosts of their country's history are as interesting as with their mothers."[12] The ghosts of their country's history were a clear reference to the profound and persistent psychic legacy of slavery and its aftermath. But were there Jewish ghosts that were emerging in the moment, her own or Freud's or that of her patients (perhaps, for instance, the Orthodox Jewish couple she treated on the show)? If so, Guralnik never mentions them, except indirectly in speaking of "the collectives we belong to." In an era so insistently marked by the return of the repressed, it is striking to witness the formation of new forms of Jewish hiddenness, different modes of Jewish silence.

The shift in the relationships between Jewishness and whiteness that might be traced from Fanon to Appiah is evident as well in the field I have been calling the Jewish Freud. An earlier generation of scholarship had understood psychoanalysis as a response to European racial schemes that, according to Sander Gilman, considered Jews physiognomically black and Jewish men both effeminate and hypersexual. These were neither new nor purely "racial" stereotypes, in Gilman's view, "for the association of the Jew with blackness is as old as Christian tradition." By becoming European, European Jews unconsciously took on European views of their own racialization, "as if confronted with the reflection of their own reality."[13] They also internalized colonial attitudes toward others; for Daniel Boyarin, Theodor Herzl's "early determination that the

Jewish State must be founded in Africa or South America" follows the logic of European colonialism as part of "the broader project of becoming 'white men.'"[14] As evidence that Freud internalized European views of Jews as nonwhite, Boyarin takes his 1922 correspondence with the Indian psychoanalyst Girindrashekar Bose, who sent him a portrait by a family friend that, in Freud's view, missed "certain racial characteristics" in his appearance and depicted him as if he were a British officer.[15] Boyarin comments:

> As this anecdote suggests, Freud's origins as *Ostjude* impeded his aspirations as a bourgeois European; he was both the object and the subject of racism. From the colonized perspective, Freud might look like a white man; from his perspective, and that of dominating white Christians, he was a Jew, every bit as racially marked as the Indian. In the racist imaginary of the late nineteenth century, Jews most often appeared as mulattos. The best denotation for the "race" of the European Jew seems to be off-white.[16]

While Freud's racial position was the subject of intense scrutiny in this scholarship, it was rarely juxtaposed with the racial positions of these (Jewish) scholars. But this is changing: In a 2022 essay in the *Cambridge Journal for Postcolonial Literary Inquiry* exploring the meaning and potential value of Jewish collectivity (and dedicated to the memory of George Floyd and Breonna Taylor), Boyarin forthrightly refers to himself as "white." Whereas Herzl's whiteness was aspirational, and Freud's whiteness is the mistake only a (more?) racialized colonial subject could make, Boyarin's acknowledgment of whiteness recognizes his material position within the contemporary American racial order. Despite this acknowledgment, Boyarin is not entirely prepared to concede Fanon's point that (white) Jews have the advantage of being able to pass, given that the Nazis were well able to find Jews, whether because of their open Jewish affiliations or because of the "debatable features" Fanon mentioned. Nor is Boyarin willing to see the ability to pass, even if it this ability was universally true, as an unmitigated benefit:

> This "whiteness" or invisibility of the Jew is a trap as well as a refuge. Perhaps I sat on a train at a time in my life when I was not so detectable as a Jew and sitting across from me in the subway car was a Hasid from Brooklyn. "Look Mom, look, a Jew! dirty. Ikh." If I am silent at that moment, I have alienated myself from myself; if I speak, then I have

been "detected." The epistemology of the closet. Despite Fanon's envy of the Jew's alleged possibility of disappearance—notoriously it didn't work too well among the Nazis—he too understands well the psychic cost of deracination.[17]

Fanon stresses what (white) Jews gain by being white, but, as Boyarin shows, he also provides tools to understand "the psychic cost of deracination," the price exacted by white society for Jewish inclusion in its ranks. Acknowledging that Jews are "not threatened now, almost anywhere, with the soul-crushing pervasive and literally deadly racism that down-presses Blacks," Boyarin nevertheless laments that "we are indeed commanded through ideological state and ideological nonstate apparatuses to leave behind our Judaïtude, our Jewissance, and become indistinguishable in the society except in the most trivial ways."[18] Against this deracination, Boyarin appeals for a "thicker" Jewishness, not as religion and certainly not as Zionism, that strengthens Jewish collectivity by a return to Jewish languages and a sense of itself as "an aggregation of folk with a common *Lebensart* and stories about themselves and each other." Such a "Jewish nation" would and should eschew state power in favor of local engagements in the fight for justice, maintaining Jewish cultural distinctiveness alongside the distinctiveness of other groups. Boyarin's essay, almost a manifesto, ends with these rousing lines:

> A future of *doikayt* (hereness, solidarity with others in our locale: Black Lives Matter!) and *Yiddishkayt*/Judaïté/Judaïtude (creative—and critical—loyalty to the diasporic culture of the Jews everywhere) synchronously, of fervid solidarity with the people and nations we live among in the territory, in the state of our dwelling, the United States for me, as well as for our national life as members of the Jewish nation wherever and in whatever state we are. The diaspora nation.[19]

In some sense, my project answers this call, with its open fascination with the way Jewishness operates as an engine of collectivity and connectivity. Surface readings of Freud's Jewishness, those that avoided the trope of the hidden Jew, have the advantage of leveling the field between open and hidden Jews, Jewish studies professors and those whose Jewishness they expose and scrutinize. Part of what has evaded scrutiny by the hermeneutics of suspicion is what might be called the Jewish "racial thinking" *shared* by the scholar and her subject, by which I mean not only Freud's wrongheaded adoption of European misconceptions but also those places where what

Freud is saying is something Boyarin (or I) might also say or believe—for instance, that Jews are not quite white or even that there are people who are Jews. The work of Benjamin Schreier, Lila Corwin Berman, and others has brought attention to the modes by which Jewish studies not only studies Jews but also constructs, frames, imagines Jewishness.[20] In their view, Jews need to understand how they racialize themselves and what it means to see or recognize someone as Jewish. From this perspective, it is no longer clear that the racism evident in Freud and Herzl should be understood as borrowed from European colonialist models (leaving the racism of Jewish studies professors unexplored). There are indigenous Jewish categories that might shape the racial consciousness of even assimilated Jews, whether they are attempting to understand themselves or others.

The concept of Jewish "racial thinking" is at the core of the provocative argument that Eliza Slavet makes in *Racial Fever*, which begins with an exploration of how "ordinary Jews" think about Jewishness. Slavet claims that Jews tend to think of themselves in racial terms, even if they no longer use the word "race." Jewishness is believed to be passed "through the blood" as a powerful and enigmatic inheritance that is not easily shed. It is precisely because Jewishness is not entirely obvious, because it fails to conform to what Fanon calls "an epidermal racial schema," that it often gives rise to a certain obsession that Slavet calls "racial fever." Slavet points out that

> within Jewish communities and families—both observant and secular, both conservative and liberal—there is often an almost obsessive desire to know whether a person is Jewish. The definition of Jewishness in these cases is almost always purely genealogical in that the question is not whether a person feels, acts, thinks, or looks Jewish but whether such suggestive signs are evidence of "the real thing"—the fact that the person has a Jewish parent (or even a grandparent), the fact that the person "really" is Jewish. Indeed, it is not uncommon to hear (both Jewish and non-Jewish) people say that someone is "half-Jewish" or a "quarter Jewish" or even a "mixed breed," even as they are fully aware of the racial (and possibly racist) logic of such descriptions. For better and often for worse, the concept of race is a historical reality whose influence reaches far beyond the color line.[21]

The almost obsessive desire to know whether someone is Jewish, which Slavet sees as accompanying these racial conceptions of Jewishness, manifests itself in a fascination with genealogy and the pursuit of "ancestral memories that can somehow explain the tensions and compulsions of the present, and to reconstruct and return to these narratives as if they were indisputable history and palpable facts."[22]

Jewishness is thus a racial/corporeal/genetic inheritance; a set of myths and narratives about what Jewishness is and means; and the hunger for these myths and for Jewish connections. From this perspective, "racial thinking" is the very foundation of my book, both in the phenomena it describes (the chord Roback struck in Freud, the fascination with Freud's Jewishness in the popular Jewish press, the Jewish connections woven by his Jewish translators) and in its writing (my obsessive collecting of Jewish Freudiana, my immersion in Freud in his most nakedly Jewish embodiment). The most radical feature of Slavet's work is that she avoids the usual framing of Freud as propagating European racial schemas, viewing him as struggling alongside us (Jewish studies scholars, ordinary Jews) to articulate the persistent and inescapable character of Jewishness, as both bodily inheritance and cultural memories (occluded by repression and forgetting). *Moses and Monotheism* splits the difference between body and story by naming the murder of Moses (a founder and non-Jew) as the event that is passed down as Jewish (bodily/literary) inheritance. However idiosyncratic Freud's ideas are on this score, Slavet accords his arguments the respect she believes they deserve, of constituting an attempt to come to terms with a conundrum that remains a conundrum, of participating in a fever that remains at fever pitch for us as for Freud.

Slavet describes her book as "an attempt to explore race beyond the realm of physical variation and to consider racial thinking without reducing it to racism."[23] She is not alone in her concern about when and where Jewish racial thinking steps over that line. Boyarin is clear that his call for "creative—and critical—loyalty to the diasporic culture of the Jews everywhere" is of a piece with "fervid solidarity with the people and nations we live among in the territory."[24] Responding to Boyarin's call in an essay titled "Communities Are Complicated; Indeed, They May Not Even Be Communal," Sander Gilman expresses skepticism that Boyarin's project can ever truly be "an ethical form of Jewish collective continuity." Recalling the Freudian-Lacanian critique of the violence inherent in the psychology of a group, which is built on "the construction of difference through the drawing of symbolic borders," Gilman suggests that any "given, self-limited definition of the 'Jew'" would inevitably be constituted through exclusion of (some) Jews as well as non-Jews: "Each constituted community creates their own authentic or inauthentic 'Jews,' and therein lies the problem."²⁵ And while Boyarin's *Judaïtude* relies on Fanon's *Négritude* as a model, it does so without, in Gilman's view, taking into account Fanon's critique of the movement: "The central problem with using *Négritude* as an answer to cosmopolitanism is that rather than being an alternative, it simply registered the code switching demanded in the colonial (and I may add the postcolonial) world of Francophonie."²⁶ While Gilman's earlier work on Freud had laid out Freud's adoption of colonial racial schemes, in 2022 he was turning his attention to those who believed that such schemes might be avoided, since such proud attempts at self-determination were only apparently liberated from the forces they claimed to oppose.

The debate between Gilman and Boyarin, which played out in the *Cambridge Journal of Postcolonial Literary Inquiry*, had an urgent counterpart in a blog post published in October 2020 in *In geveb*, an online journal that aims "to be the home for the next generation of Yiddish scholarship."²⁷ The blog featured a roundtable discussion, "'Black Lives Matter' and Talking about Blackness in Yiddish," with Jonah Boyarin (Daniel's nephew), Ri J. Turner, and Arun Viswanath. The discussion explored the concrete issue of finding an appropriate, "authentic," collective, and historically resonant Yiddish translation for the phrase "Black Lives Matter," while recognizing the symbolic systems of differentiation that Gilman emphasized, the places where Yiddish racial thinking slid into racism. This debate in some sense enacted the *Yiddishkayt* and *doikayt* Daniel Boyarin movingly called for, as theory and in practice—the activists took it for granted that Yiddishists were going to BLM marches and carrying Yiddish signs. Turner put the question directly: "What do I write on the placard I'm taking to this majority-Anglophone protest tomorrow?" That is, "How do you say 'Black Lives Matter' in 'authentic' Yiddish?" Does one rely on how Hasidic Jews would say it, "since they're the ones with a critical mass of native speakers and thus the ability to demonstrate 'organic' linguistic evolution that's driven by the 'authentic usage of the masses'?" More generally, "How does one speak respectfully about Blackness and Black experience . . . for an audience of Yiddish speakers?"

As intricate and important as these questions were, they did not touch directly on the broader one of why someone would want to carry a Yiddish sign to a BLM march, where white allyship was being invited and manifested. My book focuses on the role of Jewish languages in establishing Jewish connections in relation to Freud and his translation and reception, but these languages were doing a different kind of work on contemporary political signs and posters. These languages did not all work the same way. The Hebrew references to Exodus 23:9 ("for you were strangers in the land of Egypt"), for instance, which were so ubiquitous on posters at immigration rallies in the early years of the Trump administration (at least in New York, where I spent 2016–17) created different kinds of associations than the more complicated and difficult attempts to translate "Black Lives Matter" into Yiddish. While the biblical references on the immigration signs worked to tie together Jewish experiences immigrating to the United States, the ethical vision of the Bible and the Jewish ethnic connection with it, and the natural home of Jews on the left at this moment, the meanings generated by writing "Black Lives Matter" in Yiddish or in a recognizably Jewish script were far less clear. If this was virtue signaling, what was Yiddish (virtue) signaling? These differences also spoke to the distinct political cultures of Hebrew and Yiddish studies; scholars of Hebrew had long been compelled to reckon with Zionism and its effects, but such reckoning had no real corollary in Yiddish studies, which appealed to many students and activists precisely because they saw it as untainted by Zionism, as a culturally rich and politically diasporic Jewish language. At least some participants in the roundtable took it for granted that Yiddish was an entirely appropriate language for a BLM sign, given what Jonah Boyarin described as "the shifting, multifaceted beauty of diasporic Jewish languages and cultures," a diasporic beauty grounded in "our rooted . . . interchange with neighboring people." If Yiddish did not always signal such interchanges in an entirely straightforward way, the reason was that the language and culture had been "stunted in America by whiteness . . . bourgeois aspirations in Jewish communities; the segregation of white Jews from communities of color, including Jews of color; and the Holocaust."[28] Yiddish BLM signs were thus aspirational for contemporary progressives, who could not rely on the language as they had been taught it to convey what they wanted it to convey. Whatever the historical processes that had brought Yiddish to this point, the speakers were painfully aware that a number of Yiddish terms, whatever they had meant in earlier periods, now registered (particularly at the borders of Yiddish and English) as racial slurs. This "internal," shameful character of Yiddish thus stood at some tension with its vaunted history of participation in progressive causes and solidarity across racial lines. The problem was partly that Yiddish was often half-known, fragmented, and appropriated in English and other languages rather than understood in richer cultural context. Vishwanath described the issue:

> The Yiddishist circle is concerned with ownership over the language in the face of a broader Jewish and non-Jewish world that frequently coopts and adapts Yiddish words. A common reaction to those who object to the term *shvartser* is "But that's a *kosher yidish vort* (legitimate Yiddish word)" or "But it's a completely neutral descriptor!" In other words, why should the use of this word as a slur in English by people who don't even speak Yiddish—or even the fact that actual Yiddish speakers sometimes utter the word in a denigrating and racist tone—be allowed to dictate how Yiddish speakers without racist intentions use their own language?
>
> At the same time, the Yiddish language is in many ways the most compact and symbolic manifestation of what the majority of American Ashkenazi Jews have lost (or given up, or had taken from us) in accessing American whiteness. As a result, it makes sense that for those of us who haven't given it up or have chosen to reclaim it, it becomes one of the battlegrounds at the intersection between the benefits of white privilege and the costs of assimilation.

Turner brought the discussion back to the urgent practical matter of the Yiddish signs: "If we have to choose for the time being between a racial slur and an American/English-centric term like the loanword *blek*, the latter may not be a perfect solution but there's not really any question which option is better. And that's what's going to happen anyway; people are going to use *blek* or *Afro-Amerikaner, Afro-Eyropeer*, etc. or *mentshn fun Afrikaner opshtam* because these are the non-pejorative options that we have at hand and then we'll see what's going to happen from there."

The roundtable seemed to agree that the racism expressible in Yiddish could be traced to "what the majority of American Ashkenazi Jews have lost (or given up, or had taken from us) in accessing American whiteness." It was not a pure fantasy to assume that Yiddish speakers who had not fallen for the supposed benefits of American whiteness were capable of the solidarity that both Boyarin and the *In geveb* activists saw as part of what *yidishkayt* had to offer. It was an act of scholarly solidarity for Max Weinreich, a central figure in conceptualizing Yiddish for moderns, to turn to the American race theorists of his time for methods and approaches to the study of Jewish youth, recognizing parallels between their experiences and those of Black adolescents in the Jim Crow South. But the reputed talent of Yiddish and Yiddishism for racial solidarity, with American Blacks above all, was also being questioned in the pages of *In geveb*. In the blog, the June 2021 special issue dedicated to "Race in America, *af yidish*," and elsewhere in the journal, scholars who had been drawn to Yiddish studies at least partly for its leftist history were rereading Yiddish antiracist literature to see whether it retained its appeal, asking whether the *yidishkayt* that had appealed to them had ever truly existed. Jessica Kirzane (editor in chief of *In geveb*) read David Opatoshu's story "Lintsheray" (Lynching) as expressing Opatoshu's critical sense that the move from Europe to America produced not only "a cultural gap" between the generations but more troublingly "an ethical gap—the newer generation grows not simply away from Jewish cultural, linguistic, or religious practices but toward lawless violence."[29] But Marc Caplan, reading the same story, depicts Opatoshu himself as falling into the racism Kirzane sees the author as criticizing in his younger characters, in the dehumanizing and racist language used in depictions of lynching victims, a discourse Opatoshu "inherited . . . from white racism."[30]

The racial reckoning in the field of contemporary Yiddish studies, while dealing in real time with the most concrete immediate concerns, also turned back to the ideological foundations of the field of Yiddish. In a 2016 essay, Miriam Schulz explores "the epistemological interdependence between the philological discipline and the racial paradigm in general."[31] Because philology and "racial science" were so deeply interconnected in the nineteenth century, attitudes toward Yiddish and the racial character of Jews also went hand in hand, with Yiddish-speaking Jews understood as a backward "mixed race" that deviated from the European model of "one language—one race" and that thus threatened the entire racial-national-language paradigm. In combating or transvaluing these denigrations, Yiddishist ideologues regularly asserted the superiority of Yiddish in one regard or another. Borochov, arguing for the longevity and distinctiveness of Yiddish vis-à-vis German, turned the usual historical sense of Yiddish on its head by claiming that German, in his view an impoverished mishmash of dialects, was required to borrow from Yiddish. Where previous generations of Jewish intellectuals had viewed *Daytshmerish*, the Germanized Yiddish style, as a kind of upgrade of Yiddish, Borochov accused those speaking it of actually bringing Yiddish *down* "to the level of a dirty jargon."[32] In quoting such attitudes, Borochov was also despite himself embracing "the racialist terminology prevalent in fin-de-siècle philology" and repeating its gestures in demanding that Yiddish "be cleansed of foreign elements."[33] For early twentieth-century linguists, philological questions were inevitably also racial ones; so Borochov's discussion of the different components in Yiddish leaned heavily on racial assumptions, in asking whether "'Jew-talk' was more Semitic or more Aryan, more Germanic or more Slavic? Or is it maybe, possibly simply Yiddish?"[34] Borochov's categories merely repurposed the old systems of exclusion, demonizing speakers of "inauthentic" Yiddish, who "tainted" the purity of the tongue with an alien language. The old terms of debate were reversed, but the discriminatory systems remained the same in their prejudices and exclusions. This is the structure of mimicry Gilman cautions us to recognize in all forms of group formation, even those that intend to oppose rather than imitate the unsympathetic views about Jews and Jewish languages in the dominant culture.

For Schulz, Weinreich carried on where Borochov left off, similarly "convinced of the civilizational power and identitarian force of language," an interest that spilled over to his comparative work on Jewish and Black adolescence. Weinreich was struck by the parallels he recognized between American Blacks in the South and European Jews under the shadow of Nazism, but he also saw "one important difference" between the communities: "In fact, the great masses of African Americans do not have a way of life of their own, and have no aspiration to develop a distinctive culture. The norm they strive for is that of white America, *their language is English.*"[35] By contrast, a Jewish child

> conceives of his *yidishkayt* only by dint of speaking Yiddish at home, through a Yiddish sign at the door. That is how the child will grow up with the awareness that there are different groups of people living in the world, and we are one of them, no better or worse than the others.[36]

As we have seen, Weinreich took the experiences of Black Americans in the South as a close parallel to that of the Yiddish-speaking masses who were his primary object of study. But his (perhaps surprising) view was that Blacks were in crucial sense more white (!) than Jews were, since they lacked "a distinctive culture." A more precise parallel would compare Black Americans with those Eastern European Jews who spoke a European tongue; Weinreich points out that Polish Jews in fact had begun referring to their Polonized coreligionists as "Warsaw Negroes," a reference to Antoni Słonimski's 1928 satirical play about assimilated Jews. In Weinreich's view, Polonized Jews were increasingly subjected to the same antisemitism as their more identifiably Jewish counterparts among the Yiddish-speaking masses but, like American Blacks (as he saw it), lacked the linguistic or cultural means to psychically protect themselves from this racism. Yiddish did important psychic work by maintaining Jewish distinctiveness; but Weinreich also insisted that the language conveyed the message that Jews were "no better and no worse" than others.[37] Despite this assertion, Weinreich makes clear that he himself views Jews as "better" than others, at least insofar as he views those ethnic groups that maintain their own language and culture as psychically healthier than those that lack a distinctive language and culture.

As outrageous as it is to claim that American Blacks fall into this latter category, the distinction—as Gilman might have predicted—also excludes many Jews from the superior psychic position that accrues to members of minority groups who maintain their own languages. Nor is Weinreich being entirely straightforward about what Yiddish itself conveys about Jewish superiority, since he identifies the language in both *The Path to Our Youth* and *History of the Yiddish Language* as a tool to inculcate Jewish difference precisely as superiority. It is true that in *The Path to Our Youth* Weinreich defends such linguistically reinforced expressions of Jewish superiority as a compensatory response to the cultural denigration of Jews, and in his *History* he describes Yiddish *lehavdil-loshn* (differentiation language) as part of its traditional and premodern repertoire: "There are words," Weinreich writes, "applied to Jews (or even neutrally, when no differentiation is intended), and these have a parallel series that has to begin with a derogatory connotation or one of disgust."[38] In a note to this discussion, Weinreich asserts that this differentiation language has "either withered or completely dropped out" among secular moderns, but his own assertions about the psychic transmission of Jewish culture, discussed in the last chapter of this book, open the question of whether and how these or related modes of discrimination might persist in post-traditional Jewish culture, his thought, and indeed my own.[39] How do the old forms of Jewish differentiation, moreover, map onto the American racial order most at issue here? Appiah begins his essay on why white-passing Jews should self-identify (at least on official forms) as white by asserting that "**Like Jacob and** Esau, the racial designations 'white' and 'Black' were born twins"; perhaps he is delicately alluding here to the traditional Jewish discourse that takes Jacob and Esau to represent Jews and non-Jews and thus reminding Jews that their own culture has its own long history of racial thinking, its own set of hierarchies, that is ultimately not so different from the "epidermal" order of contemporary America.

It seems to me that, even in this moment of racial reckoning, many of the apologetic assumptions about Jews and Yiddish put forward by Weinreich continue to operate. From Boyarin's critique of Herzl to Schulz's deconstruction of Yiddishist nationalism and Kirzane's reading of Opatoshu, Jewish racism is associated with assimilation, distance from the Jewish tradition, and non-Jewish influence. Herzl dreams of a colony in Africa or South America as a Jewish mimicry of British colonialism; Yiddishists borrow racial philology from those who target them through it; the younger son in Opatoshu's "Lintsheray" is more racist than his immigrant father because he is closer to American culture. Such assumptions leave intact the vision of a traditional Jewish collective free of racial hierarchies and exclusions. Even Weinreich, who devotes pages to the Yiddish "differentiation language" that privileges Jews over others, explains these propensities as reactions to anti-Jewish attitudes. It may be a different kind of compensatory mechanism to locate Jewish racism solely in assimilationism, colonial mimicry, or the justified response of a persecuted minority. But can we really distinguish Freud's ("borrowed") from Weinreich's (ostensibly "indigenous") racism? And where did my own racism come from: the Yiddish-speaking, ultra-Orthodox, economically disadvantaged world in which I was raised or the Anglophone, largely middle-class, and white world in which I now spend my time? If Yiddish transmitted and transmits racism along with cultural distinctiveness and rich life-forms, the work of antiracism will have to be targeted not only at the "assimilationists" and social strivers but also at ourselves, by which I mean also at myself, as a Jewish studies scholar, a champion of *yidishkayt*, and a regular, even professional, indulger in the pleasures of Jewish connection. Like the refuge of "whiteness," the pleasures of *yidishkayt* might also be a trap, for someone else's fingers if not my own.

5

Touching, Feeling, Translating Freud

> [Archive Fever] is a compulsive, repetitive, and nostalgic desire for the archive, an irrepressible desire to return to the origin, a homesickness, a nostalgia for the return to the most archaic place of absolute commencement.
> —Jacques Derrida, *Archive Fever: A Freudian Impression* (1996)

> What is found in translation is . . . translation.
> —Emily Apter, "The Wolf-Man, Found in Translation" (2007)

On November 7, 1955, the French psychoanalyst Jacques Lacan gave his famous lecture at the Vienna Neuropsychiatric Clinic that was later expanded and published as "The Freudian Thing, or the Meaning of the Return to Freud in Psychoanalysis."[1] Calling for a "return to Freud" in the very city from which he had been exiled, Lacan spoke lyrically and movingly of "the Freudian message" that "rang out from the Viennese bell to echo far and wide" but was muffled by the First World War and then again with the persecution and "immense human wrenching" of those who propagated psychoanalysis to the world. As Lacan put it, "It was on the waves of hate's tocsin and discord's tumult—the panic-stricken breath of war—that Freud's voice reached us, as we witnessed the Diaspora of those who transmitted it, whose persecution was no coincidence." While many of the persecuted bearers of the Freudian message found refuge in the United States, Lacan insisted that this refuge was a false one, since America was a place "where history is denied with a categorical will that gives enterprises their style."[2] In their flight, these bearers of the psychoanalytic message were compelled to jettison the cultural treasures they had brought from Europe, relinquishing the European historical sensibility, the psychoanalytic commitment to bridging "modern man and ancient myths," because of "the assimilation required" to be accepted in the United States. Freud's exile from Vienna thus forced the exile of his thought not only from German to English but also from history itself, to the flatter horizons of the Anglo-American social sciences.

The echoes of Lacan's lament were heard only decades later in the society Lacan (and Freud) spoke of with such disdain.[3] In 1982, Bruno Bettelheim published a *New Yorker* article, later expanded into a book, decrying the ways that James Strachey's canonical English translation had stripped Freud's work of its humanistic, philosophical, and literary soul in favor of a positivist, pseudo-scientific jargon accessible only to adepts.[4] In a misguided effort to win psychoanalysis a place in the Anglo-American social and medical sciences, Strachey had substituted such Latinate terms or opaque neologisms as "id," "ego," "free association," and "parapraxis" for ordinary, transparent, and easily comprehensible German words such as *es, Ich, Einfall,* and *Fehlleistung* (the last is a Freudian coinage that brings together two transparent German terms nearly opposite in meaning—failure and achievement).[5] Anglo-American culture of the day prized objectivity, neutrality, professionalism, and medical training, values signaled by the technical vocabulary in which it clothed psychoanalysis. But, in Bettelheim's words,

> the erroneous or inadequate translation of many of the most important original concepts of psychoanalysis makes Freud's direct and always deeply personal appeals to our common humanity appear to readers of English as abstract, depersonalized, highly theoretical, erudite, and mechanized—in short, "scientific"—statements about the strange and very complex workings of our minds. Instead of instilling a deep feeling for what is most human in all of us, the translations attempt to lure the reader into developing a "scientific" attitude toward man and his actions, a "scientific" understanding of the unconscious and how it conditions much of our behavior. . . . [But] one cannot be expected to get an understanding of the soul if the soul is never mentioned.[6]

By the 1950s, psychoanalysis had indeed established a place for itself within psychiatry and the social sciences, but, as Bettelheim saw it, acceptance had come at a price. As for Doctor Faustus, the price was no less than a man's soul, the *Seele* that animated Freud in Vienna and breathed life into his German writings but was utterly lost—sold to the Mephistopheles of pseudo-science—in Freud's English afterlife (where *Seele* was translated as "psyche" or "mind"). What the world knows as psychoanalysis is only a distorted echo of Freud, although in the *Standard Edition* it mistakenly imagines itself in possession of a primary source. This impression was bolstered, moreover, by the long delay of a critical edition in German, which led to what Strachey described as the absurd situation in which "a couple of unknown English people . . . set themselves up as editors of a German classic," a German classic that borrowed its structure and critical apparatus from the *Standard Edition*.[7] Strachey was modest enough in his dedication of the *Standard Edition*, referring to the translation as a "blurred reflection" of Freud's thoughts and words.[8] Nevertheless, Sander Gilman writes, "After decades of reading Freud in English, Freud has become 'Englished' in our sensibility, just as the 'real' Bible is the King James translation, not the Hebrew or Greek *Urtext*."[9] The James Strachey translation, in fact, is reportedly known among witty psychoanalysts as "The King James Version."[10]

Laments over the distortions that accompanied the Freudian linguistic and geographic diaspora are the requisite preludes to the lamenters' recovery projects—if very different ones: Bettelheim aims to recover a humanist Freud, restored to his native discourse of cultured European philosophical thought and accessible to an educated layperson as an integral part of the Western literary tradition.[11] By contrast, Lacan insists that the achievement of Freud's "Copernican revolution" was precisely to decenter European humanism, since "owing to [Freud's] discovery the veritable center of human beings is no longer at the place ascribed to it by an entire humanist tradition."[12] Attacked from various sides, and with the copyright lapsed, in 2003 the long reign of King James finally ended with the launch of the new Penguin Library series, in which individual works were rendered by different translators, none of them psychoanalysts, who were specifically asked not to collaborate with each other or consult Strachey's standardized "technical terms."[13] The Penguin Library editor, Adam Phillips, considers psychoanalysis a branch of literature, "a form of persuasion closer to poetry than medicine." Grouped thematically rather than chronologically, Freud appears in the Modern Masters series alongside writers such as Joyce and Proust. What Phillips aims to restore that had been lost is "an unconscious and a conscious ambiguity in [Freud's] writing, and an interest in sentences, in the fact that language is evocative as well as informative."[14] It is striking, then, that "despite the fact that the translators worked in isolation" (like the legendary translators of the Septuagint), so many terms were retained, evidence of how powerfully the *Standard Edition* had reshaped the English language.[15]

The vicissitudes of Freud's life in translation played out differently elsewhere. In France, after decades of individual translations published at an array of presses, the long-delayed *Oeuvres complètes* began to appear in 1988, edited by Jean Laplanche, Pierre Cotet, and André Bourguignon. In contrast with Phillips' views, the French editorial team advocated for a unified approach to Freud's writings, to be achieved by closely following the unfolding of key concepts over the duration of his long career; unlike Strachey, they justified this holistic approach on literary rather than scientific grounds. Suggesting that Freud intended for *Seele* to evoke *both* the psyche or mind *and* the soul, Laplanche and his coeditors view the polysemic German word as a "guiding thread that enabled Freud to show how the conscious and unconscious 'processes of the soul' are projected into a 'metaphysical' image of the soul."[16] Where Strachey and the Glossary Committee aimed to standardize psychoanalysis in a bid to secure its legitimacy, Laplanche and his coeditors aimed to register the meaningful repetitions and latent connections that wove together Freud's writing and lent resonance to individual works. Discussing Laplanche's translation of Freud's "Deckerinnerungen" ("Screen Memories"), Darius Gray Ornston Jr. notes that "the word 'cover'—*Decke*—appears throughout the German essay as a kind of leitmotif, a feature carefully respected in the French edition [*Oeuvres complètes*] but somewhat concealed in the Standard Edition," where the German root form *Decke* is covered with an English "screen" in the title and lost in such divergent local renderings as "table laid for a meal," "coincide with," and "conceals."[17] For Laplanche, Ornston, and others, Freud's writings invite a unified approach not because he constructed a professional terminology that translators are tasked with reproducing over the evident shifts in his thought but because his writings are expressions of "the style of one man."[18]

Beyond English and French, and beyond the narrow problem of translation, the scholarly world has followed a general trajectory from the scientific to the philosophical or literary Freud, with Freud retaining his status as an important modern thinker in the humanities even as the status of psychoanalysis has precipitously dropped in many corners of psychiatry and the social sciences. It is within this shift to the humanities that Jewish studies has staked its own claim in the Freudian recovery project, seeking to restore not so much Freud's "soul" as his *neshome*. Rather than aim—with Lacan and Bettelheim—to find the German writer lost in translation, these scholars hope to recover, more specifically, the secular fin-de-siècle Viennese Jew. These recovery projects, writ large, very nearly define the study of Freud in our own time, with the insistence on the German urtext behind the English translation, the tragic Greek behind the scientific Latin, the bearded philosopher behind the white-coated scientist, the persecuted Viennese Jew behind the Dead White European Male, the Yid behind the id. As Cuddihy memorably puts it, the "unspoken premise" of Freud's work "can be put in lapidary if vulgar form as follows: the id of the 'Yid' is hid under the lid of Western decorum (the 'superego')."[19]

To be clear, Cuddihy's "vulgar" rhyming of *Yid* and *id* is not his own invention. The near pun appears in a 1924 letter sent by James Strachey to his wife, Alix, who was spending the year in Berlin being analyzed by Karl Abraham and improving her German. James detailed to his wife a meeting he had just come from with Ernest Jones, Freud's disciple and biographer, and Joan Riviere, Jones's brilliant analysand and the first English translator of *The Ego and the Id* (1923), who had coined the term "id" for *es*; the meeting brought together the available members of the Glossary Committee (composed of the Stracheys, Jones, and Riviere), which had been formed in 1921 to standardize psychoanalytic terminology in English:[20]

> I had a very tiresome hour with Jones & Mrs Riviere from 2 to 3 today. The little beast (if I may venture so to describe him) is really most irritating. However, I hope I preserved my suavity.—One thing I foresee fairly clearly. Our names will be ousted from the title-page [of the *Collected Papers of Freud*] all right. Mark my words.
>
> They want to call "das Es" "the Id." I said I thought everyone would say "the Yidd." So Jones said there was no such word in English: There's "Yiddish," you know. And in German "Jude." But there is no such word as "Yidd"!—'Pardon me, doctor, Yidd is a current slang word for a Jew.'—'Ah! A slang expression. It cannot be in very widespread use then.'—Simply because that l.b. hasn't ever heard it.[21]

The l.b. won the battle over "id," but Strachey won the war—James and Alix Strachey appear as editor and translator of the *Collected Papers* (five volumes, 1924–25, with Riviere also listed as translator); more importantly, James was also appointed general editor of the *Standard Edition* (twenty-four volumes, 1953–66).[22] As interesting as it is to hear a fractious group of English-speaking gentiles discuss the worrisome question of whether readers of Freud's work might associate the id with "the Yidd," this early eruption of a Jewish language beneath Strachey's English prose reminds us that the potential for such eruptions is not limited to modern

Jews. What is at stake in translating Freud into English is not only the relationship between German and English but also the Yiddish (and the yid) liable to make an appearance behind either or both of these languages.

Attempts to conceptualize the role of translation in psychoanalysis sometimes begin with the recognition that Freud himself constructed an implicit theory of translation. Patrick Mahony noted decades ago that Freud had made an "enormous contribution to the critique of translation,"[23] a contribution often obscured—ironically and appropriately—in English translation. Throughout his writings Freud used the terms *Übersetzung* and *Übertragung* ("carrying over," "transfer," with "translation" as a secondary meaning) to describe and link in a single semantic network a host of psychic operations: symptom formation; jokes; dream work; the secondary narration, elaboration, or interpretation of a dream; the transition from one life stage to another; and transference and countertransference. Robert Young points to one of the earliest uses of the concept of translation in Freud's writing, in the 1895 case history of "Katharina." After Freud asks the suffering girl to recall what was happening to her at the time she fell ill and Katharina responds, "I was so frightened that I've forgotten everything," Freud adds a parenthetical comment: "(Translated into the terminology of our 'Preliminary Communication,' this means: 'The affect itself created a hypnoid state, whose products were then cut off from associative connection with the ego-consciousness')."[24] As Young writes, the parenthetical translation provides no new insight; it merely rephrases "the subject's own speech" so it is "translated into the scientific discourse that enables that experience to be understood as a function of the psyche or the body as it is understood in the realm of medical science."[25] The circular style here is deliberate: Young wryly asks "to what extent this psychoanalytic translation is more than a translation: to what extent does translation offer real understanding or explanation as opposed to a translation into its own specialized idiom, setting the one above the other? . . . to what extent is it *nothing but a translation*?[26] If so, what matters in Freudian translation is not the elucidation of meaning but a transfer into another, more respected, mode of discourse. In the case of psychoanalysis, the translation is "upward," from the incoherent suffering of a village girl to the professional language of those who claim to understand her. But if so, psychoanalysis also models another kind of translation, a translation "downward," as in the Baroness's from French to German to Yiddish, which Freud suggests is more efficacious and meaningful a translation, since it moves closer to rudimentary truth.

If psychoanalysis, as Young claims, is the practice of translation from psychic suffering into medical discourse, in Freud's view the psyche itself is just such a serial translator, from one sign system to another. In dreaming, the psyche translates "an occulted original" into images and scenes.[27] Ken Frieden writes that, in *The Interpretation of Dreams*, "both the dream work and the analytic work resemble translation, and are characterized by the multivalent word *Übertragung*. Dream images are like primitive hieroglyphics that ambiguously translate dream-thoughts; the work of interpretation attempts to return from the pictorial language of dreams to ordinary waking expressions."[28] Freud often mobilizes fine-grained detail in this guiding metaphor, for instance, in describing "dream-thoughts" as undergoing an *Übertragung* (transcription) into a different "mode of expression"; the thought is deciphered only by a comparison of the original and the *Übersetzung* (translation):

> The dream-thoughts and the dream-content are presented to us like two versions of the same subject-matter in two different languages. Or, more properly [*besser gesagt*], the dream-content seems like a transcript [*Übertragung*] of the dream-thoughts into another mode of expression, whose characters and syntactic laws it is our business to discover by comparing the original and the *translation* [*der Trauminhalt erscheint uns als eine Übertragung der Traumgedanken in eine andere Ausdrucksweise, deren Zeichen und Fügungsgesetze wir durch die Vergleichung von Original und* Übersetzung *kennen lernen sollen*].[29]

Freud's attempt to describe this knotty translational relationship begins with him supplying a familiar definition of translation: "two versions of the same subject-matter in two different languages." But he quickly feels the insufficiency of this conception and tries again: what distinguishes dream-thoughts and dream-content is that they are different kinds of language, with (at least) one "unknown in its characters and syntactic laws." Despite this difference, one language functions as a transcript of the other, touching it even more intimately than translation in the sense that the material features of the language and not only the meaning are also captured. Translation is a useful metaphor for Freud, but only once he revises the term, abandoning its humanist underpinnings in an ideology of the transparency and potential equivalence of languages. Rather than French and German serving as models, as they are often called to do in Western translation discourse, for Freud the primary model of translation involved at least one ancient or dead language, the kind deciphered over the course of the nineteenth century. In taking hieroglyphics as his regular example, and in suggesting that dream-content is a *transcription* of dream-thoughts into another "mode of expression" (*eine andere Ausdrucksweise*), Freud also points to the significance of what Damrosch calls "scriptworlds," the material networks and semiotic systems created by different alphabets and scripts.[30]

Comparing the (opaque) original and its (back)translation leads Freud to a kind of typology of (mis)translation. Dreams distort the content they translate along two distinct lines: *Verdichtungsarbeit*, which Strachey translates as "condensation," but for which Darius Gray Ornston suggests the alternative "the work of poetic intensification," and *Verschiebungsarbeit*, which Strachey renders as "displacement" and for which Ornston suggests "the work of shifting things around, delaying, or smuggling" (Lacan views these categories, in structuralist fashion, as expressions of the fundamental linguistic operations of metaphor and metonymy).[31] Dream-content translates hidden thoughts by intensifying them, combining multiple events, people, or affects into "overdetermined" images. Dream-content also "smuggles" forbidden thoughts past psychic censors by distorting or otherwise masking them. The pressures that propel and deform these translations continue through the stages that follow: the dream-content that translates (intensifies, smuggles in) a thought is reconstructed in fictional form in the "secondary revision" of a dream from half-remembered and jagged fragments by the censor of the waking mind. In describing this process, Freud writes that "ob uns diese Rückübersetzung ganz oder nur teilweise gelingt, der Traum behält seine Rätselhaftigkeit unverringert bei," rendered in the *Standard Edition* as "whether we succeed in making this re-translation wholly or only in part, the dream remains no less enigmatic than before."[32] This retranslated dream—or, more literally, this back-translated dream—despite its still-enigmatic and fragmentary character and its own displacements and condensations, lays the groundwork for the work of analysis and interpretation, which deconstructs the narrative back into its fragments and then back to the thoughts that generated them, attending at each stage to the intensifications and displacements that characterize each of these transformations. For Freud, translation is the connective tissue not only of the psyche but also of psychoanalysis, which follows its jagged paths and produces its own.

Among the notable features of Freud's idiosyncratic, implicit translation theory is the attention paid to the temporal dimension of translation, a dimension that unsettles the normative project of translational equivalence. In an 1896 letter to Wilhelm Fliess, Freud described the psyche as having "come into being through a process of stratification: the material present in the form of memory traces being subjected from time to time to a rearrangement [*Umordnung*] in accordance with fresh circumstances—to a retranscription [*Umschrift*]." Memory is preserved not within a single imprint, as it were, but "several times over," since a person's life is structured by a succession of "epochs" separated by a boundary, across which "a translation of psychic life takes place." In these translations, memories are not only layered but also reorganized through this layering as new "imprints" retranscribe old ones. This translation is neither precise nor smooth: according to Freud, maturation from one life stage to another involves not only retranslation of older experiences but occasionally also a "refusal of translation [*Versagung der Übersetzung*]."³³ Whether "rearranged" or "refused," the transmission of "imprints" from one stage of life is never precise or complete: mistranslation is a feature rather than a bug of the system. As Andrew Parker puts it,

> Moving behind the veil or around or through it, Marxism and psychoanalysis commonly translate backward (*zurückübersetzen* is the repeated verb form) from copy to original, symptom to source, superstructure to base, consciousness to lie, the manifest to the latent, literary fiction to scientific truth. By definition, all such translations always succeed—sense in this model never fails to reach its destination—which poses the question of whether *mis*translation can ever pertain to styles of reading in which errors make as much sense as sense.³⁴

Beyond the narrow question of textual translation, the always meaningful operations of displacement or condensation also characterize other types of phenomena, for instance, Anna O.'s *Übertragungsliebe* for Breuer, rendered in Strachey as her "transferential love," a concept standardized as "transference." Psychoanalytic interpretation, as the "back-translation" of translations that "condense" and "displace" one kind of love into another, dreams into thoughts and words, traumas and memories into symptoms, is complicated by the disparate sign systems these translations connect and by the distortions and slippages that constitute the connections. If difficult memories and feelings succeed in moving from one sign system to another and surviving from one epoch into another, they do so only by shape shifting and distortion: combining two people into one, concealing one incident behind another, substituting one body part for another, or expressing an unacceptable thought in the form of a joke. Freud's conception of translation (as of sexuality) is thus distinct from and more expansive than the ordinary usage of the term, which Roman Jakobson refers to as "interlingual translation, or translation proper." Unusually, or improperly, Freud is less interested in "interlingual translation" than in the two other types of translation Jakobson identifies: the *intralingual* (rewording or paraphrase) and especially the *intersemiotic* (translation between different sign systems).[35] These are hardly discrete operations: Freud presents complex examples of psychic translation that combine Jakobson's three types. Mahony points to a footnote added in 1910 to the section on "Bungled Actions" in *The Psychopathology of Everyday Life* describing how the habitual absentmindedness of the Hungarian psychoanalyst Sándor Ferenczi translated his unconscious thoughts: One day, anxious that he had made a mistake in a treatment, "throughout the day he stumbled several times (a representation of his *faux pas*)."[36] Ferenczi's stumbles are intersemiotic, translating an anxious thought into the sign system of bodily actions; interlingual, in the appearance of French in an otherwise German phrase "(Darstellung jenes *faux pas* in der Behandlung)"; and intralingual, if we can so term the "rewording" that connects a (verbal) mistake metaphorically with a faux pas, and then literally translates it into/as a (physical) "false step." While a translation that works through *condensation* is imaginable, these translations, whether intralingual, interlingual, or intersemiotic, generally work through the *displacement* Freud identifies in dream work. Speaking more narrowly of the sign system of the body, Ferenczi's slip functions as a *downward displacement* from tongue to foot, a variation on the better-known upward displacement of penis to nose or eyes.

Perhaps the most interesting explorer of the intersection between translation studies and psychoanalysis is Jean Laplanche, student and analysand of Lacan and head of the editorial committee that produced the first complete edition of Freud's works in French. Laplanche took up his teacher's invitation to "return to Freud," focusing in particular on what Laplanche considers a fateful mistake in the development of psychoanalysis: the abandonment of the "seduction theory." Revising and generalizing Freud's theory of "infantile seduction," Laplanche argues that seduction is in fact an ineluctable feature of the asymmetrical relationship between adults and children; the mother who breast-feeds her infant also "proffers to a child verbal, nonverbal and even behavioural signifiers which are pregnant with unconscious sexual significations." These messages, felt but not understood, through their "excess" and "disequilibrium" present the infant with "the need to translate." So, too, are gender distinctions and roles, for Laplanche, among the most fundamental and enigmatic messages from the adult world to the infant.[37] Drawing on the letter to Fliess that conceives of maturation as translation, Laplanche views the infantile unconscious as constituted by the *enigmatic messages* of the other, in which nonlinguistic communication that fails to be "metabolized" persists in and *as* the unconscious. The psyche is the language of the unassimilated other. In John Fletcher's view, Laplanche sees clearly what Freud himself missed and which led to Freud's failure to complete the "Copernican revolution" of decentering the human subject. Initially catching sight of "the consequences of the priority of the other in the constitution of the . . . sexual human being," Freud then fell short in recognizing the ramifications of his thought, "in an almost inevitable recoiling" from the disturbing insight that sexuality is set in motion by the sexuality of the other, sent to an uncomprehending infant-translator.[38] Fletcher draws out Laplanche's implicit translation theory, writing that "for every process of translation, there is a remainder, something resistant to metabolization that remains *à traduire*, yet to be translated. Laplanche sees these untranslated remainders as designified signifiers—i.e., signifying elements that are disconnected from their original context and reified by repression, and that consequently lose their ordinary semiotic functions, assuming a congealed, thinglike status in the unconscious."[39] The unconscious structured like language, in Laplanche's view, includes signifiers that function more as material "things" than as immaterial vessels of meaning. Translation theorists have taken notice. For Elena Basile, Laplanche helps open the craft of translation to unconscious sexuality, discovering "the complex affective vicissitudes of seduction, transference and identification through which the translator negotiates her relation both to the alterity of the text of the other, and to the alterity of her own text-to-be."[40]

Laplanche's mobilization and revision of Freud's conceptualization of psychic translation also brings to the fore—belatedly—its temporal dimension, returning attention to the Freudian concept of *Nachträglichkeit*, which Strachey (failing to perceive it as a psychoanalytic term) variously translated as "deferred action" or "aftereffect" or even "later," and which Laplanche proposes to name, in French, *après-coup*, or in an English neologism, "afterwardsness." As Andrew Parker writes, this "uniquely psychoanalytic conception or temporality and causality . . . has itself become legible only 'after the fact' of the *Standard Edition*."[41] In Laplanche's application of this psychoanalytic conception to translation (and vice versa), a new "epoch" in psychic life is an occasion to translate historical "imprints," if those are not encountering obstacles to their transmission. As in the psyche, for translators a lapse of time provides new opportunities for and channels of transmission and resignification. According to the retrospective logic Freud saw as part of the psychic drama of maturation, a poorly "metabolized" episode of child sexual abuse might register as trauma only in its reinscription at a later stage of life. The psychoanalysis session, through its limits, norms, and refusals—especially the refusal of the analyst to counsel or pretend to *know* the analysand—is engineered to encourage the retranslation and resignification of the enigmas of childhood. Psychoanalysis is thus a space for addressing and redressing the "radical absence or default of the translation and binding process," in which we "remain possessed by those messages we are unable to translate or metabolize—messages whose violent positivity . . . persecutes the psychotic subject."[42]

The translation that is psychoanalysis and the translation of Freud's writings into French were Laplanche's double life project (along with the family business of winemaking, another translational operation), in which he seized belated, retrospective opportunities for the "detranslation of old translations" in order to "facilitate . . . the reencounter with the enigma of the imaginary other . . . to grasp anew the not-said and the not-heard in what was signified."[43] In his lectures on the meaning and significance of the Freudian *après-coup*, Laplanche asks:

> Why then invoke a theory, a translational model of *après-coup* and, more generally, a translational model of the theory of seduction and even a translational model of the constitution of the human being? It is because there is no mental process that captures the double movement better than translation, the indivisible double movement of the "being carried forward" and of "referring back." The "being carried forward" is nothing other than what I designate as a "fundamental to-be-translated": a demand to translate the message of the other.[44]

Laplanche's restoration of the paradigmatic role of translation in the infantile unconscious, and the continuing role of translation in maturation and indeed in psychoanalysis, also shapes his own practice as translator and editor of Freud's work. The translator's encounter with enigmatic messages is a belated opportunity for reengaging Freud's obscure words through reinterpretation and resignification. Rejecting normative notions of translation that efface the scandalous lapse of time between original and translation by "reconstructing" the author's original intention or the text's original effect, Laplanche draws psychoanalytic potential and literary power from the *delay* that separates source and target text, creating a productive *difference* between an enigmatic original and its translation.[45] The enigma, far from an obstacle to translation, is its very engine, generating thinking for Laplanche about his own German-French translation work. In an essay written with his two coeditors on the *Oeuvres complètes*, Pierre Cotet and André Bourguignon, Laplanche cites Antoine Berman's 1984 book *L'épreuve de l'étranger* to describe his own view of translation as a "test of alienness" that responsible translators should make "no attempt to domesticate or acclimatize." While Berman more conventionally locates foreignness in the differences between national languages, Laplanche and his colleagues suggest that strangeness resides in every translational encounter: "The 'alien' is not only the German language but also the 'stranger' that Freud reveals: the strangeness of his discovery and of the words he uses to express it."[46] Freud often alluded to the strangeness of what would seem to be the products of "our own" minds, for instance in *The Interpretation of Dreams*:

> Our scientific consideration of dreams starts off from the assumption that they are products of our own mental activity. Nevertheless, the finished dream strikes us as something alien to us. We are so little obliged to acknowledge our responsibility for it that we are just as ready to say "mir hat geträumt" [I had a dream, literally, a dream came to me] as "ich habe geträumt" [I dreamt]. What is the source of this feeling that dreams are extraneous to our minds?[47]

Or, rather, as he asks even more strangely in German, "Woher rührt diese 'Seelenfremdheit' des Traumes?," which might be roughly glossed as "From where does this 'soul-strangeness' of dreams come?" Like the strangeness of our own dreams, every translational encounter has an alien quality, which is in fact the secret of its power, since, as Laplanche writes,

> any genuine translation is not only put to the "test" of that "alien" which is the work but also, in turn, puts the work to the test of that alien which

is the experience of translation itself. What is latent in the work only an alien can discover and only the transition into an alien, foreign language can carry through the development and destiny of the work.⁴⁸

The psychoanalytic conceptions of translation I have been summarizing here provide a series of insights about the vagaries of Freud in translation. Translation has a meaningful and distinctive temporal structure; the movement from one language to another can operate as a (productive) psychic swerve; body, affect, sexuality, and "intimacy" play a role in the work of translation; translation involves not only communicable content but also enigmatic and "undigested" messages; translation participates in the ceaseless process of, in Laplanche's metaphor, weaving, unweaving, and reweaving language that is part of the life of the psyche; and the relationship between translator and author is a form of transference, moving along signifying chains and affective channels with long and meaningful histories. Subjectivity *in itself* is intersubjective: Laplanche, speaking of gender, claims that it is "the child *in the presence of* the adult who asks himself the question about this difference that is present in adults."⁴⁹ The same is no doubt true for Jewishness: Avgi Saketopoulou and Ann Pellegrini have shown that gender "assignment" is often accompanied by "assignment to religious membership," at times simultaneously, for instance, in the Jewish ritual of *brit milah*, which includes both the circumcision and "a naming ceremony in which the boy's Hebrew name is announced." In these twinned assignments ("ongoing" rather than singular), "religion and gender meet and co-articulate at the braid of word, body, and communal witnessing."⁵⁰

Freud's interest in language, so crucial to psychoanalytically oriented translation theorists, has not escaped the notice of Jewish studies scholars. Following some of the arguments already laid out in Roback's *Jewish Influence in Modern Thought* (1929), David Bakan in *Sigmund Freud and the Jewish Mystical Tradition* (1958) associates Freud's dream interpretation with Jewish mystical writings, whose "allegorical, paradoxical, and obscurant features invite the greatest latitude with respect to interpretation and constrict clear-cut assertions."⁵¹ As do the mystics, Bakan argues, Freud invites his readers to follow patterns of wordplay, free association, and the sound and shape of words (to put it in linguistic terms, the material signifier), features of language central to Jewish traditions of interpretation but often neglected or disparaged in Christian and mainstream Western sign theory.⁵² Bakan makes the more provocative claim that Freud practices dissimulation in his writing, a feature of Jewish mystical writings that can be traced both to mystical stylistics and to the political conditions under which esoteric or antinomian Jewish texts were produced and circulated. According to Bakan, what Freud hid, often enough, was Jewishness, a concealment with a long religious history; Freud, for instance, disguises his own experiences by ascribing them to a Herr Y., about which Bakan comments: "The choice of the letter Y is interesting. The *yod* (Y) often designates a Jew."[53]

Susan Handelman brings these insights into a poststructuralist framework, linking Freud's focus on language more closely to rabbinic than to mystical traditions. Glossing Freud's remark that, in his approach to dream interpretation, "we have treated as Holy Writ what previous writers have regarded as an arbitrary improvisation," Handelman writes: "Many of Freud's methods of approaching this 'Holy Writ' bear striking similarity to . . . rabbinic hermeneutic rules" and calls Freud a "Talmudic dialectician and midrashic commentator, scrutinizer of texts, pursuer of secrets, and believer in hidden unities."[54] As Handelman recognizes, the rabbinic focus on the signifier—the "body" and materiality of language, primary sites of linguistic difference—has political as well as theological or philosophical dimensions. Rabbinic hermeneutic traditions take not only a different but in fact a counterpcultural stance to the Christian and/or Western valuation of the immaterial signified that normatively transcends linguistic differences, and they do so by linking a focus on the irreducibly distinct material signifier with a keen recognition of the social landscapes in which Jews similarly registered as irremediably different; the focus on the signifier alluded to such differentials and to the minority power dynamics that shaped rabbinic texts. When Freud casts psychic repression as similar to political censorship, "perhaps this theme," Handelman hazards, "had, again, deeply to do with Freud's Jewish identity."[55]

It is hardly necessary to reach back to the rabbis or kabbalists to recognize a Jewish element in the linguistic character of psychoanalysis, whether in the founding case studies or in the cultural milieu in which psychoanalysis emerged. The fateful turn to translation overlaps with the earliest, most foundational moves of psychoanalysis: first the abandonment of biology and heredity in accounting for the etiology of neuroses and then the turn from hypnosis and suggestion to "evenly suspended attention" and "the talking cure." Mahony suggests that once Freud put his stakes in language, he could hardly avoid integrating translation into his thinking: "Laboring under the communicative obstacles of the individual patient and contending with and in a lexical heritage of broken signs," Freud learned "to listen to the jagged path of meaning" in order to achieve what Mahony calls "a repatriation of alienated signifiers," the task Mahony sees as the core and aim of the psychoanalytic project.[56] But it was more particularly a Viennese Jewish multilingual who discovered the talking cure, coining that term in a nonnative English in the context of a hysterical illness that left her stuttering, silent, and aphasic. If Freud is working within what Mahony calls "a lexical heritage of broken signs," we have to attend not only to persistent Jewish cultural patterns but also to their post-traditional fragmentation and loss. Translating Freud thus also involves lost and half-forgotten languages—hieroglyphics on shattered stelae.

Translation was not only a metaphor in psychoanalysis. Jaqueline Amati-Mehler, Simona Argientieri, and Jorge Canestri point out that in Freud's Vienna, "polylingualism and polyglottism were more or less the order of the day."[57] Freud switched back and forth between various languages (often in a single sentence) in his practice and in his writing.[58] Multilingualism continues to matter for psychoanalysis: alongside the words spoken in a session is also the question of which language they are spoken in—a language learned in childhood or adulthood, a language associated with one parent or another, a language in which a traumatic event occurred or one that covers a raw wound. Code-switching takes on psychic meaning within the psychoanalytic session: Amati-Mehler and her colleagues describe how a language learned in adulthood might function for a patient as a "'safety barrier' against the tumult of primitive emotions raised by a mother tongue."[59] A 1935 study by Eduardo Krapf, a German-born, Buenos Aires–based psychoanalyst who carried out his work in no fewer than seven languages, discusses the association of childhood languages not only with the id, as might be expected, but also with the superego (particularly in its auditory character), as an introjection of commands and prohibitions directed at the infant.[60]

Among the psychoanalytic explorations of multilingualism are some that focus on Hebrew or (more usually) Yiddish. The French psychoanalyst Robert Samacher describes how his first language, Yiddish, that constituted "the particular bond with my mother, was repressed: I forgot it except in her presence, it was reserved for her. . . . Yiddish, my mother's language, made me close to her, attracted me and was refused in the same movement. . . . Yiddish introduced an intimacy and a proximity against which I had to defend myself. I defended myself by answering in French."[61] Samacher's description of his relation to Yiddish appears in the introduction to a study that focuses on the slightly different role the language played in Louis Wolfson's psychic landscape, as laid out in *Le schizo et les langues*.[62] "The student of schizophrenic languages," as Wolfson refers to himself, experiences the English language as a painful assault.[63] Wolfson was born in New York in 1931, and English is both his mother tongue (as of this writing, he is still alive) and the language in which his mother spoke to him. Along with the French in which he preferred to converse and write, Wolfson learned German, Hebrew, and Russian well enough so that he could mentally "translate" the English spoken in his hearing into these other languages, using principles of phonetic similarity to "convert" painful English words into bearable French, German, Hebrew, or Russian "equivalents." When someone calls him a screwball, the insult is ameliorated by Wolfson's internal translation, which allows him to hear, rather, the confusing, nonsensical *un ecrou-balle* (a bullet-nut). Jean-Jacques Lecercle comments that Wolfson offers us "an inverted image of 'normal' translation. . . . The only level which normal translation dismisses, the phonetic (if I cannot have both sound and sense, and I usually cannot, I will plump for the sense), he respects to the bitter end."[64] In contrast with how he experiences English, Wolfson finds Yiddish—the mother tongue of both his parents—bearable, expressing gratitude when first his father, mostly absent from his life, and then finally his mother consent to speak Yiddish with him, which he understands because of its closeness to German.

Lecercle reads Wolfson's "abnormal" translation practice as only partly effective in alleviating his hatred of English, since within the tongues that translate it, "the foreign words persist or subsist, like the Freudian repressed."[65] Buffering the assault of the mother tongue only takes him deeper into what he is evading. As Lecercle puts it,

> Wolfson, through his translation device, is indeed going back to his origins. He is making, through language, the same journey his parents made on a boat, only in the other direction. They left Europe behind them, and then, when they reached America, tried, rather successfully, to replace their mother tongue with English. Without leaving New York, Wolfson goes back. He renounces English, his mother tongue, and his construct is a fantastic form of Yiddish. As everyone knows, Yiddish is a Wolfsonian tongue, made up of words from Hebrew, German, Romance, and Slavic.[66]

Samacher similarly considers it significant that Wolfson goes back not to the Yiddish that was his mother's only language until she immigrated at age eight and his father's only language until he was fifteen but to its German, Hebrew, Slavic, and Romance components. In the less stigmatized "national languages" that serve as building blocks of the feminine, lowly Yiddish, Samacher asks, might Wolfson have aimed "to find and found an origin that allowed him to reintroduce and construct the Name-of-the-Father, which might protect him from the invasive *jouissance* carried by the mother tongue?"[67]

What a mother tongue is and how it functions, what or how German or Yiddish *means*, cannot be predetermined in any particular circumstance, even if broader historical relations and ideological and cultural patterns and currents also run through them. While Samacher's personal relationship with Yiddish accords with the wider cultural perception of Yiddish as charged with intimate, familial, maternal affect, for Wolfson it is English that arouses the most heated passions and Yiddish, and more particularly a deconstructed Yiddish, that allows some distance from (while also providing proximity to) the mother tongue. Wolfson might be a symptom of a different cultural knot than the one that caught up the Baroness von Feilchenfeld: Yiddish, cast so regularly as the language of the traditional past from which modern Jews flee in search of integration, might also serve as a channel of escape from the very language to which their forebears had fled. Louis Wolfson's case, unique and idiosyncratic as it may seem, might shed light on a peculiar feature of Jewish language politics in modernity: Two of the major architects of modern Yiddishism, Nathan Birnbaum and Max Weinreich, were native speakers of German; a third, Ber Borochov, was a native Russian speaker; Birnbaum and Borochov learned Yiddish as adults, and Weinreich picked it up as an adolescent. The Yiddishist ideologies that cast Yiddish as the native tongue of Ashkenazic Jewry are in fact the product of estrangement and loss, "a lexical heritage of broken signs." The tensions between personal and collective conceptualizations of a mother tongue are even closer to the surface of the Hebrew revival, which championed Hebrew as an ancestral mother tongue even as almost no one could claim it as their first language and as actual mothers struggled to speak it, sometimes learning it from their children. Nevertheless, the rhetoric of maternal language was critical in the struggle to create a Hebrew-speaking populace: Liora Halperin quotes Eliezer Ben-Yehuda, the "father of the Hebrew revival," describing a national language—by which he meant Hebrew, despite its long dormancy as a vernacular—rather graphically (for what was after all a metaphor) as "that which a person imbibes along with his mother's milk, that which he sucks from her nipples, that which accompanies him all the days of his life regardless of the circumstances, those spiritual phrases in which he thinks his dearest thoughts."[68] On the ground, however, pedagogues worried that their students were learning a defective and unusable language, since, as Halperin wryly puts it, "Hebrew, the 'mother tongue' of the collective, was not the mother tongue of many mothers."[69]

It may be no coincidence that, decades before the French psychoanalytic obsession with Wolfson's "phonetic" translation practice, psychoanalysts in pre-statehood Palestine were noticing similarly "improper" translation practices among the new Hebrew speakers of the Zionist yishuv. Immanuel Velikhovsky's 1934 paper asks, "Can a newly acquired language become the speech of the unconscious?," focusing on the multilingual wordplay within the dreams of new speakers of Hebrew, a "newly revived language with no inherited memory traces." He notes that the dreams of native speakers of Russian, Arabic, or Yiddish are rich in aural wordplay, which do the work of making Hebrew meaningful on the unconscious level by linking it with words that sound similar in other languages that do have "inherited memory traces" by virtue of being mother tongues or childhood languages. Thus, when Velikhovsky's native Arabic speakers dream in Hebrew about a *kos* (a drinking glass), the word aurally translates to its true meaning, the Arabic *kus* (vagina); Velikhovsky acknowledges that this is not the best example of aural translation, "since 'drinking glass' is also a visual symbol for the vagina."[70] A better example appears in a dream about mice (Yiddish, *mayzlekh*), an aural translation of the dreamer's hopes of getting lucky (Hebrew, *mazelekh*) with the lottery.[71] Here, the "native" Yiddish mice scurry along the surface of the dream, while the newly learned Hebrew is its latent, hidden meaning. And indeed, Velikhovsky rejects the ready notion that the newly acquired Hebrew, lacking memory traces, must represent the more "superficial" level of a dream, with the native language always working as its unconscious. The unconscious, too, might learn Hebrew, even if belatedly and partially and for its own purposes. Even new speakers' dreams exhibit real sophistication in their Hebrew wordplay, as in the image of a suit (*beged*) that occludes and expresses the dreamer's fear of a spouse's infidelity (*begidah*, with the same Hebrew root). Velikhovsky hypothesizes that rabbinic hermeneutics might help explain the ubiquity of such interlingual and intralingual punning in his patients' dreams, not because Jews have inherited a propensity for wordplay but because the consonantal writing of Hebrew language encouraged the word associations of both rabbis and modern dreamers: "By omitting vowels, words invite comparison; and if the comparison is odd (*davar* [word] can be read as *dever* [plague]), they invite jokes."[72] The Hebrew unconscious, however raw and new, was structured like the Hebrew language, mobilizing its distinctive root system to string along chains of associations that reached back to antiquity.

The workings of Jewish languages in the multilingual psyche are present in Freud's writings as well. Mahony demonstrates the operations of psychic translation by analyzing the footnote in *The Psychopathology* about Ferenczi's faux pas as a translation between French and German, mouth and foot, language and body. But the very same section of the book recounts a similarly intersemiotic and interlingual "blunder" by Freud himself, and this example involves both Jewish languages and what Lecercle calls "phonic" or aural translation. Freud's blunder occurs as he is rushing out the door to diagnose whether a patient who is unable to walk has a somatic or hysterical paralysis; in leaving, he accidentally pockets a tuning fork rather than the reflex hammer beside it that he needs for the diagnosis. Asking "why it actually was that I took the tuning fork instead of the hammer," Freud resists the easy answer that this was an innocent mistake made in haste:

> "Who was the last person to take hold of the tuning fork?" was the question that sprang to my mind at that point. It was an *imbecile* child, whom I had been testing some days before for his attention to sensory impressions; and he had been so fascinated by the tuning fork that I had had some difficulty in tearing it away from him. Could the meaning be, then, that I was an imbecile? It certainly seemed so, for my first association to "hammer" was "*Chamer*" (Hebrew for "ass") [*Allerdings scheint es so, denn der nächste Einfall, der sich an Hammer assoziiert, lautet "Chamer" (hebräisch: Esel)*]. But why this abusive language?[73]

Freud answers his own question, which recognizes in the association an insult directed at himself, reflecting a deep-seated anxiety driving his blunder. As was the case with Ferenczi's faux pas, the anxiety was about making a mistake in treatment. While Ferenczi believed he had in fact blundered, Freud claims to be afraid that he will be perceived as making a mistake, as happened in a similar case when he missed a patient's multiple sclerosis. Although he had succeeded in relieving the patient's neurotic symptoms, the cure was inevitably only partial and "the impression left was that a grave error had been made." The error of picking up the tuning fork instead of the reflex hammer, he writes, "could thus be translated into words as follows, 'You idiot! You ass!' [*Der Mißgriff . . . ließ sich also so in Worte übersetzen: Du Trottel, du Esel*]."[74]

Freud thus makes a mistake because he is afraid of making a mistake and curses himself in advance, as it were, for making that mistake. The blunder strikes at the heart of his anxieties around the still-new practice of psychoanalysis, treading the tricky boundaries between psyche and body against those colleagues who "are of the opinion that I make a diagnosis of hysteria far too carelessly when graver things are in question."[75] While Freud believes he cured the neurosis, his blunder tells a different story: The problem may be graver than mistaking mind for body (or ear for knee), or vice versa, since *both* the tuning fork *and* the hammer spell failure, albeit in different ways, the former through its (stubborn) association with an imbecilic child who refuses to let it go (and for being the wrong instrument to take to diagnose a paralyzed patient) and the latter through its aural echo of—its attunement with—the word *Chamer*. There is another impropriety lurking here, too: Like the "student of schizophrenic languages," who also wields weapons against insults, Freud is caught up in the "body" of language—its material sound rather than immaterial meaning, an "abnormal" translator in choosing sound over sense. These errors leave their mark in the flurry of expansions, retranslations, and insertions into his German prose. As with those infantile failures of translation Laplanche describes, an untranslated (Hebrew) residue remains that shows itself (like the instrument it translates) as an undigested "thing."

Given another of his famous worries, that psychoanalysis would be perceived as "a Jewish national affair," it is worth lingering over the fact that Freud's initial association with the hammer he has forgotten is an introjection of a critical voice that speaks a Jewish language, which succeeds in communicating itself aurally in/as German, and which Freud transliterates in a non-Jewish script—translation operations at least as complicated as the schizophrenic student's. These anxieties are not, in any obvious sense, introjections or "internalizations" of antisemitic voices. On the contrary, the critical voice in Freud speaks a Jewish language and insults the psychoanalytic project using indigenous Jewish tools. But who is speaking in this voice, and what is he/it saying? Along with the necessary displacement of a Jewish into a non-Jewish language (in which the Jewish language remains audible), Freud's blunder translates from languages to things; from one thing (a reflex hammer) to another (tuning fork); and from the *idiotisches Kind* who won't let go of the tuning fork to the imbecile who is a (mis)diagnosing doctor and the writer who tells the story about him(self). Given that Freud's worries are not his alone, the hypercharged affect that propels and troubles these translations hardly ends at his words. While Brill, the first English translator of the *Psychopathology*, refers to an "idiotic child" who prompts Freud's worry that he is also an idiot, Alan Tyson's retranslation for the *Standard Edition* presents us instead with "an *imbecile* child" who provokes the thought that Freud is an imbecile, replacing "idiot" with "imbecile" and adding an emphasis to the noun. The result is an upgrade in register: while idiot had both "neutral" medical and pejorative connotations in the early twentieth century, "imbecile"—in the noun form and with the emphasis that implies a technical term—conveys, at least to my ear, the notion that Freud was not insulting but rather *diagnosing* the child. Medical terminology of Freud's time reserved the term "idiot" for those with more severe developmental delays than "imbeciles"; Freud's translators were thus also nudging the term "upward" toward a less severe impairment. These translations and the affects that propel them have social reverberations beyond Freud's clinic or the translator's study. The English terms "idiots" and "imbeciles" (but not "screwball") feature in the US Immigration Acts of 1882 and 1907, which codified the exclusion from the country of initially "idiots" and then also "imbeciles."[76] The *Standard Edition* Freud, in Tyson's political bid for intellectual immigration into the English language, thus expresses slightly less unseemly irritation and slightly calmer diagnosis, precisely what Freud was stymied from achieving by idiotically pocketing a tuning fork when what he needed was a reflex hammer.

The fear of being an idiot, far from being resolved in this retranslation performance, moves along the double trajectory Laplanche identifies as part of the temporality of translation, stirring up earlier traumas and extending beyond Freud's words and life to those who carry and miscarry him forward. The psychoanalyst and Hebrew translator Eran Rolnik reminds us in an essay on the singularity and oddity of Freud's prose style that Freud carried with him the sting of a high school teacher who called his writing "idiotic." Since, as Rolnik puts it, "Freud—the *Freud imago*—has a unique place in the internal object world of each analyst," translators, too, might well feel implicated in the operations of Freud's work, in which the epistemological, discursive, medical, ethical, and perhaps also ethnic status of psychoanalysis seems to hang in the balance.[77] Worries about Freud's diagnostic acumen, which make themselves felt in the eruption of Hebrew into Freud's German, also shape the difficult passage of this indigestible message from German into English.

In contrast with the footnote on Ferenczi's faux pas, this passage highlights Freud's own acts of translation: Freud plays the metaphorical translator in aurally conflating the Hebrew *Chamer* with a German *Hammer*, but he is also literally a translator, providing a parenthetical gloss on the meaning (rather than sound) of *Chamer* for his German readers "(*hebräisch: Esel*)." If Mahony reached downward for an example in Freud's footnotes, avoiding the plain nose on the text, it may have been because he was brought up short by the opacity of this *Chamer*, in contrast with Ferenczi's more transparent (for Mahony) faux pas. In sidestepping Freud's blunder/translation in favor of one that trips up German, French, English, Mahony sets implicit (national? European?) limits to the psychoanalytic translation theory he reconstructs and misses Freud's quite overt translation performance in the same text: "*Chamer* (*hebräisch: Esel*)." Derrida points to a similar parenthetical gloss in André Chouraqui's French translation of the biblical word "Babel" as a symptom of the inadequacy of translation in cases in which the original (an original that tells the story of why translation is necessary) is *already* an accomplished, condensed translation: "Recourse to apposition and capitalization ('Over which he proclaims his name: Bavel, confusion') is not translating from one tongue to another."[78] To borrow Derrida's insight for this passage, despite Freud's explicit translation gloss, the "recourse to apposition" in Freud's text cannot fully translate *Chamer* into German, since this word is *already* a condensation of German (in its aural similarity to *Hammer*) and Hebrew (in its meaning, which can be translated into German as *Esel*). Thus, and despite these multiple translations and extended explanations, this blunder functions as a Laplanchean *enigmatic message*, an untranslated residue in or as the unconscious of the text, which in its opacity declares the inadequacy of translation and thus spurs de- and retranslation.

But is *Chamer* really a Hebrew word? The German transliteration is a telltale sign, if one were needed, that Freud is pronouncing the word in its Ashkenazic and/or Yiddish form, as he would have to do for the similarity to the German *Hammer* to apply. He is also hearing this word, context shows, not as a quote from a high-register Hebrew original—the Bible, for instance, which has its share of asses—but in its metaphorical displacement as Yiddish insult. (As it happens, this insult was once or twice in my childhood flung at me, though I cannot remember when or by whom, in the Yiddish form "di chamereyzl!"; of this term, Derrida would comment that it cannot be translated because it is already a translation in a different sense, stringing together a Hebrew word [*chamer*] with its Yiddish translation [*eyzl*] in characteristic Yiddish form to produce, in English [non]translation, the insult "you donkey[H]-donkey [Y]!"[79] This half-remembered childhood insult, which emerged in the course of my own free association-cum-academic writing, may also exert some pressure on my reading of Freud's sensitivity to the imputation that he is an idiot, suggesting my worry that I am, too.) Lest one assume that this "abusive" language constitutes an internal core or primary stratum within a layered psychic-language landscape that erupts in Freud's blunder, it is worth pointing out that, while it is safe to assume that the Yiddish insult emerges from Freud's childhood memories, the insult comes "from outside," originating in the communication of the other. Perhaps this other is Freud's father, and the Yiddish is a chastising aural voice introjected as the superego. The untranslatable Hebrew-Yiddish term, unassimilable residue of an enigmatic message, is hurled by Freud both at the imbecilic child who will not let go of the tuning fork and at himself, who is or was this child—the child *in the presence of the adult . . . receiving messages* from the adult.[80] Freud nearly succeeds in making explicit these painful affects and associations, which leave him exposed as both a perpetrator and victim, abuser of children and purveyor of false diagnoses who himself is abused, himself unfairly accused of fraud. Nevertheless, the gloss "'*Chamer*' (*hebräisch: Esel*)" works as a brake to halt the translation machine one stop before its final "downward" destination, suppressing the shift that takes the Hebrew designation into Yiddish territory, in which the ass (donkey) takes its full meaning of ass (idiot).

At stake is also Freud's identification as a Jew who knows at least a few words in Jewish languages. *Traduttore traditore*—that old canard that Freud loved to quote—has another and nearly opposite sense, that to translate is to risk a kind of "self-betrayal," reversing an already accomplished assimilation through a slip toward rather than away from the truth. Freud's self-betrayal in this passage is accomplished both by revealing the Jewish languages that threaten to erupt in his psyche and by letting them say what they want to say about him. For the languages that "human beings keep hidden within them," Freud reminds us in relation to Dora, nevertheless also speak, since "no mortal can keep a secret. If his lips are silent, he chatters with his finger-tips; betrayal oozes out of him at every pore."[81] *The Psychopathology of Everyday Life* provides a Jewish example of such self-betrayal in the already discussed passage about Herr A./Victor Tausk of a convert from Judaism to Christianity, who "was obliged to learn the lesson that the 'faith of our fathers' cannot be disavowed with impunity if one is a son and has sons of one's own."[82] Translation—like lineage—is an operation that transcends the individual psyche. It is not only one's own unruly tongue, under the pressures of unconscious drives or self-censorship, that threatens to speak the "faith of the fathers." Our children speak what we do not allow ourselves to say, or we take the words out of their mouths in the very fear of what they will say about us and those whose words we also carry. Beyond the translation operations of each individual psyche, extended kinship structures and social networks trip over each other in the pressure to express and suppress themselves through our unruly tongues. Freudian psychoanalytic translation, in theory and as practice, similarly overflows the borders of a single psyche, both "backward" to the father and "forward" to the children, backward to the "original" and forward to its translation.

What is the difference between these complicated blunders and Ferencz's also painful faux pas? To put this differently: What difference do Freud's *Jewish* languages make to any translation theory we might derive from psychoanalysis? Certainly any language (or any fragment of a language within another language) carries specific affective and ideational charges, both for the individual psyche and for cultural collectives: the use of Latin in English—as in the *Standard Edition* translation of psychoanalytic terms—registers as *science*, as French conveys *sex*. Speaking of his forthright talk with Dora about his diagnosis of her cough as a hysterical representation of and response to (thoughts of) fellatio, Freud writes: "I call bodily organs and processes by their technical names, and I tell these to the patient if they—the names, I mean—happen to be unknown to her. *J'appelle un chat un chat.*"[83] However, the function of French in this passage is anything but direct: Jane Gallop remarks that "at the very moment [Freud] defines non-prurient language as direct and non-euphemistic, he takes a French detour into a figurative expression. . . . And to make matters more juicy (less 'dry'), *chat* or *chatte* can be used as vulgar (vulvar) slang for the female genitalia. So in this gynecological context, . . . he takes a French detour and calls a pussy a pussy."[84] But Latin also, perhaps not surprisingly, could signify *sex*, in and through *science*. Reading Freud's letter to Fliess in which he described an early memory of seeing his mother *nudam* on a journey they were taking together, Anne McClintock suggests that according to Freud's own principle that "a foreign language [inserted into a text] marks a repression," it is no accident that Freud reached in this case "for Latin, the ancient mother language of his nurse's church, to describe his arousal for his other mother, thereby marking the place of doubling and defense."[85] Here and elsewhere, languages convey, cover, and displace meaning, carrying particular charges not so much "in themselves" as in their presence as *Fremdwörter*—aliens, foreigners, and guests in other languages.

The Jewish languages in Freud participate in a broader linguistic landscape occupied by a diverse range of specifically charged languages, occasionally as discrete languages but mostly in their appearances as (familiar) strangers within other languages. Citations to Jewish languages strike me as super-conveyors of a range of meanings, affects, and ideologies beyond their narrow signification. These can hardly be charted on a single axis: Hebrew or Yiddish, buried within or erupting from non-Jewish languages, signifies a shameful backwardness, registers the echoes of an exalted lineage, mends frayed connections, exacerbates Jewish difference: ideologies upon shifting ideologies, given that Jewish languages traversed epochs in which old stories were reorganized and retranscribed, "revived" and transvalued.

Jewish languages do not merely add discrete elements to the rich language landscape Freud inhabited, among other Jewish or non-Jewish Europeans. Individual and contingent as they are, they are also organized in recognizable patterns. In describing European Jews as "Mercurian" shapeshifters, Yuri Slezkine asserts that a complex, collective multilingualism shaped this identity:

> As professional internal strangers equally dependent on cultural difference and economic interdependence, [Jews] speak at least one internal language (sacred, secret, or both) and at least one external language. They are all trained linguists, negotiators, translators, and mystifiers, and the literate groups among them tend to be much more literate than their hosts—because literacy, like language generally, is a key to both the maintenance of their separate identity and the fulfillment of their commercial (conjoining) function.[86]

Max Weinreich describes traditional Jewish multilingualism as comprising both "internal" and "external" bilingualism: alongside two hierarchically organized internal Jewish languages, a "high" scriptural tongue and a "low" vernacular, Jews regularly also speak an external non-Jewish language. By contrast, French and German, whatever the complexity and ambivalence of their mutual relations, function primarily as ostensibly complete-in-themselves national languages, meeting as equals across a language border and mixing within the psyches of bilinguals in relatively individual and contingent fashion. Mahony's illustration of Freud's theory of translation through Ferenczi's faux pas traverses languages and the spaces between language, body, and event. But it retains the (nationalist) fiction of languages as essentially parallel sign systems, with well-ordered borrowings in one direction or another (even as the familiar borrowing here represents a stumble). The very transparency and established relationship between languages allows the faux pas to appear untranslated in an otherwise German (or English) sentence, marking psychoanalysis as another contribution to the well-trodden borders across which European philosophical thought circulates. By contrast, Hebrew and such Jewish vernaculars as Yiddish are part of no such mutual and transparent network, still struggle to achieve the status of national languages, function as "insider" languages, and acquire their meaning through participation in diglossic cultures. Between Yiddish and German, finer distinctions intrude, since the languages have tangled roots and Yiddish has been historically seen as a Jewish "deformation" of German. Translation between these languages is always translating (like marrying) *up* or *down*, *in* or *out*, and sometimes (as in *Chamer/Hammer*) both at once. In these isolated words, German also encounters what Weinreich calls a Jewish culture system, which has its own differentiations and hierarchies and its own way of mobilizing the full range of languages at its disposal to create meaning. Thus, a Yiddish "differentiation" word like *sheygetz* (non-Jewish boy) borrows a biblical term (*shekez*, abomination) through a principle he calls *cross-translation*; through a characteristic and familiar process, Yiddish also enacts Jewish identity through *deformation*, which renders Christian terms like *tefilah* (prayer) as *tiflah* (tastelessness or vanity) or mocks its targets by *shm reduplication* (fancy-shmancy). But in an even trickier reversal, Yiddish has flexible tools for *semantic reversal*, in which that same *sheygetz* might be used to affectionately describe a young Jewish boy as "you rascal."[87] These linguistic operations, which in the case of Yiddish assert, subvert, and ironize Jewish hierarchies within a minority context, are not so distant from Freud's *condensation* and *displacement*, operating as culture but also shaping the individual psyche.

The haranguing voice—"You idiot!"—in which Freud is both accuser and accused is perhaps sufficient warning to those of us who try to understand the force of this voice and identify the language(s) it speaks. Neither language nor Jewish languages will hold still for long enough to make clear whether it is the father or his son who speaks and whether his message is diagnosis or insult, the truth or a naked display of power or fear. Is the question "Who speaks?" not the central question of translation, in which subjectivity folds on itself, languages reach across boundaries to touch, in which one person's thoughts become another's? This is not to reassert the transparency and humanism of the old model of translation: Translations negotiate between rivals, fail to see what is staring them in the face, discover and expose or conceal and displace latent meanings, resist or succumb to the push of censorship and pull of desire, communicate sotto voce what cannot be heard on the surface, discover unexpected convergences where none are anticipated, sneak through fences and repent their transgressions, forget meanings, mislay words—all the adventures and blunders that befall any human being who wants to pick up a tool of his trade or navigate a sidewalk without tripping over his own feet.

In the letter to the YIVO Press included "in place of an introduction to the Yiddish edition" of his *Introductory Lectures in Psychoanalysis*, Freud wrote, "It has given me great joy to hear that the first volume of my *Vorlesungen* in Yiddish translation is about to appear, and it was with great respect that I took the first sheet in hand. A pity, that I could not do more."[88] Freud could do no more, but in translating him into an idiomatic Yiddish (Freud takes the page in hand with *derekh eretz*), Weinreich returns Freud's respect by rendering it in the language of his readers, an act, in Zohar Weiman-Kelman's view, "all the more striking because the text imitates the letter form, while erasing the act of the letter's translation. This serves to Yiddishize Freud's disavowal of Yiddish at the same time as it makes Weinreich's translation a kosher psychoanalytic text."[89] Freud built his dream theory on the translational operations that separate a recognizable language from the unknown tongue it nevertheless expressed. Here, equally powerful currents flow between the language he knew and the one he could only identify as belonging to a Jewish scriptworld. Weinreich's translation returned the fragments of Yiddish in Freud's writings "whole," transforming a language of insult into a language of respect, where this respect was accorded not by Yiddish to Freud but rather by Freud to Yiddish (and this respect is signaled, as well, by the fact that Yiddish now possesses a name). In his "Return to Freud," Lacan gave expression to one of the drives that propels the field of Freud-in-translation, the drive to bring Freud home to Vienna, to his own tongue. But there were other languages, too, that drove this desire and other homes to inhabit.

אָנשטאָט אַ הקדמה צו דער יידישער אויסגאַבע
בריוו צום אויספיר־ביורא פון יידישן וויסנשאפטלעכן אינסטיטוט פון 30טן אפריל 1936

פּראָפ׳ ד״ר פרויד   וויען XIX, שטראַסערגַ׳ 47.

זייער חשובע הערן:—

איך האָב זיך שטאַרק דערפרייט מיט אייער ידיעה, אז דאָס ערשטע העפט פון מײַנע Vorlesungen אין דער יידישער איבערזעצונג גײט אַרויס גאָר אין גיכן, און איך האָב מיט גרויס דרך־ארץ גענומען אין האַנט אַרום דעם ערשטן בויגן וואָס איר האָט מיר צוגעשיקט. אַ שאָד, נאָר ווי מער ווי דאָס האָב איך דערמיט ניט געקענט טון. אין יונגער צײַט, ווען איך בין געווען אַ תלמיד, האָט מען ניט געלייגט קיין אַכט אויף קולטיווירן די נאַציאָנאַלע טראַדיציע; האָב איך זיך ניט געלערנט לייענען ניט העברעיש און ניט יידיש, וואָס הײַנט פאַרדריסט דאָס מיך זייער. פונדעסטווענגן בין איך פאַרט געוואָרן אַ גוטער ייד, הגם, ווי איר וויסט מיסתמא, ניט קיין גלייביקער.

פאַרלאַנגט ניט בײַ מיר קיין הקדמה. מיט אַ פאַר יאָר צוריק האָב איך מוסר־מודעה געווען, אַז מער וועל איך קיין הקדמות ניט געבן, און צו פיל מענטשן וואָלטן געהאַט פאַראיבל, ווען איך זאָל איצט ברעכן יענעם פירגעם.

אַ האַרציקן דאַנק פאַר אײַער טירחא וואָס וועט אויפווענקן דעם אינטערעס צום פסיכאָאַנאַליז בײַ אַזוי פיל אינטעליגענטע מענטשן.

אײַער זייער איבערגעגעבענער

פרויד (—)

Figure 1. "Instead of a Preface to the Yiddish Publication." Letter to the Executive Office of the Yiddish Scientific Institute, April 30, 1936. Sigmund Freud, 47 Strassergasse, Vienna XIX. Strassergasse 47 was the Freud summer residence between 1934 and 1937. Source: Library of the YIVO Institute for Jewish Research. Reprinted with permission.

Kasia Kosinen argues that the literary and linguistic focus of translation theorists has led to a neglect of the lived experience, hopes, habits, and needs "of the people involved, translation and interpretation scholars included. In short, to understand translation, one also needs to understand its affective side."[90] While attention to affect has sometimes been taken as a corrective to the "linguistic turn," there is no reason to oppose affect and language, bodies and signs. As Margaret Wetherall argues, "It is the discursive that very frequently makes affect powerful, makes it radical and provides the means for affect to travel."[91] And not only the discursive dimension of language: Freud's most remarkable and direct comments on his own Jewishness were written under the affective sway of seeing his own words translated into a language he couldn't read but whose script he could nevertheless recognize. As Freud says about the Jewish feelings these translations gave rise to, these affects are hard to pin down. They span an affective and layered spectrum, from the Hebrew/Yiddish *Hammer/Chamer* to *derekh eretz*, the phrase passed back and forth between Freud and Weinreich, and many points in between. And they travel as well to and through us, belated readers and translation scholars, shifting, reinscribing and rearranging themselves in each iteration. Translation travels these affective currents because it is also, like affect, what Brian Massumi calls "transversal," which means that it cuts "across the usual categories. Prime among these are the categories of the subjective and the objective."[92] A generation of scholars have by now recognized that, in taking translation as a metaphor for the psyche and its operations, Freud also developed a translation theory. In writing the prefaces and letters of introduction that he did, Freud developed, more particularly, a translation theory that also accounted for affect, the currents of feeling that could flow through translation, particularly (for him and, differently, for me) the translation of his German into Hebrew or Yiddish. The two texts I have been juxtaposing, the Yiddish insult that creeps in, unnamed, to Freud's *Psychopathology*, and the (translated) letter he wrote to the Yiddish translator of *Introduction to Psychoanalysis*, emerge from different epochs in Freud's life and in the relationship between German-speaking Jews and the language they eventually came to call Yiddish. As Laplanche shows, these epochs provide opportunities for reinscription, *rearranging*. This is translation, too, and it hasn't yet ended.

6

Psychoanalysis for Diabetics

> Psychoanalysis was the disease of emancipated Jews; the religious ones were satisfied with diabetes.
>
> —Karl Kraus, "On Psychoanalysis and Psychology" (1913)

In the summer of 1930, the New York daily *Forverts* advertised a "Freudian Lullaby Contest" in its Sunday English supplement, for a prize of "fifteen (count 'em, fifteen) dollars" to be paid for "the cleverest Freudian Lullaby for a Jewish Baby."[1] On September 14, the paper reported "Lullaby Contest Won by David Greenberger," noting that the offices had received eleven hundred entries from thirty-six states, Canada, Mexico, and the British Isles.[2] The newspaper published many of these lullabies in that issue and the next, including the winning poem, "Freud-ekind" (Joy [or illegitimate] Child). Greenberger's lullaby, in which the titular baby confesses to a "Mutter-Kuh [mother-cow] Komplex," is in German, but others in English also managed to pun on Freud's name, as in Milton Dickman's groaner, "I'm Affreud." The lullabies are illuminating as well as entertaining, shedding light on an intersection between psychoanalysis and Jewish experience beyond its usual nexus—Freud's Jewishness. In imagining what a "Freudian lullaby for a Jewish baby" might sound like, the jokes of the contest participants did the work of constructing a more culturally specific Oedipus (and Jocasta) than Freud had described, revealing the scope of their knowledge of psychoanalysis in the process.

Dickman's knowledge was particularly impressive: the lullaby describes a precocious Freudian baby who is suddenly no longer content with the "tinkly tunes / About tree-tops and the moon" that his mother regularly sings to him. "Baby said, 'Stop!' He was really annoyed. / 'Sing,' said baby, 'the Epic of Freud!'" It is not only Homer this baby could cite. If Dickman was not an actual psychoanalyst, he was certainly remarkably well read in the field; his baby name-checks important psychoanalysts in Freud's circle, other famous psychologists, and even the zoologist Ivan Schmalhausen. The lullaby also invokes the pioneering French psychologist Pierre Janet, mispronouncing his name for the rhyme and misattributing to him the Oedipal complex.[3] The Freudian baby commands his mother:

> Sing of regressions, repressions, the sexes.
> Psychoses, the trauma, the state paramnetic,
> Of all of the various psychic complexes.
> And also somatic, and psychogenetic.
> Sing in soft numbers of sonorous tones
> The findings of Breuer and Dr. E. Jones,
> Of Martin and Rivers, and Prof. L. S. Hollingworth,
> And Mrs. M. Sanger who writes on controlling birth;
>
> *(You'll make an Oedipus of me yet,*
> *If you hold me so close, says Dr. Janet)*
> To strains of Gotterdammerung
> Sing of Schmalhausen and also of Jung:
> In a similar strain, sing of rationalization,
> Anaesthesia and, logically, hallucination,
> Conditions hypnoidal, conditions hypnotic.
> And also of people who're autoerotic.
> For surely it gives me delight and a thrill
> To hear all about the Impulse and Will
> As expounded by Drs. Ferenczi and Brill.

By the time Dickman's Freudian baby has finished this recitation, his mother is fast asleep. Part of the familiar humor of the lullaby is its commentary on the absurdity and pointlessness of exhausted parents trying to persuade wakeful, talkative children to sleep; but perhaps there are also other jokes wrapped up in this lullaby, including the notion that the "delight and a thrill" the baby is after is less about erotic sensations than about the excitement of erotic *discourse* provided by talk about Freud. As for why it is a baby confessing to seeking such pleasures, the lullaby may be referring to the intellectual gap that opened up during this period between a younger generation fascinated by Freud and an older one that preferred to let sleeping complexes lie.

Dickman's baby is certainly Freudian, but not particularly Jewish (unless we read precociousness and fascination with psychoanalysis as ethnic markers). Claire I. Shapiro played a more overtly Jewish game with her Freudian riff on the traditional Yiddish lullaby "Ruzhinkes mit mandln" (Raisins and almonds), borrowing its well-known chorus to sing, as the traditional lullaby does, to a sweet "ben yochid," the beloved only child:

> Sweet Ben Yochid
> Hush-a-bye, my sweet ben yochid,
> Close your tired little eyes.
> Rest the head that soon will toy with
> All the wisdom of the wise.
> Ai-lu-lu-lu, ben yochid,
> Ai-lu-lu-lu-lu
> Do not twirl your toes, my darling,
> Do not kick your little feet,
> Goodness knows you may be thinking
> Thoughts that are most indiscreet.
> So Ai-lu lu, my darling, Ai-lu-lu-lu
> Do not gurgle so, my dear one,
> That's a flame from hidden fires,
> From that nasty old libido
> Loosing your suppressed desires!
> So ai-lu-lu-lu . . .
> Do not speak in dreams, my angel,
> Murderous thoughts your waking hid,
> Push against that "cellar" top
> With consciousness upon the lid!
> So ai-lu-lu-lu.

The baby in Abraham Goldfaden's well-known version of the lullaby, popularized in the 1880 Yiddish operetta *Shulamis*, is named Yidele, a diminutive of the name Yehuda (Judah), as well as a term for a little Jew; the second interpretation is bolstered by the name of his mother, the widow Bas Tziyon (daughter of Zion), whose words to her child express fearful premonitions of his future. The lullaby is thus a national allegory for the Jewish destiny known to mothers but not yet to the infants to whom they sing. Goldfaden's version of the lullaby (which has many variations) envisions this fate as economic—the baby is destined for the life of a wandering merchant trading in "raisins and almonds," but other versions sing of the baby boy as a future Torah scholar, perhaps echoed here in Shapiro's prediction that this infant will "toy with all the wisdom of the wise." Shapiro's lullaby, more interested in diagnosis than prophecy, takes a drastic plunge in register after the opening stanza. This "angel" is no innocent, teeming as he is with aggression and libido, just as would be predicted by Freud's theories of childhood sexuality, the most famously upsetting of his discoveries. Translating a beloved "only son" from its Jewish into a Freudian context challenges not only sentimental European ideas about childhood innocence but also the tender Jewish affect wrapped up in the Yiddish "ben yochid." Such tenderness was apparently ripe for Freudian deconstruction: In 1912, the *New York Times* ran a story with the rather sensational headline that asked: "Is an Only Son a Menace to Society: This Doctor Says He Is," quoting the psychoanalyst A. A. Brill in the subheading, "Spoiled by His Parents, He Grows Up in a Wrong Environment and Becomes a Neurotic."[4]

If heightened or exclusive expressions of parental love (beginning with God's preference for the Jewish people or, alternatively, for his "only-begotten Son") are dangerous, as Brill implied, that may be because the grown-up singers of lullabies that appear in the lullabies published by the *Forverts* also teem with sexual and aggressive impulses, bringing Laius and Jocasta back into focus in a story that sometimes draws more attention to their unfortunate son. Psychoanalysts have long recognized maternal aggression, grief, and rage as the subtext of lullabies the world over, unacceptable and restive emotions cloaked in the soothing rhythms that allow the lullaby to accomplish its desperately desired goal.[5] Many of the contributors seem to have seen the lullaby in just this light, taking "Freudian" to mean in this context the exposure of uglier parental emotions. Samuel Abott's "Semmy My Son" uses parentheses to mark this voice: "His laughter is enthrilling / (Quit laughing, you dirty brat.) / It reaches to the ceiling— / because he's nice and big and fat."[6] The parenthetical phrase that interrupts the lullaby deflates the just-asserted encomium to the baby's "enthrilling" laughter. The parent sings *about* the child to an unnamed other who watches the relationship from outside and can be bamboozled. Between the parentheses, between parent and child, lies the unadorned truth of their relationship.

Abott is not alone in getting comic mileage by veering wildly between "high" parental sentiment and "coarse" parental aggression. William Sunners's lullaby, included in the next week's paper, plays a similar game, although in this case the move is not between sentiment and insult but between insult and wheedling bribery, bringing to light the desires of both parent and child: "Sleep, you chozzer [pig]; don't you know, / I want to see a movie show. / If you sleep, I'll buy you toys / Like you saw by Levy's boys."⁷ Along with many of the other writers of lullabies, Sunners makes use of the reliable comedy of immigrant speech, peppering his English with Yiddish slurs and calques ("by Levy's boys"). The division of labor is clear: Yiddish supplies the insult or expresses the aggression that underlies the required parental sentiment, which speaks proper English.

The mixed-language lullabies are of course part of a venerable multilingual literary tradition mobilizing Yiddish for just such deflationary purposes. Benjamin Harshav illustrates this process with a Hebrew-Yiddish proverb in which the first half is a "pious," lofty sentiment in Hebrew, quoting a canonical rabbinic source, and the second half is its "coarse" Yiddish "translation": *bemakom she'eyn ish, iz afile a hering a fish* (where there are no men [Hebrew], even a herring is a fish [Yiddish]):

> The rhyme in the "herring" example [between *ish* (Hebrew for man) and *fish*] . . . brings the two components of the proverb together, ironizing their juxtaposition while reviving and undermining the traditional dictum at the same time. Placed as it is, after a Hebrew phrase and parallel to it, the second clause looks like a translation or explication of the first; but it actually opposes the emphatically "simple," "coarse," and smelly herring to the lofty and moralistic Hebrew style. Substituting for the original "man," the herring becomes a metaphor for whoever is the object of this sentence ("small fry"), degrading or ironizing him.⁸

The proverb recommends low expectations and standards when only herring is available, using Yiddish to bring the grandiose Hebrew *ish* down to earth (or sea) by "rhyming" him with a smelly *fish*. Yiddish is particularly well poised to play this game in relation to Hebrew, the acrolect in the hierarchical "internal bilingualism" of Ashkenaz. But it can perform this function also in relation to German and other European languages, which have a similarly "high" status as respected national tongues rather than "jargons." This function is visible in Alexander Freud's unpublished manuscript, "The Interpretation of Dreams," an exposition of his own reported dreams and those of his friends that Marinelli and Mayer describe as part of "a playful culture of lay interpretation [of *The Interpretation of Dreams*], somewhere between confirmation and skepticism, in [Freud's] social circles and in those of his family and friends." In the parody of his brother's distinguished German book, Alexander deflates and domesticates

Sigmund's lofty project by posing his own dream theory, which he claims rests on "the innumerable chalomes of my friends, as well as my own."⁹ The earnest, dry language of scientific verification and meticulous data collection that Robert Young regards as a central but often overlooked "translational" dimension of the psychoanalytic project is parodied, interrupted, and punctured by a Jewish vernacular, with Alexander's insertion of the Yiddish word for these "innumerable" dreams suggesting the strong associations of dreams not only with psychoanalysis but also with Jewish "dreaminess" and impracticality.¹⁰ Yiddish similarly ironizes the pieties of bourgeois parenthood in the *Forverts'* lullabies, whether as a Jewish weapon capable of exposing European social falsity or as an internal Jewish tool for deflating its own also-ripe-for-deflation high culture, for instance, the sublime national pathos of "Raisins and Almonds."

The *Forverts* hosted its contest in a regularly featured English section titled "For the Younger Members of the Family." Despite the implication that the page was directed at children who might read English more easily than Yiddish, the articles in fact regularly address parents among other readers of the Yiddish paper who might be trying to improve their English. Sharing a page with the second installment of the Freudian lullabies is an article titled "Foreign Accent a Handicap" by the etiquette expert Lillian Eichler, a frequent contributor to the English section. Eichler warns her readers,

> To instil in your boy or girl the love of fine English, the habit of correct daily speech, it is essential that you watch your own choice and use of words. The important thing is to speak always so carefully that the child, patterning himself from you, speaks carefully also. The accent should be watched, pronunciation, grammar—even the tone of voice. A loud, harsh or rasping voice can so influence a child that his own voice takes on the same undesirable qualities. For foreign-born parents who have an accent difficult to overcome, the problem is a little more complicated. The child is bound to acquire some of the characteristics of the parents' speech; and the only way to counteract this is to see that the youngster hears perfect English at every opportunity.¹¹

The *Forverts* might be suspected of ambivalence with the mixed messages it was sending on this page. In the column on the left, an article in stern, authoritative, and "correct" English instructs readers to restrain their Yiddish accents and tone in the service of the next generation; on the right, the winners of the lullaby contest are rewarded for imperfect English, rasping tones, and unruly emotions. On one side, an etiquette expert counseling pedagogical Americanization and "perfect English"; on the other, a parent hurling Yiddish insults at an infant son. Predictably, many of the Freudian lullabies mention the Oedipal complex; but there was another unnamed complex that also troubled them, the interrupted cultural and linguistic transmission that was the inevitable effect of mass migration. The family triangle in the Oedipus myth, we might recall, is torn apart not merely by the tensions inherent in kinship but more specifically by kinship complicated by expulsion, which opens a space between parents and son for misrecognition, mistranslation, and incest. The Oedipal and immigrant dilemmas are thus not parallel but interarticulated complexes in which the currents of language and culture and the psychosexual forces of psychic development flow with and against each other. This was the context, of intergenerational immigrant dramas, in which the *Forverts*' confused bilinguals were invited to sing a lullaby in whatever languages they could find to their Freudian, Americanizing babies.

The Freud craze was also in evidence beyond New York or other urban centers and served other purposes than helping immigrants acclimate to a new culture while holding on to something of the old one. Mikhoel Burshtin's 1937 Yiddish novel *By the Rivers of Mazovia*, which takes place in a small Polish town, includes among its cast of characters "Di Froydiske fun Smolin" (the Freudienne of Smolin). The Freudienne is a teenaged girl named Baltshe, whose father, the town rabbi, scrapes together enough money to send her to a gymnasium, or secondary school, in town and who comes back home changed by her glimpse of these wider horizons. No longer comfortable among the girls who stayed behind, Baltshe sits in the women's section of the synagogue, "sunk into her books."

> From Freud she learned that she's suffering from a complex. But what kind of complex? Where did her sufferings come from? The doctor, Gabriel Priver, might be able to shed some light on it to her, but Baltshe is too embarrassed to talk to him about it. He might suspect her of repressed things. . . . Baltshe withdraws into herself, digging deeper and discovering ever more weaknesses, instincts, and traits that she inherited from both her father's and mother's sides. Baltshe knows very precisely that her subconscious life [*unterbevustzinik lebn*] is full of dark chasms and perils. That her character is warped.[12]

Baltshe dreams of studying psychology and, peering at her face in the mirror, worries that "apart from her eyes, which are pleasant, she possesses nothing, nothing that might awaken a man's libido."[13] The scene draws on familiar tropes (or stereotypes) of Eastern European Jewish literary history: the dreamy girl reading alone and waiting, waiting for her dimly glimpsed romantic future to materialize. Y. Y. Trunk paints a literary portrait of the "aristocratic" daughters of his great-grandfather, the Hasidic Rabbi Shayele Kutner, who "would sometimes sit by the windows and read thick Polish and German novels, their eyes streaming tears, sighing at the passionate loves depicted in them."[14] Except that it is not romantic novels that consume the long days of Burshtin's rabbi's daughter, as might have been the case a generation or two earlier. It is Freud, here invested with something of the passions and habits that earlier generations had felt for the heroes of romance novels. If the secularization of Jewish culture as a system for organizing romantic, sexual, and family life had not one but two stages, the first sentimental and the second sexual, Freud was the very emblem of the second stage.[15]

Burshtin does not spell out what Baltshe is reading that provides her with such a lexicon for her longing and sorrows, but by the 1930s, when the novel takes place, she would have had her choice of Yiddish reading material on psychoanalysis. Even before the first of the Yiddish translations of Freud appeared in 1928, his terms and ideas were circulating through the popular press. They were also being propagated through public lectures, a notable feature of the landscape of Yiddish high culture throughout the world. Among the biographies of journalists, actors, and activists in interwar Poland in Melekh Ravitsh's *My Lexicon* (1947) is a wry portrait of the journalist and lecturer Dr. Avrom Gliksman (1883–1943), whom Ravitsh calls "The Eternal Student": Gliksman spent nineteen years in Leipzig, Jena, Zurich, and Paris studying business, political economy, philosophy, and the social sciences, occasionally also writing for English and German publications (including the *Economist*). In 1920, after his wealthy Hasidic family finally withdrew their support, he was compelled to return to Poland to try to earn a living among Polish Jews. Gliksman turned to Yiddish journalism and the lecture circuit, delivering high-minded talks on Plato, Kant, "the unique character of Yiddish literature," "the power of love in our spiritual lives," "woman and her eternal secret," "Baruch Spinoza as intellectual leader," and the question "Does religion still have anything to offer modern man?"[16] But it was Freud who was his particular specialty:

> When the Freud-fashion hit Jewish Poland, Dr. Gliksman's star ascended, with big and small towns literally begging him to grace them with a lecture about the great psychologist. But since Dr. Gliksman was even less capable of speaking to a general audience than of writing for one, his popularity began to wane, until someone advised him to sprinkle a few jokes into his material. Gliksman heeded the advice and the invitations began to flow again. But in one shtetl, the audience found his jokes so sidesplittingly hilarious that the convener had to pound on the table: "You immature brats, wagon drivers—the professor is providing a serious lecture and you laugh like impudent schoolchildren." The room grew somber as a funeral, and no one dared to even smile at any of the jokes that followed.[17]

Humorous and anecdotal as it is, Ravitsh's sketch nevertheless sheds light on the role of lectures in spreading the "Freud-fashion" among Yiddish speakers in interwar Poland. As Ravitsh makes clear, Gliksman rode the craze for psychoanalysis in Poland, but he did not create it. However knowledgeable he was on the topic, Gliksman had to contend with a fickle audience that knew something about the subject and had their choice of lecturers. Ravitsh also helps us see how Gliksman was able to function as an agent of cultural transfer in his peripatetic movements from Kutno to Warsaw, Germany, Switzerland, and France, and back to Warsaw.[18] As Gliksman helps us see, Freud's arrival in Yiddish-speaking Poland was also a return; with Gliksman he comes *back* to Poland, *back* to Yiddish. The role played by the (discarded) Hasidism of Freud's father in the deep structure of psychoanalysis may have been minimal, but Gliksman's (rejection of) Hasidism clearly shaped his own version of psychoanalysis, the version he circulated in the lands from which Freud's ancestors had come.

The circular and "horizontal" transfer of knowledge from Eastern to Central to Eastern Europe also tells a more "vertical" story about class hierarchies: Gliksman is kept afloat by the family he has left behind before he becomes an unemployed philosopher scrounging for gigs among the unwashed masses. Gliksman's career thus stretches between the more acculturated and bourgeois German sphere and the more impoverished Yiddish-speaking Jews of Poland. Ravitsh presents his public lecture on Freud as a scene not only of cultural translation but also of instruction and disciplining. Just as Baltshe's reading habits also signal something about her class aspirations, going to lectures spoke to the desire for cultural "improvement." While Gliksman learns to bend to reach his audience, the "immature brats" listening to him learn to control their impulses, to keep a poker face at his hilarious jokes. Along with the details of psychoanalysis, they are imbibing the rules of bourgeois comportment and acquiring worldliness and sophistication, a realm in which sex, the stuff of jokes, is translated into high culture. The psychoanalytic session may be designed to invite the (verbal) expression of a patient's unacceptable desires through the permission granted by free association, but the psychoanalytic lecture—at least in this context—follows different rules, teaching new forms of restraint to unruly audiences and translating their suffering, like the unfortunate Katharina's, into "the realm of medical science."[19] Ravitsh's biography of Gliksman pokes fun at the long-winded, self-important Gliksman and stereotypes Yiddish-speaking audiences as uncouth. Psychoanalysis speaks to both sides of this cultural equation, as a specialized subject with a technical scientific vocabulary and as preoccupied with the transgressive misbehavior that greeted Gliksman's remarks.

High culture and its bawdy disruption was a recipe that repeated itself elsewhere in the Yiddish reception of Freud, as evidenced in the Freudian lullaby contest. It may be that psychoanalysis was a popular subject in the Yiddish press because it had the rare distinction of being able to fulfill both basic functions of the newspapers at one stroke—educating and entertaining readers. Freud provided readers with intellectual sustenance that was both nourishing and sensational. The formula worked whether psychoanalysis was being promoted or (as it often was by culturally conservative journalists) treated with skepticism or outright dismissal. This was not so different in the case of the Hebrew press, despite its generally more intellectual character. In both languages, psychoanalysis was first treated as a subject in highbrow journals, before Freud, its fascinating discoverer, became a regular feature in the 1920s in the popular dailies. Hebrew and Yiddish writers discovered psychoanalysis rather belatedly: the first mention of Freud's name in Hebrew that the archives yield is in a 1912 Hebrew article, "Mental Illnesses," which appeared in the Vilna biweekly *Hazman*, in which M. Asya describes Freud's discovery of the unconscious, calling him the "master/teacher of [*rabban shel*] the school of psychiatric psychologists."[20] The first Yiddish mention came a year later, in the article "Multiple Personalities" by A. A. Roback, the Yiddishist and psychologist who corresponded with Freud in the 1930s; the essay appeared in *Dos naye leben*, a New York monthly devoted to "social and cultural questions." Asya doesn't mention Freud's Jewishness; Roback does. What the two articles share is an emphasis on the novelty, modernity, and revolutionary character of modern psychology, emblematized above all by Freud's approach. Asya vividly describes the sad state of the treatment of mental illness before modern psychology succeeded in bringing clarity to the field: "In previous generations mental illness was the mischief of evil spirits, demons, and imps. A mentally ill person was like a ruined structure with a no-longer-functional mezuzah, in which clowns and *dybbuks* dance with Lilith's daughters. The cure was obvious: the *dybbuks* had to be exorcised, the soul cleared of devilish imps." Because of thinkers like Freud (who, although Asya did not say so, also used the metaphor of a ruin to describe a mentally ill person), it was now understood that these difficulties arose not from invading imps but from the thoughts, emotions, and life history of an individual.[21] Roback took a similar approach to the narrower topic of multiple personalities (perhaps also meaning psychosis), stressing that the condition was well-known to traditional society under a variety of folk guises, as in the demons Jesus cast out (a case Asya also mentioned) or the Jewish *dybbuk*. These demons afflicted moderns at least as regularly, given the alienation of modern lives. Moreover, they were a feature of normal life as well as the mental landscape of those more seriously affected. Modernity, while not healing this suffering, nevertheless provided some perspective on it: Roback credits "the Jewish intellectual Freud who constructs his theory on the foundation of sexual life" with having succeeded in "distinguishing the normal from abnormal expressions" of the multiplicity and splits inherent in each human psyche. Qualifying this praise rather vaguely, Roback continues: "But Freud's theory has not been widely accepted among orthodox psychologists, on methodological grounds."[22]

The decade or so that followed these first mentions saw increasing attention to psychoanalysis in the Hebrew and Yiddish press. In 1915, the New York daily *Dos yidishes togeblat* devoted an article by K. Berkovski to the "scientific dream theory" of A. A. Brill, duly acknowledging Brill's debt to "Professor Sigmund Freud of Vienna" while citing Brill's own psychoanalytic writings.[23] The next year, the same newspaper devoted another glowing, but more substantive, article, also by Berkovski, to what it called "The New Scientific Institution of Dreams," praising the scientific advances made in dream interpretation by modern psychology:

> In the literature of all peoples it is possible to find "Keys to Dream Symbols," most of which are built on fantasy and popular superstition, even if one can still glean some truth from them, including the truth that humans have always been interested in the symbolism of dreams. But

recent work by Professor Freud, in Vienna, as well as by Adler, Havelock Ellis, Brill, Jung, Stekel, and Wasserman, shows how far modern science has allowed us to build on this foundation. The entire psychoanalytic *Wissenschaft*, everything we can learn from literature, and all the laboratory methods have been mobilized to help explain our mysterious night life, our dreams. The chaotic days when we resorted to old wives' tales or Gypsy Tarot Card readers are behind us. Dreams may be analyzed scientifically, in the same way that astronomy emerged from astrology and chemistry from alchemy. Just so have we exchanged the Dream Books for a scientific understanding of dreams.[24]

These early journalistic reports about psychoanalysis in the Jewish press stress the same point, that psychoanalysis is a modern, scientific advance in the understanding of the psyche, rendering obsolete older and more traditional ways of interpreting dreams and mental illness. While one article mentions Freud's Jewishness, for the most part Jewish tradition is relevant to psychoanalysis only in the context of what has been left behind by these advances as part of a broader range of benighted religious and cultural ideas about demons and the prophetic power of night visions that Freud was finally and decisively putting to rest.

By now, we are so familiar with the narratives that draw a connection between Freud's theories and their religious "precedents"—linking his dream interpretation and the biblical Joseph, rabbinic hermeneutics, or mystical language theory, for instance—that these associations seem obvious or inevitable. But the ramifications of Freud's Jewishness for his discoveries were slow to make themselves felt in the Jewish press, slower, certainly, than in Freud's immediate Viennese context. Writers took the cue from Freud himself in distinguishing his method from biblical dream interpretation or from the old manuals of dream symbolism that viewed dreams as emerging from a shared cultural lexicon rather than an individual psychic vocabulary. Freud had argued that Pharaoh's dreams were the patently "artificial" and flat-footed constructions of a biblical writer, which bore only the faintest relationship with the confused, obscure, and fragmented dreams of reality. Moreover, "the idea of dreams being chiefly concerned with the future and being able to foretell it—a remnant of the old prophetic significance of dreams"—obscured the extent to which dreams were remnants of the past.[25] Freud's first Hebrew and Yiddish interpreters got the point clearly enough: As B. Albin put it in a 1924 article in the Buenos Aires daily *Di idishe tsaytung*, "The old beliefs that dreams are a way for God or an angel to signal the future of an individual are incorrect; but the modern belief that dreams are insignificant nonsense is also wrong. Dreams are meaningful signals of a dreamer's buried wishes and their conflicted past."[26]

Things changed: the dead arose from their graves, the cast-out demons found their way back, the *dybbuks* and imps danced again. Roback's correspondence with Freud began when Roback sent him an inscribed copy of *Jewish Influence on Modern Thought* (1929), which included a long section linking Freud's discoveries with Hasidism and other currents in traditional Jewish thought; Roback described Freud as yet another Jewish "dreamer who is struck by an idea which subsequently develops into a grand vision," an attribute Roback linked with Israel Zangwill's 1898 novel *Dreamers of the Ghetto*. Freud's thought was also in line with Hasidism, by virtue of his "humanism," "the mystic halo surrounding his doctrines," and his success at "creating disciples instead of merely training pupils, as most of the other psychologists have done."[27] Roback was thus among the founding members of what Eran Rolnik calls the school of "Ethnic Maximalists" in Freud studies, consisting of the many scholars "who view Freud's work as a direct outgrowth of his Jewish origins, and even view psychoanalysis as a 'Jewish science.'"[28] If the history I have been tracing is any indication, the "ethnic maximalism" that Roback seems to have inaugurated was preceded by the prior trend of "ethnic minimalism" evident in the Hebrew and Yiddish press until 1924 or so, in which writers simply assumed that Freud's Jewishness was an interesting biographical datum but, in Rolnik's words, "as irrelevant to psychoanalysis as Einstein's is to the theory of relativity."[29] These writers may have occasionally noted his Jewish origins, but what captured their attention was not the Jewish character of Freud's thought (whether "ambivalent" or direct) but its scientific status, the novelty of his methods, and the divergence of Freud's discoveries from Jewish and all other religious traditions. This, too, might have been a distinctively Jewish approach to psychoanalysis: Antisemites might persist in seeing the fingerprints of Freud's Jewishness all over his discoveries, but Jews could avoid participating in this ugly game by respecting the way Freud presented his own work.

If in 1929 Roback was an outlier in spotting the Jewish character of psychoanalysis, writers over the decade that followed increasingly began to stress the connections rather than differences between psychoanalysis and the Jewish tradition. The very act of describing Freud's discoveries in Jewish languages helped propel this process: To reword *The Interpretation of Dreams* in Hebrew (or to describe its insights in Yiddish) was to tip the balance toward comparison and away from contrast. To refer to Freud as a "dream interpreter" in a Jewish language, or to translate the title of his German work as *Pesher hahalomot*, a title that lent Mordechai Brachyahu's 1959 translation its "pleasantly biblical tone," was to invite—intentionally or not—the association with Joseph as a *poter halomot* (interpreter of dreams) or with the biblical word for dream interpretation, termed *pesher* in Daniel 2:4 and elsewhere.[30] Language speaks. Even with the buffer of German around his thought, Freud himself could hardly avoid such associations. Despite the distance Freud is careful to take from the biblical Joseph, he acknowledges that he cannot escape his long shadow. Recounting a dream involving a colleague named Josef, Freud points out in a footnote that "the name Josef plays a great part in my dreams (c.f. the dream about my uncle). My own ego finds it very easy to hide itself behind people of that name, since Josef was the name of a man famous in the Bible as an interpreter of dreams."[31] Along with Josef the colleague and Joseph the biblical dream interpreter, there is a third Josef, too, Freud's parenthetical uncle, connected with the biblical figure by the accident of name rather than chosen profession. Freud describes this uncle as "unfortunate" without also disclosing that he was a convicted counterfeiter. The current of associations, as Freud (and Jesus) taught us, "bloweth where it listeth," and Freud's attempt to distance himself from these characters or their deeds can hardly be the final word. Freud's early popularizers in Hebrew and Yiddish may have praised him for his revolutionary scientific discoveries and marked his distance from benighted superstitions and entrenched tradition. But in translating Freud's thought into Jewish languages, it was perhaps inevitable that they also followed an unconscious path (their own or Freud's or mine, who can say?) through the thickets of a language that connected Jews and their history and literary tradition, through recycled names and occupations and dreams.

The Hebrew and Yiddish press grew considerably in the 1920s, and with it so did the circulation of Freud's teachings in these languages. Freud's sixtieth birthday passed without much notice in the Hebrew and Yiddish press, but by his seventieth birthday in 1926, Freud was a go-to staple of the booming Jewish newspaper culture across many regions, from the highbrow journals of Poland, New York, Argentina, and Palestine to the sensational popular Yiddish dailies in Warsaw and New York. Avrom Novershtern writes that, in the 1920s and 1930s, "roughly fifty daily newspapers were published in many countries—Argentina, Canada, England, France, Latvia, Lithuania, Poland, Romania, the Soviet Union, the United States, and Uruguay. . . . Every ideological camp in the Jewish world endeavored to have its own publication wherever Yiddish speakers were present in significant numbers."[32] Freud was covered by the anarchists and the Zionists and all points in between—only the Orthodox press managed to ignore him (at least for a while). In Yiddish-speaking Buenos Aires, where psychoanalysis was particularly popular, *Di idishe tsaytung* published no fewer than ten articles on the subject between June 1924 and November 1926, many of them lengthy. The offices of the daily, in the bustling Jewish neighborhood of Once, abutted such other Jewish cultural institutions as the YIVO, the Jewish Theater, and the Teachers' Seminary; advertisements in the paper attest to the interest in psychoanalysis in all these institutions and, more generally, among the city's Yiddish-speaking intellectuals.[33] In November 1926, for example, *Di idishe tsaytung* presented a detailed summary of a lecture, "The Unconscious and Its Role in Our Psychic Lives," sponsored by the Russian Cultural Society and delivered by Dr. Paulina Rabinowitz.[34] As elsewhere in the Yiddish world, public lectures were popular leisure activities as well as significant sources of income for professionals and intellectuals, and newspapers regularly advertised lectures and summarized them for those who had not attended. Mariusz Kałczewiak suggests that Freud may have had particular cachet in the city precisely because its Jewish inhabitants perceived themselves as peripheral: "Buenos Aires culture makers strived to present Buenos Aires as a city involved in the global currents of Yiddish culture."[35] As elsewhere, psychoanalysis allowed Yiddish speakers in Argentina to swim in deeper waters than they could otherwise expect.

Lest it be supposed that interest in psychoanalysis in 1920s Yiddish Buenos Aires was a Jewish offshoot of the famous craze for psychoanalysis in the city, it is worth pointing out that historians of psychoanalysis in Argentina date its popular interest in the city no earlier than the 1930s. Cecilia Taiana asserts that, before 1930, "Freud's theories and psychoanalytical practices were still novel and discussed by only a few neurologists, psychiatrists, and psychologists."[36] Mariano Ben Plotkin provides a similar periodization, writing that "by the early 1930s, psychoanalysis had piqued real interest, not only in intellectual circles but also at the level of popular culture."[37] Unlike the United States, which saw a wave of analysts fleeing Nazi Europe in that period, Argentina welcomed a mere handful of refugee analysts, including Marie Langer, who arrived in Argentina in 1942, with her student Heinrich Racker following shortly after. Argentinian psychoanalysis was mostly a homegrown affair, although, as Taiana writes, "the contribution to psychoanalysis of Argentinean-born neurologists, psychiatrists, and psychologists of Jewish ancestry—whose families arrived in Argentina in the early twentieth century—was vital to its emergence."[38] The widespread interest in psychoanalysis in Yiddish-speaking Argentina flourished precisely during the decade Taiana calls "pre-Freudian," among the immigrants whose children would later spur its homegrown development.[39] If so, then the burst of interest in Freud evident in the Yiddish press of the mid-1920s and apparently absent from the broader Spanish-speaking scene played a hitherto unrecorded role in the famous flourishing of psychoanalysis in Buenos Aires.

The Hebrew press saw a similar fascination with psychoanalysis in the 1920s, driven at least in some part by Freud's public involvement, beginning in 1920, with plans to build the Hebrew University; in 1925, he was among the first, with Albert Einstein, to join what was called the Board of Governors of the university. In truth, there were tensions behind the scenes, which came to a head in the early 1930s, over his hopes that psychoanalysis would find a home at the university; but Freud was more likely to express reservations about Palestine and Zionism in private correspondence than to inquiring journalists.[40] In a 1933 letter to Judah Magnes, president of the Hebrew University, he acknowledged that "for me, a trip to Jerusalem is perhaps possible from a physical point of view . . . but not from a psychological one."[41] But the connections Hebrew readers felt with a famous Jew who supported a cause so dear to their own hearts set the tone in the press. The philosopher and first director of the Jewish National Library, Hugo Bergmann, marked Freud's seventieth birthday in 1926 with an article in the liberal Zionist daily *Ha'aretz* that spoke to these felt connections: "Today the world is celebrating the seventieth birthday of Sigmund Freud. Among those who congratulate him will be counted our land [*artsenu*], with which Freud has tied his name by joining the Board of Governors of the University."[42] In other words, for Hebrew and Yiddish journalists, Freud was not merely the subject of a news story in a language he couldn't read. In addition to joining the rest of the world in congratulating Freud on his birthday, Zionists in Palestine, with Bergmann as their representative, felt themselves in possession of a special *right* to congratulate Freud, by virtue of Freud's connection to *them*. And because Freud's birthday was celebrated around the world, when Hebrew readers joined in the chorus of congratulations, they were not only contributing to but also drawing symbolic capital from his glory and fame.

While the Jewish press found numerous opportunities to crow about Freud's involvement in a variety of Jewish causes and organizations, these stories often included a regretful note. In 1920, the Zionist weekly *Ha-olam* reported that a Basel planning meeting for the Hebrew University had unfortunately been postponed; on the bright side the postponement had given organizers time to garner more support for their project, including from "the famous physicist Albert Einstein, who wrote that he intended to do what he could to push forward the Hebrew University, and Professor S. Freud, the famous inventor of psychoanalysis, who expressed his great interest in the idea of the university."[43] In 1925, it was Freud who provided that rueful note in begging off attending the ceremonial opening of the university, although he sent greetings that were faithfully reported across the Jewish press. In the 1920s and 1930s, the Zionist press repeatedly dangled the thrilling prospect before its readers that Freud was planning a visit to the Holy Land or even intended to settle there; readers took what comfort they could in the polite regrets he sent in response to various invitations on the grounds of illness.[44] In 1932, Freud participated (apparently as an honorary member) in the committee convened to prepare a welcome reception for the Hebrew poet Hayim Nahman Bialik, who was visiting Vienna; but he publicly apologized to Bialik that he could not meet with him personally or attend the gala because of his poor health.[45]

This pattern played itself out, at a delay of a few years, in the Yiddish cultural scene, which forged ties with Freud in the summer of 1925 when he agreed to join the Presidium, or honorary board, of the newly organized YIVO.[46] In 1935, a report in the Warsaw *Literarishe bleter* on a conference in honor of the tenth anniversary of the founding of YIVO published Freud's greetings to the attendees alongside those of Albert Einstein, also a member of the honorary Presidium, who also failed to attend. Freud wrote that "approaching my eightieth year is perhaps no enviable circumstance. My health leaves much to be desired, making it difficult for me to make the journey to participate in your jubilee conference. Please accept, in my place, this expression of deep sympathy for your efforts."[47] Ill health was a reliable excuse, and indeed the unfortunate reality. While the Hebrew press could find some measure of compensation for Freud's absence from the Holy Land when his disciples began arriving in large numbers in 1933, the New York Yiddish press sometimes consoled itself for its distance from

Freud by making do with the closer Dr. A. A. Brill, Freud's first English translator, the first practitioner of psychoanalysis in America, and (as the Yiddish press rarely failed to mention—it loved its doctors and professors) a Columbia University professor, who was often called on to mediate psychoanalytic ideas not only for American audiences but more specifically for its Yiddish-speaking members.

It was not only the aura of sophistication that readers found appealing in psychoanalysis, in an era of social "betterment." For the popular Yiddish dailies of New York and Warsaw, the whiff of scandal, notoriety, and sensation that lingered around psychoanalysis also reliably sold papers. The New York press associated psychoanalysis with both mental illness and crime, particularly crimes of passion. A 1921 article in the New York daily *Der tog*, titled "What Parents and Girls Can Learn from the Glickstein-Reizen Tragedy," turned to psychoanalysis to help untangle the circumstances that led to a widely reported Brooklyn murder in which a married doctor was shot by a newlywed woman with whom he had once been involved without a word exchanged between them. Y. Sanino, who covered the story, defended the murder victim as blameless on the grounds that

> the very fact that the young woman had gone to see a Christian Science healer before she was sent to Dr. Tannenbaum, a psychoanalyst, shows that she was carrying around a tangle of strange feelings and strange ideas, a kind of madness caused by something that presses on the soul. Dr. Freud has written extensively about that, and showed us how to discover what that oppressive feeling is and how to heal it.[48]

Sanino associates Freud with writing about the kind of "strange feelings" that might result in murder but charitably lets him off the hook of actually causing the madness. Other stories more directly implicated Freud in the seedy underworld of modern urban life, viewing psychoanalysis as partly to blame for its unruly passions. The Warsaw daily *Haynt* ran a story in 1926 provocatively titled "Sigmund Freud as 'Murderer'" about a nineteen-year-old student who shot his twenty-three-year-old teacher, an enthusiastic proponent of Freudianism, for the offense of psychoanalyzing a dream without being invited to do so by the dreamer.[49] (That Freud considers uninvited psychoanalyzing of someone else an ethical offense is clear from his description of a "sacrifice" of one of his beloved antiquities as an unconscious "penance" for this "crime.")[50] It was not only the Yiddish press that associated psychoanalysis with criminality. Peter Gay reports that when Leonard and Virginia Woolf visited Freud in London in 1939, Leonard repeated a "charming anecdote" he had read in the paper about a man who had been caught stealing a book by Freud, and "the magistrate who had fined him had said he wished he could sentence him to read off of Freud's works as punishment." Freud was not charmed, grumbling that "his books had made him infamous, not famous."[51] The associations of psychoanalysis and criminality were undoubtedly fed in many contexts by antisemitic sentiments. But the popular Yiddish press was not immune from this toxic brew, in part because it too was culturally conservative, a conservatism it sometimes combined with political progressivism and sensationalism, a mix of prudery and voyeurism that kept both the fascination with and critique of Freud at high simmer.

Freud saw what he portended for America: In a famous anecdote that Lacan claimed to have heard from Jung in 1954, as their boat sailed into New York harbor, Freud said to Jung, "Don't they know that we're bringing them the plague?"[52] Journalists seem to have concurred in this assessment, whether they breathlessly circulated sensational stories or took the high moral ground of condemning "Freudianism," if not Freud himself, for the social ills and sexual permissiveness of modern society. In the view of many in the American Yiddish press, even if Freud happened to be a Jew, "Freudianism" was contagious and alien, an import from decadent Europe. In a 1918 article in the New York *Di varhayt* titled "The Latin Quarter from the Inside: The Cradle of All the 'Isms" in America," B. Finkel excoriated the culture of Greenwich Village, the American "Latin Quarter," which had absorbed all of Europe's pernicious 'isms.' It was Greenwich Village that "made Sigmund Freud famous in America, with his cure for—forgive the vulgarity—those damned human weaknesses, sexual and otherwise." And why did Freud catch on so readily with that crowd? "Because for him sex is the engine of the whole human machine. That's why! And because sex is so 'modern,' these new theories about sex are seen as fresh products, imports from those great cultural revolutions in Europe." Finkel informed his reader that Freudianism was only the most notorious among many other unpleasant "isms," including "onanism, Futurism, and neo-Realism."[53] The impression of Freud as unsavory and of Europe as the source of all that was dangerously new persisted throughout the interwar period. In the 1936 article "The Ugly End of an Ugly Soul," the *Forverts* recounted the arrest and conviction of the writer and pornographer Samuel Roth, laying blame for this scandal squarely on the pernicious effects of psychoanalysis: "About twelve or fifteen years ago, America suddenly became 'sex conscious.' Suddenly everyone was interested in sexual problems. The writings of Sigmund Freud had an extraordinary effect on the reading public."[54] From Freud to *Lady Chatterley's Lover* to the Lewisburg Federal Penitentiary (where Roth served seven years) was a mere two degrees of separation.

Whether Freud was to blame for the ills of the age or was the only hope for its cure, it was simply the case that he was arguably the most famous Jew of his time, and the Yiddish-reading public hungered for any crumb that could be offered about his life or work. In New York, this was a curiosity shared with the English-language tabloids. Even the more sophisticated *New York Times* was hardly above covering the publicity stunt that was Samuel Goldwyn's journey to Europe in December 1924, with great fanfare, to pay a visit to "the greatest love specialist in the world." Goldwyn's more specific purpose was to "prevail upon the expert in psycho-analysis to commercialize his study and write a story for the screen"; Goldwyn was prepared to pay Freud one hundred thousand dollars for a script about Antony and Cleopatra. Once again, Freud disappointed: his refusal to meet with Goldwyn was duly reported a month later.[55]

Beginning with his seventieth birthday, birthdays and such honors as winning the Goethe Prize or having a plaque attached to his childhood home in Moravia were breathlessly covered in the Yiddish and Hebrew press. In contrast with articles in the non-Jewish press, Hebrew and Yiddish news stories about Freud and his work rarely failed to mention his Jewishness, eagerly passing around tidbits of information that could shed light on his Jewish activities, Eastern European heritage, purportedly Jewish appearance, and so on. Fascination with Freud extended to his family. In 1917, *Dos yidishes togeblatt* reported on the appeal to the New York Court of Murray Cohen, student at Columbia University, for permission to take his wife's maiden name: "She is Hela Bernays, a niece of the famous Viennese Jewish Professor Sigmund Freud."[56] (Cohen took on his wife's family name not because of the connection to Freud but in the absence of a male descendant to carry on the Bernays name.) The Bernays family was wealthy and philanthropic, and the act of a man taking on his wife's family name was rare enough that the press might have covered this piquant story in any case; but by 1917 the connection with Freud was also an obvious hook. In the dark spring of 1938, a different niece (or great-niece) found her way into a Yiddish paper purely by virtue of this relationship. The report in the *Forverts*, "Professor Freud Has a Niece in Hunter College; She Is Studying

Psychology," focused on the concerns Shirley Fuchs and her family had for the precarious political situation of her brilliant uncle. Fuchs, who was studying psychology with the aim of becoming a policewoman, asserted that she had enormous respect for uncle although she did not always agree with his theories, generously adding that "everyone makes mistakes." "And why did Freud's great-niece decide to become a policewoman?" the reporter asked. "To help unfortunate women," the young woman answered; her study of psychology would aid her in police work, and her personality was suited for this work.[57] Freud was long denied the professorship he coveted because he was Jewish, a painful slight that Freud recounted and Yiddish journalists repeated. But the Yiddish press awarded him this title over and over again, taking pleasure in the title along with Freud.

Freud's fame was not only a reflection of the enormity or interest of his discoveries, an assessment of his place in intellectual history. Freud was also famous simply for being famous, among plenty of people who knew almost nothing else about him. His fame is duly noted in the regular formula by which journalists introduced him, as "the famous Jewish Viennese Professor" (and its variants). It also linked him with a small handful of similarly famous-for-being-famous Jews, always Einstein and sometimes also Henri Bergson, and occasionally a longer list of such luminaries. In the 1920s and 1930s heyday of the Jewish press, editors on the hunt for items to fill its pages and attract subscribers regularly featured lists of famous or "great Jews," lists that occasionally set off heated debates. In 1936, the critic and novelist Lewis Lewisohn published a list of "the ten greatest living Jews" in the *New York Times*, dividing his list into two subgroups, the first four (Einstein, Freud, Bergson, and Buber) "who are first-rank geniuses," and the remaining six who are "not of the same divine spark."[58] The *Times* reported a few days later that Rabbi Stephen Wise, who (coincidentally or not) was ranked among the less sparkly, had publicly objected to Lewisohn's classificatory system on the grounds that it failed to distinguish between "great Jews" and "Jews who are great men but who are not great Jews."[59] Wise specified, however, that Einstein, Freud, Bergson, Buber, and Justice Louis Brandeis deserved both titles (as, surely, did he). This was a transnational sport: In Pinsk in 1938, *Unzer pinsker leben* asked the question: "Who Are the Most Famous Jews in the World Today?" and answered it with a more generous list of sixteen; as always, Freud and Einstein were listed, among those who needed no introduction; Yehudi Menuhin, by contrast, was described as "the young violist" (he was twenty-two at the time) and Elizabeth Bergner (a rare woman on these lists) was described as "the famous actress."[60]

The ubiquitous linking of Freud and Einstein as the two most famous Jews in the world may explain why, on January 2, 1927, while Freud and his wife were visiting their son Ernst in Berlin, Einstein and his wife thought to pay them a visit, about which Freud wrote: "He is cheerful, sure of himself and agreeable. He understands as much about psychology as I do about physics, so we had a very pleasant talk."[61] (In 1932, they had a more substantive exchange, initiated by Einstein as part of the International Institute for Intellectual Cooperation under the auspices of the League of Nations, on the question of "Why War?") While Freud joked about their mutual ignorance of each other's discoveries, there were differences between how they were treated in the press. Outside scientific publications, Einstein's theories generally warranted at most a few sentences (gravity, light, energy, relativity, "$e = mc^2$," etc.) before most readers' eyes could be expected to glaze over. By contrast, Freud's ideas were endlessly interesting and amenable to summary, even though, Freud ruefully complained, they were often wildly misunderstood.[62] Freud's oeuvre comprised works addressed to both academic and popular audiences, which correspondingly provided material for the highbrow and popular press. And not only. The YIVO Archives hold a program for a Warsaw Yiddish production of Antoni Cwodziński's wildly popular *Freud's Theory of Dreams* (1937), directed by Jonas Turkow and translated by Diana Blumenfeld.[63] In the Yiddish discourse on psychoanalysis, which traversed high and low culture and circulated throughout the Jewish world, Freud served as one of the most visible signs of the international republic of letters that was Yiddishland, connecting secular Yiddish-speaking intellectuals around the world and connecting them as well with the curious masses, while signaling the cultural ambitions and cosmopolitanism of both groups. As Karolina Szymaniak describes Freud's iconic role in Polish Yiddish culture in the 1930s,

> The dailies followed Freud's milestone birthdays, always adding biographical information. These regular mentions express more than just pride in the achievements of a Jewish intellectual. Freud—a misunderstood, persecuted, heroic figure, who fought for and triumphed with his truth—was the icon of a culture whose producers and recipients were excluded and increasingly threatened with violence.[64]

Szymaniak makes clear that the Jewish press was interested not only in

Freud's Jewishness but more particularly in the discrimination against Freud and dismissal of psychoanalysis on those grounds. Freud's resistance to persecution made him a heroic figure and icon for those in Poland who were threatened with similar treatment. Along with its heroic founder, psychoanalysis itself could help readers understand the crisis they were facing:

> Psychoanalysis in the 1930s was one of the languages in which young Jews communicated with one another, and in which they dealt with the political and cultural identity crisis and with the growing anti-Semitism of the time. Psychoanalysis was in all its expressions a modernist project, but it was also specifically promoted to young Jews by the adherents of Yiddishism—the project of creating a modern Jewish nation in the diaspora—who used it to help diagnose this identity crisis.[65]

If psychoanalysis could help Jews come to terms with rising antisemitism, the antisemitic attacks on its founder could help Jews come to terms with psychoanalysis. Even readers who took Freud's theories as a distant rumor, a source of alarm or bemusement, were fascinated by the story of a famous and controversial Jew who was attacked for his audacity. With Freud's eightieth birthday widely covered in the Jewish press, it is not surprising that the occasion also saw the release of Sh. Z. Wulf's *Sigmund Freud: The Inventor of Psychoanalysis* (Zigmund Froyd: Der shefer fun psikhoanaliza), as number 271 of the Groshn-bibliotek (Penny Library).[66] The Groshn-bibliotek booklets, published on cheap paper in a standard format of sixty-four pages and priced to sell, were issued weekly and directed at Yiddish-speaking workers. David Mazower and Lyudmila Sholokova write that the series began in 1930 with the booklet *Mata Hari: Dancer and Spy* and followed that with "a tabloid agenda of spies, love, sex, crime, and assassinations."[67] But by 1936, the series was taking on more serious topics, covering antisemitism and Soviet Communism; Freud, Leon Blum, and Genghis Khan were among the subjects of the final booklets published. Wulf's lively and accessible style imagined dialogue for Freud's life that other sources failed to provide. Anna O. haltingly describes her disgust for the governess that allowed her dog to drink out a glass and, after this recitation, calls out: "I beg—wa-ter!" Wulf continues, "The two doctors tremble as if they had witnessed the Splitting of the Red Sea [*krias yam suf*]. They both run to get water."[68] If psychoanalysis had translated the suffering of ordinary people into medical discourse, the Groshn-bibliotek reverse-engineered that process, producing popular literature out of science. This is not to say that Wulf contented himself with such dramatic reenactments; aside from chapters on Anna O., the role of America in "discovering" Freud, and "Freud the Jew," he also ably introduced readers to the unconscious, the Oedipal complex, and even the death instinct.

While the Groshn-bibliotek was clearly directed at working-class readers, its aims (at least by the mid-1930s) were not so different from those of the Yiddishists who worked to position Yiddish as "a fitting vehicle for a sophisticated high culture."[69] Cecile Kuznitz describes the Yiddishism of Chaim Zhitlowsky, an important ideological precursor for YIVO's more institutionalized cultural agenda, as a yoking of the poles of populism and elitism:

> Paradoxically, Zhitlowsky's concern for the common people spurred his advocacy of elite literature in Yiddish, including philosophical and scholarly writing as well as the translations of classics from other languages. He sought to develop the tongue into a suitable medium for all topics and forms of expression, for only in this way, he argued, could ordinary Jews have access to world culture and all Jews live a fully Jewish life without the need to turn to "foreign" sources. And only in this way could they raise the status of their national language and, by implication, of themselves as a national group.[70]

The paradoxical combination of "concern for the common people" and "advocacy of elite literature" is in fact a regular feature of national and/or "democratizing" pedagogical projects, for instance, the nineteenth-century translation of world classics into English for female and working-class readers described by Sukanta Chaudhuri or Ernest Benn's Sixpenny Library, which published more than 180 titles on a range of topics (including two on psychoanalysis, numbers 125 and 153, both by Ernest Jones), between 1927 and 1939.[71] Chaudhuri sees a double-edged ideology in the translation project he studies, in which readers "struggling for a foothold in the world of classically trained elites" were provided access, in inexpensive editions, to high-status and difficult literary and philosophical works. On the one hand, these translations broadened intellectual horizons and allowed readers to transcend their milieus, bridging the world of great ideas and ordinary readers. On the other hand, it also "'placed' them within their socially determined echelon," underscoring the chasm that separated these readers from the lofty ideas and rarefied social worlds to which they were now exposed and allowing them to see themselves as they were seen in the eyes of the elite, bringing into stark relief their own inadequacies. These

Figure 2. Cover of Sh. Z. Wolf, *Zigmund Froyd: Der shefer fun psikhoanalisa* (Freud: Discoverer of psychoanalysis), No. 271 of the series (Warsaw: Groshn Bibliotek, 1936). Source: Library of the YIVO Institute for Jewish Research.

translations, then, both "enlightened them and confined them, liberated and defined them."[72]

The translation and popularization of Freud in Yiddish, it could be argued, had the similar effect of bridging and underscoring the gap that separated ordinary Yiddish readers from the worlds opened up in Freud's writings, from which they were separated intellectually and socially; Freud both spoke to them through these translations of his words into a Jewish vernacular and "placed them" in their class, marking their distance from his Viennese bourgeois context. The paradoxical effect had a dimension lacking in the translated world classics Chauduri studies: Unlike the enormous gap between the world of the classics and that of the working class, female readers of their English translations, the distance between Freud and his Yiddish readers is less measurable or stable, distinguishing as well as connecting the acculturated Viennese Jew and the Yiddish-speaking Eastern European masses. Yiddish writers and translators seeking to overcome the resistance of working-class readers to psychoanalytic ideas had tools others did not, spinning the web of Jewish pride and ethnic connection across otherwise yawning chasms. As the advertisement in the first edition of Lerman's translation implied, Freud was worth reading because he was famous, and important, and learned, and because through Freud Jews could both show how modern they were and become more modern. To add to the attraction, editors were quick to remind readers that, for all his fame and success, Freud too was Jewish and persecuted for his Jewishness. Wulf's allusion to the two doctors "trembling as if they had witnessed the Splitting of the Red Sea" makes witty use of the watery context, finding an appropriate idiom in which to describe the miracle of Anna O.'s talking cure for her hydrophobia. But by describing the doctors as atremble with what they were witnessing, as at "the Splitting of the Red Sea," Wulf also reminded his readers of what they shared with these important doctors (and not only their suffering patient).

Jewish newspapers took particular delight in tracing Freud's Eastern European ancestry and Galician forebears (occasionally reprinting his family tree or taking the measure of his "noble Jewish forehead").[73] If popularizing or translating the world's great works into Yiddish allowed Jews "to live a fully Jewish life without the need to turn to 'foreign' sources," translating Freud—a Jew who wrote German—multiplied this effect. The translation and popularization of Freud in Yiddish combined the lofty, cosmopolitan, and scholarly with the homey (*heymish*), enclosing his strange and unsettling concepts in a familiar Jewish "scriptworld" in a manner that echoed and inverted how Freud himself experienced the *Umheimlichkeit* of his familiar ideas in an unreadable Jewish alphabet.[74] Precisely the circumstance that constituted one of the most insurmountable obstacles in the reception of psychoanalysis—Freud's Jewishness—was thus his major calling card for the Jewish popular readership, an incentive for even unsophisticated readers to overcome their resistance for long enough to wrap their minds around the unconscious or take a nibble at the totemic feast.

On the very day the Groshn-bibliotek published its booklet on Freud, the *Forverts* began a five-issue series on psychoanalysis by Max Weinreich, also in honor of Freud's eightieth birthday.[75] The headline and lede capture something of what psychoanalysis meant in this environment:

> PROFESSOR SIGMUND FREUD, FAMOUS RESEARCHER INTO MENTAL ILLNESSES, TURNS EIGHTY TODAY
>
> "Psycho-analysis," the means of healing nervous patients, which Sigmund Freud invented.—The difficulties Freud faced in his career because he was Jewish.—What is a "psychological" or "nervous" Illness?—The curious case of a young girl who suffered from such an illness.—How she was healed through hypnotism.[76]

The lede touches all the bases: Freud's fame, his Jewishness and the persecution he suffered because of it, the discovery of psychoanalysis, the interesting illnesses it treated, and the intriguing girls who suffered from these illnesses. Even hypnosis, by then a distant memory in psychoanalytic practice, merited a mention.

But even sympathy for Freud in the face of his treatment by antisemites could not always overcome the resistance triggered by so many aspects of psychoanalysis. An editor's note introducing the *Forverts* article acknowledged Freud's importance and the significance of the occasion, but given the controversial character of psychoanalysis, it also sought to establish that the publication of Weinreich's article was not intended as an endorsement:

> We on the editorial staff know full well that many people think psychoanalysis is a fraud, a way to make money. Nervous women go to a doctor, and pay them high fees to sit there and listen to them talk. The doctor recommends that they come every day for half a year, or even a full year, and that's supposed to cure them. But we have such respect for

Dr. Max Weinreich, an educated man of absolute integrity, that we have decided to allow him to introduce Freud to our readers.[77]

Weinreich was indeed the most effective, respected, and knowledgeable spokesperson for psychoanalysis in the Yiddish-speaking world and would become more so when he released the first volume of his Yiddish translation of Freud's *Introductory Lectures on Psychoanalysis*, also on Freud's birthday. But by the time he was working on his translation, Weinreich could build on two decades of press coverage, which had paved the way for the public understanding of psychoanalysis (even as it propagated misunderstandings) and forged a psychoanalytic lexicon that translators could follow (the subject of the next chapter). Reading the forgotten precursors to this field makes clear that Hebrew and Yiddish discourse on Freud only gradually discovered that Freud's Jewishness was not merely a biographical curiosity, relevant primarily for explaining why his contributions were sometimes reviled. The notions that undergird "the Jewish Freud," in which scholars first discovered "the influences of Jewish thought" on Freud and then moved on (more interestingly) to thinking about how Freud's ambivalence about or attempts to conceal his Jewishness might provide insight into psychoanalysis—these developed over a period of decades.

Is it possible to locate the very moment that the ethnic minimalism of Freud's initial coverage in the Jewish press morphed into the ethnic maximalism that is now so familiar? And what might have occasioned this shift? The Yiddish press stands as evidence that the maximalism so evident in Roback's work was preceded by a pioneering effort in this regard. Moreover, a close reading of this turning point demonstrates that "the Jewish Freud" was an accidental discovery, a by-product of the language in which psychoanalysis was being described. This turning point comes not in the first but rather in the second installment of a six-part series on psychoanalysis that began to appear in the prestigious Warsaw literary weekly *Literarishe bleter* a few months after its 1924 founding. The series was by Dr. Gliksman, the lecturer whose audiences needed to be taught not to laugh too hard at his jokes. The series declared its intention to apply psychoanalysis to Jewish sources; this itself did not signal the shift, since the project as thus conceived remained very much along the lines of similar work in the psychoanalytic journal *Imago*, founded by Freud, Hanns Sachs, and Otto Rank in 1919 to explore the relevance of psychoanalysis in the full range of the arts and humanities. Gliksman's stated initial aim was thus to show that Freud could help his readers understand Jewish sources, and not the reverse—that Jewish sources could help explain Freud's methods or ideas. Because Freud's work had not yet been translated into Yiddish, the project also required a preliminary exposition of psychoanalysis.[78] According to Ravitsh, most of Gliksman's editors fought to simplify and condense the learned "treatises" he submitted, but the highbrow *Literarishe bleter* was clearly willing to give Gliksman room to spread out over many pages and six issues. The first article began by bracketing the controversial question of the efficacy of psychoanalysis, laying out an argument that Freud's major contribution was in unifying the fields of medicine, philosophy, and literature. Freud's most valuable insight, that human beings were possessed of what Gliksman called (in English) a "double consience" [*sic*], glossing the phrase as "two souls" (*tsvay neshomes*) within a single person, had already been worked out by writers like Tolstoy, Dostoyevsky, Edgar Allan Poe, and Henrik Ibsen. But Freud "introduced this 'Ibsenian' structure into psychiatry, thus opening new vistas before our eyes."[79]

Gliksman was not the first to translate Freud's *Seele* as *neshome*; by 1924 it was the established term in the Yiddish press. But rendering the Freudian (single but) stratified psyche as "two souls" resonated with folkloric beliefs in the "extra soul" that the Sabbath mystically bestowed on those who observed it. Despite these echoes, Gliksman's long genealogy of proto-psychoanalytic philosophers, playwrights, and novelists includes not a single Jewish writer, although Spinoza is mentioned as such in the following installment. Gliksman's express intention was to *apply* psychoanalysis to Jewish sources; he seemed not to have entertained the thought that Jewish traces might already be there. However, by the second article, in which Gliksman turned to his exposition of core psychoanalytic concepts, the "echo chamber" of Jewish sources had begun to do its work, manifesting the resonances between Freud's new ideas and their old Jewish counterparts.[80] Describing how psychoanalytic treatment is supposed to work, Gliksman writes:

> 1. Through talking things out. Through confession [*vidui*] the individual comes on his own back to the true content of his soul. (Recall the role that confession plays in various religions, particularly Catholicism.) Psychoanalysis heals the split in the soul, the "life-lie." The "unconscious" [*unterbavuste*] becomes conscious, known, and the person becomes whole again—his life unified, without conflict.
>
> 2. In many cases, the patient can be shown that he was wrong to suppress his desire [*tayve*], and that it is not too late to revive it.

3. By understanding its causes and using his common sense [*sekhel*], a person can conquer his evil inclination [*yetser hore*] (as Spinoza already said!) and unite the present and past of his life.

4. The doctor can succeed in ennobling [*oystsueydln*] the sexual energy [*tayve-energiya*] (libido), raising up the emotions of the patient and constructing a substitute for his sexual desires [*tayves*] and thus make them a productive source of life-power. Freud calls this process "*Sublimierung*."[81]

The religious ghosts Gliksman was raising were not lost on him, and Gliksman spelled them out in the sentence that followed the reference: "We can here insert the [Hebrew] kabbalistic expression, 'to purify and raise the sparks to their roots' [*levarer u-leha'alot hanitzotzot el shorsham*], which precisely captures the profundity of Freud's method."[82] Gliksman begins his summary of Freud's methods by reference to the "talking cure," which he associates with Catholic confession (as Pappenheim and Foucault do). But the word he uses for confession, *vidui*, has powerful Jewish meanings that complicate the Catholic connection; as he continues, the Jewish resonances of his translation of psychoanalytic concepts gather steam before emerging full-blown. Given Gliksman's distinctly non-Jewish genealogy in the first article, the profusion of profoundly Jewish and religious terms that emerge when he begins to explain Freud's ideas is remarkable. The first article stands as powerful evidence that Gliksman had no intention of clothing psychoanalysis in Jewish garb or of rendering term after term with religious concepts that would strike his readers as deeply familiar. This ultra-Jewish Yiddish discourse seems to have arisen without any conscious intention on Gliksman's part, emerging, as it were, from the language itself. But how and why did that happen? Did Gliksman turn to the traditional vocabulary and Hebrew components of Yiddish for lack of less religiously charged language at his disposal? Or perhaps, in forging an academic and highbrow Jewish psychoanalytic discourse from scratch, Gliksman (consciously or unconsciously) reached "higher" for the Hebrew (and thus more traditionally Jewish) components of Yiddish, by a process roughly parallel to Strachey's reaching for Latin. Where Strachey translates the concept of *Fehleistung* as "parapraxis," Gliksman goes for the Hebrew *to'es*, even though for that word he had at hand the equally available Germanic cognate *feler*. This could not have been because Gliksman was hoping to establish psychoanalysis as a respectable science, which religious language could hardly accomplish. Hebrew perhaps struck him as the more sublime component of the language, appropriately for a sublime intellectual pursuit, and for the description of what it meant to sublimate something. And so it was that Freud met with and found a point of origin in the Kabbalah, at this point not in the deep recesses of his Jewish unconscious but in those of his Yiddish translator. Of course, the operations that transpire in the "black box" of translation are notoriously hard to bring to view. If "the talking cure" was an accidental discovery by a native Yiddish speaker who found herself speaking only English, "the Jewish Freud" may be the accidental discovery of a native Yiddish speaker who found himself reaching for Hebrew—for a host of reasons that can no longer be untangled, if they ever could be.

By the fifth article in the series, "Slips and Obstacles" (*To'esim umikhsholim*), Gliksman had sufficiently prepared the reader for the project of applying psychoanalysis to Jewish literature. There was no need, Gliksman explained, to apply it to non-Jewish literature, since Freud had already done that, acknowledging the poets and playwrights whose recognition of the unconscious preceded his; in the *Psychopathology of Everyday Life* Freud cites Portia's slip of the tongue in *The Merchant of Venice* that reveals that it is Bassanio that she desires. Following Freud here, Gliksman shows that Jewish writers too understood the workings of "Freudian slips," not only before Freud but also before Shakespeare:

> For the Jewish reader I will here mention as illustration a classic Jewish tale in the spirit of Freud, and which is older than Freud's own illustration—a tale from our *humesh-Rashi* (Bible with Rashi's commentary). When Abraham sent his servant Eliezer to procure a wife for his son Isaac, Eliezer said, "Perhaps the woman will not want to go with me." Rashi transmits the teaching: The word *ulay* (perhaps) is written without the letter *vov* so that it reads *elay* (unto me). And Rashi, following rabbinic tradition, comments that Eliezer wanted Rebecca for himself . . . for his own son.[83]

Gliksman argues that this interpretation of a missing letter in a biblical speech is characteristic of the rabbis, for whom "an error must have meaning." The psychoanalytic method resembles the hermeneutic habits of the rabbis, "who spent so much time squeezing meaning out of every letter, and waging war against the evil impulse, and who unconsciously painted the image of a delectable Rebecca (*a tsatske fun a rivke*)." Out of piety, the rabbis displace their own desires onto "the innocent Eliezer," just as

Abraham—the first in this long chain of displacements—subcontracted the job of providing a bride for his son onto his servant.[84] Gliksman adds that Jewish literature has many more examples of the same principle, in which Jewish interpreters are both unconscious of their own desires and strikingly acute in reading "mistakes" as signs of a more profound truth.

Gliksman introduced this fifth article as moving from laying out basic psychoanalytic concepts to "the application of psychoanalysis to Jewish literature." Whether he realized it or not, he was doing something more radical—laying the groundwork for an alternative literary genealogy of Freud's insights than the one either Freud or he himself had earlier traced. Gliksman was both "applying" psychoanalysis to the rabbis, who were unconscious of the mechanisms that guided their interpretations, and naming these same rabbis as precursors to Freud; both Freud and the rabbis, after all, believed (though for different reasons) that "an error must have meaning." What is implicit in the second installment of his series here emerges full-blown, not as a linguistic resonance between Jewish mysticism and Freud's theory of sublimation but as the identification of parallels in the rabbinic and Freudian modes of interpretation. Gliksman's narrower and more conventional project, of contributing another illustration of the relevance of psychoanalysis, gave way—apparently despite himself—to the project of discovering (or inventing) Jewish precursors to psychoanalytic insights. If Gliksman was indeed, as he claimed, the first to psychoanalyze Jewish culture in Yiddish, he was also the first to reverse that dynamic in the process, using Jewish culture to understand (or imagine) the origins of psychoanalysis.

Beyond the coverage of Freud's ideas, the Jewish-language press and its readers in the 1920s and 1930s were driven by curiosity about his Jewish life, a hunger for details about his Jewish ancestry, family, and personal relations—the "racial fever" that Eliza Slavet associates with "Jewish racial thinking," both Freud's and his readers'.[85] As Freud's fame grew, the Hebrew and Yiddish press sought opportunities to play Jewish geography with Freud, hoping to establish connections between the exalted, faraway, German-speaking professor and the ordinary Jew. Evocations of Freud's ancestral connection to Galicia; reproductions of the family tree that traced him back to the great-great-grandmother who bequeathed her name, *Freyde*, to him; discussions of how Jewish his features were—all these helped connect readers with the famous man and his struggles.

The interest in Freud's family and circumstances was never stronger than in the spring of 1938, in the days after the March 13 annexation of Austria by Germany, as rumors of Freud's arrest and detention, and the confiscation of his and his wife's passports, circulated globally.[86] The Jewish press was ablaze with conflicting rumors of threats to Freud and his family, Freud's health, and the plans under way to save him. On March 21, *Ha'aretz* reported that the National Council of the Medical Union in Palestine had unanimously voted to lobby the Jewish Agency to provide Freud and Professor Neumann immigration certificates to Palestine, noting that both men had expressed an interest in Zionism and that Freud was a member of the honorary board of the Union.[87] On March 25, the *Forverts* reported that the Freud family had given up on plans to leave Vienna for Palestine, had received invitations to come to the United States, but had tentatively decided to immigrate to the Netherlands.[88] On March 31, the same newspaper reported that plans were afoot to bring Freud to America.[89] Two days later, on April 2, a front-page article reported that Freud had been deprived of his passport and had informed his relatives in Holland that he would not be able to join them.[90] The following day, *Ha'aretz* reported from Palestine, also on the front page, that Freud's son Ernst had denied that the family had Dutch relatives.[91] On April 6, the *Unzer Byalistoker ekspres* reported: "Professor Sigmund Freud in Nazi Hands: The Great Tragedy in the Dusk of His Life."[92] On May 20, the Warsaw daily *Unzer ekspres* reported that Freud was headed for Paris.[93] Freud had long been a big story in the Jewish press, but in the spring of 1938 he was an almost daily presence, often on the front page. So feverish was the focus on the Freud family that *Ha'aretz* felt the need to remind its readers that other Jews were in danger, too.[94] As in the non-Jewish press, Freud's actual flight through Paris to London (June 4–6), his warm reception in London, the honors bestowed to him by the Royal Society, his visits to his dog in quarantine, and other piquant details of his post-Viennese life were followed closely by the Hebrew and Yiddish press in its various centers. As before, they did not always have their story straight: the *Forverts*, for instance, reported on June 5 that Freud was en route to New York.[95]

Freud's predicament in the spring of 1938 made the already intense affective attachments to Freud in the Jewish press that much stronger. On March 14, 1938, Yehuda Leyb Teller (who also wrote for *Commentary* as

Judd Teller) published a story in the New York *Morgn Zhurnal* titled "The Jewish Community of Vienna Now under the Shadow of Hitlerism," describing a trip he had taken to Poland, Germany, and Austria in the spring of 1937:

> Vienna is the fourth largest Jewish city in the world, and among the most interesting Jewish communities in the world. In Vienna, all the different branches of the Jewish world come together in one community. In Vienna resides Sigmund Freud, the great genius of psychoanalysis and a Jew. A few streets away lives the Chortkover Rebbe, among other Hasidic leaders who were evacuated along with their courts during the Great War.⁹⁶

Hasidic rebbes had lived near Freud before 1938, of course (along with the Chortkover, there were courts in interwar Vienna connected with Husiatyn, Boyan [until 1922], and others); but the threat they now shared brought into focus the proximity of the Godless Jew and his God-besotted Hasidic neighbors. Freud's joke about the Galicianer and the acculturated German Jew with whom he shared a train compartment had done similar work of forging Jewish connections within a context of fraying or disavowed ties—but this was no joke. What Freud was as a Jew, and how his connection to other Jews should be understood, was all shifting in the late 1930s, under the recognition that despite his fame, he was a Jew among Jews, under the same threat that all were facing.

In his 1937 visit to Vienna, Teller had had occasion to meet Freud, "a small man with a stone-gray face and clever Jewish eyes and a vest buttoned up to his tie." Freud "the great expert on the soul, the seer of human depths" spoke with Teller about Vienna, in that year before the Anschluss, as "a city whose senses are already completely dulled."⁹⁷ Ken Frieden notes that Teller did not elaborate on the conversation, except insofar as a poem he published in 1937, five months after the visit, "appears to be a displaced expression of the meeting."⁹⁸ Teller's poem, "Jud' Süss Oppenheimer during His First Visit to Sigmund Freud," imagines a scene in which Freud is consulted for treatment by none other than Jud' Süss Oppenheimer, the wealthy eighteenth-century court Jew who, sentenced to death on charges of fraud and other crimes, refused to convert to Christianity to save himself (the antisemitic Nazi film on Jud' Süss appeared in 1940, after the publication of Teller's poem cycle). Frieden points out that the German *Jud'* "echoes Yehuda Leib Teller's chosen English name: Judd."⁹⁹ Jud' Süss, the historical figure, and Jud' Süss, the character in the multiple retellings of the story, including Teller's, already illustrates the problematic of coming to terms with the alienating and violent antisemitic gaze. Nor is this dynamic limited to Jud' Süss or Yehuda Leib/Judd Teller, since Freud, too, can hardly be named without a similar entanglement in stereotype and projection. The first references in the poem, to Freud, are already caught up in that problem:

> That's you—the Eternal Jew.
> Of Esau's lullaby, of Gentile legend.
> And I am your nephew—Jud' Süss Oppenheimer.
> You, seer, who can see far, see clear, see through,
> You may say that I—am not really I,
> That one who craves balls and shikses
> Is not—Jew Süss.[100]

Freud, misread and miscast according to "Esau's" fantasies, is nevertheless a "seer" who can recognize the truth of who Jud' Süss is, beyond how he imagines himself (a man who craves balls) and beyond how he is seen by others. The clarity of sight is a sign not only of Freud's wisdom but also of the clarifying pressure of being hanged in the morning, of the antisemitic perspectives crowding so threateningly around the treatment couch (if Teller did not know what was in the offing, it is certainly remarkable that this poem names not one but two of the most notorious Nazi films, *Jud' Süss* and *The Eternal Jew*, both released in 1940). The poem is the first of a six-poem cycle titled "Psychoanalysis," which takes as its double subject psychoanalysis and antisemitism, read by Teller as the return of both a repressed ancient hatred and a repressed Jewish consciousness. To be healed of his psychological torments, Jud' Süss must dredge up his ancestral inheritance, the Jewish lessons he unconsciously imbibed that survival depends on suppressing one's rage—a rage against gentiles that Teller's poem allows him to express. In the fourth poem in the cycle, "Sigmund Freud on His Eighty-Second Birthday," Teller describes Freud as at an age that spells psychological peace, since he has overcome his fear of death and "smoked out" his youthful complexes. But this peace is only apparent, since, as for Jud' Süss, his Jewishness was returning to consciousness ever more pressingly. It turns out that something does remain of his childhood fear of death.

> It's something else, and just as old.
> By day, he looked out the window,

Saw the arms in salute.
The Swastika. He smelled with his clever nose
The old evil blood
In young Aryan *shkotsim*.

. . .

Shkotsim. Those whose name he carries
Have chewed the word in Hebrew-Joodish-Yiddish,
Chewed it like matzoh, kneaded it like challah
Braided it like Havdolah-candles—
Orel. Esau. Goy.[101]

Where Teller's article had described Freud as having "clever Jewish eyes," the poem—claiming access to Freud's internal sensorium—gives him instead a "clever nose," whose Jewishness can hardly be in doubt, since what it sniffs out is the "old evil blood" of antisemitism in "young Aryan *shkotsim*." Teller's use of *shkotsim*, a derogatory term (lit., "abominations" or "vermin") for non-Jewish boys or young men, might be understood as the poet's own Yiddish translation of Freud's German thoughts about the Hitler Youth. But in repeating the word, Teller makes it clear that this word emerges from Freud's own mind or, perhaps more precisely, from the psyches and indeed bodies of those "whose name he carries," who "chewed it like matzoh." In the litany of Yiddish insults or derogatory terms for non-Jews, including *orel* (an uncircumcised man), Teller is evoking what Max Weinreich called *lehavdil loshn*, the Yiddish "differentiation language" that traditionally distinguished Jews and non-Jews, Jewish and non-Jewish spheres.[102] For Teller, the rise, the return, of the old evils of antisemitism plunged even such assimilated Jews as Freud back into the old Jewish mind-set, which rested on stark distinctions between Jews and others. There is nothing in Teller's report on his visit with Freud that suggests that they exchanged a Yiddish word of any kind. But in the poem that refracts and displaces this meeting, Freud (or Freud's ancestors) and the Yiddish poet spoke in the powerfully particularistic Jewish idiom of a Jewish language. Teller's report on the 1937 visit draws attention to just how close Freud's apartment was to the Hasidic courts on neighboring streets. But his own proximity to Freud was also being measured, not in city blocks but in the link that Yiddish forged between the younger poet and the great seer, whose ancestors had chewed the same language, with both of them spitting out the Yiddish term *shkotsim*, a word that captured these thugs better than German cared to.

I do not mean to overstate or sentimentalize these Jewish affective ties, the momentary acts of communication in these circumstances, which were (as Dan Ben-Amos would predict) built over yawning chasms and under enormous pressure. Stefan Zweig describes the "community of expulsion" he witnessed in 1938 at a London travel bureau crowded with desperate refugees searching for any refuge they could find. These were people, Zweig wrote in the closing pages of his autobiography, who had lost whatever had traditionally connected them to their social milieux and had lost as well the religious concepts that could have lent their suffering meaning:

> Only now, since they were swept up like dirt in the streets and heaped together, the bankers from their Berlin palaces and sextons from the synagogues of orthodox congregations, the philosophy professors from Paris, and Rumanian cabbies, the undertakers' helpers and Nobel prize winners, the concert singers, and hired mourners, the authors and distillers, the haves and the have-nots, the great and the small, the devout and the liberals, the usurers and the sages, the Zionists and the assimilated, the Ashkenasim and the Sephardim, the just and the unjust besides which the confused horde who thought that they had long since eluded the curse, the baptized and the semi-Jews—only now, for the first time in hundreds of years the Jews were forced into a community of interest to which they had long ceased to be sensitive, the ever-recurring—since Egypt—community of expulsion.... And thus, with smarting eyes, they stared at each other on their flight: Why I? Why you? How do you and I who do not know each other, who speak different languages, whose thinking takes different forms and who have nothing in common happen to be here together? Why any of us? And none could answer. Even Freud, the clearest seeing mind of this time, with whom I often talked in those days, was baffled and could make no sense out of the nonsense.[103]

This was an unevenly shared persecution, in which Jewish connections could be a death sentence or haven from the storm. Freud, given here nearly the same sobriquet Teller had awarded him, of clarity of vision, nevertheless "could make no sense out of the nonsense." But the Jewish associations that arose from this "community of expulsion" may explain the strangeness of a July 1938 portrait of Freud in the Warsaw daily *Haynt*, which described the inside of his treatment rooms not in the usual terms—as adorned by "gods" and fetishes and statues—but as lined with "shadowy portraits of his grandfathers: Jews from Dusseldorf and Kovno, long ago merchants and scholars, with rabbinic yarmulkes . . . and full great beards, caught up in rabbinic questions."[104] The shadowy portraits, as in Teller's poem, were a psychological projection and thus both a deep reading and distortion of Freud's Jewish condition. But the grandfathers were perhaps not wholly imagined. A 1941 article by Dr. M. Greenwald, later reproduced in the *Yizker bukh* (Memorial book) of the town of Buczacz (now in Ukraine), found occasion to reproduce Freud's family tree, as part of the unspoken processes whereby Hebrew and Yiddish readers and writers measured their own more ethereal kinship with the famous professor. According to the accompanying description, the family name was bestowed by an Austrian official in 1812, while the family tree was reconstructed in Buczacz, using cemetery records, in 1914 with the approval of the Freud family.[105]

In the article, Greenwald, an acquaintance of the Bernays family in Hamburg, recounts meeting Freud at a lecture he delivered in 1898 on the topic of the antisemitism in Hermann Sudermann's recently premiered play *Johannis*. Freud was asked to formally introduce Greenwald at the dinner that followed, and Greenwald recalled that Freud joked that, when he heard that he would be introducing a rabbi, he had imagined someone along the lines of John the Baptist in a prophet's cloak, not the stylish young man in an elegant frock coat who had delivered the lecture. Greenwald writes: "I thought to myself, how distant this man must be from Jewish life, if he can only imagine a rabbi in the garb of the ancient Near East!"[106] The Jewish press was certainly guilty of wishful and paranoid projections onto Freud, alternating between wishing for his arrival in the Holy Land as if he were the Messiah (or Moses) and blaming him for any spike in crime. But, as Greenwald saw, Freud's understanding of his Hebrew and Yiddish readers could be equally transferential, also shaped by projections. The introductions he wrote for the Hebrew translations of *Introductory Lectures* and *Totem and Taboo* stand as evidence that he seemed to honestly believe that this audience might be offended to learn that he was a nonbeliever.[107] If Greenwald surprised Freud by being both a rabbi and an urbane young man, Freud ended up surprising him in the years that followed. Greenwald concludes: "Freud's connection to Judaism, as far as it was clear to me, aroused astonishment when I learned that he recognized the claims of Zionism. How much more astonished I was when I heard that he had become a member of the Presidium of YIVO." The editors of *Sefer Buczacz* added an emphasis to the next line, in which Greenwald discovers the logic behind Freud's surprisingly strong Jewish attachments in his family history:

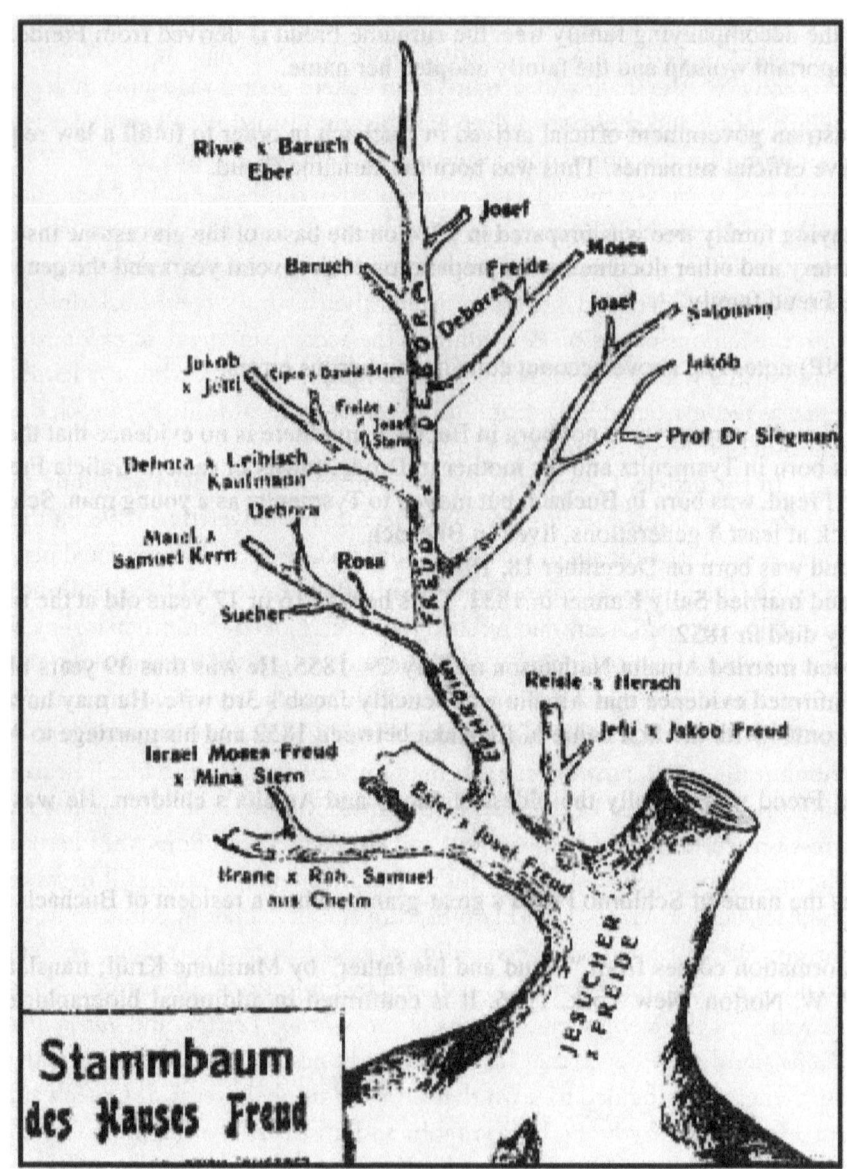

Figure 3. *Stammbaum des Hauses Freud* (Family tree of Freud family). Source: *Sefer Buchach* (Buczacz Memorial Book), ed. Yisrael Cohen (Tel Aviv: Committee for the Commemoration of Buczacz and Am Oved, 1956), 120.

Freud's father came to Vienna from Buczacz, which is in Galicia. From Vienna he moved to Freistadt in Moravia. In Vienna he worked as a broker, helping merchants from his homeland procure merchandise in Vienna. His famous son—who has repeatedly been praised to me as a son who fulfills the commandment to "honor thy mother"—in his elder years became a great supporter of the language that is spoken in the land of his birth.[108]

Freud confused Greenwald with an Essene, but Greenwald's genealogy of Freud is equally garbled—we now know that Jacob Freud was born not in Buczacz but in the Galician town of Tysmenytsia (although earlier generations were indeed from Buczacz), and he moved from Freiberg, not Freistadt, to Vienna. But the point of the article is not Jacob's journey; it is Greenwald's, from his initial sense of Freud as "distant from Judaism" to the pleasant surprise that Freud was willing to ally himself publicly with Zionism and Yiddishism, a willingness that made sense to Greenwald only after he reconstructed Freud's Jewish family tree. The telling aside about Freud's filial respect for his mother, which Greenwald associates with his support for Yiddish as the "mother tongue" of Eastern European Jewry, further cements the connection between Freud's personal family history, his reverence for Yiddish, and the broader ideology about the language. The *Stammbaum des Hauses Freud* (Freud family tree) that appears in the *Yizker bukh* as illustration for Greenwald's article cements the connection between Eastern Europe, language, ancestry, and maternity, showing the "trunk" of the tree as Jesuchur and Freide and revealing the family name to be a matronym.[109] Matronyms are not particularly unusual in Eastern European Jewish naming culture (Sorkin—Sarah's child, for example); but the *Yizker bukh* of Buczacz lays bare the often forgotten link between a long-dead matriarch and her modern descendant, a foremother who provided "the father of psychoanalysis" with his famous name. What first seems to Greenwald estrangement and distance becomes, as Freud's life progresses and as Greenwald continues to spin his tale, a tightening family circle (real or invented) that embraces Freud, Greenwald, the Bernays in Hamburg, Greenwald's Hebrew readers, and the descendants of the town of Buczacz (where my own father was born) who bask in Freud's reflected glow.

Word that Freud was about to publish a book about Moses, or about the Bible, began to circulate in late 1938, even as attention to his deteriorating health and his life in London continued unabated. One of the first Hebrew articles on the subject, "In Defense of Freud," defended Freud not against the now-familiar charge that *Moses and Monotheism* offended Jews in their hour of need but against the rather different charge, propagated by Patrick Scanlan in the *Brooklyn Tablet*, that Freud had written (and the "Jewish publisher" Alfred Knopf would be releasing) an anti-Catholic screed.[110] The book's release, in German by an Amsterdam publisher on February 2, 1939, and in English on May 19, 1939, turned the focus more squarely on what Freud's claims about Moses meant for Jews. Freud famously began *Moses and Monotheism* by expressing his concern for what he anticipated would be the Jewish reaction to his book: "To deprive a people of the man whom they take pride in as the greatest of their sons is not a thing to be gladly or carelessly undertaken, least of all by someone who is himself one of them."[111] In November 1938, corresponding with Yehuda Dvir-Dwossis in Jerusalem about a Hebrew translation of *Moses and Monotheism*, Freud felt constrained to warn him that "its contents are particularly suited to offend Jewish sensibilities."[112] Freud was not wrong to worry. In a review for the religious Zionist *Hatzofeh*, the writer Aaron Zeitlin compared Freud's argument that Moses was an Egyptian with Houston Stewart Chamberlain's declaration that Jesus was a pure Aryan, and more generally with the German higher critics' destruction of the status and unity of the Hebrew Bible:

> But the one thing even the German Bible critics could not steal from the Jews was the figure of our teacher Moses. It was true that they tried to show that he got his ideas from the Code of Hammurabi. But the man himself was left standing in his greatness. He remained the great liberator, the leader through the wilderness, founder of a nation, lawgiver who ascended to heaven and brought the divine word down to the world.[113]

Zeitlin did not suspect Freud of antisemitism, but he nevertheless regretted his decision to write such a thoughtless book, which would lend ammunition not so much to the Nazis, who had all the weapons they needed, as to those so-called friends of the Jews who would delight in the new evidence of Jewish cultural mediocrity.

Freud was right that Jews would object to his claims about Moses, but he need not have feared that he was depriving Jews of their beloved leader. Reactions to *Moses and Monotheism* in the Jewish press attest that no Jew felt so deprived. On the contrary, those Jews who felt the strongest attachment to Moses were offended but hardly threatened by Freud's arguments, finding ready compensation for whatever threat Freud posed in their unshakable sense that they knew Moses far better than Freud did. Hebrew reviewers, in particular, regularly pointed out passages in Freud's book that they found embarrassingly ignorant, flaunting their own superior knowledge of Hebrew. As did later critics, these Hebrew reviewers tended to overlook Freud's praise for what monotheism had given the Jews in terms of their intellectuality and capacity for abstraction—their *Geistigkeit*; what attracted their attention was Freud's admittedly startling hypothesis that Moses was an Egyptian and only secondarily that the Jews had murdered their leader (which one might have thought the more insulting claim). Shlomo ben Horin, reviewing the book for *Davar* in May 1939, set the tone for many of the reviews that followed in regretting that Freud had relied on Protestant scholarship rather than consulting Jewish scholars, who might have helped Freud avoid his most egregious mistakes: "On page 44 Freud decides that Amon sounds similar to Adonay, and suggests the following revision—'Hear O Israel, Adonai (Aton) is our God Adonai (Aton) is one.' Freud should have known that the original biblical word in this declaration is not Adonai but rather the unpronounceable name of God, the Tetragrammaton," for which Adonai was a substitute forged only many centuries after Moses's death.[114] Benjamin Gutsman, reviewing the book a few weeks later in *Haboker*, was more withering in his assessment, declaring that Freud had shown himself to be ignorant of things that "everyone knows." Gutsman also scorned Freud's suggestion that Moses's reliance on Aaron as a translator was evidence that Hebrew may have not been his native tongue. "But, goddammit, Aaron was his translator for Pharaoh! If Moses was indeed an Egyptian, why did he need a translator? . . . But go argue with a dreamer."[115] Where earlier writings on Freud had searched for rabbinic connections or hoped and imagined that he knew some Hebrew, in reviewing his book on Moses the Hebrew press was united in judging *Moses and Monotheism* irrefutable proof of just how little Hebrew Freud knew. For all his Galician ancestry, Freud was and had proved himself to be a German Jew, a "minor difference" that now made all the difference and helped keep Eastern European Jewish narcissism intact.

Yiddish journalists, presumably less territorial on this issue than their Hebrew counterparts, tended to be more tolerant of Freud's biblical scholarship. A few journalists even managed to find some grim humor in Freud's "stealing Moses from the Jews"; an article in the Warsaw daily *Haynt* joked about the "big fuss" that Freud had kicked up by declaring Moses an Egyptian and suggesting that Moses's lack of a grave was a sign that he had been murdered: "Not only are living Jews now insecure about their existence, but even dead Jews, whether or not they have graves, now have to worry about their Jewishness."[116] A reviewer in *Forverts* similarly sought to find the resonances between Freud's Moses and the writer's own unfortunate situation. Freud had tried to prove that Moses was an Egyptian by demonstrating that Moses was an Egyptian and not a Jewish name:

> But Freud forgot that he himself has the Teutonic name "Sigmund," even though he is nothing more than an unfortunate Jew, who in his old age was compelled to leave his Teutonic homeland. If Moses is truly an Egyptian name, that shows only that some Jews in Egypt had Egyptian names, just as some Jews in Germany and Austria had Teutonic names. ... If a "researcher" in three thousand and three hundred years comes across the name "Sigmund" or "Sigmund Freud" and uses this to show that Professor Freud, if his name will still be known then, was a Teuton, it will be based on exactly as much evidence as Freud's hypothesis that Moses was an Egyptian.[117]

Freud is mistaken in supposing Moses to be an Egyptian, but the reviewer more charitably adds that the mistake is understandable, since Zipporah made exactly the same mistake in reporting to her father that "an Egyptian saved us from the hands of the shepherds" (Ex 16:20). The midrash on this verse asks, "So was Moses an Egyptian?" answering, "He was dressed as an Egyptian, but he was a Jew." The review concludes: "Jethro's daughters were misled by Moses's garb. Professor Sigmund Freud was misled by Moses's name." In the Yiddish anarchist *Freye arbeyter shtime*, under the eye-catching title "Is Freud a Jew?," A. Almi took a similar tack, cleverly arguing that Freud's name revealed him to be German, and his mysterious disappearance from Vienna was evidence that he had been murdered, just as Moses's lack of a grave suggests a suspicious end. Almi added, "But let us suppose that Moses actually did not know Hebrew well. Is that a sign that he wasn't Jewish? Freud himself knows neither Hebrew nor Yiddish."[118] The Jewish press, which had for a decade or more lovingly traced every possible connection between Freud and Jewish languages, now went into high gear to opposite ends. Whatever threat was posed to Jewish narcissism by Freud's book on Moses was neutralized by the new consensus that rendered Freud's connection to Jewish languages tenuous and that established the advantage of even ordinary Hebrew and Yiddish readers when it came to knowing Moses and the Bible.

But even reviewers who dismissed Freud's scholarship as embarrassingly ignorant in Jewish matters occasionally found some value in the book. Eliezer Lowenstein, writing in *Davar*, acknowledged that the arguments of the book did not stand up to academic scrutiny, but the fact that it was a fantasy and fiction only increased its Jewish interest, once one recognized that the book revealed more about its writer than about a long-dead individual named Moses: "The very fact that Freud devoted his last book to Jewish subjects should pique our attention. Freud doesn't conceal that his true interest in the book is the unique and strange destiny of the Jewish people.... There is something touching and beautiful about this exposure of Sigmund Freud's Jewish heart." What the book ultimately expressed, Lowenstein thought, were the connections and disconnections Freud was feeling in relation with his "own" people.[119]

I have said that the Orthodox press generally took no notice of Freud. But the release of *Moses and Monotheism* was too great a provocation to ignore, too blatant a trespass onto turf Orthodox writers considered their own. What particularly incensed Benjamin Mintz, writing in *She'arim*, the Hebrew journal of the Agudath Israel Workers' Party in Palestine, was a review by the (formerly Orthodox) poet Shin Shalom, which argued that whatever errors critics found in *Moses and Monotheism* were secondary to the crucial fact that Freud had declared his Jewishness for all the world to see by writing what amounted to a commentary on the Bible. Mintz summarizes Shin Shalom's review with horrified irony: "The circle is complete. The greatest scientist in the world has come home; our teacher [*rabenu*, the traditional term for "our teacher Moses"] Professor Sigmund Freud has written his Torah commentary [*perusho al hatorah*]." Mintz takes issue with the idea that *Moses and Monotheism* was "Torah commentary," and thus evidence of Freud's Jewish soul, pointing out that Jew haters were perfectly capable of writing Bible commentaries. Mintz concludes in thundering denunciation: "The thing must be said clearly—we will have no further contact with Professor Freud. He has not come home. He has abused and disgraced the name of the Servant of God. He has no share in the people of Israel."[120] Religious Zionists were no less damning. An article, "Freud's War against Our Teacher Moses," in *Hatzofeh* by Rabbi Dr. Aaron Kaminka spoke for Orthodox opinion, in general, when he wrote that "the great revered Sigmund Freud earned his great international fame and translation into most of the languages of the world not because of the depth and splendor of his investigations and the sublimity of his literary thought but precisely because of its ugliness and coarseness, its obeisance to the material world and the basest forces and animal instincts in human life."[121] Whatever Jews around the world were feeling for the endangered professor, at least these Orthodox writers were having none of it.

The last tumultuous year or two of Freud's life, marked by concern for Freud's fate and disgust at his last book, also saw perhaps the most touching and intimate story about him in the Jewish press. In January 1939, *Davar* published a report by Isaac Nachman Steinberg, the Yiddishist, anarchist, and religiously observant founder of the Freeland League, recounting a visit to the ailing Freud by three London-based members of YIVO (including Jacob Meitlis, who published an account of the same visit in English, and the critic and translator Joseph Leftwich). The visit made an impression beyond the small world of YIVO's local chapter: Ernest Jones mentions it, too, dating it to November 7, 1938.[122] Steinberg describes a room filled "with books and idols," Freud's warm greeting, silvery beard, and "oval Jewish face."

> I told him briefly about the scientific work being carried out at YIVO and he expressed his sorrow at not knowing the two languages—Hebrew and Yiddish—which made it impossible to follow what was happening in the Jewish branch of the science. "And now it would be difficult for me to learn them," he joked—"yesterday I turned 82 and a half." . . . He expressed his willingness do everything in his power to help [YIVO]. "Although I haven't reached the level of the Jews of Eastern Europe, I am still a Jew, a Godless Jew. I look in your faces and see strong vestiges of my dead father. I don't know how to explain it, but there is a great commonality in our blood" (Freud spoke emotionally, and his left hand shook along with his powerful voice).[123]

After a decade or two of polite correspondence, regretful telegrams, and near misses, the organized Jewish world—not the Hebrew University but, more humbly and *heymishly*, YIVO—finally succeeded in making direct contact with the famous Jewish professor, now rescued from Vienna. It was to this intimate group that Freud confessed yet again his worry about the impending release of *Moses and Monotheism*, reading to them a letter from "an important Anglo-Jewish professor" that, while expressing the greatest respect for Freud's genius, warned that the publication of such a book would arouse hatred against Jews at a time that "they faced persecution from every direction."[124] Freud plaintively asked the men, "What should I do? Withdraw the book from publication?" The men spoke up immediately and vehemently, drawing from a halakhic vocabulary to insist on Freud's right to release the book, since "it is forbidden to subsume scientific truth to the pressures of the hour." It was no surprise to them that his work aroused opposition, since "after all he is Professor Freud, who has fought his entire life against lies."[125] By referring to YIVO scholarship as "the Jewish branch of the science" (meaning, apparently, the science of psychoanalysis), Freud acknowledged a kinship with the YIVO representatives that went beyond their shared Jewishness. In Steinberg's account, YIVO provided the support Freud needed at a critical moment, when his own faith in scientific truth was wavering. And it did so from the unexpected direction of *yidishe visnshaft*, its own commitment to both Jewishness and science.

I have suggested that this meeting was *heymish* (Yid., homey), but if so, it was also *unheimlich* (Ger., uncanny). Freud traces the experience of *Umheimlichkeit* to a variety of different phenomena, including the appearance of "a double," "the return of the dead," or an experience "which seems to confirm the old, discarded beliefs." In an often-quoted footnote on the "uncanny effect of . . . meeting one's own image unbidden and unexpected," Freud cites Ernst Mach's description of such an experience and appends his own:

> I was sitting alone in my wagon-lit compartment when a more than usually violent jolt of the train swung back the door of the adjoining washing-cabinet, and an elderly gentleman in a dressing gown and a travelling cap came in. I assumed that in leaving the washing-cabinet, which lay between the two compartments, he had taken the wrong direction and come into my compartment by mistake. Jumping up with the intention of putting him right, I at once realized to my dismay that the intruder was nothing but my own reflection in the looking-glass on the open door. I can still recollect that I thoroughly disliked his appearance. Instead, therefore, of being frightened by our "doubles," both Mach and I simply failed to recognize them as such. Is it not possible, though, that our dislike of them was a vestigial trace of the archaic reaction which feels the "double" to be something uncanny?[126]

The uncanny is associated here with aging, which discloses resemblance to our parents as it makes us unhappy strangers and "doubles" to ourselves. In Steinberg's retelling, Freud had an uncanny experience of a related but different type on that November day: while on the train he had seen himself as a stranger, but with the YIVO delegation he saw a trio of (relatively young) strangers as his own (dead) father. The history of Freud's presence in the Hebrew and Yiddish press is often a story of projection and transference, in which Jewish readers sought the comfort of their own reflections in the shiny mirror of Freud's fame and treasured Freud's Galician roots for the comforting connections they provided. These readers were treated, in the last days of Freud's life, to a different spectacle, of Freud searching out the uncanny image of his own father in their beautiful Jewish faces.

The outbreak of war and the horrors that followed did not spell an immediate end to the interest of Yiddish readers and lecture audiences in psychoanalysis. Among the most wrenching documents the YIVO archives yield in this regard are lecture notes on psychoanalysis and related subjects by Dr. Daniel Feinstein, who delivered these lectures to the *visnshaftlikhn krayz* (Scientific Circle) of the Union of Writers and Artists in the Vilna Ghetto. The notes are among the trove of books and manuscripts rescued by the "Paper Brigade," a group of Jewish poets and intellectuals who served as slave laborers in the Vilna Ghetto, in service to the Nazi effort to loot, collect, and "study" Jewish cultural treasures; in the process, they smuggled some material out and buried it in the ghetto, where after the war some of the material was unearthed and returned to YIVO.[127] Feinstein's lecture notes, in a beautiful hand, are remarkably detailed: In "The Myth of Paradise in the Light of Psychoanalysis" (delivered June 16, 1942), Feinstein begins by summarizing the documentary hypothesis and identifies the Paradise myth as part of the Yahwistic writings, which present God in an intimate and anthropomorphic light; surveys rabbinic commentary (Talmud, Ibn Ezra) and psychoanalytic scholarship (Karl Abraham, Otto Rank, Ludwig Levy) on the myth; mines Gesenius's Hebrew grammar on the biblical use of the verb "to know" to mean copulation; and compares elements of the Genesis text with stories about Paradise from other mythological traditions. Feinstein concludes with the argument that it is only psychoanalysis that can fully explain all the interlocking elements of the myth, by demonstrating that the "forbidden fruit" is the sin of incest.[128] Another document provides notes for a lecture given on September 13, 1942, "On the Familiar and the Foreign (literally, 'the Near and the Far'): A Chapter of Anthropology." The lecture begins with a historical survey of different schools of "racial classifications" (*rasenklasifikatsiyes*), moves on to a discussion of the distinct characteristics of the races, and concludes with the argument that racial mixing has a long history, given the "mutual connections in space and time" between different races.[129] A colored chart appended to the lecture demonstrates the variety of races that contributed to the emergence of the Jewish people in ancient Israel. I have spoken of the hypercharged Jewish connections under the Nazi threat, which caught up Freud in its web. What is remarkable about Feinstein's notes is not their emotion but their reasoned calm, the unwaveringly academic approach to the controversial subject of Jewish race in the face of a murderous racial regime. Feinberg's focus on ancient Israel may have reflected the pressures of censorship; alternatively, he was simply lecturing on his own area of expertise. In either case, Feinstein's focus remained on how Jews might illustrate the broader (or perhaps universal) phenomenon of racial hybridity. These notes stand as testimony that the Scientific Circle for whom Feinstein lectured in 1942 were keeping their faith in *yidishe visnshaft*, in a science whose Yiddish form and Jewish focus detracted not a whit from its ability to illuminate the human condition beyond its own borders, to see beyond the walls that enclosed it, to understand what others availing themselves of ostensibly broader vistas could not.

7

The Yiddish (Un)Conscious

Words are little houses . . . each with its cellar and garret.
—Gaston Bachelard, *The Poetics of Space* (1958)

A doctor once told me
There's nothing there that should be hurting you
He didn't understand that
What's hurting me is the nothing-there.
—Rivka Basman Ben-Hayim, "On Time" (2008)

The Israeli literary critic Dan Miron relates that, in their last conversation before Max Weinreich's 1969 death, Weinreich touched yet again on the tender subject of the New York exile of YIVO, the Vilna-based Institute for the Study of Eastern European Jews that he had cofounded and long directed. Weinreich suggested that, despite it all, YIVO's Yiddish holdings might retain some value even in their new home: "I don't know about you Israelis," he said to Miron,

> but by now I know my American Jews, young ones included. If American Jews still dream as a group, Yiddish is the language they speak in their dream. It is still the idiom of their collective unconscious. For their personality to become whole, they—at least some of them—will have to go back to Yiddish some day. . . . And there we shall be, waiting for them down in the Yiddish cellar with a strong torchlight in our hand. Somebody will have to spell out for them the contents of their dream, to elucidate the vision they saw with bleary eyes, and we, because we made Yiddish *visnshaft* [scholarship] the thing we live and die for, will be able to throw light and heal.[1]

Like Freud, whose work he translated into Yiddish, Weinreich saw himself in this conversation as a dream interpreter, with access to a language and its attendant scholarship that, because of the extravagant commitment of its guardians, could "throw light and heal." If Yiddish could do that for Eastern European Jewish youth, as Weinreich had felt in the 1930s, it could also work to heal Jewish Americans, as the language of their collective dreams, even if they themselves could hardly understand it. It is possible to follow Weinreich's train of thought toward our topic: Freud, as an acculturated German-speaking Jew of Eastern European heritage, presumably also dreamed in Yiddish, even as he interpreted his own dreams and those of others in German. If psychoanalysis, with its Eastern European past, also has a collective unconscious "cellar" where dreams unfold in a half-understood Yiddish, the Yiddish reception and translation of Freud's works might serve to decode these dreams. Beyond collecting and studying Yiddish and Eastern European Jewish culture and history, YIVO promised to clarify the muffled reverberations of this culture in its American exile; so, too, might it translate these echoes for psychoanalysis in its Eastern European prehistory, its Viennese homeland, and its global diaspora.

It was not only interpretation that was at stake in the post-Holocaust YIVO. Weinreich considered Jewish Americans to be suffering, for all their material comfort, from an "inner, psychic fragmentation" created by shame and cultural amnesia. Yiddish, the language of their past, could help heal the shame and bring the content suppressed by that shame to consciousness.[2] Part of the way that YIVO could cure what ailed American Jews was by virtue of the fact that it was a scientific institute devoted to championing Yiddish and thus bringing Yiddish under the sublime authority of science. If Yiddish was shameful because of its lowly, feminine origins, an institute founded under the title and sign of the sciences could grant Yiddish a rational, academic, and thus masculine status that might contribute to illuminating and thus healing Jewish sexual shame. Freud himself played a similar language game in a different key by translating Katharina's inarticulate sexual shame and suffering into the fluent professional jargon of a newly created field devoted to such translation.[3] Although Weinreich does not say so, the return of Eastern European Jewish language and culture—properly, "scientifically" understood—to the scene of psychoanalysis might have similar hermeneutic powers and therapeutic effects for both Yiddish and psychoanalysis.

Among the holdings of YIVO, buried within Weinreich's voluminous personal archive, is an undated school notebook with the title "Froyd laboratoriye" [Freud laboratory].[4] Despite its placement amid material from his American years, the notebook appears to date from the period in the mid-1930s when Weinreich was working in Vilna on a translation of Freud's *Vorlesungen zur Einführung in die Psychoanalyse*, a transcription of the twenty-eight lectures Freud delivered to a lay audience at the University of Vienna between 1915 and 1917; Weinreich's translation of the first fifteen of these lectures appeared in three inexpensively priced volumes in 1936, 1937, and 1938, with the first of these released on Freud's eightieth birthday, May 6, 1936. The notebook lists difficult or ambiguous German words and phrases in the order in which they appeared in the 1922 second edition of the *Introductory Lectures* Weinreich was using (he also made notes in the margin of that volume), providing the German original, organized by page number, followed by a range of equivalents in Yiddish, Hebrew, and occasionally English or Polish. Weinreich also appended hastily scribbled notes on shades of meaning and usage and a draft of a German-Yiddish glossary of basic psychoanalytic terms. As it happens, the notebook provides for Freud's German *seelisch* only the Yiddish term *psikhish*, even though writers like Gliksman had been using the Hebraic, religiously tinged word *neshome* for years by then; in other words, Weinreich used a Yiddish cognate—in the notebook and the translation—of precisely the English term Bruno Bettelheim decries in Strachey.[5] If so, then Freud lost his soul not only in English translation, as Bettelheim charges, but also in Weinreich's Yiddish. Weinreich does not cite the English translation for *seelisch*, but he may nevertheless have been swayed, like so many other translators, by its choices (even the long-delayed German critical edition of Freud's work followed the order and incorporated the apparatus of the *Standard Edition*). If so, then Yiddish, rather than recovering the original language lost in Freud's German or giving new life to the repressed Jewish soul of psychoanalysis, turns out to be (at least in this instance) no more than another copy of a copy.

There are reasons to read Weinreich's translation alongside Strachey: Weinreich's *Araynfir in psikhoanalis*, the last Yiddish translation of a work by Freud, was the only one—as the title page proclaimed—"authorized" by Freud. Beyond this authorization and all it implied, the *Araynfir* was as close as Yiddish got to its own *Standard Edition*, by virtue of Weinreich's reputation as a scholar of both Yiddish culture and Freud's thought and the institutional imprimatur of YIVO, the publisher. These circumstances make Weinreich's notebook a multilingual Jewish counterpart to Ernest Jones's 1924 *Glossary of Psychoanalytic Terms*, which Strachey used to produce the standardized and seamless professional jargon that aimed, in Bettelheim's view, to position psychoanalysis as a legitimate part of the Anglo-American medical sciences.[6] Unlike Strachey, Weinreich had no need to lend psychoanalysis a scientific patina in a cultural-linguistic context in which psychoanalysis lacked an institutional presence or clinical aspirations. If anything, it was Yiddish that gained "scientific" status by association with psychoanalysis. It is striking, then, that he—no doubt humorously—titled his notebook "Freud Laboratory." Bettelheim argues that it is the Greek mythical and literary tradition that is obscured by the "medical" Latinate terms of Strachey's English and by the misreading of Freud's appeals to *Wissenschaft* (which means not only science but also, more broadly, knowledge, learning, and scholarship) as declarations of his allegiance to the medical sciences.[7] But the attempt to position psychoanalysis as an exact science was also intended, no doubt, to refute the charge that psychoanalysis was "a Jewish science," which is to say, no science at all.

In the 1913 exchange in which he shared with Ferenczi his long and persistent worry that psychoanalysis was or would be perceived as a Jewish science, applying only to Jews or tainted by Jewish perspectives, Freud denied the coherence of such a category or, for that matter, of "Aryan science"; science must be free of the tinge of "racial" affiliation, if it is to count as such.[8] By contrast, YIVO, the yidishe visnshaflikhe organizatsiye, signaled in its name the scholarly aspirations of the organization, commitment to raising the status of Yiddish, interest in understanding Jews, and Jewish approach to scholarship.[9] Jonathan Boyarin has drawn attention to the grammatical and linguistic distinction between *Wissenschaft des Judentum*, as the science or study of Judaism, written in a non-Jewish language and taking *Judentum* as the "passive" object of its scientific study, and *yidishe visnshaft*, in which the adjective Yiddish—meaning Yiddish and Jewish, and written in a Jewish alphabet—modifies *visnshaft*. Unlike *Wissenschaft des Judentum*, Boyarin writes, which intended to scientifically "consider" and "describe" Jewishness, *yidishe visnshaft* "is ambiguous through and through. It is indeed a science, contemporary, secular. But it isn't a field of science. It's a kind of science"; as such, it "provincializes" the allegedly universal, culturally neutral category of science, calling into question the coherence of "Western discourse as a unit."[10] At YIVO, not only the objects of study but also the research language, methods, and assumptions—the hopes and dreams—of this research were explicitly and openly Jewish. Not merely an institute serving Jews who were discriminated against elsewhere, a "diploma factory" for ambitious would-be Jewish doctors and lawyers, YIVO was instead an institute that served "the collective needs of the Jewish people."¹¹ To this day, the relationship between the Jewish "influences" on Freud and the universalist and scientific claims of psychoanalysis remains unsettled.¹² The Jewish character of YIVO's scientific research was announced at the outset. Weinreich's titling his notebook "Freud Laboratory" may signal, consciously or not, that these openly expressed affiliations and ideologies could not deny that science (as in the hard sciences, those carried out in laboratories) was an intrinsic part of YIVO's work.

The translation of Freud into Yiddish, particularly but not only at YIVO, constitutes a unique set of circumstances within the global dispersion of psychoanalysis: By most standards, the reception and translation of Freud in Yiddish is a curiosity, a minor, short-lived episode in psychoanalytic history. Researchers writing psychoanalytically oriented work in Yiddish played no role in national or international organizations; to my knowledge, until the Argentinian psychoanalyst Moisés (Moyshe) Kijak began publishing his psychoanalytic readings of Yiddish literature in 1969, followed by his Yiddish lectures on Freud and psychoanalysis in 1971, the subfield included not a single trained psychoanalyst.[13] From the geographic perspective, Yiddish was a backwater in the reception history of psychoanalysis, which is more usually mapped through the decisive moves from Austria to other regions in Central and Western Europe and then, even more fatefully, from Europe to the United States—the major center after Freud's death. In the more particular realm of translation, the Yiddish renderings of Freud's writing form a meager addition to a shelf that was already crowded by the 1920s: The first of Freud's work to be translated, in 1904, was a Russian rendering of "Über den Traum" ("On Dreams," an abridged version of the *Traumdeutung* that Freud issued in 1901); psychoanalysis was immensely popular in Russia, with translations appearing regularly and selling out quickly. English readers were introduced to psychoanalysis five years after this Russian debut, with A. A. Brill's *Selected Papers on Hysteria* (1909), followed by his *Three Contributions to the Theory of Sexuality* (1910) and *The Interpretation of Dreams* (1913).[14] By 1923 Freud could boast, in his *History of the Psycho-Analytic Movement*, of translations into French, Spanish, Italian, Polish, Norwegian, Japanese, "Chinese," and other languages.[15] Yiddish, however, had yet to appear on any such list.

Despite this belatedness and marginality, Yiddish plays a unique and important role in the global history of psychoanalysis by virtue of its status as being, at the very least, Freud's "heritage language." Although Freud rarely spoke about the place of Yiddish in his family history, he provides us with ample tools to conceptualize the language as a repressed fragment of a buried past, a feature of what Christopher Hutton calls "the 'unconscious' ('Jewish') self repressed in the process of socialization."[16] Weinreich was not unique in associating Yiddish with the collective unconscious of acculturating Jews; Hutton describes this conception (along with Yiddish "femininity" and "maternity") as in fact "the dominant ideology of Yiddish."[17] Along these lines, the French psychoanalyst Max Kohn begins his book on Yiddish and psychoanalysis with the more personal assertion that "mon inconscient parle Yiddish; c'est une certitude" (My unconscious speaks Yiddish; that is certain).[18] Yiddishist psychoanalysis was thus simultaneously charged with exploring the associations of Yiddish with the (Jewish) unconscious and investigating the possibility, coherence, and value of *yidishe visnshaft*, which might raise the Yiddish unconscious to the rationalist heights of science.

The translations of Freud from German into Yiddish thus navigated a double imperative, toward science and toward the Jewish unconscious. Moving from German to Yiddish also required the traversal of a particularly dense language border, given the complex, politically and culturally charged, mutually implicating historical relationships between Yiddish and German. These circumstances were not external to Freud's work but reflected within it in intricate ways, given the Yiddish sprinkled through Freud's writings and the implications that Yiddish might be understood as a kind of marrow of Freud's Jewish identity, even where it was not visible on the surface. Given the persistence of ideologies that embrace traditional views of Yiddish as a feminized "jargon," and as the denigrated vernacular, it's worth remembering that Freud also publicly participated in the twentieth-century reclamation and championing of Yiddish as a Jewish national language, one perfectly suited for scientific discourse. Freud went further at times, speaking of YIVO and psychoanalysis as parallel institutions, or even—according to one report—describing YIVO as "the Jewish branch of the science."[19] In Freud's view, the two institutions both pursued similar projects and were similarly endangered, in need of refuge from the persecution they faced in their homelands; in a letter to Weinreich, for instance, Freud compared himself and Weinreich to Rabbi Yohanan ben Zakkai, who escaped the besieged Jerusalem for Yavneh to start a yeshiva where learning might be pursued, just as he and Weinreich were seeking refuge to reconstitute their own yeshivas.[20] In this sense, YIVO and psychoanalysis were both "Jewish branches of the science."

To speak of Freud as having a relationship with the language we are calling Yiddish is already to mischaracterize a major aspect of the story. Freud's early writings that might bear on that relationship—particularly (with Breuer, 1895) *Studies in Hysteria* and *Jokes and Their Relationship to the Unconscious* (1905)—were composed in an entirely different "climate of opinion" in relation to Yiddish than his later works. As in so many other contemporary depictions of the language, Yiddish appears in Freud's early writings as a degenerate, grotesque, laughable, mongrel jargon, the speech of a backward culture and the unruly body. In Anna O.'s case it may also be a symptom of her hysterical aphasia, if we read the description of her German "decomposing into Jargon" in this light. Freud's references to a coarse or repulsive Yiddish are part of a larger narrative of modernity and Europeanization, in which Jews were expected to earn and achieve integration by abandoning their backward and ugly Jewish vernacular for German and other European tongues. But the story does not end there: David Roskies describes the beautiful twists by which Yiddishism unsettled the "colonial" hierarchy that had dictated the relationship between German and Yiddish. For Yiddishists, Yiddish was a language in its own right, rather than an ugly and distorted mixture of "proper" tongues like German, Hebrew, and Slavic languages, which Jews would do well to learn.[21] The attempts to realize Jewish hopes for emancipation and integration by learning European tongues gave way, in the manifestos and keynote addresses of early twentieth-century Yiddishism, to a different moment, in which Yiddish sought its own emancipation from German, proclaiming its independent status among the family of languages. While nineteenth-century maskilim had sought to write a Germanized Yiddish that would soon enough be upgraded into "proper" German, Yiddishists worked to expand the distance between the languages, emphasizing those (Jewish) elements that distinguished Yiddish from German rather than those that betrayed their kinship.

Yiddishists sought not only to democratize the relationship with German but sometimes also to reverse its historical hierarchies by claiming for Yiddish, for instance, the status of preserving linguistic strata of German that had otherwise been lost. In other words, Yiddish could illuminate not only the deep history of Ashkenazic Jews but also that of their medieval and early modern Christian neighbors. In this regard, Yiddish knew things that German had once known but no longer did. This was an ideological revolution but also an affective and psychological one, seeking to heal Jewish shame by means of Jewish pride; replacing the "kitchen language" with a language at home in the laboratory; countering the failed projects of emancipation and integration with Jewish nationalism—using Yiddish and Yiddishism, in other words, as therapy and cure for the wounds of Jewish modernity. These were sexual wounds, too: Zohar Weiman-Kelman draws attention to the parallels between sexology and philology, noting that "Yiddish philology shared a similar drive [to the sexologists working toward 'a less perverse future'], as a science attempting to normalize the language, and thereby also its speakers."[22] This revolution was headquartered in Vilna, in the newly built building of YIVO; according to Roskies, Weinreich was "the chief ideologue and driving force of this Yiddish renaissance."[23] But the mood caught up Freud and other Central European Jews as well. In the April 30, 1930, letter to YIVO that was published in Weinreich's translation of *Introduction to Psychoanalysis* "in place of an introduction to the Yiddish publication," Freud writes of his "great pleasure in hearing that the first volume of the *Vorlesungen* was about to appear in Yiddish translation" and adds:

> It was with great respect [*groys derekh-eretz*] that I took in my hands the first pages that you sent me. It is a shame that more than that I could not do. When I was a student, they took no trouble to instill the national tradition; so I did not learn to read either Hebrew or Yiddish, which saddens me today. Nevertheless I am a good Jew, although not, as you probably know, a believer.[24]

Freud here clearly distinguishes his present stance from the earlier attitude toward Jewish languages that conditioned his own education and led to his failure to learn to read (or to retain what he learned) both Hebrew and Yiddish, rendered here as a language fully equivalent to Hebrew. What is shameful is not Yiddish but his own "sad" ignorance of Jewish languages. By 1930, Freud was speaking movingly and "with great respect" about the emotions aroused in him by seeing his thought embodied in Yiddish, which is to say, in the Hebrew letters that conveyed meaning even if he could not read them. The transformation of Freud's early disinterest in or disgust with jargon (if that's what it was) into evident appreciation for Yiddish is, of course, part of a much broader historical process of increasing the symbolic value of what Freud could now call "the national tradition," the central aim of Yiddishism at YIVO and beyond. If Yiddish might be psychoanalytically understood as the buried fragments of a painful past, psychoanalysis could also illuminate the workings of Yiddish nationalism as an emancipatory process that encourages this past to speak and thus to lay its traumatic aftereffects to rest. From the perspective of psychoanalysis, the past and its languages can never be entirely abandoned, since they will persist in some form or another—as dream, symptom, accent, body, memory fragment, trauma. So, too, do the teachings of psychoanalysis suggest that talking might function as a remedy for this condition, reversing trauma and healing fragmentation by recovering abandoned, ostensibly forgotten, shameful speech. The interconnections between Yiddish and the unconscious have long been recognized; what I am suggesting here is something slightly different—that psychoanalysis and *Yiddishism* are in many ways parallel phenomena.

I have said that Yiddish-speaking Eastern Europe was a backwater in the global dispersion of psychoanalysis, the strongest and most fateful currents of which flowed in the westerly direction. But it is also true that this region, apparently so distant from the nerve centers of psychoanalysis, was the ancestral home of psychoanalysis. A backwater interwar Poland may have been, but it was Freud's backwater, from which he himself, or at any rate his family, had come. It was not only Freud's personal history that was shaped by this geography. The journey from Yiddish to German, from East to West, was undertaken by many besides Freud or his parents; ambitious young men and women, in the wider and broader stream of such emigrants from the Eastern provinces of the Austro-Hungarian Empire to Freud's Vienna, formed the core of early psychoanalysis—the Vienna Psychoanalytic Society included at least nineteen members who had been born and reared in Polish lands. Helene Deutsch, the founder of the society, recognized the significance of the circumstance that she and her colleagues came from "the center of the earth"; Paul Roazen, Deutsch's biographer, suggests that Freud drew so many disciples from Polish lands because, for the centuries of partition, Poland persisted as an idea rather than a recognized political entity, an idea that had powerful effects on the continent in the same way that the unconscious invisibly guided human affairs.[25] In a recent reconstruction of the beginnings of psychoanalysis in Polish lands, Edyta Dembińska and Krzysztof Rutkowski explain that "one of the reasons why this history has been hard to reconstruct—or has remained less visible or pertinent to mainstream psychoanalytic historiography—is the fragmentation of the Polish Kingdom itself," in its partition among Russia, Prussia, and Austro-Hungary.[26] The unconscious character of Polish psychoanalysis continues into the Soviet period. As Ewa Kobylińska-Dehe and Paweł Dybel put it the introduction to *Psychoanalysis in Poland in Polish-German-Jewish Cultural Contexts*,

> Our research is grounded in two hypotheses. First: psychoanalysis was

not present in Poland, since until the 1990s no one was interested in the subject and no one studied its history. Second: Psychoanalysis was not present because it was not accepted, worked through, and integrated into Polish culture and society. These two hypotheses, which are by no means mutually contradictory, give rise to various questions and research foci.[27]

The history of psychoanalysis in Poland thus itself needs to be rescued from various forms of psychologically and culturally charged amnesia. What is recovered in this process, among other discoveries, is the presence of a Polish-Russian-German-Jewish cultural sphere. Rejecting the relevance of Eli Zaretzky's view that European psychoanalysis flourished amid the urban alienations of "the Second Industrial Revolution" for the "culturally backward" Polish lands, Dybel suggests that psychoanalysis in that region emerged from the particular cultural antagonisms of this context as part of an already simmering "cauldron of ideas" that especially appealed to leftist intellectuals from assimilated Jewish families:

> At the turn of the 20th century, a veritable "cauldron of ideas" bubbled, leading to the political and social mobilization of the intelligentsia and the middle class. One result of this was an increase in ethnic and social antagonisms and a deepening of political and cultural divisions within these groups. It is in the context of this "cauldron of ideas," rather than the economic and civilizational processes which Zaretsky calls the Second Industrial Revolution, that we should analyze the beginnings of the psychoanalytical movement in the entire region. This movement was joined mostly by Jewish graduates of medical studies, who perceived Freud's theory not only as an innovative scientific theory offering a new mechanism for human mental life and as a proposal for a new method of therapy for mental disorders, but also as a theory which, when implemented in therapeutic practice, would lead to a fundamental change in the functioning of the "economy" of human mental life in terms of the role played by sexual drives and aggression. This would open the way to the emergence of a human being who would be able to cope better with the threats generated by these drives. And in the longer term, it would allow for the emergence of a new psychoanalytically enlightened society and emancipate it not only regarding sexuality, but from anti-Semitic prejudices.[28]

While Dybel is describing the early twentieth century, Freud's ancestors also emerged a generation or two earlier from the same Polish lands, however one construes that geography or cultural landscape. Lest we suppose he felt a special kinship with his Polish colleagues and followers, so geographically close to Vienna, Dembińska and Rutkowski cite his bemused response to an excited telegram he received from a 1909 neurological congress in Warsaw at which Ludwik Jekels (the one signatory Freud knew) presented the first psychoanalytic paper on Polish soil, humorously writing to Jung that the telegram had been signed by "seven illegible and unpronounceable Poles."[29] If many early Jewish psychoanalysts came from or in some sense, wherever they went, still inhabited an unrecognized "Poland," many also emerged from an even less recognized or authorized "Yiddishland" that was itself repressed and fragmented within the fragmented, repressed Poland and that remained even more so in the post-Holocaust era. (It is probably also the case that Poland is repressed within Yiddishland.)[30] Even the return of the Polish repressed, for instance, in the founding of the independent republic of Poland in 1918 or the revival of psychoanalysis in post-Soviet Poland, could not alter the status and character of Yiddishland, which was hardly confined to those borders.

Locating Yiddish within the global reception of Freud's writing is thus an oddly bifurcated enterprise: Within the institutional history of psychoanalysis, Yiddish is simply nonexistent, appearing in no list of psychoanalytic societies or institutes and rarely mentioned in mainstream psychoanalytic publications. But Yiddish is also nearly everywhere in the development and circulation of psychoanalysis, far beyond the authorized or unauthorized Yiddish translations and the influence of Freud on YIVO's research agenda and methods. Long before Freud's work appeared in Yiddish translation, the language was woven into the fabric of the prehistory, development, and dispersion of Freud's writing and of psychoanalysis as a movement, given how many of Freud's first followers were of Eastern European Jewish descent. Brill (1874–1948), Freud's first English translator, emigrated from the Galician town of Kańczuga to New York at the age of fifteen; if Brill's German was acquired "via" Yiddish, as it seems to have been (and as my own German was), Yiddish would hold the status of an unacknowledged channel, filter, or "pivot language" between Freud and his first English readers (which might also help explain why Brill's translations were soon rejected in favor of those produced by Freud's London-based disciples). Sándor Ferenczi, the first psychoanalyst in Budapest, had family roots in Galicia and, like Freud, reportedly spoke Yiddish with his mother; as it was for Freud and many of their colleagues, Ferenczi's German was more accurately described as a variety of the language infused with local and "minor" characteristics—including, in Ferenczi's case, a particularly Hungarian Jewish flavor—within the linguistic kaleidoscope of Central European culture in which Yiddish (however conceptualized) played a ubiquitous and persistent if often unspoken part.[31] These examples, of course, could be multiplied many times over.

The travels and displacements of these early psychoanalysts similarly trouble the neat geographic listing of psychoanalytic societies in the regular bulletins of the International Psychoanalytic Association. Dybel describes the absurdity of the competing Wikipedia pages for Ludwik Jekels: "Just a few years ago, in the Polish version you could read that Jekels was a Polish psychoanalyst, in the German one he was called an Austrian analyst, and in the American version he became American."[32] Such difficulties in establishing the place of such peripatetic psychoanalysts within rigid political maps of the kind faithfully adhered to within the international organizations of psychoanalysis are compounded for those seeking to establish where in this world one might locate Yiddish. How does one mark the workings of Yiddish, spoken or ancestral or part of a "cauldron of ideas" in the thought of the Polish-born Rudolf Lowenstein, credited with founding the Paris Psychoanalytic Society; the German-American-Mexican-Swiss psychoanalyst Erich Fromm; the Warsaw-born Polish psychoanalyst Gustav Bychowski, whose father attended the First Zionist Congress and who studied with Eugene Bleuler and Freud, translated Freud into Polish (as did Jekels), returned to Warsaw where he established a free clinic for children, escaped to New York in 1939, and died (on vacation) in Fez in 1972; or the Odessa-born Moshe Wulff, who studied with Karl Abraham in Berlin, returned to Russia, cofounded the Moscow Psychoanalytic Institute, translated Freud into Russian, returned to Berlin after it was shut down, left Berlin with Eitingon in 1933, settled in Tel Aviv, added Hebrew to the languages of his psychoanalytic publications, and served as the president of the Psychoanalytic Society of Palestine (and then Israel) from 1947 to 1954?[33] While Hebrew became a full-fledged psychoanalytic language when Eitingon founded the Palestine Psychoanalytic Society on October 15, 1934 (even as German remained in everyday use), Yiddish never saw a similar development: even those psychoanalysts who spoke (or dreamed in) Yiddish generally lived their professional lives in another tongue, and often many other tongues.

But a language not spoken may also have its place in psychoanalysis, as a dream tongue, a mechanism for reviving fraying Jewish ties, a native tongue "interfering" with a later-acquired spoken language, a language that hovers just out of comprehension, a forgotten but still unconsciously operative *Muttersprache*, a fragment of an "enigmatic message," a symptom healed by being transformed into a rallying cry, and so on. The Austrian-Chilean-American psychoanalyst Otto Kernberg (b. 1928), who served as president of the International Psychoanalytic Association from 1997 to 2001, wrote of his experiences as

> a polylingual psychoanalyst with bilingual and polylingual patients whose "other" language coincided with one or another of my own, and the transference and countertransference implications of this silent yet ever present, overlapping and resonating set of linguistic and experiential worlds.
>
> I could reconfirm, in my experience, that, as patients shift from one language to another, they indicate in the process shifts in the transference and in the relationship to their unconscious past as well. I was reminded of patients whose apparent forgetting of an early childhood language was undone by their reencounter with that language as part of the acceptance of a repressed past; and I thought of patients who made use of skillful navigating among various languages to express their "as if" characteristics in order to escape from a specific, dreaded relationship linked to a particular language. I thought of my own difficulties in struggling with subtle emotional implications of the language of patients forming part of a culture to which I was a newcomer.[34]

The intricate linguistic relationship between the polylingual analyst and analysand includes not only the words actually uttered but also "silent yet ever present" languages that may be part of a larger "overlapping and resonating set of linguistic and experiential worlds." Such a dynamic may have been present from the start of psychoanalysis, in the extraordinary case of Sholem Dov Schneierson, the fifth Lubavitcher rebbe (known as the Rashab), who in 1903, when he was forty-two, was introduced to Freud and the psychoanalytic method after seeking neurological treatment in Vienna for paralysis and loss of sensation in his left hand and arm. While there is no record of such a visit in Freud's writing, and the Rashab's own references to this episode are understandably guarded, Maya Balakirsky Katz has discovered the case history of a forty-two-year old *rabbiner*, suffering from a similar set of symptoms, in a 1908 work by Wilhelm Stekel, an early follower with whom Freud later broke; according to Stekel, Freud referred the rabbi to him and supervised the treatment closely, since he was Stekel's first patient. Stekel's disguise of many aspects of the Rashab's identity—his position as a Hasidic rebbe, his marriage at fourteen (which Stekel placed at the more respectable eighteen)—not only safeguarded this particular patient's privacy but also hid the fact that he was an *Ostjude*. Stekel "doctored" the case history, Balakirsky Katz surmises, "to avoid distracting readers with non-essential facts that might lead them down incorrect diagnostic paths (i.e., that the rabbi's neurosis was related to his Jewish Eastern European ancestry)."[35] Balakirsky Katz sees Stekel's reference to the language the rabbi spoke, "a gibberish of German and Hebrew words," as a further attempt to disguise the Eastern European rebbe as a Central European *Rabbiner*; but it is also possible that Stekel simply heard Yiddish as gibberish (as Breuer understood Anna O.'s Yiddish as *Jargon*), even as he apparently understood it well enough to carry out the analysis and write up the case.[36]

The London psychoanalyst Joseph Berke, who is skeptical that Stekel's *rabbiner* was in fact the Rashab, raises the question of why Freud would have directed such an eminent patient to Stekel, "who at the time was a junior colleague," entertaining but ultimately dismissing the theory that Freud was "trying to get rid of a deeply spiritual and religious patient whom he found disturbing."[37] But perhaps it was Stekel's ability to understand Yiddish (despite not considering it a language) and his knowledge of Hasidic life that recommended him for this case: Stekel was born in and throughout his youth often visited relatives in the Bukovina town of Boyan (Boiany, now Ukraine), home to a lively Hasidic court that was the town's economic and social engine. It is not only the Rashab's identity that is obscured in the case history: the languages and culture of Stekel's childhood also disappear from view. If so, we are in the thick of one of those complicated relationships that might arise between polylingual analysts and analysands that Kernberg described: The analysand spoke a ("mixed," polylingual) language that Stekel understood (at least in part), since it was familiar to him (even if disavowed) from childhood. Given the disgust that palpably shapes Stekel's case history, it will come as no surprise that the Rashab did not find complete relief under Stekel's care. On what linguistic or affective level did Stekel's attitude toward his patient's language communicate itself to the Rashab? The transferential and countertransferential currents between a Hasidic rabbi analysand and his recently acculturated and brand-new (but already on his way out) psychoanalyst-in-training continue to make themselves felt in the projections and transferences of the scholarship working through this remarkable relationship, aided or misled by the partial historical record and shaped by ever-shifting ideological and psycho-affective currents. With new generations of scholarship, new forms of transference emerge within the expanding field. But these do not necessarily signify that what creeps in is only new mistakes. As these events in the early history of psychoanalysis recede in time, occasionally the "phase-effect" that characterizes both psychoanalysis and scholarship (as well as translation) allows this history to swim into closer view.

The place of Yiddish in a psychoanalytic encounter such as may have transpired between Stekel and the Rashab cannot be confined to the individual subjectivities of the psychoanalyst or analysand. Yiddish occupied or comprised a *third*, or "third space," of the session, the intersubjective in-between site of analytic encounter traced by Jessica Benjamin, among others.[38] If so, we can posit that Yiddish also takes its place more generally within the "overlapping and resonating worlds" that connect Freud and so many other psychoanalysts (perhaps even until the present day) with their patients, even if Jewish languages remained entirely unspoken in these encounters or erupt only in fragments. Evidence that Yiddish formed a fragmentary presence in at least one of Freud's analytic relationships lies in the case notes for the Rat Man, the only process notes—notes taken after a session (Freud did not write during sessions)—that Freud did not manage to destroy. The published case study gives no hint that the Rat Man (Ernst Lanzer) was Jewish, but such an impression would be hard to avoid by anyone perusing the notes. In shorthand, Freud describes a session with the Rat Man, who, acting like "a man in desperation . . . buried his head in his hands, rushed away, covered his face with his arm, etc." while relating his fear that Freud would beat him and speaking of people passed on the stairs that he imagined were members of Freud's family:

> Another horrible idea—of ordering me to bring my daughter into the room, so that he could lick her, saying "bring in the *Miessnick*." He associated to this a story about a friend who wanted to bring up guns against the café he used to visit, but who wanted first to save the excellent and very ugly waiter with the words, "*Miessnick*, come out." He was a *Miessnick* compared with his younger brother.
>
> Also play on my name: "*Freudenhaus-Mädchen*" [girls belonging to a House of Joy—prostitutes].[39]

The case notes do not appear in the *Standard Edition*, but the *Freud Reader* supplies the helpful footnote for *Miessnick*, "Yiddish for an ugly creature."

The sexual hostility of these thoughts, directed against Freud through his daughter, is hardly separable from the Yiddish language of the insult. In form and content, *Miessnick* is an intimate assault on the Jewish domestic interior of Freud's world. Although the play on Freud's name that follows is German, it recalls (perhaps only to me) that Freud's name is a matronym, going back to his great-great-grandmother *Freyde*; in other words, there really is a (Jewish, Yiddish-speaking) woman inhabiting this particular "Freudenhaus." Freud's daughter is only the first *Miessnick*. The Rat Man associates this same insult with a friend of his who has violent fantasies (or plans) of shooting up a café but who wants to rescue one person from the bloodshed: an ugly waiter he describes to his friend using the same Yiddish insult. This second use of the term suggests that an insult can signal intimacy, relationship, even affection, a function Max Weinreich calls *semantic reversal* and views as particularly characteristic of Yiddish insult.[40] The Rat Man found a Yiddish insult for Freud, too, not contenting himself with insulting Freud's daughter and "house"; he reports to Freud the thought, "20 *kronen* are enough for the *Parch*." For *Parch*, the footnote here provides "Yiddish for a futile person," softening the definitions in Uriel Weinreich's dictionary: "canker, ulcer; (vulgar) rat, stingy person." The equivalent "(vulgar) rat," is striking—Freud assigns Ernst Lanzer the protective pseudonym of the "Rat Man" for Lanzer's many associations with all things rat; but the case notes stand as evidence that Lanzer also called Freud (something like) "rat" *first*, and in Yiddish. Somewhere between the German publication and the Yiddish words uttered in the private session and accidentally preserved for posterity, Jewish words reveal and cement the (grotesque, redemptive, aggressive, transferential) connection between analyst and analysand, writer of case notes and their belated readers. The unwelcome *Fremdwort* in Freud's house suggests that Yiddish (or rather Yiddish-in-German) potentially functions in the third space of at least his sessions with the Rat Man as intimate aggression, aggressive intimacy.

Fragments and hints of Yiddish are everywhere in Freud's work and in psychoanalytic history. But psychoanalysis also has a place in Yiddish culture, with a small canon of works easy enough to catalogue. Along with the articles in the popular and highbrow press and three Yiddish translations of books by Freud that appeared between 1928 and 1938, a popular biography of Freud by Sh. Wolf was published in Warsaw in 1936. A more sophisticated explication of psychoanalysis by Max Weinreich, collecting his 1936 series of articles on psychoanalysis in the *Forverts*, appeared in 1937. In 1935, Weinreich published a sociological study of Jewish youth that mobilized psychoanalysis among other methods. After his death, Freud seemed to have a Yiddish afterlife mostly in Argentina, where a lively Yiddish scene combined with an interest in psychoanalysis. In 1957, the Buenos Aires literary quarterly *Davke* devoted its thirtieth issue to Sigmund Freud, with eight essays on Freud and psychoanalysis (two, by Ferenczi and Ernst Cassirer, were translated from German into Yiddish), and Yiddish translations of selected letters from the Roback-Freud correspondence, particularly those that concerned Yiddish and Freud's Eastern European roots.[41] This history seems to have ended in 1971, with Moisés (Moyshe) Kijak's volume on *Freud and Psychoanalysis* (*Froyd un der psikhoanaliz*), based on lectures delivered at YIVO Buenos Aires.[42]

The first of the Yiddish translations of Freud's writings, Sarah Lerman's 1928 *Group Psychology and the Analysis of the Ego*, appears to have been a hit, with a second edition appearing that same year and two more in 1929 and 1931.[43] Sarah Lerman is evidently a pseudonym: the dedication (to a friend in New York) is signed by *der ibersetzer* (the [male] translator).[44] In 1932, a Yiddish translation of *The Future of an Illusion*, by Y. Dodnik, appeared in Cleveland.[45] The last of the translations is Weinreich's "authorized" but unfinished version of the *Introductory Lectures*, planned as six volumes but with only three appearing—in 1936, 1937, and 1938—before events intervened.[46] These were individual translations, appearing in three different cities, under the auspices of no society and with no overarching project uniting them. Nor was it initially clear that there was a readership for such material. The first edition of Lerman's *Group Psychology* includes an advertisement on the back jacket, not so much for the book at hand, with which it shows only a glancing familiarity, as for its author:

> Who is Professor Sigmund Freud?
>
> In the contemporary field of inquiry into the human soul [*mentshlekher neshome-forshung*], Prof. Sigmund Freud is among the greatest researchers.... There is no language of culture whose literature has not gathered into itself the highly valuable work of this great intellectual.
>
> This volume brings into Yiddish for the first time one of his most interesting investigations, on the masses and the "I," and their reciprocal relations. This book must be read by every thinking person.[47]

By the second printing later in 1928, such an advertisement may no longer have been necessary; the inside cover advertises a different book recently published by the same press, translated not from German but Russian. The advertisement may have been written by the same person, since it uses a similar compliment to the "intelligent" reader to sell Nikolai Bukharin's *Theory of Historical Materialism*, "translated by Sarah Lerman from the latest, 1925 Russian edition," as of interest to all "deep-thinking people, whether followers or opponents of this philosophy" but particularly to "class-conscious workers interested in understanding the conditions of their own lives."[48] In combining attention to psychoanalysis with an interest in Marxism, Lerman's translation agenda fits squarely in the international trend of "Freudo-Marxism," centered in the 1920s in Germany and the Soviet Union but certainly part of the "cauldron of ideas" in what was now Poland. YIVO was a diverse and collective enterprise, but there, too, a left-leaning range of political positions combined with diaspora Jewish nationalism, Yiddishism, and an interest in psychoanalysis.[49] *Group Psychology* may have particularly appealed to Lerman's readers, who bought out the first edition in a matter of months, for a variety of reasons: Yiddishist culture, with its strains of socialism and nationalism, its youth movements and critique of the family, had a vested interest in conceptualizing collectivity. Freud's particular attention to the hypnotic dark forces unifying the masses and energizing such conservative institutions as the church and the army must also have struck readers as all too relevant and timely. As Kenneth Moss has argued, Freud's analysis of the hostility among groups, a "Hatred of Others" that was "terrifyingly *natural*," was of profound interest to a population struggling with the horrifying visibility of just such hatred. The translation of *Group Psychology* contributed to what was already a concerted attempt by Jewish intellectuals to wrestle with the psychology of antisemitism. As Moss writes,

> Already in 1924, the Warsaw Bnai Brith lodge—a gathering place for Polonized but Jewishly engaged elites—hosted a lecture titled "The Psychology of Antisemitism." In 1932, the lodge revisited the question in a talk titled "Antisemitism in the Light of Psychoanalysis," by Gustav Bychowski.[50]

Bychowski, who had trained with Freud before moving back to Warsaw in 1921 and who was the Polish translator of *Introductory Lectures on Psychoanalysis* (the same book Weinreich translated), visited Freud in 1935 to ask for Freud's advice on an era when "waves of hatred shake the foundation of the human world."[51] Given the transnational and multilingual attempt to mine psychoanalytic insights for widely shared political predicaments, it is not surprising that *Group Psychology* was also the first of Freud's monographs to be translated into Hebrew, and in 1928, the same year. (A brief exposition of psychoanalysis by Dr. A. Litvak appeared in 1925, and Freud's first translation into Hebrew, of "Resistances to Psychoanalysis" was published in a periodical in 1926.)[52] Alternatively, Eran Rolnik suggests that the organization of Hebrew teachers chose Freud's *Group Psychology* as the work that would "bring the message of psychoanalysis to the Hebrew-reading public" because the book was "devoted to the origins of social justice and to the formation of the tribe, two subjects that concerned the Yishuv's educators."[53]

Yiddish interest in Freud's ideas and biography, as this brief summary suggests, was less centered on the technical aspects of psychoanalytic treatment or the structure of the psyche than on those areas of Freud's thought that addressed broader social, cultural, and political matters of interest to a general audience. Gliksman, in his 1924 series on psychoanalysis, made it clear that Freud had much to offer in the realm of the humanities. Weinreich similarly acknowledged in his introduction to the first volume of his Yiddish *Introduction to Psychoanalysis* (appended to the end of the volume) that, aside from his obvious contributions to the fields of psychiatry and psychology, Freud had valuable insights to offer "criminologists, pedagogues, sociologists, historians, literary critics, and artists. And the ordinary person [*mentsh fun a gantz yor*] has also found much of interest in this work."[54] Indeed, for many Yiddish readers, Freud was a figure of interest even if the fine details or actual practice of psychoanalysis remained out of reach. Freud's eightieth birthday, covered so widely in the Jewish press and beyond, aroused new interest in his discoveries. The back cover of the first issue of Weinreich's *Introduction* announced that YIVO, which counted Freud as a member of its Presidium, was launching the translation on the very day of Freud's eightieth birthday, "with the permission of the author."[55] That same day, May 6, 1936, Weinreich also launched the first of his series of articles on Freud in the *Forverts*; these articles were assembled and published as a book the following year.

From the purely linguistic perspective, translating psychoanalysis involved navigating a shifting terrain, given the proximity that connected and distance that separated German and Yiddish. In fact, the path to the earliest Yiddish translations had already been paved, given that the journalists and lecturers who aimed to convey the substance of psychoanalysis in the years before 1928 had already been compelled to find or construct Yiddish equivalents for such concepts as "the unconscious," "the Oedipal complex," the "id" and "ego," and so on. In many cases, German and Yiddish were so close that the concept of translation seems hardly warranted—what Yiddish word could a translator possibly use for *ich* (German) other than *ikh* (Yiddish), or *es* for *es*? For a taste of where German and Yiddish readily met and where they diverged, here are the first lines of Freud's *Massenpsikhologie* and Lerman's translation:

> *Der Gegensatz von Individual- und Sozial- oder Massenpsychologie, der uns auf den ersten Blick als sehr bedeutsam erscheinen mag, verliert bei eingehender Betrachtung sehr viel von seiner Schärfe.*
>
> (Strachey: The contrast between individual psychology and social or group psychology, which at a first glance may seem to be full of significance, loses a great deal of its sharpness when it is examined more closely.)[56]
>
> *Di stire tzvishn der individualer un sotzialer oder masn-psikhologiye, vos zet undz oys ofn ershtn blik tsu zayn a zeyer bataytndike, vayzt zikh gornisht oys azoy sharf nokh a gruntlekher batrakhtung.*

Although Yiddish possesses a cognate term for *Gegensatz* in *kegensatz*, Lerman begins with a rather sharper Hebraic-Yiddish term, *stire*, which means "contradiction" rather than "contrast" and carries with it the flavor of Talmud study, of fine distinctions and the movements of thought and counter-thought. But most of the sentence reflects the ease with which Yiddish could accommodate technical scholarly terms such as *Massenpsychologie* through transliteration; find equivalents or near equivalents for words such as *Blick*, *bedeutsam*, and *Schärfe*; and discover idiomatic and even folksy Yiddish ways of capturing German turns of phrase; the way Lerman describes Freud's distinction between individual and the group that, on reflection, *vayzt zikh gornisht oys azoy sharf* (seems not quite so sharp) captures, to my ear, more of Freud's idiomatic German than Strachey's more formal and abstract "loses a great deal of its sharpness." Where the *Standard Edition* sought consistency in translating *masse* as "group" (although the broader *masse* could, as the editors note, mean "crowd" or "masses") and rendering *Massenpsychologie* as "group psychology," Lerman, who includes no glossary of terms, felt free to vary its usage throughout the text.

If the proximity of German and Yiddish could ease translators' paths, it could also lead them to assume equivalence when the historical development of the two languages had diverged, creating "false friends" in which words that appear similar mean entirely different things. This was the case with the German *Unbewusstsein* (the unconscious), which Lerman and Dodnik translated as *umbavustzayn* and Wulf translated as *unterbavustzayn*. Weinreich was still using *umbavust* in his 1935 sociological *The Path to Our Youth* but rejected the term for the 1936 translation on the grounds that, in Yiddish, the root adjective *bavust* meant not "conscious" but "known" (as in famous).[57] Mordkhe Schaechter, in an essay on the translation, notes that the word *bavust* in that ordinary Yiddish meaning appears quite a few times in Weinreich's Yiddish translation, and if he had also used the word to mean "conscious," its ordinary German meaning, "that would have caused major confusion."[58] In its place, Weinreich revived the old Yiddish term *visik*, producing also *umvisik*, *untervisik*, and *umvisikayt* for the "unconscious," the subconscious, the "preconscious," and so on. Weinreich's term had the virtue of being transparent in its connection with *visn*, "to know or be aware of"; distinct from ordinary German usage—always considered an advantage in his Yiddishist milieu; and archaic, evoking psychoanalytic concepts in its reach down to an earlier stratum of the language. The ingenious solution, Schaechter writes, "was immediately taken up by Z. Rayzen, Prilutzki, Gininger and others. But the Holocaust interrupted the spread of YIVO terminological accomplishments, and so *visik* and *visikayt* did not receive the attention they deserve."[59] Even Uriel Weinreich, in his 1968 *Modern English-Yiddish, Yiddish-English Dictionary*, split the difference, providing both *bavust* and his father's *visik* as the two equivalents for the Freudian "conscious"; but Kijak's 1971 Yiddish monograph on psychoanalysis reverts unapologetically to *bevustzayn* and *umbevustzayn*.[60] If Yiddish is the Jewish unconscious, it may not be surprising that we still do not know how exactly to say that in Yiddish, given that the discourse that might have answered the question was interrupted by genocide and cultural amnesia.

Weinreich abandoned the Freud translation when the Second World War broke out, turning his attention away from psychology and sociology toward linguistics and the task of rebuilding YIVO on American soil. But the concepts of the conscious and unconscious play a role in these spheres, too, as might be inferred by Weinreich's suggestion that YIVO was, in some sense, the collective unconscious of American Jews. Among the most influential scholarly contributions of Weinreich's magnum opus, *History of the Yiddish Language*, is his argument that what distinguishes Yiddish from other languages is not its character as a fusion language (*shmeltzshprakh*)—Yiddishists were long united in arguing that such hybridity was a feature of most if not all languages, however fervently nationalists might imagine their own languages as "pure." What distinguishes Yiddish is that, for contingent historical reasons, its speakers have a heightened *awareness* of this characteristic, to a degree rare among speakers of other (similarly "fusion") languages. Even uneducated Yiddish speakers possess, to some degree, what Weinreich called *komponentn visikayt*, or "component consciousness," using the term Weinreich had coined to translate Freud's "conscious":

> Every sophisticate among Jews in eastern Europe is a kind of comparatist. He prays in *Loshn-koydesh*, and occasionally also looks into a *Loshn-koydesh* book; he dwells among Slavs; he encounters German in business or at work. (In certain social categories, German books were also read and German spas were visited.) Therefore recently one could still find simple people of the older generation who really did not know German, but in given situations they could easily and at once change *dray khodoshim* (three months) to *dray monatn* or *matone* (gift) to *geshank*.[61]

If Yiddish was the unconscious language of assimilated Jews, among traditional Jews it was also a language of (hyper)consciousness. What was unconscious for the speakers of most national languages—the multiple components and checkered history of the tongues they called their own—was an intrinsic, concrete, and culturally generative aspect of Yiddish linguistic consciousness. Yiddish speakers thus had ready access to what for speakers of other languages remained deep, mostly imperceptible history. Only the most poetic or educated of English speakers is aware of and feels the difference between, for instance, the Romance and Anglo-Saxon elements of the language, although this history shapes the language even in being lost or buried. Yiddish in this sense tells truths about all languages (but especially German) that these languages have suppressed; perhaps this explains why it was long treated with such hostility (by speakers of German above all). "Component consciousness," so striking a feature of the speech community as a whole, was certainly heightened for translators between Yiddish and German, plying as they did the charged, blurred, and shifting border that connected and divided Yiddish and its main component language.

By the time Weinreich set out to translate Freud in the mid-1930s, the existing store of Yiddish psychoanalytic terms included a few that domesticated Freud's strange ideas by mobilizing the distinctively Jewish components of Yiddish. However they came by their choices, translators and popularizers were aware that such techniques could help overcome resistance to psychoanalysis by casting its insights as native Jewish wisdom. A 1931 article by the psychologist Tz. Rudy assured his readers that there was no reason to be disturbed by the term *libido*, since "sexuality, or *libido*, is simply what the Jewish vernacular calls the *yetzer hore*, the 'evil inclination.'"[62] And in fact Yiddish translators did regularly refer to the sexual drive through the term *yetzer*. Among the most persistent criticisms of the *Standard Edition* has been that it used the word "instinct" for *Trieb*, inappropriately implying that sexual "drives" are biological in nature. If "instinct" suggests biology, *yetzer* leads us into the thickets of Jewish language and culture, with a range of biblical meanings (intent, imagination, creation) and the distinct suggestion in Genesis 8:21 (for the *yetzer* of the human being is evil from youth) that *yetzer* goes deep but is perhaps not inborn, much less "original." As Rudy suggests, Yiddish culture draws less on biblical than on rabbinic anthropology, in which *yetzer* becomes a foundational concept while splitting into two, *yetzer hatov* and *yetzer hara* (the good and evil inclination). "The evil inclination" might seem an inappropriate equivalent for the ostensibly more neutral "libido," but the rabbis read that inclination with more nuance than the term "evil" might imply, as in the midrashic apothegm "Rabbi Nahman bar Samuel bar Nachman said in the name of Rabbi Samuel bar Nachman: 'And behold it was very good' (Gen 1:31)—this refers to the *yetzer hara*. But is the *yetzer hara* indeed very good?! Were it not for the *yetzer hara*, a man would not build a home, or marry a woman, or have children, or engage in business" (Genesis Rabba 9:7).

The most elaborate exploration in the *Introductory Lectures* of the sexual *Trieb*, or *Triebregung* (the "stirring" of the drive), is in the context of Freud's analysis of a dream described over the course of a few lectures, a young married woman's dream that her recently engaged friend has been unable to get good seats at the theater so had chosen not to attend. Freud explains that, in this dream, "a visit to the theatre became an obvious substitute ... for marriage," since "simple minded girls, after becoming engaged, are reputed often to express their joy that they will soon be able to go to the theatre, to all the plays which have hitherto been prohibited, and will be allowed to see everything."⁶³ The desire to see, according to Freud, has roots in the infantile desire to witness the sex lives of the parents, "Wurzeln ins Infantile . . . Triebregung."⁶⁴ Weinreich translates *Triebregung* here through a compound neologism as *yetzer-vekung*, the awakening of *yetzer*. The compound Yiddish term is Weinreich's own, but it is rooted in and intertextually connected with traditional Jewish sources that combine to route this drive or desire through eminently cultural channels. Freud himself lends substance here to Lacan's reading of *Trieb* as mediated through language and culture. What girls desire in marriage, in this rather astonishing logic, is not the sex "itself" that marriage might be presumed to provide but their freedom as married women to go to the theater and view risqué performances, satisfying a desire that is rooted in the infantile desire to see adult sexual activity. Before it was Foucauldian, that sex and knowledge are intricately related was a biblical insight (along with the contrary but related insight that it is perfectly possible to have sex with someone without knowing who they are; cf. Jacob and Leah; or Judah and Tamar). To the visual, performative, theatrical, cultural, and linguistic paths of sexual knowledge, the *Schaulust* Freud had explored (and which Strachey translates as "scopophilia"), Weinreich contributed also the pleasures of Jewish intertextuality, which feeds the drive for knowledge about origins by providing Jewish readers with a peepshow into the sex lives of their parents and their distant biblical and rabbinic ancestors, which turn out to be not so different from their own.

Language politics certainly also play a role in these translation choices, as in Weinreich's resistance to introducing Germanisms (*daytshmerish*), even if no obvious indigenous Yiddish expressions presented themselves. Weinreich wrote in the preface to his sociological study *The Path to Our Youth* that scholars could not always rely on the Yiddish language to express their findings:

> An apology for the language of this book. Many terms will seem strange, but there is nothing to be done about that here. There simply isn't an adequate expression in Yiddish for everything, so one has to be a partner in Creation [*a shutef lemayse bereshis*] far more one wishes . . . but it's my sense that a new, still rough Yiddish word is a thousand times preferable to a Germanic barbarism.⁶⁵

Weinreich understood the importance of providing a distinctively Jewish and Yiddish version of Freud's thought to Eastern European Jews, but he also steered away from what he considered overdoing this effect. The

"Freud Laboratory," Weinreich's working notebook, cites a phrase from Yehuda Dwossis's 1934 Hebrew translation of the *Introductory Lectures* and adds the disapproving note: "too Jewish."⁶⁶ (Lerman's *Group Psychology* makes no appearance, and Weinreich made clear that he considered it a terrible translation.)⁶⁷ Yiddish had distinctive resources beyond its always-at-hand Hebrew components: Weinreich, for instance, drew attention to the stylistic use Yiddish speakers made of the word *es* (which it shared with German) as an "ambient" subject without a specific referent or lexical meaning. Freud's idiosyncratic attention to the German *es* was something Yiddish speakers could easily grasp, since their own language had taught them to recognize the workings of "absent" or "unmarked" entities in the realm of human action, as in the Yiddish turn of phrase *es vilt zikh epes*—not "I want something" but "something in me which is not quite me wants something." John Murray Cuddihy identified the id as a cover for the unruly Yid. But Yiddish saw the matter otherwise, viewing the *es* as a persistent feature of all human subjectivity, seen in its operations but never grasped in its substance. Even if this id was more readily grasped in and by a Jewish language, as an entity not identified with the *conscious* subject, it was certainly not the very essence of what made this subject "Jewish."

In these and other cases, it is clear that German-Yiddish translation invites us to rethink the stock assumption that translation always signifies loss. Yiddish translators regularly took the option of turning Freud's thought in a Jewish direction, one that generated a host of associations: with what was already Jewish about his thought or with the Jewishness Freud had abandoned, suppressed, or never known, the Jewishness of his ancestors. In the rare cases in which Freud's German was itself a translation from Yiddish (or Hebrew), Yiddish translation could function more directly as a "retroversion" or "back-translation" of or into a lost original. Freud did not bring up the story of his father's fur cap in the *Introductory Lectures*, so we cannot know whether Dwossis or Weinreich might have recognized that cap as the *shtrayml* identified by Jewish studies scholars much later. Freud does, however, relate a dream in the *Introductory Lectures* that refers to *Samstag*, although it is clear as day (but which day?) that Freud means *shabes*. Here is the description of the dream, in its entirety:

> Ein Traum besteht nur aus zwei kurzen Bildern: *Sein Onkel raucht eine Zigarette, obwohl es Samstag ist.—Eine Frau streichelt und liebkost ihn wie ihr Kind.*⁶⁸
>
> (This dream consisted only of two short pictures: *His uncle was*

smoking a cigarette, although it was Saturday.—A woman was caressing and fondling him as though he were her child.)⁶⁹

A kholem shtet zikh tsunoyf nur fun tsvey kurtse bilder: Zayn feter reykhert a papiros, hagam s'iz shabes.—A froy glet un tsertlt im vi irs a kind.⁷⁰

Interpreting this two-faced dream requires of Freud different types of translation. The first is the cultural translation that explains to his audience that the dreamer's uncle is a pious Jew so is forbidden from smoking on Saturday; a second is the psychoanalytic translation of the religious sin of smoking on the Sabbath into the sexual transgression of incest. After the dreamer free-associates from "a woman" to his mother, Freud makes the dream logic clear: If my uncle, *der heilige Mann*, were to smoke on the Sabbath, then might I welcome my mother's caresses. Weinreich follows Freud in explaining the problem with smoking on *Samstag*, but the explanation—the cultural translation—is redundant, since describing the uncle as smoking although it is *shabes* already does that work. The translation or back-translation of *Samstag* as *shabes* is also the *only* possible translation in Yiddish. Weinreich thus calls attention to the place of Yiddish as an unspoken stratum of psychoanalytic discourse, whether first buried under the German and then excavated for the benefit of Freud's audience; or suppressed by the dreamer in his secondary revision of the dream and recovered in Freud's interpretation; or lost within the dream "itself," in an earlier and deeper turn of the translational/psychoanalytic engine.⁷¹ Freud's lecture uses (a German translation of) a Jewish sin as a metaphorical vehicle for the most universal of transgressions, incest. (And, in fact, in a 1927 *Imago* essay, Erich Fromm suggests that the prohibition against work on the Sabbath, particularly agricultural work—a kind of conquest of "mother earth"—is related to the incest taboo.)⁷² But who is to say from which direction to read these twinned sins—from left to right, from particular to universal, or from right to left, from universal to particular? To put it in terms of Kosofsky Sedgwick's surface theory, perhaps they are in a relationship of "*beside* rather than . . . *beneath* or *behind*."⁷³ Translating this dream into the very Jewish language that it has been translated out of (in rendering *shabes* as *Samstag*) allows us to level the playing field that privileges original over translation. This back-translation draws attention to the role of religion, sin, and the Jewish tradition in psychoanalysis, the sins that still stir the sleep of some of his Jewish dreamers. In this way, translation recalls if it does not entirely reverse the move from one generation to the next, from "tradition" to "modernity," and from East to West—the cultural context of "deconversion" that Philip Rieff argues is necessary for the emergence of psychoanalysis in Freud and in his international reception.[74] Yiddish cannot fully tell that story, which depends on the swerve into German to explain how the meaning of a day might have been lost or buried. But in translating as he must, Weinreich also performs the psychoanalytic service of converting what had been deconverted, which is to say, of raising to consciousness what had been obscured by German for Freud's dreamer and thus shining a torchlight on "the vision they saw with bleary eyes."

8

A Godless Jew in the Holy Tongue

> He is at home here. He is part and parcel of these treasures. I have come a long way, I have brought nothing with me. He has his family, the tradition of an unbroken family, reaching back through this old heart of the Roman Empire, further into the Holy Land. "Ah, Psyche! / From the regions which / Are Holy Land!"
> —H.D., *Tribute to Freud* (1994)

> By the end of the eighteenth century, doctors discovered that a return home did not always treat the symptoms. The object of longing occasionally migrated to faraway lands beyond the confines of the motherland. . . . Yet the physicians failed to find the locus of nostalgia in their patient's mind or body. One doctor claimed that nostalgia was a "hypochondria of the heart" that thrives on its symptoms. To my knowledge, the medical diagnosis of nostalgia survived in the twentieth century in one country only—Israel. (It is unclear whether this reflects a persistent yearning for the promised land or for the diasporic homelands left behind.)
> —Svetlana Boym, *The Future of Nostalgia* (2001)

In the summer of 1933, Dr. Samuel Perlman, scholar of medieval Hebrew poetry and former dean of Hebrew College in Boston, ran into Hayim Nachman Bialik on a Tel Aviv bus, only days before the poet was to leave for Vienna to undergo a medical procedure. Perlman felt compelled to share with Bialik a dream he had been harboring of editing a series of Hebrew translations of works written by Jews in non-Jewish languages. Recent events had made the project urgent. While Jewish writers had "enriched the literature of non-Jewish nations," these countries, particularly Germany, "had thrown their work onto the trash heap or set them on fire."[1] In the meantime, Perlman lamented, "the younger generation being educated here in Hebrew cannot even read these books without learning a foreign language!" These young people, engrossed in the latest trashy novel, might never understand the richness and anguish of diaspora Jewish experience. It wasn't only the thoughtless young that stood to benefit from these translations:

> The Hebrew writer feels himself alone. The best among his brothers abandoned him to sing in a foreign tongue, leaving our internal life impoverished and split. If we return to our midst those spiritual giants who sinned against us—intentionally or unintentionally—the resonance would return to our Hebrew writers, whose voices ring out so thinly now.[2]

In that conversation and for years to come, Perlman cast the Hebrew translation project as a cultural parallel to the physical "ingathering" of diaspora Jews in Palestine, speaking of the proposed translation as a "return of the straying children [*habanim hato'im*] to their Hebrew borders."[3] Bialik would have missed neither the ideological implications nor the literary allusions of Perlman's words, which referred to the present wave of immigration while echoing Jeremiah's stirring prophecy, "For there is a reward for your labor—declares the Lord: They shall return from the enemy's land. And there is hope for your future—declares the Lord: Your children shall return to their borders [*veshavu banim legevulam*]" (Jer 31:16–17).

According to Perlman, Bialik was very much taken with the idea of such a translation series, although he was busy with his own "ingathering [*kinus*]" project, working with his longtime collaborator Joshua Ravnitzki on modern editions of the Hebrew poetry of Golden Age Spain, the area of scholarship he shared with Perlman.[4] They promised to continue the conversation when Bialik returned from abroad, but the reunion was not to be—Bialik died of a sudden heart attack in Vienna a week after the operation. Mossad Bialik, the cultural institute and press founded in 1935 to honor the memory of "the Hebrew national poet," accepted Perlman's proposal, although it was not until 1940 that Perlman could announce the forthcoming publication of the first book of the series, which bore the meaningful title *Legevulam* (To their borders). As a report on the new series explained, the delay was due to the difficult political and economic conditions of 1930s Mandatory Palestine rather than to any lack of enthusiasm for Perlman's vision. Nor were qualified translators in short supply: the series had a strong focus on German-Hebrew translation at a moment when the libraries and cafés of Jerusalem, Tel Aviv, and Haifa swarmed with underemployed German-speaking intellectuals in flight from Nazism (although, of course, many if not most of them had little Hebrew).

Legevulam ran for over two decades with Perlman as editor in chief, launching with a Hebrew rendering of a work by the Danish literary critic Georg Brandes and continuing with Solomon Maimon, Moses Mendelssohn, Theodor Herzl, Heinrich Heine, Henri Bergson, and Freud, among others. Aside from serving as the series editor, Perlman was as one of its most prolific translators, producing translations of ten of Heine's works, later collected as a three-volume set, along with many works by Herzl. It may have been his devotion to Heine (and perhaps also the taint of Theodor Herzl's son's 1924 conversion to Catholicism, which dismayed the Zionist world) that brought controversy to the series. In a 1958 interview titled "Bringing 'Straying' Sons Home," Perlman was confronted by his interviewer with the complaint of an unnamed "important person" in the Zionist establishment who objected to the fact that the series "mostly published writers who had converted to Christianity." Perlman stood firm in the face of the accusation, correcting the exaggeration but not apologizing for his approach: "Assimilated Jews and converts, too. If the writer is a deep person and gifted writer, his Jewishness will be preserved in his writing, and it will impart to non-Jewish readers a certain taste of the values of Judaism."[5] It was precisely because these assimilated writers or converts had strayed that the mission of *Legevulam* was so critical, as a symbolic salvage operation for Jews who had grown distant from the tradition that was nevertheless still "preserved" in them and who were now endangered—or their books were, at any rate—by the Nazi bonfires.

German-Hebrew translation, in such conceptions, was something different from and far more affecting than an act of lexical rewording or the displacement of an original into a foreign tongue. Which tongue was foreign and which the mother tongue, which text was the original and which the translation, where was home and where diaspora, where displacement began and where it ended—all those apparently settled issues were up for grabs again in the project. Translation itself, far from signifying loss, here was conceived as salvage and redemption, an "ingathering" and "homecoming" of prodigal sons and the foreign languages in which they wrote into the native and "original" language and interpretive community from which they had become estranged, "intentionally or unintentionally."[6] Nevertheless, as Danielle Drori shows, Zionist translators wrestled with what it meant to be translating "foreign" authors rather than obeying the imperative of creating new cultural products that expressed the pioneering and unique spirit of the time; the suspicion that translators were trafficking in "imitation" (associated in the Zionist imaginary with diaspora assimilationism) rather than "innovation" (the aspiration of cultural Zionism) hung particularly heavily over those thought to be introducing "foreign influences" to the Land of Israel.[7]

If translation continued to be necessary in the land Jews hoped to call their own, this necessity shed light on the partiality and ambiguity of the miraculous revival of the ancient Hebrew tongue; Roni Henig has described the ways that the rhetoric of "language revival" in fact occluded a host of melancholic losses in its tale of miraculous recovery.[8] Perlman acknowledged at least one such loss in speaking of the loneliness of Hebrew writers at the isolated margins of world literature in a language few could understand; for these writers, translation was a way of intimately connecting with the big world and with their Jewish counterparts who were both fortunate and unfortunate to be part of that larger world. For Zionist pioneers repressing nostalgia for Europe and European tongues, translation into Hebrew could provide some welcome immersion in what was not Hebrew, while framing this immersion as extraction and thus as praiseworthy Zionist work. If so, then the Hebrew "rescue" of straying sons was also a form of rescue for the Hebrew translators-rescuers, providing a broader intellectual horizon for a literary culture that could feel hemmed in precisely by its own successes.

As marginal and historically specific as Hebrew "salvage translation" might appear, psychoanalytic translation during those years was swimming in a similar affective current, with just such an urgent and mournful mindset. Riccardo Steiner notes that Ernest Jones initiated the project that would become the *Standard Edition* in an emotional letter to Strachey dashed off a few hours after Freud's funeral (September 28, 1939, five days after his death). Jones wrote that notwithstanding financial difficulties and the winds of war that were blowing, he was enlisting Strachey and a few others to "secure a definitive edition for generations to come" to replace the incomplete *Collected Papers* that had been published in 1924–25. Jones, who had turned sixty that year, was clearly feeling his own mortality, warning Strachey that "if it is done after our time, it can never be done so well."[9] A few weeks later, after Sir William Baggs, president of the Royal Society, rejected his request for support on the grounds of the war that had just broken out, Jones urged him to reconsider, precisely because of Germany's bellicosity:

> I am persuaded that you would share the view that to salvage from the

Moloch of destructiveness something of our cultural and scientific treasures is an aim worthy to rank even with the patriotic duty of winning the war. Most decisive of all, however, is the consideration that those of us who worked personally with Freud, partly in his more active years, are few and old and it is on them that the burden of the undertaking would fall. It is very much a question of uniformly editing and annotating his writing in a way that would elucidate allusions and references the meaning of which would otherwise be lost for those after us.[10]

The impression Steiner gives of the heated emotional and political context in which the *Standard Edition* was launched could hardly be further from Bettelheim's description of the *Standard Edition* as propelled by cold calculation and professional strategy. The *Standard Edition*, as this correspondence makes clear, was a passion project, intensely charged with the emotions stirred by Freud's recent death and the outbreak of war in Europe, involving not only grief, loss, and intimations of mortality but—as Freud would have predicted—all the complicated emotions that flow between the founder of a movement and his fervent, ambivalent, and fractious disciples. Steiner reads Jones's mood in this correspondence as vibrating "with a sort of apostolic, almost pentecostal fervor," the mood that overcame Jesus's followers in Acts 2 when they converged on Jerusalem for the Pentecost festival, the pivotal point at which—through a miraculous translation event—disciples became apostles and the Jesus movement took its first steps to becoming a world religion. The style of the *Standard Edition*, in Steiner's view, expresses the monumentalizing impulses to eternalize a body of writing and, through this monument to the Master, establish the editors and translators as exemplary transmitters of the message. Freud's death also put a stop to the unceasing and digressive flow of his writing and thought, giving editors the opportunity to fix a canon and view psychoanalysis from the bird's-eye perspective that could lend it singularity, wholeness, and systematicity. As Steiner argues,

> It is almost as if Jones were trying to evolve a strategy in the face of the loss of the Master, no longer present to clarify queries about his message and to answer to the often flimsy attempts to unravel its subtleties; so that for Jones it was almost a question of transmitting a word which had been attributed an all but definitive form and significance, in whose tonalities it is difficult immediately to distinguish between deference towards the magnitude of Freud's achievement and honour at having been among

the elect, chosen by Freud to share in it; pain and anxiety at the loss of Freud; and the necessity of defending his work and furthering it through a translation; and it is also difficult to separate all these elements from the possible influence of the cultural and scientific convictions of Jones and his group, which must be taken into careful consideration.[11]

Steiner's reading of the powerful emotions stirred by Freud's death for the compilers of the *Standard Edition* might also help illuminate the affective currents that drove the Hebrew translation of Freud during this period. Only one of these translators, Yehuda Dwossis (later Dvir), who translated three of Freud's works in the 1920s and 1930s, had occasion to confer with the writer, and Freud's authorization was duly noted on the title pages of his last two books and in the special prefaces for the Hebrew editions Freud penned. Zvi Woyslawski, who translated *The Psychopathology of Everyday Life* in the early 1940s, was not among those fortunate translators with direct communication with the Master. Nevertheless, it is fair to assume that, in publishing with Perlman's *Legvulam* series (and, as we will see, in the style he chose for his translation), Woyslawski also saw himself as among Freud's saviors, and perhaps also among "the elect" who shared in "the magnitude of Freud's achievement," not through the direct investiture by Freud that Dwossis could claim but through the bond he shared with Freud by virtue of their being Jews. That others—including the non-Jews in London—were more evidently entitled to express their kinship with the great man only increased the urgency, for Freud's Hebrew translators, of staking a claim to their own closeness to the man and his plight. London was famous as Freud's place of refuge, a role it played on a broader level in serving as a center of world psychoanalysis, a headquarters for the rescue of Jewish psychoanalysts threatened by the Nazi regime, and the major site for the translation, standardization, and dissemination of Freud's writings. But Jerusalem, too, could serve as an alternative, far less prominent, even secret sanctuary for psychoanalysis, psychoanalysts, and Freud's embattled ideas, with Hebrew translators guiding the way.

The "salvage" of Freud's work through translation and editing in the tumultuous years in which this work seemed to call out to be rescued was aspirational, considering the yawning gap between the metaphorical rescue through translation and the political and existential realities it ostensibly mirrored: Freud himself was ultimately beyond rescue; rendering his works into another language could hardly put a halt to Nazi advances or save the lives of Jewish psychoanalysts; and even "salvage" translation had to contend with the persistent and inevitable specter of the betrayal and loss of Freud's *ipsissima verba*. In this sense, the rescue fantasy was an expression of powerlessness, shame, and guilt, concealed behind a blustering superhero facade. As it happens, Emanuel Berman, editor of the important Am Oved series on psychoanalysis (launched in 1993) that undertook to modernize Hebrew psychoanalytic translation after earlier efforts came to seem antiquated, is among those who study the role played by unconscious rescue fantasies in psychoanalytic work. In the case of many who choose psychoanalysis as a profession, Berman believes, these rescue fantasies can be traced "to the earliest ties to the mother, to experiences of loss and restitution, to a reparation of damage caused by aggression, to the need to save a depressed or helpless parent, to the rescue of oneself as projected onto the other." The influence of these unconscious factors on the psychoanalyst's work does not diminish its value or efficacy; psychoanalysis could hardly exist, or the "helping professions, in general—without a rescue fantasy." Psychoanalytic training should not attempt to eradicate these rescue fantasies but instead teach candidates to sublimate them "into a realistic therapeutic frame of reference," freed from their characteristic grandiosity, narcissism, and aggression, so clearly evident in the tendency of rescuers to "demonize an other" (often the family of the patient in need of "saving").[12] The rescue fantasies that drove psychoanalytic translation into Hebrew might serve as evidence that whether or not they ultimately derive from intimate family situations, they also find collective form in the dreams and fantasies that spur national ideologies.[13]

Translations of Freud between 1933 and 1945 throughout the world were undoubtedly affected by the existential, political dangers facing Freud, his family, his writings, and the field he had founded and by Freud's exile and then death. In the case of Hebrew, these affects were intensified by the additional complication that these were collective Jewish crises and by the intimate associations of translation and Zionist ingathering. The ingathering of Freud into Hebrew "borders" was not only a metaphor. This operation was taking place on the ground, as a feature of the immigration of psychoanalysts to the Land of Israel, whether they treated Palestine as a temporary refuge or considered it their homeland. We are fortunate to be in possession of two detailed and illuminating histories of psychoanalysis in Mandatory Palestine by Eran Rolnik and Guido Liebermann (there is another, on psychiatry, by Rakefet Zalashik).[14] According to these histories, the Zionist ingathering of psychoanalysis was a halting process: The first psychoanalyst to step foot in the Land of Israel was apparently David Eder, a Zionist activist, socialist, and the first secretary of the British Psychoanalytic Society (founded 1913), who accepted Chaim Weizmann's invitation to serve on the British Zionist Commission that arrived in Palestine in 1918. In Palestine, where he remained until 1922, Eder was kept busy with organizational and administrative issues, but he found time to consult on issues of practical concern with the psychologists and social workers of the Zionist yishuv.[15] Dorian Feigenbaum, who later cofounded and served as editor in chief of the *Psychoanalytic Quarterly*, left the Swiss Psychoanalytic Society in 1920 for Palestine, where he worked as medical director of what was then the only psychiatric hospital in Palestine, the Ezrat Nashim facility in Jerusalem. Rolnik writes that the hospital served an extremely heterogeneous population, so that "the babel of languages and cultures was an exceptional psychoanalytic challenge." From that post, Feigenbaum published on the mental problems of the Zionist settlers, diagnosing their extraordinarily high suicide rate as stemming not from the economic and physical difficulties regularly cited by Zionist leaders but from the "terrible battle in the subconscious of the Chalutz (pioneer)." As Feigenbaum wrote,

> This was a struggle with the yearning for the old parents that had been left in the old home (and who had not always consented to their sons' leaving them), a battle fought every night in dreams that, characteristically, had their scene "here in Palestine and, at the same time at home." Thus the psychoanalyst was the only witness of the silent battle the Chalutz has to fight, not only with malaria and the stony soil, but with an easily comprehensible longing that had been sacrificed to his ideals.[16]

These dreams reflected a rather different scenario than the one expressed in the Herzlian slogan "If you will it, it is no dream." This perspective countered the Zionist dream that, in immigrating to Palestine, psychoanalysis was coming "back home" with another set of dreams, silent battles with absent parents for which psychoanalysts served as sole witnesses, which showed that Zionists were less at home in the Holy Land than Herzl had imagined.

In the two years they overlapped in Jerusalem (1920–22), Eder and Feigenbaum led a psychoanalytic study group and sought other means of advancing the cause in Palestine, which as a society in revolutionary transformation was in a unique position to absorb the lessons of psychoanalysis. Those rethinking child-rearing practices or building a new kind of Jewish educational system were particularly interested in Freud's thoughts on childhood, pedagogy, and related matters. Whereas in France, famously, artists were among the first to take a sustained interest in psychoanalysis, and in the United States, it was psychiatrists (and a few philosophers) who found Freud's ideas worth studying, in Palestine, psychologists, social workers, educators, and youth movement leaders were at the vanguard. Alex Liban and Dodi Goldman have documented the pivotal part played in disseminating psychoanalysis by the educational wing of the Labor Zionist youth organization Hashomer Hatza'ir during the years it was conceptualizing and building the kibbutz movement.[17] The larger society might have had more pressing problems on its plate than rendering Freud into Hebrew, but for these pioneers, psychoanalysis was a crucial resource in the Zionist reinvention of Jewish society, both for kibbutz leaders attempting to raise a generation of children "who knew not Oedipus" and for young Zionist settlers who drew from psychoanalysis "strong justification for both abandoning the religion of their fathers" and seeking "a freer expression of their own sexual lives."[18]

Despite the serious engagement with Freud's works in at least some Zionist circles, organized psychoanalytic training and treatment in Palestine only properly began a few years into the Fifth Aliyah (1929–39), the wave of immigration that took its character from the Central European professionals and intellectuals fleeing Nazism. Among this group was Max Eitingon, a long-standing member of Freud's inner circle who financially supported many psychoanalytic enterprises, professionalized and standardized the training of psychoanalysts, and cofounded (along with Karl Abraham and Ernst Simmel) and directed the Berlin Psychoanalytic Polyclinic and Institute (the first psychoanalytic outpatient clinic and institute), making that city a lively and innovative center of psychoanalytic research and clinical practice. As Rolnik writes, "If Vienna had been, at the end of the nineteenth century, the garden in which psychoanalysis sprouted, Berlin was the nursery where it grew during the 1920s, as the discipline underwent its decisive stage of development."[19] With his personal wealth and international network of professional and family connections, Eitingon had his choice of destinations when he was forced out of his position in August 1933. Rejecting Albert Einstein's warning that "tiny Palestine" was already overcrowded with doctors and Jones's hope that he would bring some order to the "fidgety" psychoanalytic scene in Paris, Eitingon set out for the Holy Land with his wife, where he was soon joined by colleagues from Berlin and beyond.[20]

Palestine was not terra incognita to Eitingon: his father was a prominent businessman who had emigrated from Russia to Leipzig, where he combined philanthropy, Orthodoxy, and Zionism; Max himself spent a few months in Ottoman Palestine in 1910. While Zionism was far from his preoccupations during the years he was building psychoanalysis in Berlin, when forced to look elsewhere, old attachments came into play: his Eastern European religious background, his knowledge of Jewish sources and languages, his attraction to socialism, and the visible presence of Polish and Russian Jews in Zionist society (despite this, Palestinian psychoanalysts of all backgrounds were still referred to as "the Berliners").[21] Of the six psychoanalysts who arrived in 1933 and who met monthly in Jerusalem with Eitingon, four drew from this same cultural well, combining Eastern European roots with Central European training and clinical experience, commonalities that made them no less bitterly divided on a host of professional and personal issues: Moshe Wulff, who succeeded Eitingon as president of the Palestine Psychoanalytic Society after Eitingon's 1943 death, was Odessa-born; Berlin-trained; a member of the Vienna Psychoanalytic Society; cofounder of the Moscow Psychoanalytic Society in 1922; president of the Russian Psychoanalytic Society beginning in 1924; collaborator with (and rival of) Eitingon in Berlin and then in Palestine. Anna Smiliansky, born near Kiev in 1879 and trained in Switzerland, served as Eitingon's assistant in the Berlin Psychoanalytic Institute from its 1920 founding; like Eitingon, Smiliansky had visited Palestine before the First World War, leaving after a year because an eye ailment made her sensitive to the harsh Mediterranean light. Smiliansky was well connected with the Zionist elite; her brother was the iconic "writer farmer" of the First Aliyah Moshe Smilansky. Ilja Schalit was born in Riga, educated in Petrograd, Freiburg, and Zurich, and worked closely with Ernst Simmel and Max Eitingon in Berlin; he himself settled in Haifa, adding that city to Tel Aviv (where Wulff focused on children and youth) and Jerusalem as places where psychoanalytic treatment was on offer. Along with their Eastern European roots and crisscrossing educational and professional paths, these psychoanalysts shared the socialist inclinations that had expressed themselves in the commitment to free or low-cost psychoanalytic treatment at the Berlin Polyclinic, with paying and nonpaying patients to be treated alike. Despite Eitingon's diminished fortune in Mandatory Palestine, his practice there was similarly based (at least in theory) on the premise that no patient who could benefit from treatment would be turned away for lack of funds; the Palestine Psychoanalytic Society also maintained a lunch fund for needy patients, wisely recognizing that "an empty stomach is not conducive to analysis."²²

Of course, not all the German-speaking intellectuals who arrived in the Fifth Aliyah were Zionists, socialists, or of Eastern European birth. Many, including the psychoanalysts among them, simply considered Palestine another stop on an unpredictable refugee itinerary until something better (or at least cooler and not as sandy) turned up. Some who landed there by the luck of the draw became Zionists, while others who arrived as Zionists saw their ardor fade under the Mediterranean glare. The writer Arnold Zweig, a friend of Freud who became a psychoanalyst after leaving Palestine for East Germany, was one such disappointed Zionist, laid low by the pressure to abandon German for Hebrew, a language he felt incapable of mastering. Even Eitingon complained that, in moving to Mandatory Jerusalem, he had surrounded himself with ultra-Orthodox Jews and Arabs, neither population particularly eager for psychoanalysis. Nevertheless, he also seemed to believe that he had arrived at the axis mundi—he "had a world map in his study on which little flags marked the exact position of every Freudian analyst in exile," as if Jerusalem were the nerve center or military headquarters of the global movement.²³

For Eitingon and many among his circle, the Palestine Psychoanalytic Society (founded 1933) and the Palestine Psychoanalytic Institute (founded 1934), organizations risen from the ashes of Berlin psychoanalysis, were living embodiments of the Land of Israel as a place of refuge both for psychoanalysis and for Jews. In Zionist society, it was a source of pride that among its intellectuals was a distinguished member of Freud's inner circle. Formally congratulating Eitingon on his sixtieth birthday in 1941, Henrietta Szold proclaimed that "the in-gathered exiles rejoices [sic] that you have reached your three score years with them in Zion." Szold, founder in 1912 of Hadassah, the Women's Zionist Organization of America, had also moved in 1933 to Palestine, where she became acquainted with Eitingon after consulting with him on a number of projects aimed at alleviating the psychic difficulties of the immigrant population. Szold, herself past eighty in 1941, continued by delicately commenting on Eitingon's advanced age: "We are grateful that you brought your ripe sapiency, nurtured by epoch-making genius, into the land of beginnings and are training us to look abroad as well as within, within as well as abroad."²⁴ The sixty-year-old Jones in London was moved by the thought of himself as among the last of those who had personal contact with the "epoch-making genius"; Szold, in Jerusalem, saw something similar in Eitingon.

The language of diaspora and ingathering was not limited to Zionists in Palestine: Anna Freud, in a 1934 letter to Jones, describes the harried flight of scores of Jewish psychoanalysts from Germany, writing of this as "a new form of diaspora" and helpfully explaining that the term referred to "the spreading of the Jews over the world after the destruction of the temple of Jerusalem."[25] Freud himself alluded to this historical precedent in addressing the Vienna Psychoanalytic Society in March 1938, repeating the reference in a letter later that year to Max Weinreich, director of the YIVO Institute, during a period in which both men were dealing with threats to the institutions they had built. Freud, by this time safely relocated in London, offered Weinreich these historical-religious words of support:

> We, Jews, have always cherished spiritual values. Ideas have held us together and by virtue of them we have survived to this day. One of the most significant events in our history was Rabbi Yohanan ben Zakkai's plea to the conqueror, immediately after the destruction of the Temple, for permission to establish the first academy of Jewish learning in Yavneh.
>
> Once again our people are facing difficult times. They call for a mustering of all of our strength to preserve unharmed our culture and learning.[26]

Freud here takes a Jewish view on the psychoanalytic diaspora, in contrast with Paul's mission to the gentiles that Lacan had implicitly alluded to in his 1955 lecture in Vienna. During this critical period, Freud was immersed in biblical literature and history, and entire critical studies have been built around his ostensible identification with the figure of Moses. But in these repeated declarations, Freud explicitly identified himself not with Moses, who failed to arrive in the Promised Land, but with the rabbinic figure of R. Yohanan, who succeeded in escaping a besieged city and built a rabbinical academy at Yavneh (sometimes written as Jamnia or Jabneh), where his work could be carried forward. Freud also mentions R. Yohanan in his last work, *Moses and Monotheism*, praising him as recognizing the destruction of the Temple as an invitation to "dematerializ[e] . . . God," the spiritual and intellectual advance that for Freud constituted the greatest achievement of the Jewish people: "The nation's political misfortune taught it to value at its true worth the one possession that remained to it—its literature. Immediately after the destruction of the Temple in Jerusalem by Titus, Rabbi Johanan ben Zakkai asked permission to open the first Torah school in Jabneh. From that time on, the Holy Writ and intellectual concern with it were what held the scattered people together."[27] If Freud was familiar with Rabbi Yohanan, he may have also been aware of the Talmudic legend that describes the smuggling of Rabbi Yohanan out of the besieged city in a coffin, which Daniel Boyarin reads as the primal scene of the birth of rabbinic-textual Judaism from the death of Second Temple priestly Judaism.[28] The Pauline narrative of the translation of a Jewish teaching into a universal tongue is the drama that plays out on the public stage, as the general backdrop against which Bettelheim and Lacan view Freud's exile and the dispersion of his thought. But alongside this narrative is a more private Jewish tale that remains hidden in its own coffin, in which an unheroic remnant barely escapes danger, saving the intellectual treasures he can from the mass destruction. If so, historians of psychoanalysis have more than one model by which to understand what happened to psychoanalysis in its global dispersion and development. Alongside the displacement-as-assimilation (as Bettelheim sees it) of Freud's German into Strachey's English, for instance, we might also recognize a different and more intimate drama, in which Freud's *Traumdeutung* was "rescued" in Hebrew form when Mordechai Brachyahu translated it as *Pesher haholomot*, published by a Tel Aviv press called Yavneh.[29]

Psychoanalysis stood at a precipice in these years, with Freud newly gone and those who had known him themselves no longer young and now scattered around the world or at grave risk in Nazi Europe. Psychoanalysis, Szold implied, was by now an old man's game, brought to a land that venerated youth. But that was precisely what constituted its most precious contribution. Young Zionists were rightly focused on the concrete tasks they faced, but those who were past the age of draining swamps and building roads could also contribute to the collective enterprise, using Freud's genius to both enlarge the cultural lens of the Zionist yishuv and turn it "within," adding cosmopolitanism and breadth, as well as interiority and depth, to the rough-edged Zionist culture. At the same time, Zionism brought honor to psychoanalysis, offering an authentic welcome in a world that could not be counted on for such hospitality, rich soil for psychoanalysis to strike deep new roots, and a laboratory to rethink old cultural patterns anew.

Although Szold did not touch on certain sore points, it was not entirely true that the Land of Israel was hospitable to Freud's thought, as evidenced by the protracted failure, after hopes were repeatedly raised and dashed, to establish an academic chair in the study of psychoanalysis at the Hebrew University. Freud was gratified to learn, Peter Gay tells us, that his name (along with those of Einstein and Bergson) was invoked by Lord Balfour, resplendent in his Cambridge robes, as "one of the three men, all Jews, who had had the greatest beneficial influence on modern thought" in his address at the formal opening of the Hebrew University on April 1, 1925.[30] Despite this accolade, the appointment of a professor in psychoanalysis was a controversial undertaking, with many Orthodox professors and others (most famously, Martin Buber) on the faculty opposed on the grounds of Freud's atheism, ostensible lack of scientific rigor, and/or the marginality of psychoanalysis within the field of medicine or psychology (that psychoanalysis was "a Jewish science" was one issue that posed no obstacle). If Freud regularly disappointed those who awaited his arrival in the Holy Land, Freud and his boosters in Palestine were similarly disappointed in their expectation that psychoanalysis would finally find an academic home in the institution on whose board of governors Freud had long served. Nor was the practice of psychoanalysis entirely at home in the Land of Israel or in the Hebrew language. It was true that the Palestine Psychoanalytic Society was invited to work alongside the Hebrew Language Academy on a glossary of psychological and psychoanalytic terms, with Eitingon joining the committee in 1935. Despite the publication of the glossary and a Hebrew psychoanalytic journal, and despite ongoing initiatives to translate Freud's writings into Hebrew, Guido Liebermann tells us that "German remained the official language of the Institute for many years."[31] Both patients and psychoanalysts had to wrestle with "a complex linguistic reality and the inherent difficulties of the Hebrew language."[32] The distance between ideological aspirations and realities on the ground was of course not limited to psychoanalytic circles, as Liora Halperin has shown in her aptly titled *Babel in Zion*. Welcoming immigrant psychoanalysts to Palestine or rendering Freud's works into Hebrew reflected the desire to rescue psychoanalysis or return Freud to his Jewish origins rather than the accomplished mission.

Among his earliest Hebrew translators, the hope that Hebrew might uncover subterranean connections between Freud's discoveries and Jewish sources found expression in a heightened Hebrew style infused with biblical and rabbinic references. As was the translation into a Jewishly infused Yiddish, the motivation for this style was overdetermined, reflecting unconscious and conscious impulses shared with Hebrew translators working on writers other than Freud and with Freud's translators into other languages. Thus, Hebrew translators, along with their English counterparts, reached for a higher stratum of the language than Freud had generally mined in his German style, which leavened professional and "scientific" discussions with idiomatic and even novelistic passages. But where the translators of the *Standard Edition* reached for the "scientific" Latin for which their own educations had prepared them, Hebrew translators reaching higher inevitably bumped up against the biblical and rabbinic Hebrew of their traditional educations. If the effect of these borrowings on the *Standard Edition* was, as Bettelheim saw it, a "flat" scientism, the effect for Freud-in-Hebrew was to infuse psychoanalysis with affectively resonant Judaism, striking deep into the network of childhood associations and paving the way for a recognition or construction of pathways between traditional Jewish culture and Freud's discoveries. The pattern was set by the first three book-length translations of Freud, all of them by Dwossis-Dvir (but released by three different publishers): *Group Psychology and the Analysis of the Ego* in 1928 (the same year Yiddish saw Lerman's rendering); *Introductory Lectures in Psychoanalysis*, in three volumes in 1934–35 (a year or two before Weinreich's unfinished Yiddish version); and *Totem and Taboo* in 1939.[33] Sharing this small shelf of Hebrew translations is Yohanan Tversky's "Resistances to Psychoanalysis," which appeared in the American Hebraist weekly *Hado'ar* in 1926, and Freud's brief response to Einstein's question, "Why War?," which appeared in 1935 in a sixteen-page pamphlet that was reprinted in 1940.[34] Anna Freud, with her focus on childhood, was also of interest in this environment, and a compilation of her work directed to educators was published in 1930.[35] As Rolnik writes, from the 1920s through the 1940s, Hebrew translations of Freud shared a "prophetic biblical style," expressing, consciously or not, "the desire to impart Freud's teachings to Hebrew readers in a prophetic-biblical style, to turn him into a kind of ancient prophet."[36] Freud was not immune to such associations, writing in his 1930 preface to the Hebrew translation of *Introductory Lectures on Psycho-analysis* that the translation had "clothed" his words "in the ancient language which had been awakened to new life by the will of the Jewish people." He continued: "The author can well picture the problem which this has set for its translator. Nor need he suppress his doubt whether Moses and the Prophets would have found these Hebrew lectures intelligible."³⁷ Freud's doubt about whether Moses would understand psychoanalysis in Hebrew garb might seem to mark the distance of his thought from the Jewish tradition until one remembers that the Talmud, in a quite extraordinary passage in Menahot 29b, imagined an equally uncomprehending Moses listening to the teachings not of Freud but of Rabbi Akiva (Moses is comforted when Rabbi Akiva explains to a student that his teachings, as unfamiliar as they may seem, are in fact also "the law of Moses from Sinai").

Despite the casual attitude toward copyright of the period, Hebrew shared with Yiddish the distinction of boasting an "authorized" translator of Freud's work. This implied no association with organized psychoanalysis: Dwossis, like his successor in the field, Zvi Woyslawski, was a Bible scholar and educator rather than a psychoanalyst. While Max Weinreich became Freud's authorized Yiddish translator before he published his first (and only) translation of Freud's work, Yehuda Dwossis seems to have established contact with Freud only after publishing his first Hebrew translation, of *Group Psychology*. The men communicated by phone as well as mail: Rolnik writes that since Dwossis had no telephone at home, "Freud would, at a pre-established time, call a café in Jerusalem's Ein Kerem neighborhood."³⁸ It was Freud who encouraged Dwossis to work on the more accessible and foundational *Introductory Lectures*, swallowing his misgivings about Dwossis's own choice of *Totem and Taboo*, the translation that followed. In 1930, Freud wrote a preface for both the *Introductory Lectures* and another one, which at Dwossis's request was more personal and "warmer," for *Totem and Taboo*; the translations themselves only appeared in 1934–35 and 1939.³⁹ Freud hoped for more from Dwossis; a 1938 letter from London expressed his anticipation that Dwossis, having completed *Totem and Taboo*, would take on the forthcoming *Moses and Monotheism*, which Freud described as a continuation "of the themes of *Totem and Taboo*, applied to the history of the Jewish religion."⁴⁰ Freud was not just hanging his hopes on Dwossis's (narcissistic?) attachment to the book he had just translated; he was clearly counting on what he assumed would be Hebrew readers' interest in "the history of the Jewish religion." In the letter Freud was responding to, Dwossis had informed Freud that his Hebrew translation of *Totem and Taboo*, which was already in press, included—"in the form of footnotes—many citations from biblical and Talmudic literature, which provide material that confirms and corroborates the claims of your book, and occasionally also shed new light on them."⁴¹ Rolnik points out that Dwossis's footnotes contradict Freud's insistence in the preface he had provided in 1930 that the book "adopts no Jewish standpoint"; but Freud was hardly in a position to object to Dwossis's additions, hidden as they were for him in a foreign tongue. It is striking that Dwossis and Freud were working during the same years on parallel projects—in Dwossis's case, writing footnotes that could shed biblical and Jewish light on Freud's book; in Freud's case, on writing a book that applied "the themes of *Totem and Taboo* . . . to the history of the Jewish religion." For a few years in the 1930s, psychoanalytic authorship and its Hebrew translation were not disconnected, successive projects but parallel or even overlapping investigations.

The prophetic-rabbinic style Dwossis shared with other translators was of course not limited to Freud: an allusive style characterized the fiction and poetry, translated as well as original Hebrew writings in this period. Intertextual allusions were hardly avoidable in a language still in the process of vernacularization, whether wielded deliberately and artfully or just awkwardly adopted in the absence of better alternatives. The Hebrew translations of Mandatory Palestine were also shaped by the circumstance, with multiple psychoanalytic and translational ramifications, that translators, psychoanalysts, and their patients were generally nonnative speakers of Hebrew. This is the cultural context in the background of Immanuel Velikovsky's "Kann eine neuerlernte Sprache zur Sprache des Unbewußten werden?" [Can a newly acquired language become the language of the unconscious?], which appeared in 1934 in *Imago*, the journal edited by Freud, Otto Rank, and Hans Sachs and dedicated to the intersection of psychoanalysis and the humanities.

The glossaries that accompany these early translations and the German terms supplied alongside the Hebrew in the body of the text might seem to signal a stable psychoanalytic Hebrew lexicon, but in fact they show that Hebrew lacked such a lexicon. Even after the 1935 publication of the Hebrew Glossary of Psychological and Psychoanalytic Terms, the glossaries included in translations were inconsistent, with the standardized terms ignored and each new translator reinventing the wheel. It was true that satisfying or obvious equivalents for basic terms were arrived at fairly early: *ani* for *Ich*; *stam* for *es*. As they could in Yiddish, Freud's first translators could sometimes rely on coinages that had already appeared in writings about psychoanalysis or other topics; Elon Gilad has shown that Dwossis borrowed both *toda'a* for consciousness/*Bewusstsein* and *tasbikh* for complex/*Komplex* from "Hebrew Speech," a 1912 essay by Isaac Epstein.[42]

But other terms were slower to settle: Freud's *Lust* (translated in the *Standard Edition* as "pleasure") was *hemda* for Dwossis; in a nice stroke, he mobilized the root for his translation of clitoris as *hamdan*. The word did not stick—the 1930s also saw *dagdegan* (tickler), which remains the colloquial term for clitoris.[43] Dwossis himself was inconsistent, translating the word "unconscious" as *bilti-muda* in his first Freud translation and *lo-muda* in his second; Dr. A. Litvak, author of the booklet on psychoanalysis in 1925, had used an entirely different term: *mimata lehakara* (beneath recognition). In 1954, Menahem Aylon used *oneg* for *Lust* in his Hebrew *Three Essays on the Theory of Sexuality*. *Sublimierung* (sublimation) was *idun* for Aylon, but either *ha'atzalah* or *idun* for Mordechai Brachyahu, whose translation of *The Interpretation of Dreams* appeared in 1959. Hebrew translators groped their way toward renderings that might find more than temporary purchase: Woyslawski translated *Fehlleistung* (parapraxis, in Strachey's notorious neologism) as *ma'aseh shegaga* in 1942, Brachyahu as *ma'aseh shegaga keshel* in 1959, and Aryeh Bar as *ma'aseh keshel* in 1968, a translation that gave way in 2015 to Adam Tenenbaum's *keshel bitsu'a*, a translation that finally managed to capture the oxymoronic character of an "unintentional failure" that was also a kind of "achievement." Translational failures, as this daisy chain of renderings demonstrates, can also be steps toward achievement. The very absence of a stable psychoanalytic vocabulary and psychoanalysts or translators who were native Hebrew speakers opened a linguistic void that could reward creative translators and into which older strata of the Hebrew language could easily flow.

The biblical and rabbinic allusiveness of these early translations only in part distinguishes the Hebrew translations of Freud's work from their Yiddish counterparts, since the Hebraic strata of Yiddish could allow Yiddish translators to mobilize Jewish intertextuality to powerful effect. There were many other similarities between the projects of Hebrew and Yiddish translation of Freud: The choice of *Group Psychology* as the first of Freud's work to be translated, in the same year, into Hebrew and Yiddish is a sign that cultural commonalities operated across linguistic, cultural, and geographic borders (that the book is relatively short might also have played a part). Both translation projects participated in a larger cultural enterprise of modernizing and secularizing a language with a religious history (a more ancient one in the case of Hebrew). Both projects mobilized translation to produce a functioning "monolanguage" where diasporic multilingualism had previously held sway. Hebrew and Yiddish translators shared the pride of affiliating themselves with world-famous Jews and demonstrating their broadminded worldliness through attention to psychoanalysis. In both spheres, psychoanalysis found an interested public of Jewish readers fascinated by Freud and drawn to the Jewish dimensions of psychoanalysis, whether as these related to Freud's Jewish background or what was understood to be the "Jewish influence" on his thought. These were cultural contexts in revolutionary ferment, and Freud often took his place alongside Marx in both contexts. In Hebrew as in Yiddish, the twin concerns of collectivity and youth shaped the reception of psychoanalysis. Finally, Hebrew and Yiddish translators alike resisted the deeply rooted parochialism of their inherited Jewish cultures by compelling Hebrew and Yiddish to serve as vehicles for broader (if not universal) scientific and philosophical thought.

But the distinctions between these translation projects are not insignificant. On the one hand, we are faced with the asymmetrical, charged proximity that constitutes the entanglement of German and Yiddish; on the other hand, we have the much greater linguistic distance between German and Hebrew, which despite this mutual distance have more evenly matched claims to the status of language, a status that, in Max Weinreich's frequently quoted aphorism, depends on possession of an army and a navy. Yiddish translators worked in a language closely related to German if differentiated by its script (which it shared with Hebrew) and religio-cultural affiliations. Practically speaking, Yiddish translators constructing a psychoanalytic lexicon, if they were truly at a loss, could just "Yiddishize" Freud's German by transliteration. For instance, Lerman translates the term *Urhurde* (primal horde), so abundant in both *Group Psychology* and *Totem and Taboo*, with the *daytshmerish* (Germanism) *ur-hurde*, for lack of an idiomatic Yiddish term. Dwossis, working in the unrelated language of Hebrew and equally lacking a modern equivalent, could hardly do the same. His solution was the striking and barely translatable phrase *mahaneh-bereshit*. While *mahane* (camp, in its multiple meanings) and *bereshit* (in the beginning) are perfectly ordinary and transparent Hebrew words, their juxtaposition is novel, taking *bereshit* adjectivally to signify primordial and yoking Freud's anthropological (and ostensibly secular) temporal frame to a mythical, biblical primordiality.[44]

While the Bible and its famous beginning play a role in this phrase, Dwossis also mined postbiblical Jewish sources for equivalents to Freud's German. In *Totem and Taboo*, Freud summarizes the archaeologist Salomon Reinach's "twelve articles of Totemism" by calling them "a catechism, as it were, of the totemic religion."[45] Freud's (dated and colonialist) witticism is itself a kind of translation, conflating Catholicism with "Totemism," and the systematic theology of Catholics about their own religion with Reinach's anthropological attempts to systematize totemic religion. Perhaps Freud also planted an extra barb in his joke in casting the radical Jewish secularist Reinach as a Catholic priest. Dwossis follows the logic of Freud's wit here, although he describes Reinach's "twelve articles of Totemism" not as a Catholic "catechism" (however that might be translated into Hebrew) but as the *Shulḥan Arukh* of the totemic religion, a reference to the canonical sixteenth-century Jewish legal code by Jacob Karo.[46] There is a joke here, too, but a different one, building on the alleged incongruity (concealing a telling congruity) not of Catholicism and (anthropological attempts to systematize) Totemism but of secular and religious Jewishness, in which an avowed opponent of religion and particularly of Jewish law such as Salomon Reinach could nevertheless find himself (unconsciously?) following in the path of his rabbinic ancestors in codifying the finicky prohibitions of a religious culture as odd as Judaism.

Dwossis's attempts to clothe Freud in biblical and rabbinic garb are most evident in the copious "translator's footnotes" to *Totem and Taboo* that he described to Freud in the 1938 letter, which only rarely do the standard work of clarifying ambiguities in the text or defining terms potentially unfamiliar to readers. While Dwossis represented these footnotes in his letter as supporting Freud's claims, they often function instead as a tissue of citations from Jewish sources that bear an indirect relation to Freud's text; in these cases, Dwossis leaves it to his readers to draw their own inferences from the resonances and suggestive parallels he notes. One such footnote is appended to Freud's description of the "horror of incest" that governs the relationship between a mother-in-law and son-in-law. The passage already has Freud's own footnote, citing J. G. Frazier's 1910 *Totemism and Exogamy*; to this Dwossis adds a second note asserting that "this point has a few substantiating sources in the writings of the Sages" and adding citations to four Talmudic passages that warn against too much conversation between a mother-in-law and her son-in-law. Two paragraphs later, Freud's mention of "marriage by capture" elicits a biblical reference to Judges 21:19, where the men of the tribe of Benjamin, deprived of wives by other tribes, "seize a wife from among the girls of Shiloh."

Dwossis generally did aim to bolster Freud's arguments, but (although he did not report this to Freud) he occasionally objected to whatever point Freud was making, particularly in areas Dwossis considers his own scholarly turf. Thus, the second chapter of *Totem and Taboo* begins with Freud's assertion that "taboo is a Polynesian word. It is difficult for us to translate, because the concept it connotes is no longer in our possession." Freud continues: "It was still current among the Romans. . . . So, too, the 'αγος' of the Greeks and the '*kadesh*' of the Hebrews must have the same meaning as is expressed in taboo of the Polynesians and many analogous terms in America, Africa (Madagascar) and North and Central Asia."[47] Freud thus begins the chapter by suggesting that translations for taboo are abundant but often misleading, because the once widespread concept has lost its familiarity. Reading Freud's warning on the challenges of translation as warrant for his own intervention, Dwossis suggests in his footnote that the Hebrew word *herem* and its Arabic cognate *haram* are actually "a closer fit for taboo" than *kadesh*.[48]

It is not only ancient Jewish culture that makes an appearance in the margins of Freud's Polynesia. Dwossis appends a particularly lengthy footnote to the seventh article of Reinach's "catechism" of the twelve tenets of Totemism, which asserts that "clans and individuals adopt the names of animals—viz. of the totem animals":[49] The footnote begins with a string of biblical citations that describe the tribes as various animals. "Judah is a lion's whelp," "Issachar is a strong-boned ass," "Dan shall be a serpent by the road," "Naftali is a hind let loose," "Benjamin is a ravenous wolf" (Gen 49:9–27.). To this Dwossis adds a number of other Hebrew names that also mean animals, including Hulda (rat), Aryeh (lion), and Ze'ev (wolf).[50] These notes imply that the Bible should (contra Freud) also be counted among the totemic cultures; but given that the practice of naming Jewish children after animals continues into the present day and, indeed, increased in the Zionist culture that prized Hebrew names over those derived from other languages, it is clear that Jewish Totemism is no "dead religion." We have evidence that Jewish totemists were in fact among the neurotics who sought psychoanalytic treatment in the Holy Land: The one clinical study included in the memorial volume for Eitingon published by the Israel Psychoanalytic Society in 1950 presents the case study of a young man whose "horror of incest" extended beyond his mother, whose name was Haya (life, or wild animal), to any woman who bore an animal name (Tziporah, Devorah, Rachel, Yael, etc.).[51] Unfortunately for the young man, these were (and are) common Jewish names, even if, over the centuries, the animal meanings had become dead metaphors, more or less forgotten in their daily association with the Jewish humans who bore them. By creating a Hebrew-speaking culture that brought to life the meaning of these names, the Hebrew revival also succeeded in reviving the repressed biblical Totemism they carried, awakening the animals asleep for centuries within traditional Jewish naming practices.

Despite the disillusionment with Freud provoked in many of his Hebrew readers by the 1939 publication of *Moses and Monotheism*, Perlman still chose Freud as the second of the writers to be translated in the *Legvulam* series, after Brandes. The work selected was *The Psychopathology of Everyday Life*, and the translator assigned to this work was the prolific scholar and editor Zvi Woyslawski (who later translated Marx, Hermann Cohen, Georg Simmel, and Martin Buber). It was an excellent choice: the volume saw at least five editions between 1942 and 1967 and was not retranslated until 2015—by contrast, Haim Isaac replaced Dwossis's 1939 *Totem and Taboo* with his own rendering in the five-volume *The Writings of Sigmund Freud* (1965–68), by which time Dwossis's translations had fallen out of print. Woyslawski, like Perlman, was an Eastern European Jew who had studied in various yeshivas and had received a doctorate at a Central European university before moving to Palestine; he thus combined German fluency with a deep knowledge of Jewish sources.[52] Rolnik writes that, when the committee awarded Woyslawski the Tchernikhovsky Prize in 1942, they "emphasized that the excellence of his translation of Freud's book lay in its use of the language of the Mishnah and midrash, creating an illusion that 'one of our ancients' wrote the original."[53] Woyslawski's prose is as steeped in traditional Jewish literature as Dwossis's translation, although he does not go so far as to "bolster" Freud's findings with his own biblical and rabbinic examples. Freud's *Vergreifen*, which Brill translates as "erroneously carried-out actions" and Alan Tyson as "bungled" actions, is rendered in Hebrew as *ma'asey shegaga*, which carries the tinge of halakhic discourse— the phrase might be expansively translated into English, along the lines of translations of the Talmud's telegraphic prose, as "[transgressive] acts that are [in the halakhic category of] unintentional." In the chapter by that title, Woyslawski translates Freud's discussion of such an "accident" by an overworked engineer in a laboratory of an institution of higher learning (*im Laboratorium der Hochschule*) as an act that took place in a *ma'abada shel beit hamidrash hagevoha*, the "laboratory" of the "higher house of study."[54] The Hebrew translator's own workshop similarly wavers between (psychoanalytic) laboratory and (rabbinic) study hall; the yeshiva with eight thousand students in Lakewood, New Jersey, is technically called Bais Medrash Govoho (BMG).

As translational parapraxes, *ma'asey shegaga* and *beit midrash* vacillate between "mistake" and "triumph," the binary that Roland Végső views as the constitutive elements of translation. Summarizing Bettelheim's critique of what he considers the wrongheaded translation of *Fehlleistung* as "parapraxis," Végső writes, "What happens in *Fehlleistung* is simultaneously—albeit on different levels of consciousness—a real achievement and a howling mistake—this should indeed convince us that we are now talking about translation."[55] Despite or because of its opacity and singularity, "parapraxis" thus is not only an excellent translation of *Fehlleistung* but also a powerful term for translation, first because "parapraxis" recognizes translation as "a form of praxis":

> Second, however, the prefix indicates that this praxis is not quite praxis: it is located "beside" praxis. As a dislocated form of praxis, it happens to be "beside itself," a praxis without a unified identity. Third, this inherent lack of identity does not mean that it never has any identity whatsoever. Rather, the point is that translation is a form of doing that is best understood as the practical interruption of a praxis by the unpredictable emergence of an unconscious truth.[56]

If all translations are in some sense parapraxes, that certainly holds true for the Hebrew translation of *The Psychopathology of Everyday Life*, a mixture of mistake and achievement, a text "beside" and "outside" itself, displaced from its original location by the unconscious truths that propel and deform it. This double operation might be traced in the section of *The Psychopathology* devoted to the breaking of such objects as vases, statuettes, inkstands, and household china, which presents the everyday realia of life in their intended uses (praxis) and in their propensity to mishap (parapraxis). The parapraxes described by and embodied in the translation shed light on the unconscious forces that render household objects liable to breakage: a superstitious attempt to assert control over life's vicissitudes; a desire to fix a mishandled friendship; the tensions between employer and employee that complicate care of the household; the family rivalries that trouble even the most serene of bourgeois Viennese households, including Freud's own—rather overstuffed, he acknowledges, with fragile objects. The Hebrew translation, taking shape beside the German, is susceptible to the failures to grasp something correctly, a failure that occasionally generates its own powerful achievement. Thus, when Freud knocks over "a handsome glazed Egyptian figurine [*ägyptisches Figürchen*]" as unconscious penance for psychoanalyzing a friend without being asked to, Woyslawski's rendering allows us to hear the biblical resonances of the penance (*teshuva*), the "little sculpture" (*psalsal*), and the propitiatory sacrifice (*korban minha*).[57]

In the Hebrew, Freud's overdetermined act of breakage becomes even more overdetermined than in German, since Freud, like a few of his famous ancestors the Hebrew cannot help bring to mind, is both sacrificing a personal possession and smashing an idol (*pesel*). So, too, does the "minor epidemic of broken glass and ceramic ware" (*onat-shevirah shel klei zkhukhit veharsina*) that overtakes the Freud household during the engagement of his oldest daughter echo (at least in Hebrew) the divine accident and cosmic catastrophe of *shevirat hakelim* (the breaking of the vessels) that figures so fatefully in the Lurianic Kabbalistic narration of Creation and that appears, many centuries later, as the mystical background of the translator's task of repairing "fragments of a vessel which are to be glued together," in Walter Benjamin's "The Task of the Translator."[58]

Freud brings antiquities into his home for the secular purpose of anthropological display; his Hebrew translators, too, mine the ancient ruins of the Hebrew language in search of the words they need to render Freud's supremely modern thought. But in Freud's household and its Hebrew translation these words and objects do not always stay put, as if their unmooring from ancient religious contexts to Freud's chambers had unleashed ancient powers. Gershom Scholem believed something similar about the Hebrew revival, for all its ostensible secularism.[59] In Galili Shachar's paraphrase, "The Zionist attempt to transform Hebrew, the language that carries God's words, into a spoken and useful language, is . . . bound up, Scholem argues, with the forgetfulness of the abyss, the deep, hidden, unrepresentable element of language." Through "a false, profane articulation of holy names and in the danger of their return from the silent, forgotten layers of the language, lies the *Unheimlichkeit* of the New Hebrew, its unfamiliarity, its homelessness, its terrible faith."[60] If Hebrew is a repository of irrational, religious, and apocalyptic energies, translating Freud's work about unreason, primeval history, and ancient religions into that tongue created multiple opportunities to raise the ghosts buried in both Freud's German and the Hebrew of his translators.

As Rolnik demonstrates, Freud's Hebrew translators often intentionally or inadvertently imposed a Jewish religious flavor on Freud's German prose, which on the surface is more taken up with sexual, familial, and "universal" concerns. But it is not always possible to say what translators impose and what they discover; nor are the sexual and the Jewish so easily disentangled. The passage in *The Psychopathology* that describes "a minor epidemic of broken glass and ceramic ware" provides an example of such overdetermination—when Freud describes the epidemic as "easily explained," it is a sure sign that we are in deep waters. Here is the passage in German and two English translations:

> Vor kurzem gab es in meinem Hause eine Zeit, in der ungewöhnlich viel Glas und Porzellangeschirr zerbrochen wurde; ich selbst trug mehreres zum Schaden bei. Allein die kleine psychische Endemie war leicht aufzuklären; es waren die Tage vor der Vermählung meiner ältesten Tochter. Bei solchen Feiern pflegte man sonst mit Absicht ein Gerät zu zerbrechen und ein glückbringendes Wort dazu zu sagen. Diese Sitte mag die Bedeutung eines Opfers und noch anderen symbolischen Sinn haben.[61]

Brill's translation:

> Recently, we passed through a period in my house, during which an unusual number of glass and china dishes were broken. I myself largely contributed to the damage. This little endemic was readily explained by the fact that it preceded the public betrothal of my eldest daughter. At such festivities, it is customary to break some dishes and utter at the same time some felicitating expression. This custom may signify a sacrifice or express any other symbolic sense.[62]

And Alan Tyson's for the *Standard Edition*:

> Recently we passed through a period in my house during which an unusually large amount of glass and china crockery was broken; I myself was responsible for some of the damage. But the little psychical epidemic could easily be explained: these were the days before my eldest daughter's wedding. On such festive occasions it used to be the custom deliberately to break some utensil and at the same time utter a phrase to bring good luck. This custom may have the significance of a sacrifice and it may have another symbolic meaning as well.[63]

The sexual symbolism of the broken crockery needs no commentary, since the previous section was devoted to the vase and similar receptacles as "an unmistakable symbol of a woman." Freud has also just described how breaking a cherished object might serve as penance or a "propitiatory sacrifice to avert evil." Marriages, after all, are not entirely joyful events (and certainly not for the father "losing" his daughter), just as mourning—in Freud's reading—involves more than pure grief. These discussions take us a long way toward understanding the "sacrifice" of symbolic vessels at traditional betrothal and wedding ceremonies, sacrifices that might be carried out even in the absence of a traditional framework, as seems to have been the case in the Freud household. Although Freud does not comment on it, the "accidental," post-traditional repetition of a deliberate folk custom surely adds another layer of significance to the action: Freud may be mourning losing (his grip on) his daughter, along with parents at a similar fateful moment in many traditional societies, but his unconscious reenactment of a traditional ceremony further suggests that he is also mourning the religious framework that would have lent meaning to the moment, ritualizing and sublimating what otherwise is just a pile of broken dishes. To add to the complexity of this reenactment of engagement rituals, it is not entirely clear what ceremonies he is reenacting, given that similar rituals accompany Jewish and German-Christian betrothals and marriages (and no doubt those in many other cultures, too). Is Brill right that we are talking about a "public betrothal" (whatever that might be), or is Tyson correct in reading *Vermählung* as "wedding"? Is Freud unconsciously and incestuously taking the Jewish role of the bridegroom who stomps a glass under the wedding canopy? Or is he, less scandalously, breaking a plate the way the parents (or, more usually, the mothers) of the bride and groom do at a Jewish betrothal ritual? Or perhaps he is playing the role of a guest at a *Polterabend*, in which guests break plates and other ceramic vessels outside the house of the bride on the night before the wedding; the *Polterabend* was customary at both Jewish and non-Jewish weddings in Germany, though I have not managed to discover whether or not Freud's own September 14, 1886, wedding to Martha Bernays included such riotous festivities.[64]

It may be relevant to understanding the epidemic of broken china that, as the biographers report, Freud counseled his daughter about her insecurities around the time of her engagement, playing the role of healer, but he had no part in her choice of a mate.[65] Mathilde Freud met Robert Hollitscher, a banker, entirely on her own, while on holiday. Peter Gay writes that "Freud, then in the first glow of his friendship with Sándor Ferenczi, told Ferenczi that he would have preferred him as a son-in-law, but he never begrudged his daughter her choice. Hollitscher quickly became 'Robert,' a member of the Freud clan in good standing."⁶⁶ Freud behaved himself, but the feelings were perhaps stronger than Gay suggests. The father of the bride wrote to Ferenczi the very day of his daughter's 1909 wedding to say, "I can now admit to you that in the summer I would have liked to have seen you in the place of the young man who, having since endeared himself to me, has now gone away with my daughter."⁶⁷ Freud here appears in the guise of a traditional rabbi or head of yeshiva, sizing up (or falling in love with) his unmarried students for their son-in-law potential, just as Rabbi Abraham, father-in-law of the Besht (the Ba'al Shem Tov, founder of Hasidism) "became attracted to the Besht's soul and their souls were in one accord."⁶⁸ In breaking a plate, Freud (impotently) asserts his participation in a marriage that was contracted without his input. Stymied from integrating psychoanalytic disciples into "the Freud clan," Freud nevertheless paid homage to the traditional role by acting it out, to no effect on Mathilde but wreaking havoc on her stand-ins in the kitchen cabinets.⁶⁹

This constellation of events, blunders, history, and affect (which did not end there, since Freud was intimately involved with Ferenczi's romantic life for decades to come) draws not only from sexual anxieties and deep religious impulses but also from the post-traditional condition. It is only the narrowest—and most Oedipal—reading of the family romance that fails to recognize the erotic energies and frustrations that might spill over from the love story at central stage, encompassing not only the bride's father (and displaced lover) but also the desired-by-the-father, rejected-by-the-daughter son-in-law. The "nuclearization" sociologists identify as central to the modern restructuring of the family entails not only a reduction (and Oedipal intensification) of traditional extended family but potentially also its disavowal, the expulsion of the parents and particularly father-in-law from the scene of the marriage arrangements, and the repression of the homosexual ties between a charismatic master and the appealing young man he hopes to bind himself to through marriage.⁷⁰

Translators of this passage are called on not simply to render Freud's ostensibly transparent German but also to parse, if they do not simply repeat, the twin motions of amnesia and (cultural) recovery, explaining what it is Freud is describing in this passage even as he himself does not quite know or say. Despite the shards on the kitchen floor, these gestures of recovery and reconstruction resemble ethnography more than archaeology, the reconstruction of lost customs from fragments of language and memory. For what is Freud's body exactly saying, and what is his German describing? Does Freud's *glückbringendes Wort* refer to the "mazel tov" that accompanies the ritual plate and glass breaking of Jewish betrothals and weddings—and which is also, more humorously, shouted (perhaps even in the Freud household) when plates are broken by accident? Or does Freud have in mind the adage associated with *Polterabend*, that *Scherben bringen Glück* (shards bring luck)? Brill was perhaps hedging his bets or conceding confusion in translating the phrase, vaguely, as "some felicitating expression." Nor could Hebrew bring back this custom in its full transparency and presence: Woyslawski writes, "Bram, mahalah kalah umekomit zo mistaberet benakel; hayu elah yamim shekadmu le'erusei biti habekhirah. Besimhot elah nohagim bederekh klal lenafetz kli ulevarekh al hashverim." (However, this minor, local illness is easily explained; those were the days preceding my eldest daughter's betrothal. At these celebrations it is generally customary to shatter a vessel and to bless the shards.) As charming as it is to hear these customs described in the habitual present tense, and to hear Mathilde's *Vermählung* rabbinically rendered (and in line with Brill, who may have been consulted) as *erusin*, the odd locution about "bless[ing] the shards" suggests that Woyslawski, too, is having a hard time pinning down "these celebrations" that Freud sees as the obvious motivation for his breakage.

Rey Chow has written about this particular intersection between ethnography, modernity, and translation, reading a description of a traditional funeral in Ba Jin's classic novel *Jia* (Family, 1931) as an ambivalent form of cultural translation: The funeral, "like the depiction of other family rituals, practices and superstitions throughout the novel," is presented as "an exotic ethnographic find, whereupon an indigenous custom receives the spotlight not for the significance it carries in its conventional context, but rather for a displaced kind of effect—as an absurd drama seen with fresh—that is, foreignized—eyes."[71] The narrator of *Jia*, doing the work of mediating between a traditional practice and modern readers, "transcribes it into another code, another language and literacy, against which the original scene becomes newly legible precisely by being disparaged and devalued."[72] The depiction of a funeral, translating between indigenous customs and modern sensibilities, swings between mourning and mockery; Freud and his translators, depicting a wedding, similarly move between traditional customs and modern sensibilities, humor (but not mockery), and suppressed mourning. The inability of Freud's translators to settle on whether this ritual is still observed (Brill: "it is customary to break some dishes"; Woyslawski: "nohagim bederekh klal le-nafetz") or a feature of the past (Tyson: "it used to be the custom") repeats Freud's own blurring of the boundaries between present and past, ritualized custom that is abandoned and then returns as unconscious slip. When mourning shades into melancholy, the beloved deceased cannot be fully mourned, since the grief is stifled by disavowed hatred and ambivalence. Freud's secular melancholy has a nearly opposite structure. What has been disavowed—religion, folk traditions, the role of the father in traditional marital arrangements—cannot be truly laid aside, given the love (erotic and Jewish both) that persists after the burial and renunciation.[73] Benjamin views the task of the translator as gluing together the "fragments of a vessel" that has broken.[74] Barbara Johnson comments that the "loving gesture that translation is said to be is one that does not seek to repair what is broken." Rather, translation sometimes "heightens the fragmentation, its rough edges."[75] If these translators cannot heal the breach, it is because they, too, are inheritors of the same broken traditions that slip through Freud's hands.

The ingathering of Freud in Hebrew translation was not a one-time event, signed, sealed, and delivered when psychoanalysis found an institutional home in the Land of Israel. Evidence that Freud's homecoming to Israel was not a settled matter is how often and insistently he was described as coming home, how often he needed to be brought home again to a place where he was evidently still not at home, a place he glimpsed but, like Moses, never entered. A 1976 report by the Jewish Telegraphic Agency on the establishment of a Sigmund Freud Chair at the Hebrew University began with a declaration by Dr. Charles Ansell from Encino, California, who had been involved with creating the chair: "The Hebrew University will now stand as the center of Freud's thinking. In some mystical sense, Sigmund Freud has come home at last."[76] In August 1977, when the Congress of the International Psychoanalytic Association convened for its Thirtieth Congress in Jerusalem, the first time it met outside the European continent, the president of the Israel Society, Rafael Moses, greeted the guests assembled at the Binyanei Hauma Convention Center (including Mayor Teddy Kollek) with a related thought about the appropriateness of the venue: "Jerusalem has been viewed as the navel of the world, the birthplace of ideas and of religions." By suggesting that Jerusalem had spawned not only (as everyone knew) religions but also ideas, Moses reminded his fellow psychoanalysts of Freud's praise of the *Geistigkeit* within monotheism, the sublime idea behind the apparently primitive religion. Psychoanalysis itself was apparently among the "ideas and . . . religions" born in Jerusalem, either because of the ongoing psychoanalytic research there or the more symbolic notion of Jerusalem as the ancestral birthplace (and ultimate destination) of every Jew, Freud included. The choice of Jerusalem for the Congress "was not entirely fortuitous. Freud had an emotional relationship to Jerusalem."[77] To his credit, Moses was forthright in also acknowledging the ambivalence of Freud's emotional relationship with the city and its university:

> Throughout his life, Freud identified himself unequivocally with the Jewish people and their fate. In 1932, Freud proposed to Judah Magnes, Rector of the Hebrew University, that the first Chair of Psychoanalysis in the world be established at "our university." When this suggestion was not accepted and an academic psychologist was appointed instead, the Hebrew University became, for Freud, "your university." What was being omitted then is being rectified now, 45 years later. The Hebrew University is establishing now the first regular academic chair in psychoanalysis, with tenure, to be set up anywhere. The breach between Freud and the Hebrew University has been healed.[78]

The four-day Congress (August 22–25) was well attended despite worries that participants would stay away because of the heat, political tensions, high cost of travel, and the question of whether "by meeting in the Jewish State, would psychoanalysis compromise its neutrality? Bluntly, would it seem to be siding with the Israelis over the Arabs?"[79] The organizers were proud to report a robust attendance of over fifteen hundred, equaling that of the London Congress two years earlier (at the time, the International Psychoanalytic Association had around four thousand members; it now has triple that number); Hebrew newspapers noted that participants came from Europe, the United States, South America, Mexico, India, South Africa, Japan, and elsewhere.[80] The theme, appropriately enough, was "Affect." Among the presentations of interest to local observers was a special session on the intergenerational effects of Holocaust trauma, with a paper by Martin Bergmann, the New York–based son of Hugo Bergmann, the philosopher and founding director of the Jewish National Library.[81] Along with the papers and plenaries, a full musical program contributed to the high emotions. We are fortunate to have a detailed description by the New England–based psychoanalyst and professor Paul Schwaber: The Congress opened at 9 a.m. on Monday, August 22, with a concert of Haydn music; the psychoanalysts dined to the accompaniment of "mellifluously sad *shtetl* music"; and—most memorably—dinner was followed one evening by folk dancing to "the rhythms of many nations," culminating in the delegates "linking arms for a hora. Hundreds and hundreds of psychoanalysts dancing a hora—it was not something one sees every day, or even dreams about."[82] Schwaber delicately alludes here not only to the famous psychoanalytic association with dreams but also to the equally well-known conceptualization of the State of Israel as a realization of the Zionist dream—in Herzl's words, "If you will it, it is no dream." The Congress itself, for Schwaber and no doubt many others, was just such a realization, making clear "the actuality of psychoanalysis and of the State of Israel." The actual meeting of the two dreamers came at some delay. Although Herzl and Freud lived across the street from each other in Vienna, the men never met, despite Freud's sending Herzl a copy of the *Traumdeutung*, apparently in hope of a review. Holding the Congress in Jerusalem provided "a sense of progeny finding one another though their ancestors could not." Psychoanalysis had suffered from its association with a Jewish founder and his Jewish patients, colleagues, and followers; but, as Herzl had intended, the founding of a Jewish state was something of a solution to "the fear-driven cycle of anti-Semitism" that put so many obstacles in the path of psychoanalysis in its European home.[83]

A culminating moment in what Schwaber called the "long-delayed meeting of the children of Herzl and the children of Freud" was Anna Freud's Inaugural Lecture for the newly established Sigmund Freud Chair of Psychoanalysis at the Hebrew University, to be held by Rafael Moses.[84] Anna Freud was too ill to attend, and her lecture was read by Arthur Valenstein at the amphitheater of Mount Scopus at the site of the old Hebrew University.[85] Roy McLeod points out that the amphitheater, where Balfour had delivered his 1925 address on the opening of the university, was "a deeply symbolic location . . . enclosed by groves of rustling trees that looked east across the Jordan towards the hills of Gilead and Moreh, and towards the place where, according to tradition, the children of Israel had first entered the promised land."[86] Despite Anna Freud's absence, Schwaber comments, "she proved the most memorable participant, the one most finely tuned to significant change."[87] The lecture was memorable for referring directly to the troubled relationship psychoanalysis had historically had "with various academic institutions":

> It has also, repeatedly, experienced rejection by them, been criticized for its methods being imprecise, its findings not open to proof by experiment, for being unscientific, even for being "a Jewish science." However the other derogatory comments may be evaluated, it is, I believe, the last-mentioned connotation that can serve as a title of honour.[88]

Schwaber describes the powerful effect of these words: "People hesitated, turned, wondered: A Jewish science!" These words "faced down the old issues, unexpectedly transvaluing values. The very quality of unencumbered statement suggests that the tension had not been resolved but dealt with differently. Nonetheless, with proximate distance, she bespoke a changed attitude. An historical moment."[89] Along with dealing differently with the persistent question of the Jewishness of psychoanalysis, in Schwaber's view the Congress also seemed to be providing new psychoanalytic perspectives on religion, if the psychoanalysts touring Jerusalem's sacred sites were any indication. "What might I infer," Schwaber asks, "about those analysts, still sporting their 'IPAC 1977' badges, walking slowly among the bustle of praying groups? What of the young delegate with his eyes closed, swaying among the Hasidim?"[90]

Schwaber's unresolved questions also involved the intersection of psychoanalysis and Zionism. What did it mean for psychoanalysis to find itself in this particular outpost, with Israel's "social and political inequities, still no peace and major disagreements about what to yield to get it and economic scandals?"[91] Along with the other upheavals Schwaber alludes to we might count the emergence in 1971 of the Black Panther protests against discrimination against Mizrahi Jews and the calamitous Yom Kippur War. August 1977 was a mere three months after the cultural earthquake that was the May 17 election, which brought to power, for the first time in the thirty-year history of Israel, a right-wing government, Menachem Begin's Likkud. Schwaber felt himself to be witnessing the extinction of old fantasies about Israel as a democratic utopia, a refuge for the Jews, or "a land without a people for a people without a land." As he wrote, "Even in the Promised Land—that was the bitterest lesson—they were still as if in the Diaspora, needing support from the Exile communities."[92] Shelley Orgell, reporting on the Symposium on Training held before the Congress, expressed a similar thought, writing that "a Pre-Congress marked by much sharing of personal information" encouraged her to speak openly about what it meant to her to participate in such a meeting in Jerusalem:

> I want to suggest that, for me, there *is* a real consonance between *one* meaning of Israel and what is essential in our work and our view of man. Both aim to cure sickness. But both recognize that the cure is slow and uncertain, and that dark places in the human mind, buried in long-forgotten and repressed pasts, need to be brought into the light of confrontation and self-acknowledgement, and that wounds which seem to heal too quickly on the surface may fester interminably underneath, that one must suffer, and create structures for this humane purpose, to keep memories alive in order to approach the peace of true reconciliation with the human history we all have in common. In this sense, the meanings of psychoanalysis and a Pre-Congress on Psychoanalytic Training are intertwined with the meanings of this city and State.[93]

For intellectuals of an earlier era, Freud belonged in the Holy Land because it was his homeland, as it was every Jew's. So, too, were the missions of psychoanalysis and Zionism parallel—to cure sickness, that is, the sickness of the diaspora Jew. Orgell adds another element to this story, a "but" that follows this aim, expressing the difficulty of achieving these goals because of unresolved memories and trauma. Although Orgell does not say so explicitly, she seems to be talking about Holocaust trauma, an important topic of scholarly discussion at the Congress. The Palestinians are only implied in this report, indirectly through Orgell's hope for peace and reconciliation. This, too, is (and now appears to us as) a form of repression.

The reunion between Freud, in the person of his daughter, with the children of Herzl, the Holy Land, and the institution that had initially denied him a home was thus belated, incomplete, and still unsettled on both sides. This may have been inevitable: not Freud but his daughter, and not her physical presence (as "return") but a lecture read in English by yet another diaspora Jew, to a land that itself was now dependent on the support of the Jewish diaspora. The "title of honour"—that psychoanalysis, after all, was a "Jewish science"—could finally be avowed, but what it was that was being asserted by this phrase, after these generational and geographic displacements, and now that psychoanalysis had found a place in so many national contexts, was no longer clear, if it had ever been.

In a 2002 lecture at the Freud Museum in London later published as

Freud and the Non-European, Edward Said suggested that something of what Schwaber was beginning to feel in Jerusalem that August could already be discerned in *Moses and Monotheism*, which he reads as Freud's attempt to undermine any doctrinal attempt to put Jewish identity on a solid foundation, whether religious or secular. Contrasting Freud's openness to the non-Jewish other with Israeli governmental policies, Said argues:

> Quite differently from the spirit of Freud's deliberately provocative reminders that Judaism's founder was a non-Jew, and that Judaism begins in the realm of Egyptian, non-Jewish monotheism, Israeli legislation countervenes, represses and even cancels Freud's carefully maintained opening out of Jewish identity toward its non-Jewish background. The complex layers of the past . . . have been eliminated by Israel.[94]

Said recalls that, in a 1930 letter to the Jewish Agency, Freud condemned, with what Said sees as remarkable prescience, the transformation "of a piece of Herodian wall into a national relic, thus offending the feelings of the natives."[95] For Jacqueline Rose, Said's respondent at the lecture, what Said was pointing out was that Israel's suppression of Palestinians also signified that "Israel *represses* Freud" and perhaps nowhere more so than at the "piece of Herodian wall" that so appealed to the psychoanalysts with their IPAC badges.[96] This book has focused largely on the affective ties by which translators, scholars, and readers forged a particularly Jewish connection with Freud, against a more general backdrop of universalizing European thought. In his lecture at the Freud Museum, the Palestinian-Egyptian Said made it clear that those were not the only options.

Along with the major difference between a translation project aligned with the ideology of a nation-state and one that embraced the possibilities of diaspora, another distinction of the Hebrew as opposed to Yiddish writings on Freud is that Yiddish psychoanalysis all but ceased after 1939 (with the exception of a brief afterlife in Argentina), while in 1939 Hebrew translation was just getting off the ground. In 1966, the Dvir Press launched its five-volume *Kitvei Sigmund Freud* (*The Writings of Sigmund Freud*), the first (and still only) attempt at such a collection; the series was introduced as bringing Freud's important thought, which had become "flesh of the flesh" of world culture, to those "dissatisfied with superficial, third-hand summaries of his thought. Henceforth, the Hebrew reader might drink directly from the well."⁹⁷ For Zvi Zohar, reviewing the collection with the release of its second volume, the sentimental and quasi-biblical language of the introduction was yet another sign of what was still wrong with Hebrew translations of Freud. Despite the laudable attempt at providing Freud's collected writings in a single edition with a single "scientific" editor (Haim Ormian, a psychologist who had served on the committee of the Hebrew Language Academy that produced the glossary of psychological and psychoanalytical terms), the collection was unprofessional and haphazard. It began with Haim Isaac's rendering of Freud's *Introductory Lectures on Psychoanalysis* (which it mistranslated as *Introduction to Psychoanalysis*, as Weinreich had also done); as logical as such a beginning might seem, Zohar pointed out that Freud's lectures were very partial in what they introduced. The second volume, translated by Aryeh Bar, comprised short essays that were thematically related but, as Zohar pointed out and indeed was clear enough to see, were not chronologically arranged.⁹⁸ More generally, the collection lacked an editorial board or statement of principles, provided only the briefest of introductions, and made no discernible effort to cover Freud's major writings or otherwise account for the development of his thought. Stylistically, the translators were both infected with a linguistic "purism" that led them to seek indigenous Hebrew terms for Freud's German concepts; as Zohar wrote, it was "sheer luck that the term *psychoanalysis* escaped unscathed from such treatment, which might have turned it into *nitu'ah nefesh* [investigation of the soul], or something similarly 'purist.'"⁹⁹

While the style of the Dvir edition hearkened back to earlier trends, Zohar's review stands as evidence that the tide was turning. In the decades since, Freud saw not only retranslations away from the style Zohar excoriated but also re-retranslations. Emanuel Berman, editor of the influential Psychoanalysis translation series at the Am Oved Press that launched in 1993, explains that "Hebrew is a language that develops fast and therefore also ages quickly; translations from 40 years ago (of fiction and poetry too) sound dated." Berman also recognized that psychoanalysis, as at its Palestinian outset, was facing an era of renewed interest in Freud's work beyond the "closed circle of analysts." Berman writes:

> When I started approaching publishers about it, I faced skepticism: This will not sell. But they were wrong. The Psychoanalysis Series published by Am Oved Publishers in Tel Aviv since 1993—with the support of the Israel Psychoanalytic Society—sells very well, and several of our

books became bestsellers. We translated Freud, Ferenczi, Winnicott, Balint, Hanna Segal, Manonni, Kohut, and Ogden. Our consistent success with over a dozen books (mostly classics, a couple of creative original books) prompted additional publishers to join the field. Now, for the first time, I can teach an introductory course on the history of psychoanalysis using only Hebrew texts, which increases the chance that beginning students will fully comprehend the readings. . . . I make every effort to make our Hebrew texts crisp and lively, to avoid any stale formulations, any expressions that an average psychologist will not use, or could misunderstand.[100]

More recently, the Libido series at Resling Press has taken center stage, along with *Ma'arag*, a prestigious Israeli journal devoted to psychoanalysis that began publishing in 2010. Unlike Perlman's *Legvulam*, which paired Freud with other "straying [Jewish] sons," the Am Oved series places Freud in the context of other psychoanalytic and post-Freudian thinkers; Resling's Libido series (which is divided into the categories Translation, Film, Sociology/Anthropology, Theology, and History) places Freud alongside Arendt, Barthes, Bourdieu, de Beauvoir, Derrida, Foucault, Jung, Lacan, Levinas, Said, and Žižek. Writings by Jews of course appear on this list, with Levinas, Jacqueline Rose, Rosenzweig, and Steven Nadler (on Spinoza) rubbing shoulders with Giorgio Agamben, Camille Paglia, Victor Turner, Abd al-Rahman al-Kawakibi (on "Mecca as the Mother of Cities"), and Susan Buck-Morss (on "Islamism and the Left"). As did Adam Phillips's Penguin series (and indeed also as in the second volume of Dvir Press's *Writings of Sigmund Freud*), translators and editors generally organize Freud's shorter writings thematically rather than chronologically or according to his own book titles, with collections of his writings on *Culture, Religion, and Judaism* or *Inhibition, Symptom, and Anxiety*. As evidence of how far we have traveled from the series *Legevulam* (To their borders), Resling Press takes its name from Barthes's famous essay "The World of Wrestling."

If earlier generations had imagined that psychoanalysis had come home in Hebrew translation, Berman, editor in chief of the Am Oved Freud translation series, writes that his homecoming involved going back to Poland in the years he was participating in the post-Soviet reconstruction of Polish psychoanalysis:

> This period reconnected me with the Polish language, my mother tongue, which, until then, was frozen for me at a 4-year-old level. I

came to learn the words for transference, drives, object relations, and so on. Initially, I read my papers in English, but gradually I managed to read them in Polish (after correcting and editing translations made by Polish colleagues) and even answer questions in my imperfect but understandable Polish. Although my work has been translated by now into French and German, Italian and Hungarian, Spanish and Turkish, nothing compares to my excitement when my papers appear in a Warsaw psychoanalytic journal. Whereas my Israeli identity is quite strong, this definitely feels like a homecoming.[101]

So we have come full circle to yet another point of origin, "the Polish lands" from which Freud's descendant Berman, like Freud's ancestors, first set out.

In this cultural context, the questions of which country is the homeland and which language is the mother tongue have been released from the heavy ideological overlay of an earlier generation that was surer of the answers to these questions. Translators now bring to Freud's work a contemporary Hebrew with little remaining of the high prophetic tones beloved by Dwossis and Woyslawski or the "purism" of Isaac. Translators sometimes actively seek to distance themselves from the effects their predecessors prized in pursuit of a post-Zionist Hebrew Freud. The gifted and prolific translator Ruth Ginsburg (*Interpretation of Dreams* [2007], *Moses and Monotheism* [2009], *The Uncanny* [2012], *Totem and Taboo* [2013], *Beyond the Pleasure Principle* [2021]) describes Moshe Ater's 1978 *Moses and Monotheism* as "saturated in all the Hebrew language strata—biblical, rabbinic, medieval, and modern."[102] Mobilizing these historical strata allowed Ater to map Freud's ideas onto Jewish sources and Jewish experience, for instance, translating Freud's term "catastrophe" as *shoah*, as in the phrase "these Moses-people that escaped the *shoah* that hit him and the religion he established."[103] The allusive style and "sublime" register, Ginsburg recognizes, is "part and parcel of his nationalist ideology" (Ater was associated with right-wing parties that supported the ideology of a Jewish right to "Greater Israel"), mobilizing allusions to Jewish sources to make the case, advanced in Ater's epilogue, that Freud's thesis was "in complete agreement with Jewish tradition." In much the same way that Adam Phillips tried to wrench Freud away from the scientific Latin of the *Standard Edition*, Ginsburg and her peers seek to discover a Freud not yet hijacked by his Jewish admirers, who himself—Ginsburg reminds us—read the Bible in German translation.

Ginsburg's *Moses and Monotheism* "did not involve only translating Freud's 'catastrophe' as 'disaster' (*ason*) instead of 'shoah'":

> Nor was it limited to my reverting to the word *monotheism* in the title, instead of adopting Ater's *emunath hayi'hud*, which is resonant with the Hebrew Bible, prayer book, hymn, commentary, and kabbalah references that immediately embed the text in Jewish religion as historically conceived. I was looking for linguistic elements, tricks even, that would estrange Hebrew and make it different, "Egyptian"—at least somewhat.[104]

If Freud is brought home in these Hebrew translations, it is to a home prior to and different from the "borders" into which Perlman placed him. As with Edward Said's "Egyptian" Freud, we are in the presence, even in "the Holy Land," of a stranger Freud than the one earlier Hebrew translators had glimpsed in the shining Jewish mirror of their prose. Said calls attention to the workings of Israeli archaeology to establish Jewish claims to the land, in which "the Bible is materially realized" and "history is given flesh and bones." Said continues,

> Such claims, of course, uncannily return us not only just to the archival site of Jewish identity as explored by Freud, but to its officially (we should also not fail to add; its forcibly) sanctioned geographical locale, modern Israel. What we discover is an extraordinary and revisionist attempt to substitute a new positive structure of Jewish history for Freud's insistently more complex and discontinuous late-style efforts to examine the same thing, albeit in an entirely diasporic spirit and with different, decentering results.[105]

By contrast to the monumentalizing of Jewish history in Israeli archaeology, Said suggests attention to the "enormously rich sedimentations of village history and oral traditions . . . remainders of an ongoing native life and living Palestinian practices of a sustainable human ecology.[106] The surface, that is, also has something to say.

Chapter 2 traced Freud's archaeological model of the multilingual psyche, which was modeled on the Rosetta Stone found in Egypt, and discussed his repeated mentions of hieroglyphics, which I argued might stand in for the Jewish multilingual monument buried in the early history of psychoanalysis, the hysteric, German-Yiddish translator, and feminist Bertha Pappenheim. But perhaps it is time again to take Freud at his Egyptian word, or let the "oral traditions" of the villagers in the vicinity of the ruins speak. Hebrew translation of Freud began with his ingathering, but in Ruth Ginsburg's *Moses and Monotheism*, even Hebrew has come to discern in Moses's words the echo of an Egyptian tongue. Hebrew did not simply demonstrate the "Jewish influences" on Freud. Translation works more mutually to expose absences as well as hidden presences, to show the foreign in the self, the familiar in the foreign. As Ginsburg writes in her reflection on translating Freud's *The Uncanny*,

> In the merciless mirror of the other language, the "original" sees its own empty spaces, the places it confronts and evades, experiences of the world for which only the other language has morphemes or words. Via the other language, the lacunae of one's own language are reflected. Indeed, psychoanalysis was not only formulated by what the German language says; it was conceived in what it and its creator, Sigmund Freud, did not, could not, or would not articulate. . . . When Freudian psychoanalysis saw itself reflected in Hebrew (in my Hebrew), what did it see? And Freud, who refused to look into the Hebrew language, what did he *not* see?[107]

9

Jews, Dogs, and Other Animals

And there shall be a loud cry in all the land of Egypt, such as have never been or will ever be again; but not a dog shall snarl at any of the Israelites, at man or beast—in order that you may know that the Lord makes a distinction between Egypt and Israel.
—Exodus 11:6–7

To keep a dog for pleasure is the behavior of the uncircumcised.
—Rabbi Jacob Emden, She'elat *Yavetz*, responsum 17
(ca. 1728–ca. 1748)

For about him till the very end were still
those he had studied, the fauna of the night,
   and shades that still waited to enter
the bright circle of his recognition
turned elsewhere with their disappointment as he
was taken away from his life interest
   to go back to the earth in London,
an important Jew who died in exile.
—W. H. Auden, "In Memory of Sigmund Freud" (1940)

In his description of their 1938 London meeting, I. N. Steinberg relates that he told Freud briefly about "the scientific work being carried out at YIVO" and that Freud expressed regret at not being able to follow "what was happening in the Jewish branch of the science," given that he lacked the ability to read Yiddish.[1] Psychoanalysis was just one of many approaches and methods in use at YIVO, and it is striking that Steinberg remembers Freud describing YIVO as "the Jewish branch of the science," apparently meaning the science of psychoanalysis. This chapter asks what it would mean to take Freud as his word, that is, to see Max Weinreich not only as Freud's translator and popularizer but also as his collaborator and fellow researcher, exploring the same general issues in similar ways but with a Jewish lens and in a Jewish language. Such a collaboration is necessarily asymmetrical, not only because Freud couldn't read Weinreich. In the 1930s, the decade in which Max Weinreich devoted himself to psychoanalysis as a translator, popularizer, teacher, and researcher, Freud was wracked by ill health, fighting threats to his family and to psychoanalysis, and finishing *Moses and Monotheism*—the time was long past for pursuing research partners or falling in love with interesting and smart young men.[2] On Weinreich's part, the use of Yiddish for his sophisticated scholarship was not happenstance but a deliberate ideological choice, a demonstration that Weinreich's work was intended as a contribution not to European *Wissenschaft* but to Yiddish high culture. Beyond Freud's inability to read his work, the cost of Weinreich's investment was high. Outside a small group of Yiddishists, and despite an interminable and insatiable curiosity about the Jewish Freud, the existence of a body of psychoanalytically oriented research into Jewishness by a scholar Freud knew and supported is almost completely unknown. Weinreich was in fact engaged with a research agenda about the origins, transmission, and nature of Jewishness comparable to the one that Freud was wrestling with during these same years and which he referred to in the 1930 preface he provided for Dwossis's Hebrew *Totem and Taboo*:

> No reader of this book will find it easy to put himself in the emotional position of an author who is ignorant of the language of holy writ, who is completely estranged from the religion of his fathers—as well as every other religion—and who cannot take a share in nationalist ideals, but who has yet never repudiated his people, who feels that he is in his essential nature a Jew and who has no desire to alter that nature. If the question were put to him: "Since you have abandoned all these common characteristics of your countrymen, what is there left to you that is Jewish?" he would reply, "A very great deal, and maybe its very essence." He could not now express that essence clearly in words, but someday, no doubt, it will become accessible to the scientific mind.[3]

Freud's *someday* has the whiff of science fiction, but during the 1930s YIVO was grappling with the very essence of Jewishness, summoning precisely the scientific tools Freud believed might be helpful in this pursuit.

If any scientific mind could elucidate the Jewish ambiguities Freud had raised, it was Weinreich, the most distinguished scholar and longest-serving administrator of YIVO, who was working precisely on the question of how Jewish identity was unconsciously formed, in what it consisted, how it was transmitted from one generation to the next, and how it persisted after acculturation, whether or not someone had "abandoned" Judaism or took no share in nationalist ideals. Abigail Gillman similarly takes Freud's comments about his Jewishness seriously, reading them as "testimony to the powerful and enduring character" of Jewish tradition as it "accrues and evolves over time and in time." She adds, "The concept of tradition pays homage to the enigma of memory: the sheer force of characters who endure, and past ideas that resurface, and the wholly unpredictable ways they do so."[4]

It is possible to draw the knot between Freud and Weinreich even more tightly. Weinreich located a certain kernel of unconscious Jewishness in the animal phobias he considered prevalent among Jewish children. Freud's one case study of a child, little Hans, involved just such an animal phobia. Although little Hans's Jewishness is nowhere mentioned in the case study, it does include one of Freud's most direct discussions of antisemitism (a core dimension of Weinreich's research), and we now know that Freud spoke about the boy's Jewishness in correspondence with his father. Weinreich and Freud, then, could be seen as working the same tangled knot of issues, although Freud trained his attention on a single child while Weinreich, working decades later and in a different language, studied the psychology of a collective.

Lest one assume that Weinreich's research was a parochial counterpart to the cosmopolitanism and universalism of psychoanalysis, it is worth pointing out that Freud delivered his first public lectures on dream interpretation in 1897 to his brothers in the Vienna chapter of Bnai Brith, while Weinreich began to work on what would become *The Path to Our Youth* as a Rockefeller Fellow in the 1932–33 Yale Seminar on the Influence of Culture on Personality, which brought together thirteen researchers from Germany, Poland, Hungary, France, Italy, Finland, Norway, Turkey, China, Japan, and India.[5] It was Freud whose field of vision was local, at least at the outset; by the 1930s, Weinreich was riding the wave of the global dispersion of psychoanalysis. The seminar, led by the anthropologist and linguist Edward Sapir and his former student, the social psychologist John Dollard, embodied those global aspirations and the questions they raised, combining a psychoanalytic approach to personality with a focus on "the relativity of cultural values" in shaping the psyche.[6] The mandate of the group was not to lay to rest such perpetual, perpetually vexed questions as whether the Oedipal dilemma (as Freud called it) or others of Freud's discoveries might apply beyond his Viennese bourgeois milieu or the borders of modern Europe. Beginning with the assumption of cultural diversity, the seminar aimed to mobilize psychoanalytic methods to understand the psychic phenomena that rendered cultures so distinctive. References to the particularities of Freud's milieu were unwelcome in the years Freud was trying to establish his claims. But by the 1930s, at least at Yale, a psychoanalysis fully alive to cultural differences, in Europe and beyond, was beginning to flourish as a legitimate area of research, and Jews were welcome to participate in the enterprise precisely for what they could contribute as Jews. This might be putting it a little too generously. Given that participants were chosen according to national categories, the representation of Eastern European Jews was made possible only by the admissions committee making a special exception to allow two participants "from Poland."

Along with assigned readings and visiting lectures by leading researchers, a crucial feature of the Yale seminar was auto-ethnography.[7] All participants were expected to answer a detailed questionnaire about family, religion, and "etiquette" in the culture in which they had been raised and that they were now studying. Weinreich, at this point in his late thirties and an experienced researcher, did not answer all the questions and took issue with some of them for betraying Protestant or American biases.[8] But a few elicited fulsome responses that he later developed in *The Path to Our Youth*. One section in the family questionnaire, on "Bodily Training of the Child," included this question: "Against what kinds of perils (situations like falling, animals, etc.) are small children warned?" Weinreich responded, "In the traditional family small children are warned against a great number of things," categorizing these prohibitions as "reasonable," "magical," or both; examples of prohibitions Weinreich considered both reasonable and magical (at least in how they were explained to children) were "don't play with fire" and "don't mimic a cripple." But the greatest portion of Weinreich's response to this question was devoted to the attitudes of Jews toward dogs, a subject that took him far beyond the narrower question the seminar leaders had posed about "perils against which children are warned":

> The tooth of a black dog worn around the neck is considered a specific remedy against a child's fear of a barking dog. If a dog is par-

ticularly aggressive, the following rhymed formulae are tried and true: "Dog, dog, close your snout. If you bite me, evil spirits will tear you apart" (*Hunt, hunt, farshlis dayn mund. Oyb du vest mikh baysn, veln beyze rukhes dikh tseraysn*). Or "Dog, dog, don't bite me. I am Jacob's child, you are Esau's child; if you bite me, the angels will tear you apart" (*Hunt, hunt, bays mikh nit. Ikh bin Yankevs kind, du bist Eysevs kind, oyb du vest mikh baysn, veln di malokhim dikh tseraysn*).

I wonder, however, whether these spells prove effective in every situation, because the fear of dogs may be considered a rather general Jewish cultural pattern. The origin of it, I think, is to be found in former days when landowners would set their dogs on Jewish peddlers and merchants. In most families children are taught this fear, albeit unconsciously, by the parents themselves; that's why later admonitions are preached to deaf ears. When I want to know to what degree a Jewish family in this country has become Americanized, I never ask whether the children continue speaking Yiddish; instead, I always inquire whether they are afraid of dogs or not.

Other perils that small children are warned against include horses and automobiles on the street, leaning against a window, etc. In very many places, and formerly as a general rule, children are supposed to be on their guard around non-Jewish children as the latter are often aggressive. I am sure, however, that the number of Jewish families is growing in which the children, particularly boys, are taught to resist in case of attack.[9]

Each of these interrelated topics is taken up at much greater length in *The Path to Our Youth*, in which Weinreich seeks to explain how a cultural pattern established in and applying primarily to "former days" might be passed from one generation to the next:

> Setting a dog on an enemy is a ubiquitous human phenomenon; but when a few thousand Jewish peddlers had to quiver each time they passed the entrance of an estate, the fear of dogs became a Jewish trait. A peddler whose fear of dogs was sufficiently implanted would see a dog from afar on his way to the synagogue with his young son and give it a wide berth. It was through such paths that the fear of dogs could be transmitted from father to son.[10]

Weinreich was careful to stress that animal phobias were not necessarily unconsciously transmitted from parent to child; they might also arise for a host of more contingent and individual (or Oedipal) reasons, for instance, "the fear of an abusive father."[11] Nevertheless, the fear of animals was widespread enough as a Jewish trait to warrant ethnographic investigation. According to Weinreich, attitudes toward animals and other similar traits were implanted in Jewish children through multiple channels: The first was "direct cultural formations," or explicit Jewish discourse of about what constituted Jewish difference. The second was through "the messages the outside world sends to the Jewish collective and Jewish individuals, for instance that walking outside the city is dangerous for Jews, because non-Jews might attack them; the fact that postmen and policemen are non-Jews; the fact that street names are written in non-Jewish languages, etc." The last channel of Jewish cultural attitudes most clearly demonstrates Freud's influence on Weinreich and is "the hardest to define, because it involves the fundamental elements of Jewish constitution." These were the elements that were fated to turn an infant into a Jew by virtue of unconscious attitudes the parents and other adults around the child had absorbed and were now wordlessly transmitting, including that "they themselves are afraid of non-Jews; they are insecure because they know that 'non-Jews have all the luck'; but also that they see themselves as important because they belong to the Jewish people, who worship the one God."[12] Even the youngest infants absorb these attitudes. The Jewish mother who holds her infant closer when walking through a non-Jewish neighborhood, aurally differentiated from Jewish neighborhoods by the sound of dogs barking, transmits a fear of dogs to her child through a quickening of the breath and closer skin contact, even before the child knows the words for Jew, non-Jew, person, dog.

For Weinreich, becoming Jewish—like becoming a woman—was a protracted and ambivalent cultural process. Animal phobias exemplified the complexities of this process not because they were central to Jewish identity but because they provided clear evidence of unconscious intergenerational transmission of Jewishness early in life (although *not* genetically); took shape at the boundaries of Jewish and non-Jewish life; were embodied and involuntary; and operated largely outside Jewish literary and religious legacies (although of course they left traces in the sources). It is because the fear of dogs and similar Jewish characteristics are largely unconscious that secularization, acculturation, conversion to another religion, or "later admonitions" by parents have so little effect.

For all his insistence on the stubborn persistence of Jewishness, Weinreich was well aware that "the Jewish character" was changing as he wrote. Deeply ingrained cultural traits such as Jewish animal phobias had reached collective consciousness, as evidenced by the fact that they were now the subject of sociological study (his own and others). They were also the subject of autobiographical self-reflections, political interventions, and deliberate changes in child-rearing style. Animal phobias and other ostensibly Jewish traits were reaching self-consciousness precisely because they were changing so rapidly. As the title reflects, *The Path to Our Youth* begins by noting the chasm that separated the older generation (youth researchers among them) from Jewish youth, a generation gap everywhere manifest but particularly marked in the Jewish community, where modernization had been so rapid and traumatic. This gap had disrupted the normal means of cultural reproduction, with children increasingly taking their cues not from home life but from "the ideals, tendencies, and illusions of Hollywood," a language their parents did not generally share. "Wherever you look," Weinreich writes, "there are conflicts, if the parents are conservative, and anxious doubts, if the parents are trying to act in the spirit of the times."[13] For well-meaning parents,

> the situation is even more difficult. Along what paths should they lead their children, when all the old rules are falling like a house of cards?! Should we teach our children to save, when we see inflation turn life savings into nothing? Should we teach our children to respect authority, when we see the public worship clownish buffoons? On the contrary, one must teach them to challenge authority: but will that not make the child overly insecure about what can be trusted?
>
> And even the "objective" rules of conduct have shifted. It was once understood that masturbation was harmful, and parents tried to root out this "sin of youth." Whether they succeeded is another question; but nowadays parents are told that all children suffer from this "ailment" and the best way to treat it is to pretend not to notice.[14]

In the face of such radical social uncertainty, Weinreich takes a radical epistemological stance. He begins his study not by assuring hesitant adults of his ability to explain Jewish youth to them but by confessing that he shares their uncertainties. Weinreich's research approach reflects this epistemological humility: Taking the youth autobiographies YIVO had collected in the contests of 1932 and 1934 as primary sources, Weinreich allowed the autobiographies to speak for themselves, excerpting lengthy passages without further comment (although selection and framing are of course also a kind of commentary). Publishing in Yiddish similarly signaled that the research, attuned as it was to the larger scientific world, was both *about* young Polish Jews and *for* them. More radically, Weinreich found frequent occasion to insist that, however profound the effects of a Jewish upbringing, individuals could never be reduced to their cultural or familial context. Weinreich thus paid homage to the process of individuation he saw as crucial to adolescence, allowing his subjects to be something other than the ideological or cultural products of the parents that had raised them, the religion that claimed to guide them, the youth movements to which they belonged, or the traumatized minority to which Polish society relegated them.[15]

Weinreich paid particular attention to the last of these contexts, recognizing the consequential role of the non-Jewish world in the making of "a Jew" and the powerful place of non-Jews in Jewish psyches. The animal phobias that arose at the boundary between humans and animals (more precisely, human animals and nonhuman animals) were symbolically, semiotically, and phenomenologically inseparable from the boundary that separated Jews and non-Jews, as suggested by the triangular structure of the magical formulae ostensibly designed to protect Jews from dogs. Weinreich was skeptical that these formulae could protect Jews from dogs or cure Jewish fears. What they accomplished was the interpellation and constitution of a (young, fearful) Jewish subject via the negation and denigration of the non-Jew/dog, a complicated form of what could be called religious or ethnic "assignment." The formulae that claim to protect Jews from dogs constitute them as Jews by virtue of their assignation as Jacob's child; the dog, by contrast, is the spawn of Esau, Jacob's "evil twin." The spirit world participates in the drama: angels fight on behalf of Jews and evil spirits tear apart dogs. Jewish animal phobias and the formulae that emerged in response to them betray a cultural structure that recognizes non-Jews and dogs as occupying a single category, against the human sphere that is represented in exemplary fashion by the Jew. While Weinreich prefers folklore to rabbinic opinions, the eighteenth-century Talmudist Jacob Emden, considering the permissibility of Jews owning dogs, remarks that only "the uncircumcised" take pleasure in dogs.[16] In these discourses, dogs fulfill the role to which they owe their domestication, eating castoffs in exchange for barking at strangers, which is to say, symbolically marking and thus policing the boundaries that distinguish (and secretly connect) Jew and non-Jew. While Weinreich does not discuss this, despite the Manichaean categories that distinguish Jews from dogs and non-Jews, and despite the cosmic interventions on behalf of Jews, the chants reveal the secret that Jew and non-Jew are in fact kith and kin, descendants of twin brothers. It is just because this is so that a (guard) dog must police the boundaries that distinguish them.

As evidence that other animals might also fill the role played by dogs in the triangular structure Jew/non-Jew/dog, Weinreich relates an anecdote he heard "from a reliable source" about an exchange that took place in Berlin, adding, "and even if it's not true, it's still a good anecdote":

> Just after the ascension of Hitler, two young boys were walking in the street when they saw a horse harnessed to a cart. Said one boy to the other:
> "Don't get too close, or that horse might give you a kick!"
> Said the other, "But how would he know I was Jewish?"[17]

Horses, in this logic, absorb the hostility of their non-Jewish owners to Jews, sharing their animus to "Jacob's child" as if they recognized themselves as Esau's kin (along with dogs) and identified with Esau's (justified) resentment against Jacob. The anti-Jewish fever that periodically swept up Berlin also affected its equine inhabitants, who participated in the deadly game of discriminating Jewish from Aryan faces and bodies. But Jews also hold or held sharp feelings of superiority in relation to the inhabitants of the mixed-category non-Jew/animal, which in Weinreich's view were aspects of the "compensatory mechanisms" by which Jews, like other denigrated people, salve their bruised egos.[18]

Jennifer Young and Leila Zenderland have shown that Weinreich's interest in the distinctive characteristics of Jewish culture was informed by the attention to race, power, and class that he acquired during his year in the seminar co-led by John Dollard, who was working during this period on the still-acclaimed *Caste and Class in a Southern Town* (1937).[19] Dollard appreciated his student from Vilna, reporting that while most seminar participants traveled over the 1932 Christmas break to nearby cities to research how immigrants from the cultures they were studying were adapting to American life, "Weinreich made a swing south, visiting [Fisk University in] Nashville, the Tuskegee Institute, and Atlanta to interview authorities on race relations in the south."[20] It was through these encounters and, Young guesses, his reading of W. E. B. Du Bois that Weinreich came to understand the ways that Jewish identity should be understood as an "attack," a blow from outside, rather than an essential or interior feature of an individual or collective (it may be relevant to this discourse that Weinreich himself was the victim of an antisemitic attack on November 12, 1913, which cost him the vision in his right eye).[21] Derrida similarly responded to a question about his Jewishness by describing the "blow" of being called a *jew* in his childhood, remembering "how the word *jew* (before 'judaism' and, most of all, before 'jewishness') arrived, how it reached me like an arrival or a first arrival, in the language of my childhood, landing in the French language of the Algeria of my first sentences."[22] This word *jew*, Derrida writes, is "deeper and more profound in me than my own name." Despite this depth and profundity,

> I do not believe I heard it first in my family, nor ever as a neutral designation meant to classify, even less to identify a belonging to a social, ethnic, or religious community. I believe I heard it at school in El Biar, already charged with what, in Latin, one could call an insult [*injure*], *injuria*, in English, *injury*, both an insult, a wound, and an injustice, a denial of right rather than the right to belong to a legitimate group. Before understanding any of it, I received this word like a blow, a denunciation, a de-legitimation prior to any right, prior to any legality. A blow struck against me, but a blow I would henceforth have to carry and incorporate forever in the very essence of my most singularly signed and assigned behavior.[23]

Weinreich, anticipating this insight, worked to delineate his understanding of Jewishness as an externally and violently "assigned" identity, distinguishing two successive stages of this assignment that he called the first and second "attack of Jewishness [*atak fun yidishkayt*]." In Weinreich's view, the first of these attacks struck deep but remained largely unconscious, only belatedly registering in the reverberations of later attacks. The second stage was the one that the youth who were the focus of Weinreich's most sustained attention were experiencing in Poland of the 1930s, a traumatizing awareness of the antisemitism that confronted them and constrained their future prospects. Weinreich's formulation is itself shocking, perhaps deliberately so: In contrast with the word "Jew" or *jew*, which Cynthia Baker shows is a pejorative term only recently transvalued and "owned" by Jews, *yidishkayt* (more than "Jewishness") is a term with normatively warm, intimate, positive connotations, an "indigenous" term by which Jews describe and praise themselves and their life-forms.[24] It is some variation of this term that

Derrida must be referring to when he writes that he encountered the term "jewishness" and the idea of "the right to belong to a legitimate group" only long after he was "struck" (from the outside) by the word "jew." The phrase the "attack of *yidishkayt*" thus approaches cultural ungrammaticality, since *yidishkayt* normally heals the attack against the *jew*, as the discourse by which Jews "own" their minority status, by which—as Cynthia Baker puts it in a response to Derrida's reflection—they "translat[e] Jew from accusative object to nominative subject . . . , a name for self, a pronouncement about identity, connection, and the contours of 'legitimate' difference."[25]

But if the Jew as "accusative object" is a hateful mischaracterization, the "nominative subject," the Jew as understood "from within," is not thereby a more accurate reading. The concept that Weinreich credits most directly to his time in the American South is the "compensatory mechanism," the alleviation of the trauma of persecution and humiliation by the grandiose fantasies and self-serving narratives by which marginalized cultures compensate for how they are seen by others. Such compensation could heal the trauma of animal phobias, for instance, which descendants of enslaved people in the American South shared with descendants of Eastern European Jews, and for related historical reasons.[26] Hearing a thirteen-year-old Tuskegee student earnestly explain to him that Blacks were the original inhabitants of North America, Weinreich writes that he initially thought to respond by asking the young man whether three centuries of living in America were insufficient for people of African descent to feel they had the right to belong.[27] Holding back from correcting the student in Tuskegee allowed Weinreich to recognize the psychological function of the boy's discourse as a mode of compensation and identify such mechanisms not only in Jewish folklore (Weinreich's particular interest) but also in or even as religion. In Weinreich's view, the Jewish religion should be understood as essentially a set of compensatory mechanisms, supplying notions of Jews as the chosen people and stories about the coming of the Messiah as ways to bolster fragile Jewish egos. But even within the Orthodox camp, Weinreich believed, religious modes of psychic compensation had worn thin under the pressure of secularization; fortunately, secular versions had arisen to fill the breach. Writing in the first-person plural, Weinreich ventriloquized these modern Jewish forms of compensation:

> It was true that Jews were a persecuted minority in many lands, but that was exactly what made us a people with a worldly outlook, and of eternal character. Or: What really do all these persecutions add up to? From the

biblical prophets until Einstein, all the greatest people have been Jews. ... In one completely assimilated Viennese family, in which the parents had taken seriously the question of how to raise Jewish children, the father related to me that his four-year-old daughter already had a strong sense of Jewishness. She had said to the maid: "Your Christmas is only two days, but our Chanukah lasts eight days!" The father felt that this Jewish superiority would stand her in good stead when she later had to face the inevitable jabs of non-Jewish society.[28]

Jewish compensatory mechanisms continued to be necessary even in assimilated Jewish families, and Weinreich was unsurprised (and perhaps relieved) to discover them there, so distant from the traditional communities where such mechanisms were most evidently on offer (though why Weinreich considered a family that celebrated Chanukah rather than Christmas "completely assimilated" remains a mystery). It was also true that such mechanisms were failing just when they were most needed, with new attacks that also targeted Jews who lacked the strong sense of Jewish superiority that could psychically shield them. Even parents who attempted to pass along Jewish ways of living and thinking were unsuccessful, since "knowing these lifeforms is one thing, and psychologically integrating them is another."[29] Within such a chasm, where the channels for transmitting Jewishness had broken down and the family was helpless, YIVO's research into what it meant to be a young Jew in such times could provide an academic alternative to the religious fantasies, ethnic narcissism, and political propaganda tasked with collective and individual self-understanding. The youth autobiographies stood as ample evidence of acute suffering, but for those for whom psychoanalysis was out of reach, it might constitute something of a talking cure, putting individual misery to collective Jewish use and thus itself serving as a modern, scientific compensatory mechanism. In the years Weinreich was attempting to rebuild YIVO in New York, he reinstituted a fourth autobiography contest on American soil (after the 1932, 1934, and 1939 contests in Vilna), asking for reflections on the experience of immigration. The 1942 contest no longer focused on youth, since YIVO lacked a language and organizational structure to communicate with young Jewish Americans. After the prizes were awarded, the entries were deposited in the archive, where they rest in peace.[30]

The "Jewish branch of the science" that was taking up the question of Jewishness was not simply applying Freud's insights in new areas where he had not ventured. In writing from right to left rather than left to right, Weinreich also reversed Freud's approach and priorities: Where Freud appends a brief comment on antisemitism (and circumcision) to his study of childhood phobias, Weinreich produces a treatise on how antisemitism shapes Jewish subjectivity and triggers such phobias. Where Freud produced many volumes on the libido, translating on behalf of individuals who could not articulate their suffering in words, Weinreich provides a brief appendix on the particular character of Jewish sexuality, allowing a contributor to his youth autobiography contest to do the theorizing, given that Weinreich feels that he "knows nothing about specific developments in the sexuality of [Jewish] youth."[31] Where Freud writes about what it means to grow up with Jewish culture in a private letter to a friend, this issue lies plain on the face of Weinreich's work for all the (Yiddish-reading) world to see.

The tightest point of convergence between these research projects involves Freud's 1909 case study of little Hans, the young boy with a crippling fear of horses. The case study, more formally known as "Analysis of a Case of Childhood Phobia," actually describes an analysis carried out by little Hans's father under Freud's loose supervision. It is by now well-known that Hans was Herbert Graf, the son of the music critic Max Graf and Olga Hönig Graf, whom Freud had treated before her marriage. Max was a participant in the Wednesday Evening Circle, the meetings that preceded the founding of the Vienna Psychoanalytic Society, where he reported his observations about his son's psychosexual development. Freud took Graf's reports as real-time evidence for the operations of the Oedipal drama in a young boy, confirming the more indirect hints he had gleaned from how the Oedipal conflict exercised its influence long after the fact (including in himself). Along with being little Hans's analyst at one remove, Freud was also a family friend, known by little Hans and his parents, as by so many others, as "the Professor." Max Graf remembered that Freud carried a large wooden rocking horse up four flights of stairs as a present for his son's third or fifth birthday.[32]

Jay Geller points out that the case study of little Hans, published in the inaugural issue (1909) of the first psychoanalytic journal, the *Jahrbuch für psychoanalytische und psychopathologische Forschungen*, appeared during a period in which Freud's anxieties that psychoanalysis would be perceived as "a Jewish national affair" were at their highest pitch, a period in which he "eschewed explicit public references to matters Jewish in his analytic writings."[33] It is not surprising, then, that Freud avoided mention of little

Hans's Jewish connections. But little Hans's Jewishness is no mere happenstance: In 1942, Graf published a reminiscence of his friendship with Freud, revealing that he had consulted with him in 1903 about whether to baptize his newborn son. Freud counseled against such a step, since, "if you do not let your son grow up as a Jew, you will deprive him of all those sources of energy which cannot be replaced by anything else. He will have to struggle as a Jew, and you ought to develop in him all the energy he will need for the struggle. Do not deprive him of that advantage."[34] Freud does not specify what energy might be provided by being raised Jewish, but this is one question Weinreich investigates at length, in his theory that Jewish culture provided compensatory mechanisms against antisemitic attack and elsewhere. In a commencement address he gave in 1945 at Baltimore Hebrew College, he said, "No escape from common Jewish fate is possible, even if it were desirable," and lamented, "this unfinished assimilation, which robbed hundreds of thousands of Jews of all pleasures of Jewishness, and left them only the kernel."[35]

Beyond the question of how the energy or pleasures of Jewishness (along with or instead of psychoanalysis) might help a frightened boy, the case revolves around the very neurosis that Weinreich considers a paradigmatic, unconsciously transmitted Jewish trait: animal phobias. As he put it in the Yale questionnaire, Weinreich believed that fear of dogs was a more reliable sign that a family had not become Americanized than that they continued to speak Yiddish; he also mentioned horses as among the dangers that Jewish children are warned about. It is true that there is not a trace of this "cultural diagnosis" in little Hans: it seems never to have occurred to Freud that Hans's problem with horses had any relationship to his Jewishness or might have been inherited by Hans from his father, whose paternal threat Freud believed the phobia to be displacing. The fear of horses derived, in Freud's view, from little Hans's castration anxiety, a function of his Oedipal desire for his mother and fear that his father would punish him for it; the case is more complicated than that, but all the complications apparently emerge from the Graf family constellation. Of course, there is no reason to reject Freud's Oedipal scenario in favor of Weinreich's implicit Jewish diagnosis; Weinreich also fully recognizes that animal phobias might arise from the fear of an abusive father, whether in actuality or only in a child's fearful fantasy.

However, Jewishness does play a role in the published case study. A famous footnote extends Freud's analysis of Hans's castration anxiety beyond the Oedipal triangle to the broader social sphere, where rumors and phobias about circumcision intersect with antisemitism:

> I cannot interrupt the discussion so far as to demonstrate the typical character of the unconscious train of thought which I think there is here reason for attributing to little Hans. The castration complex is the deepest unconscious root of antisemitism; for even in the nursery little boys hear that a Jew has something cut off his penis—a piece of his penis, they think—and this gives them a right to despise Jews. And there is no stronger unconscious root for the sense of superiority over women. Weininger (the young philosopher who, highly gifted but sexually deranged, committed suicide after producing his remarkable book, *Geschlecht und Charakter* [1903]), in a chapter that attracted much attention, treated Jews and women with equal hostility and overwhelmed them with the same insults. Being a neurotic, Weininger was completely under the sway of his infantile complexes; and from that standpoint what is common to Jews and women is their relation to the castration complex.[36]

As one of Freud's rare explicit discussions of Jewish identity or antisemitism in his psychoanalytic writings, and particularly as related to gender, this footnote (cited here in its entirety) has excited considerable attention. Geller points out that, despite Freud's confidence in "attributing to little Hans" this "unconscious train of thought," its relevance to the case at hand is murky, since "the little boys [who] hear that a Jew has something cut off his penis" and thus consider it their right to "despise Jews" would seem to be non-Jews. If little Hans was Jewish, as we know he was (although Geller writes that there is no record of his circumcision), why would Freud speak about Jews as if little Hans (or Freud himself) were not one of that group?[37] Beyond the apparent disavowal of little Hans's (and Freud's own) Jewishness, Daniel Boyarin points out that the footnote fails to provide an "indigenous" Jewish alternative to the horrified "external" gaze at circumcision, for instance, in the rabbinic view that "only the circumcised man was considered as 'whole.'"[38] Boyarin writes, "In presenting 'Little Hans' and Weininger as if they were gentiles gazing, as it were, at the Jewish penis and becoming filled with fear and loathing, Freud is actually—I want to suggest—representing himself, or at least some aspect of himself, gazing at his own circumcised penis and being filled with fear and loathing."[39] Failing to mention that he himself is circumcised, or that Weininger and little Hans are Jewish, is a symptom of the "self-contempt of the racially dominated subject," which explains why Freud found fit to "discursively closet his circumcision."[40]

Readings of the footnote that see Freud as taking a non-Jewish perspective on circumcision are not inevitable: Eliza Slavet questions the "common sense" understanding of circumcision as a transparent and immediately available "fact" available to male Jews about themselves, "since all they would have to do is look down." In fact, given "the most curious aspect of Jewish circumcision," that it is performed so close to birth, "the Jewish boy does not necessarily always already know about his difference—his difference from others, and his difference from his uncircumcised seven-day-old self." Rumors about circumcision thus "would apply equally to Jews and non-Jews," including Jewish individuals who "are aware of the fact that they are racially—that is, physically and permanently—marked."[41] For Slavet, the "proper" Jewish meaning of circumcision (for instance, that circumcision perfects a body) is in some sense permanently unavailable to the circumcised subject, marked before he can remember as a Jewish male through a ceremony whose meaning remains largely opaque. Such a subject might take on a Jewish view of what circumcision means or one propagated by others, but in either case circumcision represents—is the most dramatic representation of—the ways in which racial as well as gender identities are assigned rather than inborn and always remain external data about the self.

Slavet's reading of Freud's confusing footnote, which refuses to resolve the confusion about circumcision through the category of "internalized antisemitism," might help us read Weinreich's discussion of similar issues. For the most part, what Weinreich means in his discussion of "the attack of *yidishkayt*" is clear enough—the shock of being called a Jew by an outsider who considers this term an insult. There are two moments that complicate this insider/outsider distinction, however. In a bracketed remark (as opposed to Freud's discussion, which is a footnote described as an interruption) Weinreich acknowledges the act of circumcision itself—*before* the "nursery rumors" that (mis)apprehend it—as potentially significant in shaping Jewish character traits. Reaching for ways of understanding how Jewishness might be transmitted in infancy, Weinreich writes,

> Even if we bracket the question of the inheritance [of Jewish character traits], and further bracket the psychological effects of circumcision on Jewish boys (not because circumcision isn't important, but only because we still know nothing about its effects), we would still have to take into

> account the widespread belief that Jewish mothers are more tender with their infants than non-Jewish mothers. We have already suggested that this might be explained as the expression of a dark feeling: This child is bound to suffer so much, let it have some pleasure now. But I cannot stand behind either this explanation or the fact of such tenderness, since no one has succeeded in establishing its facticity, or finding adequate methods to research it.[42]

Weinreich leaps from the act of circumcision to the belief that Jewish mothers may be more tender with their infants because of a premonition of what they will suffer in the future, from the non-Jewish world; he does not suggest that Jewish mothers may be compensating for what at least their sons have *already* suffered, from their Jewish fathers (and rivals for this tenderness). Nevertheless, Weinreich's initial (bracketed) comment on circumcision is certainly to the point: If Freud believes that merely the rumor of circumcision in the nursery might give rise to complex psychological effects for those who hear about this act (and mistake it for castration), then perhaps the actual experience of being circumcised, its visible legacy as a bodily mark, and the deferred understanding that the act has been performed, also has consequences for Jewish psychosexual development for those on whom it is performed, on those who perform it, and those excluded from the ritual. Weinreich reaches in these hypotheses a place very similar to where Freud arrived in wondering about the deep sources of his Jewish feelings—to a kind of Jewish core that present research methods cannot reach. In both cases, folk psychology and rumor reign, widespread beliefs about Jewish mothers and nursery rumors about circumcision. The tender Jewish mothers Weinreich mentions play a role in little Hans's development, too. Although it his mother who threatens castration for the sin of masturbation, little Hans attributes the real threat to his father, who for his part suspects that his son's neurosis may derive from his wife's "overly tender" relationship with him.[43] So where do the traumas of childhood originate? In tenderness or violence? The Oedipal family or Jewish one? And what is the role of the actual animals on the streets outside the home or the dark future that hangs over childhood and makes it presence known even in the intimacy of a mother's tender touch?

A critique of Freud's too-close focus on the Oedipal triangle and obliviousness to the social circumstances of its construction has been put forward by Gilles Deleuze and Felix Guattari precisely around the issue of little Hans's fear of horses. Deleuze and Guattari view Freud's interpretation of little Hans as not Oedipal but "oedipalizing," yoking the horse to the cart of the human, the social, and the family. For Freud, "the horse's blinders are the father's eyeglasses, the black around its mouth is his moustache, its kicks are the parents' lovemaking. Not one word about Hans' relation to the street, on how the street was forbidden to him, on what is for a child to see the spectacle 'a horse is proud, a blinded horse pulls, a horse falls, a horse is whipped.'"[44] Viewing Freud as imposing a suffocating and predictable triangle of the family on Hans, Deleuze and Guattari aim to restore Hans's "relation to the street," a sphere of actual animals, of human-animal interaction, and the spectacle of human cruelty and animal suffering. Such oedipalization subsumes animals to the needs of humans and denies humans not only the realm of "the street" but also what lies outside the social altogether, their "becoming animal."

Deleuze and Guattari refrain from diagnosing Freud's inability to let animals—including human animals—be animals. Such an implicit diagnosis comes from Ernest Jones, who makes the case that Freud's characteristic disinterest toward animals was a function of his Jewish upbringing. Describing Freud's sudden conversion, at the age of seventy-two, into a fierce lover of dogs, Jones writes:

> Like most other Jews of his generation, he had had little contact with animals, but a couple of years before an Alsatian dog, Wolf, had been procured to accompany his daughter Anna on her walks through the forests of the Semmering. Freud had taken a considerable interest in observing canine ways, and from now on he became more and more fond of one dog after another—evidently a sublimation of his very great fondness for little children which could no longer be gratified.[45]

Reflecting in a different passage on why Freud was unable to recognize more than a limited number of human instincts, ignoring such contemporary zoological findings as the maternal or hunting instincts, Jones adds:

> Then again Freud seems to have followed his ancestral traditions in feeling aloof from the animal world, an attitude that may be illustrated by the saying: "If a Jew says he enjoys fox-hunting he is lying." It was only towards the end of his life that he got on to speaking terms with a dog; then, it is true, he established a close relationship of a human kind.[46]

Because Freud could not fathom the pleasures of fox hunting, he had little insight into the pleasures humans (or at least gentiles) shared with animals that hunted. And even his establishing a close relationship with his beloved dog did not quite add up to such an understanding, given that it did not involve Freud letting an animal be an animal. Jones's description of Freud's connection with his own dogs—a series of three chows—as getting on speaking terms with them, or developing a close relationship of a human kind, suggests not only intimacy and love but also projection, transference, and "oedipalization." While Jones focuses on the Jewish character of Freud's long estrangement from the animal world, Weinreich may help us see that Freud's belated interest in dogs may also have Jewish meaning, along with its non-Jewish ones: Anna's dog Wolf was procured from Dorothy Burlingham, Anna's "friend, companion, colleague, and soul mate," who moved with her four children to Vienna in 1925, looking for help with her unmanageable ten-year-old son, Bob.[47] In an introduction to Princess Marie Bonaparte's "biography" of her chow Topsy (which Sigmund and Anna translated from French into German in the last years of his life), Gary Genosko writes that "Freud's paternal fondness for Anna's dog may have been strong enough to mask the sociosemiotic significance of the presence of an Alsatian (called a German shepherd), a breed which makes an ideal police dog, in a household identified as Jewish.[48] Genosko assumes that Freud's paternal fondness for Anna's dog (which conflates dog and daughter) masks the significance of the presence of a non-Jewish dog (which is to say, a non-Jew) in the Jewish household, implying perhaps that Freud's concern for his daughter's safety was enough to trump what would otherwise have been his Jewish aversion to the dog (or its specific breed).

But if Freud's Jewish parents had transmitted to their son indifference or antipathy to dogs and the non-Jews who loved them, the Freud family could change with the times, as so many other Jewish families were doing during this period; if so, then they may also have learned (from a non-Jewish woman) that dogs could protect as well as terrify Jewish children. The love of dogs, that is, could take Jewish forms. Susan Kahn's research demonstrates that the presence of a German shepherd in the Freud household may have been part of a larger trend: it was a Viennese Jewish woman, Rudolphina Menzel, who pioneered the training of dogs for the German police force and then introduced pet ownership to Palestine when she immigrated there in 1938.[49] Freud's conversion into a dog lover was, from this perspective, of a piece with such modern Jewish movements as Zionism and, indeed, psychoanalysis itself. Yerushalmi takes the "Hebrew" name of Freud's beloved

Yofi as evidence of just how Jewish Freud was, not least when he reminded Arnold Zweig that the name was pronounced "Jo wie *Jud*."[50] But Yofi, far from being evidence in the flesh for Freud's Jewishness, is a complicated ethnic marker, given that his overestimation of Yofi also signals the distance Freud traveled from his traditional Jewish aversion to dogs, a journey he was taking along with many other Jews around the world.

As Weinreich would have predicted, Yofi played a role not only in Freud's Jewish self-transformation but also in his relation with non-Jews, including analysands. Yofi was always welcome and generally present at the foot of Freud's famous couch, where she reportedly functioned as a kind of alarm clock, signaling the end of the analytic hour by yawning or stretching (a little early if the session was tiresome). The richest description we have of the experience of being analyzed by Freud is the remarkable account of the poet H.D. [Hilda Doolittle] of her move to Vienna in 1933–34 to take up treatment (Weinreich spent that same autumn in Vienna, in analysis with Siegfried Bernfeld). When she stepped into the room, H.D. writes,

> A little lion-like creature came padding toward me—a lioness, as it happened. She had emerged from the inner sanctum or manifested from under or behind the couch; anyway, she continued her course across the carpet. Embarrassed, shy, overwhelmed, I bend down to greet this creature. But the Professor says, "Do not touch her—she snaps—she is very difficult with strangers." Strangers? Is the Soul crossing the threshold a stranger to the Door-Keeper? It appears so. But, though no accredited dog-lover, I like dogs and they oddly and sometimes unexpectedly "take" to me. If this is an exception, I am ready to take the risk. Unintimidated but distressed by the Professor's somewhat forbidding manner, I not only continue my gesture toward the little chow, but crouch on the floor so she can snap better if she wants to. Yofi—her name is Yofi—snuggles her nose into my hand and nuzzles her head, in delicate sympathy, against my shoulder.[51]

Freud's ancestors (or even his own father) may have known the peddler's fear of dogs, but by 1933 Freud was a man with his own door keeper, and H.D. was the stranger at the threshold. Whatever Freud thought of H.D.'s non-Jewishness, his Jewishness is never far from her mind. She writes that walking to her daily session, she followed a trail of swastikas "down Berggasse as if they had been chalked on the pavement especially for my benefit."[52] Her horror at Viennese antisemitism does not prevent her from also sometimes sharing it: H.D. confesses to thinking that Freud's relationship with his antiquities is mercantile; when Freud annoys her by declaring of a little bronze statue that "she is perfect," H.D. writes, "like a Jew, he was assessing its worth; the blood of Abraham, Isaac, and Jacob ran in his veins." It is true that Freud himself had a similar thought—writing to H.D. from London about the "return of the Gods," he adds, in a curiously rabbinic parenthetical phrase, "(other people read: Goods)."[53] Talking about his grandchildren, Freud strikes her as "so tribal, so conventionally Mosaic" that she felt "the old boredom of looking at historical, genealogical references in a small-print school or Sunday-school Bible."[54] The memoir as a whole is an extraordinary depiction of how the relationship between psychoanalyst and analysand was freighted, in this case, not only by the usual chains of transference and countertransference but also by the long history of Jewish-Christian difference (and more particularly Christian anti-Jewish sentiment), qualified or intensified by H.D.'s ambivalent reverence for (and overestimation of) Freud.

It is within this charged context that we might understand H.D.'s connection with Yofi, who was Jewish by virtue of being "a Freud" and hostile to "strangers" to the Freud household, but non-Jewish (like her) by virtue of being a dog (and also, like her, a female).[55] Yofi thus played the role of the "third" in the psychoanalytic session, opening up the psychodynamic dyad of H.D. and Freud to a multiplicity of transference effects. In H.D.'s treatment, Yofi formed part of the triangle that she identified as "wise-man, woman, lioness (as he calls his chow)."[56] This is an unbalanced configuration, rendered further so by the engine of transference, identification, and disidentification along multiple lines: first of all two humans and a dog, but also, the Master and his dog versus a "stranger." Their very first encounter rearranged things, with H.D. and Yofi (the two females, the two non-Jews) in a camp against the uncomprehending (Jewish) man. "Yofi—her name is Yofi—snuggles her nose into my hand," H.D. writes, ending the chapter. And begins the next one: "So again I can say the Professor was not always right."[57] The triangle in the treatment room was occasionally charged with (female) rivalry rather than solidarity: H.D. grumbles, "I feel limp and frustrated. I was annoyed at the end of my session as Yofi would wander about and I felt that the Professor was more interested in Yofi than he was in my story."[58] It was H.D. on the couch, being treated by Freud. But the presence of Yofi told a longer and more complicated cultural story—about the difficulties of facing or even healing the hostilities that complicated relationships between men and women, Jews and non-Jews, humans and animals.

If Freud could overcome his indifference to dogs (although not to cats, which he continued to dislike), perhaps it is not surprising that little Hans was rather quickly cured of a fear of horses. Freud views Hans's cure, predictably, in Oedipal terms: Hans was cured in part by revising his terrifying "sexual theories" through the acquisition of more factual information of where babies come from and women's anatomical differences. Without this knowledge, "his two active impulses—the hostile one toward his father and the tender one toward his mother—could be put to no use, the first because of the love that existed side by side with the hatred, and the second because of the perplexity in which his infantile sexual theories left him."[59] Weinreich might alert us to another possible factor in little Hans's cure. Freud had advised Max Graf that only by remaining psychically connected to Jews and Jewish culture could he provide his son with the energy to withstand the blows of the anti-Jewish world. It was Weinreich, though, who spelled out how that connection and energy worked: Secular and acculturated Jews, distant from religious forms of compensation, took solace in the prideful thought that "from the biblical prophets until Einstein, all the greatest people have been Jews." Freud is absent from this sentence, but the more usual formulation of the thought that "the most important thinkers in the world are (like us) Jewish" almost always included Freud alongside Einstein (and sometimes Marx); Weinreich perhaps omits Freud from this (familiar) litany of great Jews to avoid the awkwardness of citing folk praise of Freud alongside his own more serious mobilization of Freud's scientific insights. But I have been arguing that these two modes of engagement with Freud, the scholarly and the popular, may be more closely linked than scholars cared to acknowledge. Weinreich's intimate entanglement with Freud, through all the modes of scholarly "touch"—translating, teaching, popularizing, citing—may well have also been charged with varieties of pride, including the pride of association with such a famous Jew. Freud (along with Einstein) joined the YIVO's Presidium in 1930, no doubt providing much compensatory satisfaction during the difficult decade that followed. The names of this honorary board appeared on the letterhead of YIVO in Vilna as well as in its many chapters throughout the world, and they still appear on the home page of the YIVO website, providing me with reliable pleasure every time I happen across them.

Freud played a less public but certainly more significant role in the Graf family, as a family friend who was also (becoming) a famous Jew. Max Graf relays his pride at the unusual friendship between a musicologist with a young son and the older and more established Freud, who participated warmly in family gatherings although "he was already aging and his marvelous black hair was beginning to gray."[60] It was not only rumors about circumcision that would have reached little Hans in the nursery. He may well have been aware that "the Professor" was not only famous but also a famous Jew and could take pride in contributing to his findings. Max Graf's careful transcription of the conversations that constituted his psychoanalysis of his son suggest as much. When Hans expresses the fervent wish that his newborn sister would die, leaving him alone with his beloved mother, Max says, "A good boy doesn't wish that sort of thing, though." Hans protests, correctly and precociously, "But he may *THINK* it!" His father replies: "But that isn't good." Hans: "If he thinks it, it *IS* good all the same, because you can write it to the Professor."[61] Fear of horses, and all that implied about Hans's defective masculinity, may well be the inherited lot of even assimilated and bourgeois Jewish children. But Jewish children, as long as they recognize themselves as such, might also benefit from the affective ties that connected the Grafs, young and old, with the famous professor. Weinreich was well aware that part of what YIVO had to offer Eastern European Jewish youth was the benefit of association with an institute known to be not only Jewish but also modern and scientific, values signaled by its commitment to psychoanalysis. Along with the hatred he inspired by virtue of his Jewishness and shocking ideas, Freud aroused Jewish pride in his fame, by which he himself supplied some of the benefit he believed that belonging to a Jewish collective had to offer. Aside from its specific ideas, psychoanalysis could heal wounds just by redounding to Jewish credit. As Weinreich could explain, to anyone who could read him.

So did Weinreich know something (about Jewish children and inherited animal phobias and compensatory mechanisms) that Freud did not? Did Freud know some of these things also, only differently? It is tempting to characterize the relationship as shaped by the dichotomy between universal and particular, public and private. These are no simple oppositions:

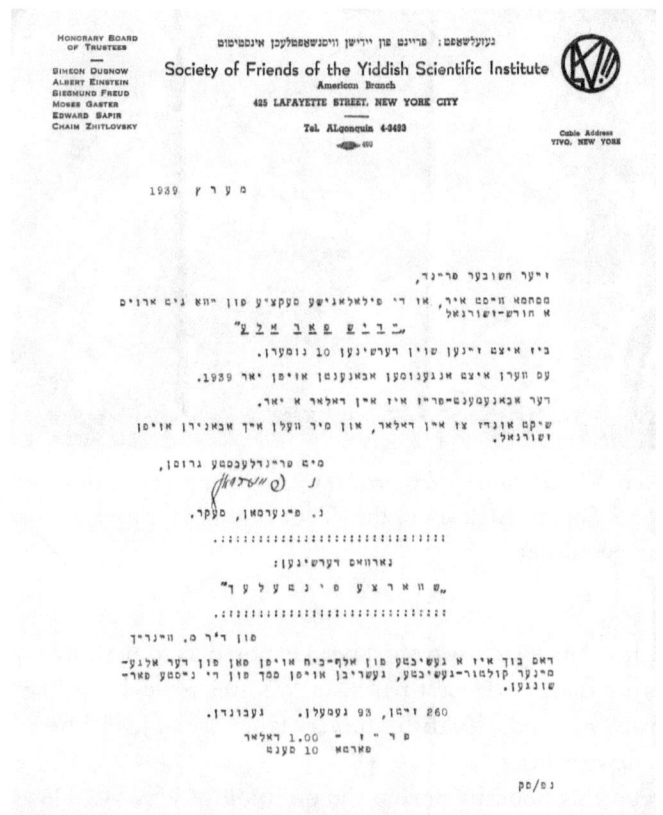

Figure 4. Letter from Naftali Feinerman, Secretary of the Society of Friends of the Yiddish Scientific Institute, American Branch (March 1939). Similar branches of the YIVO existed throughout the world. Source: Archives of the YIVO Institute for Jewish Research. Reprinted with permission.

Weinreich devoted himself publicly, though in a "private language," to the particular Jewish questions Freud considered in fragmentary and private form, in a "public language" and universalist disguise. But this scheme relies in part on the suspicious readings of Freud I have been trying to avoid, using Yiddish as a can opener to pry open the Jewishness of the professor. It was precisely Weinreich's point that it was no longer possible to say what Jewishness was, once the old compensatory mechanisms had

Figure 5. Max Weinreich (*standing, right*) with students at a seminar on psychoanalysis, 1936. Source: Archives of the YIVO Institute for Jewish Research. Reprinted with permission.

turned to dust, once *yidishkayt* had been exposed as something external to the self rather than its deepest truth. In Weinreich's awkward neologisms and borrowed methods, Yiddish, the very language of Jewishness, strained to express new realities.[62]

I began this book by posing the question of why we—Jews, Jewish studies scholars—want to know how much Yiddish Freud knew, persisting in asking the question even after it is clear that we know the answer. To know the answer is to know something fundamental about who Freud was, to expose the bedrock of a Jewish past, to arrive at Jewish truths that make themselves heard only in Jewish languages. For Jewish studies scholars as for psychoanalysts, Yiddish often serves as the punch line of the joke, as the *Ostjude* stands in for the core of the Jewish self. Having analyzed the cryptic footnote, having uncovered the father's Hebrew poem, having counted the Yiddish words, the archaeologist can pack up her picks and spade, the researcher can turn in his manuscript, put their work to bed, for a well-earned, dreamless sleep. But scholars at YIVO, a few hundred miles to the east of Vienna, were under no such illusions. At YIVO, that punch line, the *Ostjude*, was where the real work began. Yiddish, it turned out, was no bedrock for the Jewish psyche. The ground they stood on was shifting as they built their enterprise, as they sought their scholarly footing. In Weinreich's work, Yiddish itself struggled to capture how one became a

Jew and what it might mean to be one. If as Slavoj Žižek writes, "the secrets of the Egyptians were also the secrets for the Egyptians themselves," the secrets concealed from Freud in Yiddish texts were secrets for the Yiddishists themselves.[63] Along with an endlessly generative treasure trove of folklore and rich food and collectivity and a nurturing past, *yidishkayt* was also an enigmatic message, the symptom and name for the split self, the blow you didn't see coming. Like us, those cultural archivists and Yiddishists strained to understand the familiar, foreign voices that murmured just out of hearing.

Out of the Closet, an Epilogue

In the weeks after I turned in the manuscript of this book (but before I wrote this Epilogue), the Freud closet gradually began to revert to its previous status as the closet off our living room. The first crack was the other books and research objects, not strictly related to my Freud project, that drifted onto the desktop, followed by a small bookcase, with all the unrelated-to-Freud books it had held before. Because our house is small, and because nature (and everyone else) abhors a vacuum, it also seemed a natural place to store our upright vacuum cleaner, which had been exiled to a corner of the living room. Soon enough, the vacuum was tangling cords with a stand-up fan. By this point, as I type these closing reflections in a café (finally! again!), the Freud closet has been almost fully deconsecrated, becoming the dusty, crowded storeroom it was before. But it still contains its original items, so it constitutes a (buried) archive or museum of what it once was.

If the Freud closet is a shadow of its former self, it was always a shadow, a cheap substitute for the grander places I imagined I would be seeing during my research year—not only the Frankel Institute in Ann Arbor but maybe also the New York Public Library, the Library of Congress, the National Library of Israel, the various Freud museums and archives. As occurred with other researchers around the world, digital searches and emails to archivists and librarians—the academic first responders of the pandemic—took the place of physical visits. In the closet where I was maintaining my social distance, the Hebrew and Yiddish books I had assembled in the years before lockdown provided a different and more tangible itinerary.

It wasn't until December 2022 that I finally made it to the Freud Museum in London. The visit was tacked on to another engagement (the Limmud Festival in Birmingham), and I neglected to make a research appointment or meet with the archivists with whom I had corresponded. So I paid the entrance fee, put on the headphones, and trudged among the hordes, slightly irked to be just another tourist taking a selfie with the famous couch. It is embarrassing to admit that what I was looking forward to most was the gift shop, which I had passed through quickly in buying a ticket, saving it the way you're supposed to for the end. My Freud closet was in some sense a substitute for and displacement of those more authentically Freudian sites in London and Vienna. But now that I had made it to one of these "real" places, what compelled me was the prospect of adding to my collection, finding something to bring back to my closet where I could enjoy it in peace and quiet.

Such desires aren't so unusual. Kathryn R. Barush points out that pilgrimage sites have attracted souvenir shops since at least the Middle Ages (and complaints about the unholy mixture of sacred sites, kitsch, and commerce are just as old). Pilgrims often commemorated their experiences by acquiring "a physical souvenir of the journey—a bottle of holy water, a statue, a candle."[1] Beyond these souvenirs of pilgrimages actually taken, those who could not travel made or acquired substitutes for physical pilgrimage, "contact relics" that had touched those absent places or images or replicas of sacred sites made holy themselves by a "transfer of spirit." This is not only a premodern or religious phenomenon: Among the contemporary replicas and relics Barush describes is the backyard Camino de Santiago Phil Volker constructed on Vashon Island after a cancer diagnosis; an altar by the artist Gisela Insuesta in a converted prison-transport bus parked in Oakland; and the reconstruction of the grotto at Lourdes, where Bernadette was visited by an apparition of the Virgin Mary in 1858, at Our Lady of Victory National Shrine and Basilica in Lackawanna, New York, an industrial suburb of Buffalo. Barush often visited this shrine with her grandfather as a child and dates her interest in replica sites to these early pilgrimages. She finally visited the original, "authentic" pilgrimage site in Lourdes, with its miraculous spring, when she was thirty-two, as part of a larger research trip. Barush describes the visit:

> When it was finally my turn, I took a draught of the cold, mineral-tasting water and waited in the queue of pilgrims processing toward the grotto with great anticipation. Much to my surprise, when I arrived inside, I

felt I was back in Lackawanna—a reverse medial shift. The tactility of the smooth, well-worn rock, touched by so many pilgrims, transported me immediately to the smaller grotto at Our Lady of Victory, holding my grandfather's rough and strong hand—presence, communitas, embodiment, and a visit from the beloved dead.[2]

There was no grandfather back in my Freud closet, but there were other, more distant representatives of what Barush calls "the beloved dead." What I had in my closet that I missed in London was Freud-in-Hebrew-and-Yiddish; what I was missing in Maresfield Gardens, to put it differently, was the Freudian mirror in which I saw the image that could be called Freud-and-myself. I wasn't the only one looking for such Jewish traces. Describing the London Museum, Simon Goldhill writes,

> There are no signs of Jewish life in the Freud Museum. He owned a menorah, the eight-branched candelabrum used at Chanukah, but only as an art object—it is a very rare thirteenth-century example and the most valuable object in his collection. We couldn't see it, or the two kiddush cups he owned, in the displays in the house.[3]

The kiddush cups were missing (they never, as Yerushalmi tells us, made it to London), but the Freud Museum had a beautiful family tree, beginning, satisfyingly, with Solomon (Shelomo) Freud, the grandfather for whom Freud was named, and continuing on through his parents to a sepia photo of the young Sigmund and Martha, from which branch out their many descendants. But it wasn't the hand-drawn family tree I was familiar with from the Buczacz Memorial Book, the one that went back to Jesucher and Freide, the one that included more of those who might have used those kiddush cups, the one where my own ancestors touched Freud's on the page. The missing menorah Goldhill looked for, the missing Freide I sought out, that was what I had in my closet. It was true that I am not in possession of an actual object that Freud touched and brought from Vienna to London, but what I have that was almost as precious (although not in actual dollar value) is Hebrew and Yiddish translations, and these touched Freud and his words through a different kind of lateral displacement, a different "transfer of spirit." The medieval term "translation," Barush reminded me over a drink after her book talk, conflates the notions of textual and geographic movement. It was used to describe the movement of sacred relics, the remains of saints or "contact relics," from one site to another; thus, the removal of the body of St. John Chrysostom back to

Constantinople in 438, thirty years after he died in exile, is described as the Translation of Saint John, an event commemorated every January 27 in the Orthodox Church. The Freud Museum is a site of translation, as the place to which Freud's "gods and idols," his couch, and his ailing body were "translated" from Vienna. My closet is not so different, as the place that gathers the translations in which Freud's thought was moved into Jewish languages by translators who wanted to rescue it from a different kind of exile.

The museum is also a "Translation Site" in the sense Sherry Simon gives the term, as a space comprising a pendulum swing, in which "the back swing recalls the violence of voices suppressed. The forward swing embraces the struggle to reanimate and reinstate those languages and the worlds they contain."[4] The Freud Museum, swinging back and forth in time and place, is itself more than one place, since beyond Vienna and London, a third Freud Museum has been constructed from the house in which Freud was born in Příbor, the Czech Republic. In a 2006 essay in the *Guardian*, "Analysing Freud's Couch," William Cook describes the "pride of place" that the couch takes in the London Museum. "At Bergasse, meanwhile, the Freud Museum has gathered an array of artworks about couches, from Max Ernst to Man Ray. Andy Warhol's erotic movie, *Couch*, is screened every Sunday. Rachel Whiteread's *Amber Bed* lies slumped against a wall. There's a photo of Oscar Wilde lying on a chaise lounge."[5] Vienna, justifiably stripped of Freud's possessions for having stripped him of his home, mourns this evident absence through a proliferating and multimedia assortment of souvenirs and substitutes of the missing couch. H.D. suggests that the Vienna room in which she was analyzed in 1934 was already a museum, in which Freud sat, "like a curator in a museum, surrounded by his collection."[6] When Freud moved with his family and his collection to London, he tried to preserve the layout of his Viennese office and treatment room. As Goldhill writes, "Freud built, as it were, the first museum of his earlier life."[7] He adds, decades later, after Anna Freud's death: "The house has now been tidied into an exhibition of itself": museums upon museums, strata upon strata, pendulum swings upon pendulum swings.

Goldhill comments on a peculiar psychic feature of the London Museum, which applies as well to the house it preserves, to the apartment it supplanted, and perhaps also to the other museums: The antiquities are confined to one room so that "Freud's office is like the unconscious of the house, a weird other place within the bourgeois home."[8] My Berkeley home is not bourgeois, and I am less religious about the space in which I confine my Freudian tchotchkes, being reasonably sure that a refrigerator magnet belongs on a refrigerator. But my closet, too, is a kind of unconscious, a Yiddishist cellar along the lines Weinreich described to Miron, or one of the "nooks and crannies" Gaston Bachelard sees as among the places where "our memories have refuges."[9] Bachelard points out that modern cities light all spaces with the same electricity, and even in buildings that have basements, "we no longer go to the cellar carrying a candle."[10] But this may have already been true for Freud: The most precious object in his collection, according to Goldhill, the thirteenth-century menorah, was for display rather than ritual use. Freud's Jewishness invites what Bachelard calls a topoanalysis, "the systematic psychological study of the sites of our intimate lives," which would attend to the spatial, psychological, material, and temporal differences and transformations between the unconscious as (Jewish) cellar and the unconscious as (Jewish) closet, room, or museum display. What I have in my closet invites a reading not only of depths but also, as Kosofsky Sedgwick puts it, of "what is beside rather than what is beneath or behind."[11]

In the end I bought only one small souvenir from the gift shop. It turns out that the holdings—textual and material—of the Freud Museum gift shop are not so different from what I had already acquired in other places around the world or had bought on Amazon or eBay or the Unemployed Philosophers Guild website. The only objects for sale I did not already own (at least of those that would fit in my carry-on bag) were the museum's own magnets and pens. It was no bottle of holy water, but the fancier of the two pens had a transparent chamber filled with a mysterious liquid that magically allowed a couch to slide up and down against the background of Freud's treatment room (the man himself was missing). The pen is a souvenir not only of my London pilgrimage but also of my own "beloved dead," my always-traveling father, who brought back a few such pens, along with snow globes, little spoons, and plastic viewers, to show us where in the world he had been and compensate for his absence. Freud himself began to collect antiquities in the month or two after his father's 1896 death, and the paradoxical power of paternal absence plays a role in his thinking from the beginning until the end of his career.[12] With the possible exception of my bespoke Yiddish Freud mug (which serves as a penholder for the Freud pen and others), the London Freud Museum pen is the most prized object in my closet. It is true that the closet is no longer alive the way it once was, when I felt it thrumming within me even when I was away, unless it abides in this book, as the engine that drove its thought and the space that shaped its words. Describing the beloved books and other "booklike creations" that inhabit the "fringe areas" of a collection, Walter Benjamin writes of the "spirits, or at least little genii," that live within such a collection:

> For a real collector—and I mean a real collector, a collector as he ought to be—ownership is the most intimate relationship that one can have to objects. Not that they come alive in him; it is he who lives in them. So I have erected one of his dwellings, with books as the building stones, before you, and now he is going to disappear inside, as is only fitting.[13]

Notes

Introduction

1. "Jesus Shaves Heat-Changing Mug," Unemployed Philosophers Guild, 2023, https://philosophersguild.com/products/jesus-shaves-mug?_pos=425&_sid=3a7c6fa6b&_ss=r.

2. Walter Benjamin, "Unpacking My Library," trans. Harry Zohn, in *Illuminations: Essays and Reflections*, ed. Hannah Arendt (New York: Houghton Mifflin Harcourt, 1968), 67. Benjamin's reference is to a humorous painting of that title by Carl Spitzweg, circa 1850.

3. Benjamin, "Unpacking My Library," 67.

4. Benjamin, "Unpacking My Library," 60. For a recent study of Jewish books as material objects, see Barbara E. Mann, *The Object of Jewish Literature: A Material History* (New Haven, CT: Yale University Press, 2022).

5. Daniel Boyarin, "What Does a Jew Want?; or, The Political Meaning of the Phallus," *Discourse* 19, no. 2 (1997): 22. The reference is to Benita Parry, "Problems in Current Theories of Colonial Discourse," *Oxford Literary Review* 9 (1987): 27–58.

6. Eve Kosofsky Sedgwick, *Epistemology of the Closet* (Berkeley: University of California Press, 1990).

7. Sander L. Gilman, *Inscribing the Other* (Lincoln: University of Nebraska Press, 1991), 202. See also Boyarin's summary of Gilman's view in Boyarin, "What Does a Jew Want?," 28.

8. Boyarin, "What Does a Jew Want?," 33. The reference is to Tim Dean, "On the Eve of a Queer Future," *Raritan* 15, no. 1 (1995): 116–34.

9. The "Jewish closet," as a masquerade or form of double consciousness, functioning in parallel to or differently from the "queer closet," continues to animate discussions of Jewish identity in modernity, with many critics arguing against Kosofsky Sedgwick's claim that Jewishness is the more stable referent than queerness. Jonathan Freedman contrasts the gay and Jewish closets in Proust's *Remembrance of Things Past*, in which "Jewishness and perversion return over and over as topics of mystery and interrogation." According to Freedman, a comparison of these closets seems "to establish the Jew as the 'out' other, the

one whose closetedness has, at least, a local habitation and a name; indeed, since the name *Jew* has been sounded as a synonym for *other* throughout the long history of Christian Europe, sodomy appears yet more secret, yet more epistemologically unstable when brought into contact with it—it is knowable through, or is best defined by, the image of the Jew." Jonathan Freedman, "Coming out of the Jewish Closet with Marcel Proust," *GLQ* 7, no. 4 (2001): 527. In her essay on Agnieszka Holland's 1990 film *Europa, Europa*, Ruth Johnston explores the racial masquerade that allows the film's protagonist, Salomon Perel, to survive the Holocaust, citing "the epistemological space of the Jewish closet" and demonstrating "its structural affinities with the gay closet," literally, as when the protagonist dreams that he is hiding in a closet with the naked Hitler, who conceals his genitals with his hands. See Ruth D. Johnston, "The Jewish Closet in *Europa, Europa*," *Camera Obscura* 18, no. 1 (2003): 1.

10. Eve Kosofsky Sedgwick, *Touching Feeling: Affect, Pedagogy, Performativity* (Durham, NC: Duke University Press, 2003), 8.

11. Sigmund Freud, *Standard Edition of the Complete Psychological Works of Sigmund Freud*, ed. James Strachey, in collaboration with Anna Freud, assisted by Alix Strachey and Alan Tyson (London: Hogarth Press, 1953–74), 13: xv. Hereafter abbreviated as SE.

12. "Negation" (1925), SE 19: 235–39. It is worth pointing out that Freud's concept is aimed more narrowly than common usage of the term, at illuminating how a free association draws meaningful connections even when one element is denied or framed in a denial.

13. Yosef Hayim Yerushalmi, *Freud's Moses: Judaism Terminable and Interminable* (New Haven, CT: Yale University Press, 1991), 69.

14. Yerushalmi, *Freud's Moses*, 68.

15. Yerushalmi, *Freud's Moses*, 70. The citation is from Sigmund Freud, "Letter to 'Meister Arnold'" (June 17, 1936), in *The Letters of Sigmund Freud and Arnold Zweig*, ed. Ernst L. Freud, trans. Elaine Robson-Scott and William Robson-Scott (New York: Harcourt Brace, 1970), 131; emphasis in original.

16. Freud sees the fetish as a substitute for the missing maternal phallus and a displacement for castration anxiety. Sigmund Freud et al., "Fetishism," SE 21: 147–58. Julia Kristeva brings this insight to bear on language, as substituting for a lost connection to reality and the object, asking, "Is not language our ultimate and inseparable fetish?" Julia Kristeva, *Powers of Horror: An Essay on Abjection* (New York: Columbia University Press, 1982), 37.

17. Anita Norich, "A Response from Anita Norich," *Prooftexts* 20, no. 1–2 (2000): 217; responding to Kathryn Hellerstein, "Translating as a Feminist: Reconceiving Anna Margolin," *Prooftexts* 20, no. 1–2 (2000), 191–208.

18. Norich, "Response," 217.

19. Zohar Weiman-Kelman, "Touching Time: Poetry, History, and the Erotics of Yiddish," *Criticism* 59, no. 1 (2017): 116.

20. Karl Kraus, "On Psychoanalysis and Psychology," in *Anti-Freud: Karl Kraus's Criticism of Psycho-analysis and Psychiatry*, by Thomas Szasz (Syracuse, NY: Syracuse University Press, 1990), 103, see also 117. Quoted in John M. Efron, *Medicine and the German Jews: A History* (New Haven, CT: Yale University Press, 2001), 151. I thank John Efron for this

reference. On Freud, the *Neue Freie Presse*, and Kraus's attacks on psychoanalysis, see Leo A. Lensing, "The *Neue Freie Presse* Neurosis: Freud, Karl Kraus, and Newspaper as Daily Devotional," in *The Jewish World of Sigmund Freud: Essays on Cultural Roots and the Problem of Religious Identity*, ed. Arnold D. Richards (Jefferson, NC: McFarland, 2010), 51–65.

21. Freud, "Wild Psychoanalysis," SE 11: 219–27.

22. Gilles Deleuze and Felix Guattari, *Anti-Oedipus: Capitalism and Schizophrenia*, trans. Robert Hurley, Mark Seem, and Helen R. Lane (Minneapolis: University of Minnesota Press, 1983), 8.

23. Jacob Meitlis, "The Last Days of Sigmund Freud," *Jewish Frontier* 18 (September 1951): 21.

24. See J. Keith Davies and Gerhard Fichtner, *Freud's Library: A Comprehensive Catalogue* (London: Freud Museum; and Tübingen: edition discord, 2004). According to the "Introduction," 3, Freud selected only a small part of his Vienna library to bring to London, making the presence of these translations that he could not read in his London collection all the more meaningful.

25. In 1960, the linguist Roman Jakobson described this function of language as "primarily serving to establish, to prolong, or to discontinue communication." See Roman Jakobson, *Language and Literature*, ed. Krystyna Pomorska and Stephen Rudy (Cambridge, MA: Harvard University Press, 1987), 68.

26. Rita Felski, "Comparison and Translation: A Perspective from Actor-Network Theory," *Comparative Literature Studies* 53, no. 4 (2016): 750.

Chapter 1

1. Ernest Jones writes that the language of Freiberg, the town of Freud's birth, was Czech, but "the Jews would speak German (or Yiddish) among themselves"; Ernest Jones, *The Life and Work of Sigmund Freud* (New York: Basic Books, 1953), 1:11–12. The first, often-quoted report that Freud's mother, Amalie Nathanson Freud, spoke only Yiddish appears to be in Erika Freeman and Theodor Reik, *Insights: Conversations with Theodor Reik* (New York: Prentice and Hall, 1971), 80, in which Reik asserts that Freud's mother spoke to her son in "not High German but Galician Yiddish." Yosef Hayim Yerushalmi, quoting Rank, asks, "If this be so, what shall we say of Jakob Freud, who grew up in Galicia [unlike Amalie, who grew up in Vienna]?" Yerushalmi counts "thirteen Yiddish words in the portions of Freud's correspondence published to date," including not only words common in German speech but also those known only to Yiddish speakers "like *Knetcher* (wrinkles), *Stuss* (nonsense), *Dalles* (poverty), or *tomer dokh* (perhaps, after all)"; Yerushalmi, *Freud's Moses*, 69. Marthe Robert, tracing the contours of Freud's social context, notes that "just as in Berlin, Vienna, or Prague, the language of the Jews of [Freud's father's] generation was never very far from Yiddish, so that their manners, tastes, and habits of thought remained very close to their popular origins"; Marthe Robert, *From Oedipus to Moses: Freud's Jewish Identity*, trans. Ralph Manheim (New York: Anchor Books, 1976), 184n59. Marianne Krüll writes that it is probable that Freud grew up among Yiddish-speaking immigrants: "Freud must thus have been familiar with the sounds of Yiddish, the language all Galician Jews spoke among themselves, and which, we may take it, Jacob and Amalie Freud spoke

with each other. We know that Amalie spoke Yiddish even in her old age"; Marianne Krüll, *Freud and His Father* (New York: W. W. Norton, 1986), 138. Jerry Diller, who charges the translators of Freud's letters to Wilhelm Fliess with "sanitizing" Freud's Yiddish by rendering, for instance, *Stuss* as "rubbish" without indicating the Yiddish of the source, argues that despite Freud's expressed regret that he did not know Hebrew or Yiddish, he had something of a Jewish education in his youth, often employed Yiddish in his correspondence, and was familiar with Jewish ritual; Jerry Victor Diller, *Freud's Jewish Identity: A Case Study in the Impact of Ethnicity* (Rutherford, NJ: Fairleigh Dickinson Press, 1991), 21–22. Yerushalmi mentions the volumes of the Talmud in his essay "The Purloined Kiddush Cups: Reopening the Case on Freud's Jewish Identity," published as an addendum to the book *Sigmund Freud and Art: His Personal Collection of Antiquities*, ed. Lynn Gamwell and Richard Wells (New York: Harry N. Abrams; and London: Freud Museum, 1989); the addendum is titled *Sigmund Freud's Jewish Heritage* (Binghampton, NY: SUNY Press; and London: Freud Museum, 1991), n.p. These citations could be multiplied many times over.

2. Many of those who recount evidence of Freud's knowledge of Jewish languages pair this claim with an assertion that he attempted to obscure this knowledge. See Diller, *Freud's Jewish Identity*, 23–24; and Yerushalmi, *Freud's Moses*, 68. For an astute critique of these assumptions, see Christopher Hutton, "Freud and the Family Drama of Yiddish," in *Studies in Yiddish Linguistics*, ed. P. Wexler (Tübingen: M. Niemeyer Verlag, 1990), 9–22, particularly 21, where he writes that the turn to Yiddish in Jewish jokes is not a symptom of unconscious self-hatred but a deliberate act of "controlled regression" in which Yiddish is reclaimed as a badge of "the honesty of self-knowledge, intimacy, authenticity."

3. A. A. Roback, *Jewish Influence in Modern Thought* (Cambridge, MA: Sci-Art Publishers, 1929). The book was reissued in 2005 as a facsimile reprint (Whitefish, MT: Kessinger, 2005). The chapter on Jewish influences on psychoanalysis is on 152–202. Selections from Roback's correspondence appear in A. A. Roback, *Freudiana* (Cambridge, MA: Sci-Art Publishers, 1957), a curious collection of letters and essays, described in this way on the cover: "What you cannot find in any biography of Freud. Unpublished letters from Freud to the author; also letters from Havelock Ellis, Pavlov, Romain Rolland, Bernard Shaw, and others, relative to Freud's importance. Critical Essays and Reviews, Freud's Father's Inscriptions Translated and Interpreted." Roback was a Yiddishist, philosopher, psychologist, and prolific writer on all these subjects who, among other accomplishments, assembled a ten-thousand-book Yiddish library at Harvard and taught the first university course on Yiddish literature in the United States at that institution in 1929. He also served on the YIVO advisory council. The mention of a dedication "evidently written in Hebrew letters" is from the letter of February 20, 1930, in Roback, *Freudiana*, 27. The Library of Congress holds additional items of the Freud-Roback correspondence; Ernest Jones gave him permission to reprint only a selection.

4. Davies and Fichtner, *Freud's Library*, items 3003–10.

5. Meitlis, "Last Days," 20.

6. SE 20: 273–74. See also Diane Jonte-Pace, *Speaking the Unspeakable: Religion, Misogyny, and the Uncanny Mother in Freud's Cultural Texts* (Berkeley: University of California Press, 2001), 85.

7. Sigmund Freud and Anna Freud, *Gesammelte Werke, chronologisch geordnet* (London: Imago Press 1952), 17:52. Hereafter abbreviated as GW.

8. SE 17: 244–45.

9. Jonte-Pace, *Speaking the Unspeakable*, 85–86. Jonte-Pace cites an often-quoted essay by Susan Shapiro that traces the long associations of Jews and the uncanny, a persistent feature of European Judeophobia: "It is as this border-state, this spectral and ghost-like condition, that I think the trope of the 'Jewish Uncanny' is both repressed and returns in Freud's writings, especially in his 1919 essay, 'das Unheimliche' ('The Uncanny')." Susan E. Shapiro, "The Uncanny Jew: A Brief History of an Image," *Judaism* 46, no. 1 (1997): 70.

10. Roback, *Jewish Influence*, 160.

11. A. A. Roback, "Letter to Sigmund Freud" (February 20, 1930), in Roback, *Freudiana*, 27.

12. A. A. Roback, "Letter to Sigmund Freud" (March 10, 1930), in Roback, *Freudiana*, 30–31.

13. Roback was referring to Ignatz Bernstein and Benjamin Wolf Segel, *Proverbia Judaeorum erotica et turpia: Jüdische Sprichwörter: Erotischen und rustikalen Inhalts*, and subtitled, in Yiddish, *Oysgelasene un grobe shprikhverter* (Vienna: Jüdisch Liebhaberbibliothek, 1918). The seventy-page book, printed in a limited run of three hundred as an addendum to Bernstein and Segel's *Jüdische Sprichwörterbuch*, was a collection of lewd and coarse Yiddish proverbs. For an English translation, see Ignatz Bernstein, *Yiddish Sayings Mama Never Taught You*, trans. Marvin Zuckerman and Gershon Weltman (Van Nuys, CA: Perivale Press, 1975).

14. A bilingual edition of the paper, with an introduction describing the circumstances of its composition, was published as Sigmund Freud and D. E. Oppenheim, *Dreams in Folklore* (New York: International Universities Press, 1958). The paper was also included in the *Standard Edition*: SE 12: 175–204.

15. Sigmund Freud, "Letter to Dr. Friedrich S. Krauss on *Anthropophyteia*" (June 26, 1919), in SE 11: 234.

16. Sigmund Freud, "Letter to A. A. Roback" (March 24, 1930), Roback's translation in *Freudiana*, 34. In the German, Freud wrote, "Ich Weiss, diese Ausnahme kommt daher, dass Sie die jüdische Saite berürt haben, die bei mir so empfindlich nachklingt."

17. Freud used the term *Chuzba* in reference to a misunderstanding: Roback had been so assured in ascribing to him "mystical leanings" that Freud had assumed that he was "a dignified old gentleman." When Roback apologized and excused himself by reference to his youth, Freud responded that in assuming he was speaking to an established scholar, he had "overlooked the necessary result of the combination of the American democratic mind and Jewish '*Chuzba*.'" Sigmund Freud, "Letter to A. A. Roback" (March 24, 1930), in Roback, *Freudiana*, 34–35.

18. Roback, who was given permission to publish only six of Freud's letters in full, summarizes Freud's letter of March 13, 1932, in response to this request in Roback, *Freudiana*, 42. But this and other letters from Freud and his correspondence with Ernest Jones in relation to permission to republish appear in the Library of Congress, Sigmund Freud Papers:

General Correspondence, 1996; Roback, A. A., with cover letters from Roback to Ernest Jones, 1956, 1934 to 1936, Manuscript/Mixed Material mss3999001109.

19. A. A. Roback, "Letter to Sigmund Freud" (August 17, 1939), in Roback, *Freudiana*, 78. In fact, Freud's Hebrew name was Shlomo (not Sholom), the name usually transliterated as Solomon, and he was indeed named after a deceased relative, his paternal grandfather, Shlomo Freud.

20. Freud expressed the worry that psychoanalysis was being treated as Jewish in a letter to Karl Abraham explaining why Carl Gustav Jung was so necessary for the movement's success; see Sigmund Freud, "Letter to Karl Abraham" (May 3, 1908), in *The Complete Correspondence of Sigmund Freud and Karl Abraham 1907–1925*, ed. Ernst Falzeder (London: H. Karnac Books, 2002), 38–39.

21. The sketch appeared on Episode 1, Season 14 (1988). A crucial dimension of the wit of this parody, it seems to me, is that it gets important details right—the popular game of discovering whether a famous person is Jewish *is* typically played with a looser set of rules than supplied by more formal, halakhic definitions of Jewishness. For a transcript of the sketch, see "SNL Transcripts: Tom Hanks: 10/08/88: Jew, Not a Jew," SNL Transcripts Tonight, https://snltranscripts.jt.org/88/88ajew.phtml.

22. Yerushalmi, *Freud's Moses*, 68–69.

23. Yerushalmi, *Freud's Moses*, 72.

24. Yerushalmi, *Freud's Moses*, 69.

25. Yerushalmi, *Freud's Moses*, 99.

26. Yerushalmi, *Freud's Moses*, 69.

27. SE 8: 112.

28. Theodor Reik, *Jewish Wit* (New York: Gamut Press, 1962), 192.

29. Dan Ben-Amos, "The 'Myth' of Jewish Humor," *Western Folklore* 32, no. 2 (1973): 122.

30. Ben-Amos, "'Myth' of Jewish Humor," 129–30.

31. Reik, *Jewish Wit*, 192. Where Reik renders the term spoken by the Polish Jew as "Asoi!," Freud renders this joke: "Ein galizischer Jude fährt in der Eisenbahn und hat es sich recht bequem gemacht, den Rock aufgeknöpft, die Füße auf die Bank gelegt. Da steigt ein modern gekleideter Herr ein. Sofort nimmt sich der Jude zusammen, setzt sich in bescheidene Positur. Der Fremde blättert in einem Buch, rechnet, besinnt sich und richtet plötzlich an den Juden die Frage: 'Ich bitte Sie, wann haben wir Jomkipur?' (Versöhnungstag.) 'Aesoi,' sagt der Jude und legt die Füße wieder auf die Bank, ehe er die Antwort gibt." GW 6: 86.

32. Reik, *Jewish Wit*, 193.

33. See "Bageling," Jewish English Lexicon, 2012–present, https://jel.jewish-languages.org/words/36. I want to thank Sara Labaton for suggesting this connection. For a discussion on the origins and nuances of the term "bageling," see Philologos, "The Great Bagel(ing) Mystery Has Been Solved," *Forward*, October 27, 2013, https://forward.com/culture/186101/the-great-bageling-mystery-has-been-solved/.

34. Jacques Derrida, *Archive Fever: A Freudian Impression*, trans. Eric Frenowitz (Chicago: University of Chicago Press, 1996), 38.

35. As it happens, Freud died, by assisted suicide, on Yom Kippur, 5640 (more generally described in the calendars we moderns carry as September 23, 1939). Did Freud know? Or is the date significant only for me, more connected than Freud to those Jewish rhythms that still tick, like a lost watch, alongside the more secular calendar that structures my life?

36. Freud himself countered this suggestion in affirming that the scientific character of psychoanalysis meant not that it was undeniable but that it was open to correction. Freud ends "Beyond the Pleasure Principle" with an acknowledgment that he has raised more questions than answers in discussing the relationship between the pleasure principle and the death drive: "This in turn raises a host of other questions to which we can at present find no answer. We must be patient and await fresh methods and occasions of research. We must be ready, too, to abandon a path that we have followed for a time, if it seems to be leading to no good end. Only believers, who demand that science shall be a substitute for the catechism they have given up, will blame an investigator for developing or even transforming his views." SE 18: 63–64.

37. Jones, *Life and Work*, 1:12.

38. Franz Kafka, "Einleitungsvortrag Über Jargon," in *Nachgelassene Schriften und Fragmente*, by Franz Kafka, ed. Malcolm Pasley, 1:189. For the English, see Franz Kafka, "An Introductory Talk on the Yiddish Language," trans. Ernst Kaiser and Eithne Wilkins, in *Reading Kafka: Prague, Politics, and the Fin de Siècle*, ed Mark Anderson (New York: Schocken, 1987), 266. The talk introduced a reading of Yiddish poetry in Prague by the Yiddish actor Yitzhok Löwy.

39. Elias Canetti, *The Tongue Set Free*, trans. Joachim Neugroschel (New York: Granta, 2011), 10.

40. George Steiner, *After Babel: Aspects of Language and Translation* (Oxford: Oxford University Press, 1992), 121.

41. Robert Samacher, "Louis Wolfson et le Yiddish," *Recherches en psychanalyse* 4 (2005): 124. Unless otherwise specified, translations are my own.

42. Eva Hoffman, *Lost in Translation: A Life in a New Language* (New York: Penguin, 1990), 14.

43. Hannah Pollin-Galay, *Ecologies of Witnessing: Language, Place, and Holocaust Testimony* (New Haven, CT: Yale University Press, 2018), 171.

44. Rainer Guldin, "Translating Space: On Rivers, Seas, Archipelagos and Straits," *Flusser Studies* 14 (2012): 1.

45. Yasemin Yildiz, *Beyond the Mother Tongue: The Postmonolingual Condition* (New York: Fordham University Press, 2012), 7.

46. Kafka, "An Introductory Talk," 263.

47. David Damrosch, "Scriptworlds: Writing Systems and the Formation of World Literature," *Modern Language Quarterly* 68, no. 2 (2007): 195. Of the three "scriptworlds" in the ancient Near East, cuneiform, hieroglyphics, and the West Semitic group of scripts (which includes Hebrew), Damrosch writes: "The literatures of these three groups tended to stay in their respective scriptworlds" (199).

48. Steiner, *After Babel*, 121.

49. Max Weinreich, *History of the Yiddish Language*, ed. Paul Glasser, trans. Shlomo

Noble, with the assistance of Joshua A. Fishman (New Haven, CT: Yale University Press, 2008), 282–83.

50. Richard Wagner also commented on the *sound* of Jewish speech: "In particular does the purely physical aspect of the Jewish mode of speech repel us. Throughout an intercourse of two millennia with European nations, Culture has not succeeded in breaking the remarkable stubbornness of the Jewish naturel as regards the peculiarities of Semitic pronunciation. The first thing that strikes our ear as quite outlandish and unpleasant, in the Jew's production of the voice-sounds, is a creaking, squeaking, buzzing snuffle: add thereto an employment of words in a sense quite foreign to our nation's tongue." Richard Wagner, *Judaism in Music and Other Essays*, trans. William Ashton Ellis (Lincoln: University of Nebraska Press, 1995), 85–86.

51. John Murray Cuddihy, *The Ordeal of Civility: Freud, Marx, Lévi-Strauss, and the Jewish Struggle with Modernity*, 2nd ed. (Boston: Beacon Press, 1987), 20. Cuddihy quotes Solomon Litt, president of the Jewish Welfare Board, as cited in the *Jewish Digest* (September 1963), 70. According to Cuddihy, this joke has different functions depending on its audience: If told by a representative of the Jewish community, it functions as a warning to Jews not to try to assimilate; if told by an assimilated Jew, it "serves as an objective correlative of his subjectively ambiguous situation." Cuddihy does not analyze the function of this joke when told by a non-Jew and scholar such as himself.

52. On the ideological construction of the concept of a "mother tongue," see Yildiz, *Beyond the Mother Tongue*, 10–14 and throughout.

53. Steiner, *After Babel*, 121.

54. Daniel Heller-Roazen here summarizes Jakob Hornemann Bredsdorff's influential doctrine of language stratification and language change in *Echolalias: On the Forgetting of Language* (New York: Zone Books, 2005), 78.

55. Weinreich, *History of the Yiddish Language*, 247.

56. Ber Borochov, "The Tasks of Yiddish Philology," trans. Jacob Engelhardt and Dalit Berman, *Science in Context* 20, no. 2 (2007): 363. See also Barry Trachtenberg, "Ber Borochov's 'The Tasks of Yiddish Philology,'" *Science in Context* 20 no. 2 (2007): 341–52. For the Yiddish, see Ber Borochov, "The Tasks of Yiddish Philology" [Di ufgabn fun der yidisher filologye], in *Der pinkes: Yorbukh far der geshikhte fun der yidisher literatur un shprakh, far folklore, kritik un bibliografye* [Annals: Yearbook for the history of Yiddish literature and language, folklore, criticism, and bibliography], ed. Shmuel Charney (Vilna: Kletskin Farlag, 1913), 1–22.

57. Borochov, "Tasks of Yiddish Philology," 363.

58. For a reading of the sexual dimension of the relationship between Hebrew and Yiddish as the masculine and feminine dimensions of the Ashkenazic language system, see Naomi Seidman, *A Marriage Made in Heaven: The Sexual Politics of Hebrew and Yiddish* (Berkeley: University of California Press, 1997).

59. Hutton, "Freud and the Family Drama of Yiddish," 10.

60. Albert Memmi, *The Colonizer and the Colonized*, trans. Howard Greenfeld (London: Souvenir, 1974), 152.

61. Max Kohn, *Freud et le Yiddish: Le préanalytique (1877–1897)* (Paris: Economica, 1984), 7.
62. Canetti, *Tongue Set Free*, 10.
63. Elias Canetti, *The Play of the Eyes*, trans. Ralph Manheim (New York: Farrar, Straus and Giroux, 1986), 317.
64. Heller-Roazen, *Echolalias*, 176.
65. Andreas Kilcher, "Kafka, Scholem und die Politik der jüdische Sprachen," in *Politik und Religion im Judentum*, ed. Christoph Miething (Tübingen: Max Niemeyer Verlag, 1999), 92; quoted in David Bruce Suchoff, *Kafka's Jewish Languages: The Hidden Openness of Tradition* (Philadelphia: University of Pennsylvania Press, 2012), 6. The translation is Suchoff's. The connection between Jewish historical experience and the linguistic phenomenon of mixed languages in which *Fremdwörter* play an enriching or alienating role is famously explored by Theodor Adorno in "Wörter aus dem Fremde," in *Minima Moralia: Reflections from Damaged Life*, trans. E. F. N. Jephcott (London: Verso, 1974), where he famously writes that "German words of foreign derivation [*Fremdwörter*] are the Jews of language" (110). Monolingual ideology is, in Adorno's view, closely allied with the fear of the foreign that manifests as antisemitism. Adorno's essay in fact began as a response to criticism of his practice of including "words of foreign derivation" in his German works.
66. Bachelard describes the juxtaposition of claustrophobia and agoraphobia, for instance, in the poetry of Henri Michaux, which aggravates "the line of demarcation between outside and inside. But in so doing, from the psychological standpoint, he has demolished the lazy certainties of the geometric intuitions by means of which psychologists sought to govern the space of intimacy." Gaston Bachelard, *The Poetics of Space*, trans. Maria Jolas (Boston: Beacon Press, 1994), 220,
67. Jacques Lacan, "The Mirror Stage as Formative of the *I* Function," in *Écrits: A Selection*, trans. Bruce Fink in collaboration with Héloïse Fink and Russell Grigg (New York: Norton, 2002), 6–7.
68. Yehuda Leib Gordon's poem "Hakitzah ami!" (Awake, my people!) was first published in *Hakarmel* 6, no. 1 (1866): 1. This translation is taken from Michael Stanislawski's biography of Gordon, *For Whom Do I Toil?: Judah Leib Gordon and the Crisis of Russian Jewry* (New York: Oxford University Press, 1988), 49. For a discussion of the reception history and allusive power of the poem, see Gershon Bacon, "An Anthem Reconsidered: On Text and Subject in Yehuda Leib Gordon's 'Awake, My People!,'" *Prooftexts* 15, no. 2 (1995): 185–94.
69. Moshe Leib Lilienblum, "A Critique of the Collected Poems of Yehuda Leib Gordon" [in Hebrew], in *Kol kitvei Moshe Leib Lilienblum* (Odessa: M. Beilinson Press, 1911/1912), 3:34. Quoted in Bacon, "An Anthem Reconsidered," 188.
70. Yirmiyahu Yovel, *The Other Within: The Marranos: Split Identity and Emerging Modernity* (Princeton, NJ: Princeton University Press, 2009), 256. The reference is to the poet, translator, and philosopher Fernando Pessoa (1888–1935); a citation from his work serves as an epigraph to one of Yovel's chapters, "Portugal and the Fifth Empire": "Who, if they're Portuguese, can live within the narrow bounds of just one personality, just one nation, just one religion, one nation?" (187). In the second volume of *Spinoza and Other Heretics*, Yovel

devotes a chapter to the philosophical commonalities and differences between Spinoza's and Freud's thought, drawing a connection as well to their biographical positions: "To a certain extent both Spinoza and Freud exemplify the situation of the Jew who, abandoning his orthodox tradition without being integrated into the Christian world, develops a penetrating eye for both worlds and the ability to free himself from their conventions." Yirmiyahu Yovel, *The Adventure of Immanence, Spinoza and Other Heretics* (Princeton, NJ: Princeton University Press, 1989), 2:141–42.

71. Michel Foucault, *The History of Sexuality, Volume 1*, trans. Robert Hurley (New York: Vintage, 1990), 68.

72. The aphorism is one of many Pappenheim wrote, which she referred to as *Denkzettel*, memos she jotted down and distributed to friends and colleagues or included in various publications; this aphorism is the only one that mentions psychoanalysis. In Bertha Pappenheim, "Gedanken über Erziehung," *Blätter des Jüdischen Frauenbundes* 5, no. 2 (February 1929): 5; cited in and translated by Elizabeth Loentz, *Let Me Continue to Speak the Truth: Bertha Pappenheim as Author and Activist* (Cincinnati: Hebrew Union College Press, 2007), 1.

73. Nancy Hartevelt Kobrin, "Uriel Da Costa, J. M. Da Costa, M.D.—What's Freud Got to Do with It? Or How Ladino and Sephardic Culture Inform Psychoanalysis and Trauma Studies," in *Languages and Literatures of Sephardic and Oriental Jews: Proceedings of the Sixth International Congress for Research on the Sephardi and Oriental Jewish Heritage*, ed. David M. Bunis (Jerusalem: Bialik Institute, 2009), 306.

74. Jonathan Skolnik, "Writing Jewish History between Gutzkow and Goethe: Auerbach's Spinoza and the Birth of Modern Jewish Historical Fiction," *Prooftexts* 19, no. 2 (1999): 117.

75. Freud mentions Heine's joke that Spinoza was his *Unglaubengenossen* (as Freud was with both of them) in SE 8: 77. On Freud and Spinoza, see Henri Vermorel, "The Presence of Spinoza in the Exchanges between Sigmund Freud and Romain Rolland," *International Journal of Psychoanalysis* 90, no. 6 (2009): 1235–54.

76. Hartevelt Kobrin, "Uriel Da Costa," 310. On the Sephardic population of Vienna during those decades, see Martha Rozenblit, *The Jews of Vienna, 1867–1914: Assimilation and Identity* (Albany: SUNY Press, 1983), 148; according to Rozenblit, there were a few thousand Sephardim in Vienna in Freud's youth.

77. In *The Psychopathology of Everyday Life*, for instance, Freud points out a number of literary examples, including works by Shakespeare, that show that the writer "was familiar with the mechanisms and meaning of slips of the tongue"; SE 6: 96. Philosophers, too, understood the unconscious: In a 1917 essay, he wrote that "probably very few people can have realized the momentous significance for science and life of the recognition of unconscious mental processes. It was not psycho-analysis, however, let us hasten to add, which first took this step. There are famous philosophers who may be cited as forerunners—above all the great thinker Schopenhauer"; SE 17: 143.

78. Cuddihy, *Ordeal of Civility*, 20.

79. Daniel Boyarin, *Unheroic Conduct: The Rise of Homosexuality and the Invention of the Jewish Man* (Berkeley: University of California Press, 1997), 39–40.

Chapter 2

1. For an analysis of Freud's antiquity collection as a modern version of idolatry and transgression against Mosaic monotheism, see Ellen Handler Spitz, "Psychoanalysis and the Legacy of Antiquity," in Gamwell and Wells, *Sigmund Freud and Art*, 159. The photograph of Freud's antiquities collection was taken by Edmund Engelman in May 1938, shortly before Freud's departure from Vienna, to document the contents of his apartment. The identification of the two goblets as kiddush cups is described in Yosef Hayim Yerushalmi, "The Purloined Kiddush Cups," n.p., but he does not name the discerning graduate student, nor have the cups been found among Freud's possessions in London.

2. Lynn Gamwell, "The Origins of Freud's Antiquities Collection," in Gamwell and Wells, *Sigmund Freud and Art*, 22.

3. For a catalogue of these references, see Donald Kuspit, "A Mighty Metaphor: The Analogy of Archaeology and Psychoanalysis," in Gamwell and Wells, *Sigmund Freud and Art*, 133–51.

4. H.D. (Hilda Doolittle), *Tribute to Freud* (New York: New Directions, 1994), 67–71.

5. Kuspit, "Mighty Metaphor," 133.

6. SE 1: 126.

7. SE 1: 408; GW 1: 426–27. Of course, this text is itself—as are so many others by Freud—bilingual, with the Latin appearing in the original.

8. Alan Bass, "On the History of a Mistranslation and the Psychoanalytic Movement," in *Difference in Translation*, ed. Joseph F. Graham (Ithaca, NY: Cornell University Press, 1985), 102.

9. Sabine Hake, "*Saxa loquuntur*: Freud's Archaeology of the Text," *boundary 2* (1993): 151.

10. SE 2: 129.

11. SE 13: 177.

12. For an account of this friendship, a description of the Anna O. case, identification of Anna O. as Bertha Pappenheim, and credit to her for discovering the "cathartic method," see Jones, *Life and Work*, 1:223–26.

13. Steiner, *After Babel*, 121.

14. Along with the insights provided by hysteria, Anna O.'s case was foundational for the understanding of transference and countertransference in therapy. According to Jones, these played a huge role in the treatment, which Breuer broke off after the patient contracted "an hysterical childbirth (pseudocyesis), the logical termination of a phantom pregnancy that had been invisibly developing in response to Breuer's ministrations." Jones, *Life and Work*, 1:224–25.

15. The connections between hysteria and its various cultural contexts (in particular its nineteenth-century peak) are explored in Edward Shorter, *From Paralysis to Fatigue* (New York: Free Press, 1992). For a counterargument to the view that hysteria is a "cultural" mental illness, see Jon Stone, Russell Hewett, Alan Carson, Charles Warlow, and Michael Sharpe, "The 'Disappearance' of Hysteria: Historical Mystery or Illusion?," *Journal of the Royal Society of Medicine* 101, no. 1 (2008): 12–18.

16. SE 2: 24–25; GW 1: 80.

17. SE 2: 26.
18. SE 2: 26.
19. SE 2: 29.
20. SE 2: 39.

21. Sander L. Gilman, *Jewish Self-Hatred: Anti-Semitism and the Hidden Language of the Jews* (Baltimore: Johns Hopkins University Press, 1986), 260. *Mauscheln* (also called *jüdeln*) was a term—from the Jewish name Moshe—prevalent in the nineteenth century that referred to the ways Jews spoke German with a Yiddish accent or stereotypically Jewish speech patterns. On German-Jewish *mauscheln*, see Gilman, *Jewish Self-Hatred*, 139.

22. Matthew Johnson, "Faltering Language: On German-Yiddish Literature" (PhD diss., University of Chicago, 2022), 82n19.

23. The first of these translations, under the pseudonym P. Berthold, is Mary Wollstonecraft, *Eine Verteidigung der Rechte der Frau: Mit einer kritischen Bemerkung über politische und moralische Gegenstände* (Dresden: Pierson, 1899). The Yiddish translations, published under Pappenheim's own name, are *Die Memoiren der Glückel von Hameln, geboren in Hamburg 1645, gestorben in Metz 19. September 1724* (Vienna: S. Meyer and W. Pappenheim, 1910); *Allerlei Geschichten: Maasse-Buch. Buch der Sagen un Legenden aus Talmud und Midrasch nebst Volkserzälungen in jüdisch-deutscher Sprache. Nachder Ausgabe des Maasse-Buch Amsterdam 1723*, intro. I. Elbogen (Frankfurt am Main: J. Kauffmann Verlag, 1929); and *Zeenah u-Reenah. Frauenbibel* (Frankfurt am Main: J. Kauffmann Verlag, 1930).

24. The term is from Martin Buber, "Jüdische Renaissance," *Ost und West* 1 (1901): 7–10.

25. Michael Brenner, *The Renaissance of Jewish Culture in Weimar Germany* (New Haven, CT: Yale University Press, 1996), 4–5.

26. Brenner, *Renaissance of Jewish Culture*, 111.

27. Bertha Pappenheim, *Sisyphus-Arbeit: Reisebriefe aus den Jahren 1911 und 1912* (Freiberg: Kore, 1996), 149–50, 156.

28. Pappenheim, *Sisyphus-Arbeit*, 149–50; emphasis mine.

29. On Pappenheim's translation of the Yiddish "Women's Bible," see Abigail Gillman, *A History of German Jewish Bible Translation* (Chicago: University of Chicago Press, 2017), 220–30; and Matthew Johnson, "Glikl's Circulation: Editing, Translating, and Value," in *Der Wert der literarischen Zirkulation*, ed. Michael Gamper, Jutta Müller-Tamm, David Wachter, and Jasmin Wrobel (Berlin: J. B. Metzler 2023), 291–309.

30. Bertha Pappenheim, *Gebete*, ed. Jüdische Frauenbund (Berlin: Philo, 1936). Pappenheim used a hybridized German in these prayers, occasionally mobilizing Jewish folk expressions and Hebraisms: the prayer dated June 17, 1930, for instance, describes the *Malakh ha-Mavet* (Angel of Death) brushing the writer with his wings. For a discussion, see Loentz, *Let Me Continue*, 180–82. *Gebete* was reprinted in 1946, 1954, and 2003; the 1946 edition (New York: A. Stein) was accompanied by an English translation by Estelle Forchheimer.

31. I want to thank Mark Shell for this remarkable insight.

32. SE 5: 442. The full title of the section is "Absurd Dreams—Intellectual Activity in Dreams."

33. SE 5: 442.

34. SE 5: 441–42.

35. SE 5: 442; GW 2/3: 44.

36. Ken Frieden, "Sigmund Freud's Passover Dream Responds to Theodor Herzl's Zionist Dream," *Religion* 54 (1997): 242.

37. Adam Lipszyc, "The Name as the Navel: On Refinding Things We Never Had," in *Thinking in Constellations: Walter Benjamin in the Humanities*, ed. Nassima Sahraoui and Caroline Sauter (Newcastle upon Tyne: Cambridge Scholars, 2018), 43. In a footnote to the sentence about his "own Schriftgelehrte," the writer thanks Dr. Piotr Paziński, chair of the Jewish Studies Department at the Franz Kafka University of Muri.

38. SE 5: 443.

39. On his Yiddish (or German-Yiddish) accent, see Patricia Everett, who cites a newspaper report of the impression Brill made in Taos: "Shocking Taos dowagers with his easy, natural references to sexual matters or influences, he nevertheless seemed to offend no one, so obviously good-natured, wise and tolerant were his remarks. And his jollity was accentuated by the almost vaudeville-stage German-Yiddish accent, which he has never completely lost, despite his many years' residence in New York." Patricia Everett, *Corresponding Lives: Mabel Dodge Luhan, A. A. Brill, and the Psychoanalytic Adventure in America* (London: Routledge, 2018), 195. According to Nathan Hale, Brill supported himself when he first came to the United States "by sweeping out bars, giving mandolin lessons, and teaching." Nathan G. Hale, *Freud and the Americans: The Beginnings of Psychoanalysis in the United States, 1876–1917* (New York: Oxford University Press, 1971), 1:202. Paula Fass writes that he was "rather coarse, and although he had studied for a short time at the Burghölzli in Zurich and held an important appointment in psychiatry at Columbia, his manner lacked the kind of polish that could further the acceptance of psychoanalysis in the world of established medicine." Paula Fass, "A. A. Brill: Pioneer and Prophet" (master's thesis, Columbia University, 1968), 29.

40. Lydia Marinelli and Andreas Mayer, *Dreaming by the Book: Freud's Interpretation of Dreams and the History of the Psychoanalytic Movement* (New York: Other Press, 2003), 132.

41. Sander L. Gilman, "Psychoanalysis, Medicine, and the Body in the Time of Freud and Brill," in *Diseases and Diagnoses: The Second Age of Biology*, ed. Sander L. Gilman (New York: Routledge, 2010), 205.

42. On Yiddish and femininity, see Hutton, "Freud's Family Drama"; and Seidman, *A Marriage Made in Heaven*.

43. According to Leo Rosten, this joke is actually an anecdote told about the apocryphal Countess Misette de Rothschild. Leo Rosten, *The Joys of Yiddish* (New York: Pocket Books, 1968), 134–35.

44. SE 8: 81; GW 6: 86.

45. SE 8: 81; GW 6: 86.

46. Cuddihy, *Ordeal of Civility*, 24.

47. Andrew Parker, *The Theorist's Mother* (Durham, NC: Duke University Press, 2012), 104.

48. Sigmund Freud, *The Joke and Its Relation to the Unconscious*, trans. Joyce Crick (New York: Penguin, 2002), 70.

49. Freud, *Joke and Its Relation*, 70, 85. Crick's citation is to Rosten, *Joy of Yiddish*, 134–35.

50. Freud, *Joke and Its Relation*, 85.

Chapter 3

1. "Hey Alma," Instagram, accessed September 5, 2023, https://www.instagram.com/hey.alma/?hl=en. Hey Alma describes itself as a "News & media website" and "a Jewish feminist publication bringing you a diversity of voices. Home of Jew or Not Jew." I want to thank Emily Pascoe for drawing my attention to the website and game and pointing out its relevance.

2. On the problems with the game of "Jewish geography," see Alysha Ruth, "How Jewish Geography Excludes Jews of Color," *Forward*, September 13, 2018, https://forward.com/opinion/41029/how-jewish-geograph-excludes-jews-of-color/.

3. Primo Levi, *The Reawakening*, trans. Stuart Woolf (New York: Collier, 1965), 113.

4. For more on Yiddish as a postvernacular, see Cecile Kuznitz, "Yiddish Studies," in *Oxford Handbook of Jewish Studies*, ed. Martin Goodman (Oxford: Oxford University Press: 2004), 552–58; and Jeffrey Shandler, *Adventures in Yiddishland: Postvernacular Language and Culture* (Berkeley: University of California Press, 2008).

5. Yildiz, *Beyond the Mother Tongue*, 38–39, discusses the notion of German as a Jewish language, raising the question also of whether Hebrew and Yiddish are necessarily "Jewish languages." See also 225n17 for a discussion of the Palestinian Hebrew writer Anton Shammas.

6. Kalman Weiser, "Mother-Tongue, *Mame-loshn*, and *Kulturshprakh*: The Tension between Populism and Elitism in the Language Ideology of Noah Prylucki," in *Czernowitz at 100: The First Yiddish Language Conference in Historical Perspective*, ed. Kalman Weiser and Joshua A. Fogel (Lanham, MD: Lexington Books, 2010), 50.

7. Hutton, "Freud and the Family Drama," 13–14.

8. Jacques Derrida, *Monolingualism of the Other; or, the Prosthesis of Origin*, trans. Patrick Mensah (Stanford, CA: Stanford University Press, 1998), 54–55.

9. Kata Gellen, "Ein Spanischer Dichter in deutscher Sprache: Monolanguage and mame-loshn in Canetti, Kafka, and Derrida," in *Sprache, Erkenntnis und Bedeutung: Deutsch in der jüdischen Wissenskultur*, ed. Arndt Engelhardt and Susanne Zepp (Leipzig: Leipzig University Press, 2015), 300–301.

10. Georges Perec, *Ellis Island*, trans. Harry Matthews (New York: New Directions, 2021), 47.

11. Osip Mandelshtam, *The Noise of Time*, ed. and trans. Clarence Brown (New York: Penguin, 1993), 78–79.

12. Mandelshtam, *Noise of Time*, 77.

13. Robert Alter, *Necessary Angels: Tradition and Modernity in Kafka, Benjamin, and Scholem* (Cambridge, MA: Harvard University Press, 1991), 25–64. See also Vivian Liska, "On German-Jewish Thinkers Not Knowing Hebrew," *Prooftexts* 33, no. 1 (2013): 140–46. For Liska, the *idea* of Hebrew in German texts "arouses hope, and is a site of protest against the status quo" (144–45).

14. Gellen, "Ein Spanischer Dichter," 321.

15. Kohn, *Freud et le Yiddish*, 7.

16. Kohn, *Freud et le Yiddish*, 12.

17. Kohn, *Freud et le Yiddish*, 11.

18. Cecil Roth, *A History of the Marranos* (Brooklyn: Sepher Hermon, 1931), xi–xii.

19. Roth, *History of the Marranos*, 364.

20. Barbara Ferry and Debbie Nathan, "Mistaken Identity? The Case of New Mexico's 'Hidden Jews,'" *Atlantic Monthly* 283, no. 6 (December 1993): 85–88. See also Judith Neulander, "Cannibals, Castes and Crypto-Jews: Premillennial Cosmology in Postcolonial New Mexico" (PhD diss., Indiana University, 2001). In 2020, Isaac Artenstein released a documentary film, *A Long Journey: The Hidden Jews of the Southwest* (Cinewest Productions).

21. Michael P. Carroll, "The Not-So-Crypto Crypto-Jews of New Mexico: Update on a Decades-Old Debate," *Religion* 48, no. 2 (2018): 245. For a discussion of the emergence of crypto-Jewish claims in Brazil, see Bruno Feitler, "Four Chapters in the History of Crypto-Judaism in Brazil: The Case of the Northeastern New Christians (17th–21st Centuries)," *Jewish History* 25 (2011): 207–27.

22. Dalia Kandiyoti, *The Converso's Return: Conversion and Sephardi History in Contemporary Literature and Culture* (Stanford, CA: Stanford University Press, 2020), 24.

23. For a summary of the scholarly debate on the reliability of Inquisition records of Judaizing New Christians, see Howard Zvi Adelman, "Inquisitors and Historians and Their Methods: A Radical New Interpretation of New Christians," in *Historiographic Method: The Structured Analysis of Ellis Rivkin*, ed. Allen Podet (Potsdam: Abraham Geiger Press, 1992), 22–52.

24. Kandiyoti, *Converso's Return*, 18.

25. Elaine Marks, *The Marrano as Metaphor: The Jewish Presence in French Writing* (New York: Columbia University Press, 1996).

26. Erin Graff Zivin, "Introduction: Derrida's Marranismo," in *The Marrano Specter: Derrida and Hispanism*, ed. Erin Graff Zivin (New York: Fordham University Press, 2017), 4.

27. See Safaa Fathy's documentary *D'ailleurs, Derrida* (La Sept Art/Gloria Films, 1999), https://youtu.be/FG6beHNyc64?si=BbpgHV2iInF6Wfe8.

28. Abraham Joshua Heschel, "Die Marranen von heute," *Gemeindeblatt der jüdischen Gemeinde zu Berlin* 26, no. 38 (September 16, 1936): 2.

29. SE 9: 238–39.

30. SE 23: 14–15.

31. For Marthe Robert, Moses the Egyptian was Freud's expression of "an intransigent refusal of blood ties . . . the son's last protest and bulwark against the inevitable return of the fathers." Robert, *From Oedipus to Moses*, 167. In Yerushalmi's view, Freud's last book expressed instead his filial guilt: "In writing *Moses and Monotheism* he belatedly obeys the father and fulfills his mandate by returning to the intensive study of the Bible, but at the same time he maintains his independence from his father through his interpretation." Yerushalmi, *Freud's Moses*, 78.

32. Gershon Shaked, "A Response" to Michael P. Kramer, "Race, Literary History, and the 'Jewish' Question," *Prooftexts* 21, no. 3 (2001): 334.

33. Benjamin Schreier, "The Failure of Identity: Toward a New Literary History of Philip Roth's Unrecognizable Jew," *Jewish Social Studies* 17, no. 2 (2016): 103.

34. Lila Corwin Berman, "Jewish History beyond the Jewish People," *AJS Review* 42, no. 2 (2018): 274.

35. Stephen Best and Sharon Marcus, "Surface Reading: An Introduction," in "The Way We Read Now," ed. Stephen Best and Sharon Marcus, special issue, *Representations* 108, no. 1 (2009): 1.

36. Rita Felski, *The Limits of Critique* (Chicago: University of Chicago Press, 2015), 15.

37. Rita Felski, *The Uses of Literature* (Oxford: Blackwell, 2008), 1.

38. *Foucault Live: Interviews, 1961–84*, ed. Sylvère Lotringer, trans. John Johnston (New York: Semiotexte, 1989), 57–58. Quoted in Best and Marcus, "Surface Reading," 13.

39. Yerushalmi, "Purloined Kiddush Cups," n.p.

40. Shin Shalom, "Freud's Repressed Judaism" [in Hebrew], *Moznaim* 14 (1942): 319.

41. SE 6: 17.

42. Shin Shalom, "Freud's Repressed Judaism," 318.

43. SE 6: 10.

44. SE 6: 11.

45. SE 6: 11.

46. SE 6: 11.

47. SE 6: 17.

48. Shin Shalom, "Freud's Repressed Judaism," 319.

49. SE 6: 17.

50. The anecdote appears in Sigmund Freud, *Psychopathology of Everyday Life* [Psikhopatologya shel hayei yom-yom], 2nd ed., trans. Zvi Woyslawski (Tel Aviv: Mosad Bialik, 1945), 97–98.

51. Victor Tausk, "Zur Psychopathologie des Alltagslebens," *Internationale Zeitschrift für Psychoanalyse* 4, no. 3 (1916): 156–58. For an English translation, see Victor Tausk, "Contributions to the Psychopathology of Everyday Life," in *Sexuality, War and Schizophrenia: Collected Psychoanalytic Papers*, ed. Paul Roazen, trans. Eric Mosbacher (Oxford: Routledge, 1991), 231–33.

52. SE 6: 93.

53. Paul Roazen, "Introduction," in Tausk, *Sexuality, War and Schizophrenia*, 26.

54. Marius Tausk, "Victor Tausk as Seen by His Son," *American Imago* 30, no. 4 (1973): 323–35. M. Tausk writes, "I can firmly deny any statement that my father resented his Jewish ancestry or ever made a secret of it when this was a matter of any importance at all." Speaking of the conversion, he continues, "What my father did not like about the change—as far as I can tell—was the impression that he wanted to disguise some thing, which was against his very honest nature" (324). Defending his father against the charge, which he attributes to Kurt Eissler, that "the Faith of the Fathers" demonstrates Tausk's cowardice, M. Tausk points out that his father, after all, "published and analyzed the parapraxis himself" and that he sees no moral cowardice in his choosing not to engage an antisemite (333–34).

55. SE 8: 115.

56. Rita Felski, "Suspicious Minds," *Poetics Today* 32, no. 2 (2011): 227.

57. Felski is paraphrasing Paul Ricoeur in *Freud and Philosophy* (New Haven, CT: Yale University Press, 1977) in this passage. See Felski, *Limits of Critique*, 31.

58. Yael Segalovitz, "A Leap of Faith into Moses: Freud's Invitation to Evenly Suspended Attention," in *Freud and Monotheism: Moses and the Violent Origins of Religion*, ed. Gilad Sharvit and Karen S. Feldman (New York: Fordham University Press, 2018), 110.

59. SE 6: 170.

60. SE 12: 111–12.

61. SE 18: 238.

62. Segalovitz, "A Leap of Faith," 117.

63. Segalovitz, "A Leap of Faith," 131.

64. SE 5: 525.

65. John Forrester, *The Seductions of Psychoanalysis: Freud, Lacan, Derrida* (Cambridge: Cambridge University Press, 1990), 373n5.

66. Elena Basile, "The Most Intimate Act of Reading: Affective Vicissitudes in the Translator's Labour," *Doletiana: Revista de traducció, literatura i arts*, no. 1 (2007): 2. See also Elena Basile, "A Scene of Intimate Entanglements, or, Reckoning with the 'Fuck' of Translation," in *Queering Translation, Translating the Queer*, ed. Brian Baer and Klaus Kaindl (London: Routledge, 2017), 26–37.

67. Weiman-Kelman, "Touching Time," 99.

68. Zohar Weiman-Kelman, "Eroto-Philology: Sex, Language, and *Yiddish* History," *Orbis Litterarum* 74, no. 1 (2018): 65.

69. Reik, *Jewish Wit*, 175.

70. Reik, *Jewish Wit*, 180–82.

71. Simon J. Bronner, *Jewish Cultural Studies* (Detroit, MI: Wayne State University Press, 2021), 319–20. Bronner cites Zygmunt Bauman, "Allo-Semitism: Premodern, Modern, Postmodern," in *Modernity, Culture, and "the Jew,"* ed. Bryan Cheyette and Laura Marcus (Stanford, CA: Stanford University Press, 1998), 143–44.

72. Bronner, *Jewish Cultural Studies*, 322–23.

73. Frieden, "Sigmund Freud's Passover Dream," 242.

74. Lipszyc, "Name as the Navel," 43.

75. SE 23: 98.

76. Slavoj Žižek, *The Abyss of Freedom/Ages of the World* (Ann Arbor: University of Michigan Press, 1997), 50; cited in Eric Santner, *The Psychotheology of Everyday Life* (Chicago: University of Chicago Press, 2001), 6–7.

77. SE 22: 33.

78. Dan Miron, "Between Science and Faith: Sixty Years of the YIVO Institute," *YIVO Annual* 19 (1990): 5.

Chapter 4

1. Friedrich Nietzsche, *The Gay Science*, trans. Walter Kaufmann (New York: Vintage, 1974), 322.

2. Elsbeth Probyn, "Writing Shame," in *The Affect Theory Reader*, ed. Melissa Gregg and Gregory J. Seigworth (Durham, NC: Duke University Press, 2010), 76.

3. Probyn, "Writing Shame," 84.

4. Probyn, "Writing Shame," 82.

5. Elin Diamond, "The Violence of 'We,'" in *Critical Theory and Performance*, rev. and enl. ed., ed. Janelle G. Reinelt and Joseph R. Roach (Ann Arbor: University of Michigan Press, 2007), 406.

6. This argument is made most explicitly in Boyarin, *Unheroic Conduct*, 271–312.

7. Nylah Burton, "White Jews: Stop Calling Yourselves White-Passing," *Forward*, July 2, 2018, https://forward.com/opinion/404482/white-jews-stop-calling-yourselves-white-passing/.

8. Kwame Anthony Appiah, "I'm Jewish and Don't Want to Identify as White. Why Must I Check That Box?," *New York Times Magazine*, October 13, 2020, https://www.nytimes.com/2020/10/13/magazine/im-jewish-and-dont-identify-as-white-why-must-i-check-that-box.html.

9. For a critique of the "competitive memory" that sometimes characterizes these discourses, see Michael Rothberg, *Multidirectional Memory: Remembering the Holocaust in the Age of Decolonization* (Stanford, CA: Stanford University Press, 2009).

10. Frantz Fanon, *Black Skin, White Masks*, trans. Charles Lam Markmann (London: Pluto Press, 1986), 115–16.

11. Eddy Portnoy, "Richard Belzer Was a Jewish Comedian. Why Didn't His Obituaries Say So?," Jewish Telegraphic Agency, February 23, 2023, https://www.jta.org/2023/02/23/opinion/richard-belzer-was-a-jewish-comedian-why-didnt-his-obituaries-say-so. See also the English comedian David Lioner Baddiel, *Jews Don't Count* (London: TLS Books, 2022), who argues that Jews have ceased to "count" as a minority group.

12. Orna Guralnik, "Domestic Disturbance," *New York Times Magazine*, May 21, 2023, 37.

13. Sander L. Gilman, *Difference and Pathology: Stereotypes of Sexuality, Race and Madness* (Ithaca, NY: Cornell University Press, 1985), 31.

14. Boyarin, *Unheroic Conduct*, 302.

15. On Freud, Bose, and psychoanalysis in India, see Kalpana Seshadri-Crooks, "The Primitive as Analyst: Postcolonial Feminism's Access to Psychoanalysis," *Cultural Critique* 28 (1994): 175–218.

16. Daniel Boyarin, "What Does a Jew Want? or, The Political Meaning of the Phallus," *Discourse* 19, no. 2 (1997): 29.

17. Daniel Boyarin, "The New Jewish Question: To the Memory of Breonna Taylor and George Floyd, ד״יה," *Cambridge Journal of Postcolonial Literary Inquiry* 9, no. 1 (2022): 51. ד״יה is the Hebrew acronym for "May God Avenge Their Blood," appended by traditional Jews after the names of victims of the Holocaust.

18. Boyarin, "New Jewish Question," 52.

19. Boyarin, "New Jewish Question," 65–66.

20. For a summary of this discussion, see Chapter 3.

21. Eliza Slavet, *Racial Fever: Freud and the Jewish Question* (New York: Fordham University Press, 2007), 2.

22. Slavet, *Racial Fever*, 6.

23. Slavet, *Racial Fever*, 2.

24. Boyarin, "New Jewish Question," 65.

25. Sander L. Gilman, "Communities Are Complicated; Indeed, They May Not Even Be Communal," *Cambridge Journal of Postcolonial Literary Inquiry* 9 (2022): 101.

26. Gilman, "Communities Are Complicated," 104.

27. "About *In geveb*," 2023, https://ingeveb.org/about.

28. Jonah S. Boyarin, Ri J. Turner, and Arun Viswanath, "'Black Lives Matter' and Talking about Blackness in Yiddish: Stakes, Considerations, and Open Questions," *In geveb*, October 27, 2020, https://ingeveb.org/blog/black-lives-matter-in-yiddish.

29. Jessica Kirzane, "'This Is How a Generation Grows': Lynching as a Site of Ethical Loss in Opatoshu's 'Lintsheray,'" *In geveb*, June 21, 2016, https://ingeveb.org/articles/this-is-how-a-generation-grows-lynching-as-a-site-of-ethical-loss-in-opatoshus-lintsheray.

30. Marc Caplan, "Yiddish Exceptionalism: Lynching, Race, and Racism in Opatoshu's 'Lintsheray,'" *In geveb*, June 21, 2016. https://ingeveb.org/articles/yiddish-exceptionalism-lynching-race-and-racism-in-opatoshus-lintsheray.

31. Miriam Schulz, "For Race Is Mute and *Mame-Loshn* Can Speak: Yiddish Philology, Conceptions of Race, and Defense of Yidishkayt," *Judaica Petropolitana* 5 (2016): 100.

32. Borokhov, "Ufgabn fun der yidisher filologye," 2; cited in Schulz, "Race Is Mute," 111.

33. Schulz, "Race Is Mute," 112.

34. Schulz, "Race Is Mute," 108.

35. Max Weinreich, *The Path to Our Youth: Foundations, Methods, Problems of Jewish Youth-Research* [Der veg tsu undzer yugnt, yesoydes, metodn, problemen fun Yidisher yugnt-forshung] (Vilna: YIVO Press, 1935), 190; cited in Schulz, "Race Is Mute," 116.

36. Weinreich, *Path to Our Youth*, 192.

37. Weinreich, *Path to Our Youth*, 191–92.

38. Weinreich, *History of the Yiddish Language*, 193–94.

39. Weinreich, *History of the Yiddish Language*, 531.

Chapter 5

1. Jacques Lacan, "The Freudian Thing, or the Meaning of the Return to Freud in Psychoanalysis," in Fink, *Écrits: A Selection*, 107–37. The lecture was given at the Vienna Neuropsychiatric Clinic on November 7, 1955, and first published in an expanded version in *L'évolution psychiatrique* 1 (1956): 225–52, and reprinted in *Écrits* (Paris: Editions du Seuil, 1966).

2. Lacan, "The Freudian Thing," 108.

3. On Freud's distaste for America, see Ernst Falzeder, "'A Fat Wad of Dirty Pieces of Paper': Freud on America, Freud in America, Freud and America," in *After Freud Left: A Century of Psychoanalysis in America*, ed. John Burnham (Chicago: University of Chicago Press, 2012), 85–109.

4. Bruno Bettelheim, "Freud and the Soul," *New Yorker*, March 1, 1982, 52–93.

5. The issue is more complicated than Bettelheim apparently knew. The term "ego" for *Ich* was coined by Brill, Freud's first English translator. After James Putnam told Freud he thought Brill's translations were "atrocious," Joan Riviere took over, translating *The Ego*

and the Id in 1923; the term "id" for *es* is hers. Riviere mostly translated *Seele* as "soul"; by contrast, Strachey consistently used the dryer term "mind" in revising Riviere's work for the *Standard Edition*. Strachey discusses his understanding of *Seele* as meaning "mind" in the "General Preface" to the *Standard Edition*, saying that "the fact that '*psychisch*' is usually translated 'psychical' and '*seelisch*' 'mental' may lead to the notion that these words have different meanings, whereas I believe they are synonymous." SE 1: xix. On these issues and Bettelheim's argument, see D. G. Ornston, "Freud and Man's Soul," in *Translating Freud*, ed. Darius Gray Ornston Jr. (New Haven, CT: Yale University Press, 1992), 63–74.

6. Bruno Bettelheim, *Freud and Man's Soul* (New York: Vintage, 1984), 4–6.

7. Darius Gray Ornston, "Alternatives to a Standard Edition," in Ornston, *Translating Freud*, 97. Of particular importance was the care Strachey took to note the many changes and additions Freud made to his own work in later additions. The twenty-four volume *Standard Edition* was published by the Hogarth Press in 1953–74, decades after the Stracheys and Jones began to prepare Freud's work for critical publication. Edited by Alexander Mitscherlich, Angela Richards, and James Strachey, volumes 1–10 of the *Gesammelte Werke* were published by S. Fischer Verlag between 1969 and 1975. The supplement (*Schriften zur Behandlungstechnik*), coedited by Ilse Grubrich-Simitis, which added Freud's writings on psychoanalytic technique, appeared in 1975, followed by a *Studienaufgabe* that incorporated Strachey's critical apparatus.

8. The dedication of the first volume (covering the years 1886–99) reads, "To the Thoughts and Words of Sigmund Freud This Their Blurred Reflection Is Dedicated by Its Contriver." *The Standard Edition of the Complete Psychological Works of Sigmund Freud*, translated from the German under the general editorship of James Strachey, assisted by Alix Strachey and Alan Tyson, editorial assistant: Angela Richards (London: Hogarth Press, 1966). SE 1: v.

9. Sander L. Gilman, "Reading Freud in English: Problems, Paradoxes, and a Solution," in *Inscribing the Other* (Lincoln: University of Nebraska Press, 1991), 205.

10. See, for instance, Daphne Merkin, "The Literary Freud," *New York Times Magazine*, July 13, 2003, 6:40.

11. Bettelheim's view here is far from accepted. As Patrick J. Mahony writes, "A modern debate, with terminological confusion of its own, rages as to whether Freud, despite his [scientistic] intentions, developed a clinical theory that was hermeneutic rather than scientific." According to Mahoney, opinion differs on whether psychoanalysis is a branch of the humanities or a natural science, a debate complicated by the ways that "the humanistic picture of man underlies much natural science." Patrick J. Mahoney, "A Psychoanalytic Translation of Freud," in Ornston, *Translating Freud*, 28.

12. Lacan, "Freudian Thing," 107.

13. Strachey called these words "technical terms" and wrote that "I have tried as far as possible to keep to the general rule of translating a German technical term by the same English one. Thus, '*Unlust*' is always translated 'unpleasure' and '*Schmerz*' is always translated 'pain.'" SE 1: xix. The vaunted resistance to creating technical terms by the Penguin translators, however, was only partial, since many "technical terms" had become so entrenched that translators simply accepted them.

14. See Robert S. Boynton, "The Other Freud (the Wild One): New Translation Aims to Free Master from his Disciples' Obsessions," *New York Times*, June 6, 2010, B:9.

15. On this point, see Parker, *Theorist's Mother*, 93–94.

16. Jean Laplanche, André Cotet, and Pierre Bourguignon, "Translating Freud," in Ornston, *Translating Freud*, 177.

17. Ornston, "Improving Strachey's Freud," 15–16.

18. Laplanche, Cotet, and Bourguignon, "Translating Freud," 154.

19. Cuddihy, *Ordeal of Civility*, 29.

20. On the Glossary Committee, see James Strachey's obituary for Joan Riviere. In 1921, he writes, he joined "a decidedly peculiar institution called the Glossary Committee. It met in Ernest Jones's consulting room in Harley Street and consisted of him, Mrs Riviere, my wife, and me. This quite irresponsible body decided for all time how the technical terms of psycho-analysis were to be translated." James Strachey, "Joan Riviere (1883–1962)," *International Journal of Psychoanalysis* 44 (1963): 229. In some dialects of Yiddish, the word "yid" is spelled and/or pronounced as "id," making this a homophone rather than a near pun.

21. James Strachey and Alix Strachey, *Bloomsbury/Freud: The Letters of James and Alix Strachey, 1924–1925*, ed. Perry Meisel and Walter Kendrick (New York: Basic Books, 1985), 83. Interestingly, James also complains in this letter that one of his only two analysands (on whom the couple's income partly depended) had missed a session because of "The Jewish Fast [Yom Kippur]" (84). Lest one conclude from this letter that the Stracheys were better acquainted with Jews and Jewish customs than Jones, it's worth remembering that Leonard Woolf was a longtime member of the same Bloomsbury circle as the Stracheys even before their involvement with his Hogarth Press, and by 1924 Jones himself had been married for five years to Katherine Jokl, a Jewish friend of Anna Freud whom he met in Vienna.

22. Sigmund Freud, *Collected Papers* (New York: International Psycho-analytical Press, 1924–35). Anna Freud is listed as a collaborator of different translators of individual volumes, including Alix Strachey and Joan Riviere.

23. Patrick J. Mahony, *Psychoanalysis and Discourse* (London: Taylor and Francis, 1987), 3.

24. Robert J. C. Young, "Freud on Cultural Translation," in *A Concise Companion to Psychoanalysis, Literature, and Culture*, ed. Laura Marcus and Ankhi Mukherjee (Newark, NJ: John Wiley Press, 2014), 370. Young quotes Sigmund Freud and Josef Breuer, *Studies in Hysteria*, trans. Nicola Luckhurst (London: Penguin, 2004), 131.

25. Young, "Freud on Cultural Translation," 370. Young adds, in parentheses, that he is quoting from the Penguin translation, which "cannot obviate the extreme degree of this psychoanalytic transposition" into medical language, despite its stated desire to do so.

26. Young, "Freud on Cultural Translation," 370–71.

27. Young, "Freud on Cultural Translation," 374.

28. Ken Frieden, *Freud's Dream of Interpretation* (Albany: SUNY Press, 1990), 109.

29. SE 4: 277; emphasis mine.

30. Damrosch, "Scriptworlds," 195–218.

31. For these alternate translations, see Darius Gray Ornston, "Improving Strachey's Freud," in Ornston, *Translating Freud*, 12.

32. SE 4: 53. It might be more appropriate to translate the term *Rückübersetzung* as "detranslation" (with Laplanche) or "back-translation."

33. Sigmund Freud, "Letter to Wilhelm Fliess" (December 6, 1896), in *The Complete Letters of Sigmund Freud to Wilhelm Fliess*, ed and trans. Jeffrey Moussaieff Masson (Cambridge, MA: Harvard University Press, 1985), 207–8. For the German, see Sigmund Freud, Wilhelm Fliess, J. Moussaieff Masson, and Michael Schröter, *Briefe an Wilhelm Fliess, 1887–1904*, ed. J. Moussaieff Masson (Frankfurt am Main: S. Fischer, 1986), Letter 112.

34. Parker, *Theorist's Mother*, 96.

35. Roman Jakobson, "On Linguistic Aspects of Translation," in *On Translation*, ed. Reuben Arthur Brower (Cambridge, MA: Harvard University Press, 1959), 233.

36. SE 6: 156n2. "One day, however, he was blaming himself for having committed a technical error in a patient's psycho-analysis. That day all his former absent-minded habits reappeared. He stumbled several times as he walked along the street (a representation of his *faux pas* [false step—blunder] in the treatment), left his pocket book at home, tried to pay a kreutzer too little for his tram-fare, found his clothes were not properly buttoned, and so on."

37. Jean Laplanche, *New Foundations for Psychoanalysis*, trans. D. Macey (Oxford: Basil Blackwell, 1989), 126.

38. Jean Laplanche, "Exigency and Going Astray," *Psychoanalysis, Culture, and Society* 11 (2006): 188. Cited in John Fletcher, "Seduction and the Vicissitudes of Translation: The Work of Jean Laplanche," *Psychoanalytic Quarterly* 76, no. 4 (2007): 1243.

39. Fletcher, "Seduction and the Vicissitudes of Translation," 1256.

40. Basile, "Most Intimate Act of Reading," 2.

41. Parker, *Theorist's Mother*, 92.

42. Fletcher, "Seduction and the Vicissitudes of Translation," 1266.

43. Jean Laplanche, "Transference: Its Provocation by the Analyst," in *Essays on Otherness*, ed. John Fletcher, trans. Luke Thurston (London: Routledge, 1999), 254.

44. Jean Laplanche, *Après-coup*, trans. Jonathan House and Luke Thurston (New York: The Unconscious in Translation, 2017), 155.

45. Among the expressions of these notions of translation is Eugene Nida's long-influential, now-superseded theory of "dynamic equivalence," the "quality of a translation in which the message of the original text has been so transported into the receptor language that the *response* of the *receptor* is essentially like that of the original receptors." See Eugene A. Nida and Charles R. Taber, *The Theory and Practice of Translation, with Special Reference to Bible Translation* (Leiden, Netherlands: Brill, 1969), 200.

46. Laplanche, Cotet, and Bourguignon, *Translating Freud*, 140.

47. SE 4: 48.

48. Laplanche, Cotet, and Bourguignon, *Translating Freud*, 190.

49. Jean Laplanche, "Gender, Sex, and the *Sexual*," trans. Jonathan House, in *Gender without Identity*, by Avgi Saketopoulo and Ann Pellegrini (New York: The Unconscious in Translation, 2023), 100; emphasis in original. First published in *Libres cahiers pour la psychanalyse: Études sur la Théorie de la seduction* (Paris: In Press, 2003), 69–103. *Gender without Identity* aims to work through the implications of Laplanche's insights about gender, sex, and the sexual for a non-transphobic psychoanalytic practice.

50. Saketopoulou and Pellegrini, *Gender without Identity*, 59.

51. David Bakan, *Sigmund Freud and the Jewish Mystical Tradition* (Boston: Beacon Press, 1958), 242.

52. Bakan, *Freud and the Jewish Mystical Tradition*, 259. I discuss the differences between Jewish and Christian sign theories in *Faithful Renderings: Jewish-Christian Difference and the Politics of Translation* (Chicago: University of Chicago Press, 2006).

53. Bakan refers to Sabbatian and Frankist texts as the Jewish heretical sources that share with psychoanalysis a tendency toward dissimulation. Bakan, *Freud and the Jewish Mystical Tradition*, 38n1.

54. Susan Handelman, *Slayers of Moses: The Emergence of Rabbinic Interpretation in Modern Literary Theory* (Albany: SUNY Press 1983), 152.

55. Handelman, *Slayers of Moses*, 152.

56. Mahony, *Psychoanalysis and Discourse*, 4.

57. Jacqueline Amati-Mehler, Simona Argientieri, and Jorge Canestri, *The Babel of the Unconscious: Mother Tongue and Foreign Languages in the Psychoanalytic Dimension* (Madison, WI: International Universities Press, 1993), 19. Amati-Mehler and her colleagues reserve the term "polylingualism" for the phenomenon of knowing more than one language from birth rather than learning languages in succession.

58. Amati-Mehler, Argientieri, and Canestri, *Babel of the Unconscious*, 25, cites a 1912 letter to Jones, which begins in English, but after Freud curses his own English, he switches to German and recovers the ability to write in English.

59. Amati-Mehler, Argientieri, and Canestri, *Babel of the Unconscious*, 2.

60. Eduardo Krapf, "The Choice of Language in Polyglot Psychoanalysis," *Psychoanalytic Quarterly* 24 (1935): 350; quoted in Amati-Mehler, Argientieri, and Canestri, *Babel of the Unconscious*, 51. Krapf mobilized his multilingualism for technical purposes, switching from an infantile to a secondary language with one patient to "favor her unconscious need to break away from her mother" (52).

61. Robert Samacher, "Louis Wolfson et le Yiddish," *Recherches en psychanalyse* 4 (2005): 124.

62. Louis Wolfson, *Le schizo et les langues* (Paris: Gallimard, 1970).

63. Along with calling himself "the student," Wolfson also calls himself the "schizophrenic student," "the mentally ill student," "our hero," the "anal epileptic," the "fugitive," "L. W.," and "Him."

64. Jean-Jacques Lecercle, "Louis Wolfson and the Philosophy of Translation," *Oxford Literary Review* 11, no. 1–2 (1989): 108.

65. Lecercle, "Louis Wolfson," 106.

66. Lecercle, "Louis Wolfson," 114.

67. Samacher, "Louis Wolfson et le Yiddish," 133.

68. Eliezer Ben Yehuda, *Ha-halom ve-shivro*, ed. Reuven Sivan (Jerusalem: Bialik Institute, 1978), 95; quoted in Liora Halperin, *Babel in Zion: Jews, Nationalism, and Language Diversity in Palestine, 1920–1948* (New Haven, CT: Yale University Press, 2014), 6.

69. Halperin, *Babel in Zion*, 38.

70. Immanuel Velikhovsky, "Kann eine neuerlernte Sprache zur Sprache des Unbe-

wußten werden? Wortspiele in Träumen von hebräisch Denkenden," *Imago* 20 (1934): 236.

71. Velikhovsky, "Kann eine neuerlernte Sprache," 235. The Hebrew is actually "your (f.) luck."

72. Velikhovsky, "Kann eine neuerlernte Sprache," 239.

73. SE 6: 165; GW 4: 182.

74. SE 6: 166; GW 4: 183.

75. SE 6: 166.

76. See An Act to Regulate Immigration (1882), US Sess. I, Chap. 376, 22 Stat. 214; An Act to Regulate the Immigration of Aliens into the United States (1907), US Sess. II, Chap. 1134, Sec. 2.

77. Eran J. Rolnik, "Before Babel: Reflections on Reading and Translating Freud," *Psychoanalytic Quarterly* 84, no. 2 (2015): 310.

78. Jacques Derrida, "Des Tour de Babel," trans. Joseph F. Graham, in *Difference in Translation*, ed. Joseph F. Graham (Ithaca, NY: Cornell University Press, 1985), 172.

79. *Chamer*, in Freud's transliteration, points to a Yiddish rather than Hebrew meaning because Ashkenazic Yiddish/Loshn Koydesh pronounced Hebrew words differently in Yiddish conversation than they did in reciting the Torah or praying. Thus, Yiddish speakers say *Shabbes* in ordinary speech and *Shabbos* in reading from the Torah. *Chamer* follows the same pattern: *Chamer* thus means "an idiot," while *Chamor* would be used for a "Hebrew ass," and secondarily—and only in a Hebrew context—for "an idiot." *Esel* in German has the same two meanings (donkey/idiot), without distinction in pronunciation.

80. Laplanche, "Gender, Sex, and the *Sexual*," 117; emphasis in original.

81. SE 7: 114.

82. SE 6: 93.

83. SE 7: 48.

84. Jane Gallop, "Keys to Dora," in *In Dora's Case: Freud—Hysteria—Feminism*, ed. Charles Bernheimer and Claire Kahane (New York: Columbia University Press, 1990), 210.

85. Anne McClintock, *Imperial Leather: Race, Gender, and Sexuality in the Colonial Contest* (London: Routledge, 1995), 89.

86. Yuri Slezkine, *The Jewish Century* (Princeton, NJ: Princeton University Press, 2004), 20.

87. Weinreich, *History of the Yiddish Language*, 193–94.

88. Freud, "Instead of an Introduction to the Yiddish Edition," in *Introduction to Psychoanalysis*, n.p. Roback may have used the same term in his Yiddish dedication of his book *Jewish Influence on Modern Thought to Freud*, translated in the catalogue as "To Professor Freud / With reverence and sincerest wishes / for more long years of work / from the author A. A. Roback." Davies and Fichtner, *Freud's Library*, 436, item 3007.

89. Weiman-Kelman, "Eroto-Philology," 62.

90. Kasia Kosinen, *Translation and Affect: Essays on Sticky Affects and Translational Affective Labour* (Amsterdam: John Benjamins, 2020), 11.

91. Margaret Wetherall, *Affect and Emotion: A New Social Science Understanding* (Los Angeles: Sage Press, 2012), 27.

92. Brian Massumi, "Preface," in *The Politics of Affect*, by Brian Massumi (Cambridge, MA: Polity Press, 2015), x.

Chapter 6

1. "Freudian Lullaby Contest," *Forverts*, August 17, 1930, 2:15.
2. "Freudian Lullabies," *Forverts*, September 14, 1930, 2:6.
3. On the charged question of what Freud owed Janet and whether he sufficiently acknowledged his debt, see Michael Fitzgerald, "Why Did Sigmund Freud Refuse to See Pierre Janet? Origins of Psychoanalysis: Janet, Freud or Both?," *History of Psychiatry* 28, no. 3 (2017): 358–64.
4. "Is an Only Son a Menace to Society?," *New York Times*, September 8, 1912, 12.
5. For a recent survey, see Henrique T. Vicente, Ana Alexandra G. Grasina, Cristina P. Vieira, and Carlos Farate, "Lullabies and Unconscious Maternal Phantasies: An Exploratory and Comparative Study of Traditional and Contemporary Songs," *International Journal of Applied Psychoanalytic Studies* 17, no. 4 (2020): 328–44.
6. "Freudian Lullabies," *Forverts*, September 21, 1930, 2:6.
7. "Freudian Lullabies," *Forverts*, September 21, 1930, 2:6.
8. Benjamin Harshav, *The Meaning of Yiddish* (Stanford, CA: Stanford University Press, 1999), 35.
9. Alexander Freud, "The Interpretation of Dreams" [Appendix A], in Marinelli and Mayer, *Dreaming by the Book*, 151.
10. On Freud as cultural translator, see Robert Young, "Freud and Cultural Translation," in *A Concise Companion to Psychoanalysis, Literature, and Culture*, ed. Laura Marcus and Ankhi Mukherjee (Hoboken, NJ: Wiley Blackwell, 2014), 370. On Alexander Freud's parody, see Marinelli and Mayer, *Dreaming by the Book*, 19.
11. Lillian Eichler, "Foreign Accent a Handicap," *Forverts*, September 21, 1930, 2:6.
12. Mikhoel Burshtin, *By the Rivers of Mazovia*, trans. Jordan Finkin (Cincinnati, OH: Naydus Press, 2023), 72–73. For the Yiddish, see Mikhoel Burshtin, *By the Rivers of Mazovia* [Bay di taykhn fun Mazovye] (1937), in *Erev khurbn* (Buenos Aires: YIVO, 1970), 88–89.
13. Burshtin, *By the Rivers*, 74.
14. Y. Y. Trunk, *Poland: Memories and Scenes* [Poyln: Zikhroynes un bilder], trans. Ezra Fleischer (Merhavya: Sifriyat Po'alim, 1962), 151. Quotes in Iris Parush, *Reading Jewish Women: Marginality and Modernization in Nineteenth-Century Eastern European Jewish Society* (Hanover, NH: Brandeis University Press, 2004), 75.
15. On the two stages of romantic and sexual secularization, see Naomi Seidman, *The Marriage Plot: Or, How Jews Fell in Love with Love, and with Marriage* (Stanford, CA: Stanford University Press, 2016), 32.
16. For the biographical sketch of Gliksman, see Melekh Ravitsh, *My Lexicon* [Mayn leksikon] (Montreal: Committee for the Publication of *Mayn Leksikon*, 1947), 2:18–20. Advertisements for Gliksman's lectures appear throughout the 1920s; see, for instance, *Literarishe bleter*, October 17, 1924; October 30, 1924; and May 21, 1926. Gliksman worked alongside an army of popular lecturers—the 1926 issue advertises the offerings of

ten lecturers aside from Gliksman, speaking on twenty-nine topics ranging from "Antiquity" to "Zionism."

17. Ravitsh, *My Lexicon*, 2:18.

18. The project of writing a history of psychoanalysis in Poland that took full measure of the "polnisch-deutsch-jüdischen Kulturkontext" (1900–1939) and its emergence was carried out from 2015 to 2020 by a group of Polish and German researchers at the International Psychoanalytic University in Berlin, headed by the professor and psychoanalyst Ewa Kobylińska-Dehe.

19. Young, "Freud on Cultural Translation," 370.

20. M. Asya, "Mental Illnesses" [in Hebrew], *Hazman*, November 25, 1912, 2.

21. Asya, "Mental Illnesses," 2.

22. A. A. Roback, "Multiple Personalities: A Study in Abnormal Psychology" [in Yiddish], *Dos naye leben*, September 1, 1913, 32.

23. K. Berkovski, "A New Scientific Theory of Dreams" [in Yiddish], *Dos Yidishes togeblat*, September 2, 1915, 4.

24. K. Berkovski, "The New Scientific Institution of Dreams" [in Yiddish], *Dos yidishes togeblat*, October 8, 1916, 11.

25. SE 4: 97.

26. B. Albin, "Dreams—Their Secret and Interpretation: On Freud and Freudianism" [in Yiddish], *Di Idishe Tsaytung: Diaro Israelita*, June 11, 1924, 9.

27. Roback, *Jewish Influence*, 160.

28. Eran J. Rolnik, *Freud in Zion: Psychoanalysis and the Making of Modern Jewish Identity* (London: Karnac Books, 2012), 2.

29. Rolnik, *Freud in Zion*, 1.

30. Ruth Ginsburg so describes Brachyahu's title in the introduction to her own translation of Freud's dream book, which chose a less biblically charged title, *Perush ha-halomot*, that more accurately reflects the *process* of interpreting represented in the title and throughout the *Traumdeutung* rather than the completed interpretation. See Ruth Ginsburg, "We Are Asleep but Our Heart Is Awake: Freud's Roadmap" [in Hebrew], in *Perush ha-halomot*, by Sigmund Freud, trans. Ruth Ginsburg (Tel Aviv: Am Oved Publishers, 2018), 34. Evidence that Ginsburg herself is not averse to biblical allusion is her brilliant borrowing from *Song of Songs* 5:9 for the title of her introduction.

31. SE 5: 484.

32. Avrom Novershtern, "Yiddish Press," National Library of Israel, 2023, https://www.nli.org.il/en/discover/newspapers/jpress/all-sections/yiddish-press.

33. For more on this newspaper, see Mariusz Kałczewiak, "Yiddish Buenos Aires and the Struggle to Leave the Margins," *East European Jewish Affairs* 50, no. 1–2 (2020): 115–33.

34. "The Unconscious [unterbavustzinike] and Its Role in Our Psychic Lives" [in Yiddish], *Di idishe tsaytung: El Diaro Israelita*, November 4, 1926, 12.

35. Kałczewiak, "Yiddish Buenos Aires," 116.

36. Cecilia Taiana, "The Emergence of Freud's Theories in Argentina: Towards a Comparison with the United States," *Canadian Journal of Psychoanalysis* 14, no. 2 (2006): 272–73.

37. Mariano Ben Plotkin, "Freud, Politics, and the Porteños: The Reception of Psychoanalysis in Buenos Aires, 1910–1943," *Hispanic American Historical Review* 77, no. 1 (1997): 58.

38. Taiana, "The Emergence of Freud's Theories in Argentina," 289.

39. Studying a later generation of Jewish psychoanalysts in Argentina, Jeffrey Bass writes that such children of immigrants found in psychoanalysis "a way to negotiate their ethnic identity within Argentina's changing political landscape," in which authoritarian and antisemitic currents created "a certain shame about being Jewish" that a successful psychoanalytic practice allowed them to face and overcome. See Jeffrey Bass, "In Exile from the Self: National Belonging and Psychoanalysis in Buenos Aires," *Ethos* 34, no. 4 (2006): 447–48.

40. On these tensions, see Rolnik, *Freud in Zion*, 126–34.

41. Sigmund Freud, "Letter to Judah Magnes" (October 5, 1933), Freud Museum and Research Centre, London; quoted in Rolnik, *Freud in Zion*, 64.

42. Hugo Bergmann, "For Sigmund Freud: Born May 6, 1856" [in Hebrew], *Ha'aretz*, May 6, 1926, 2.

43. "On the University Conference" [in Hebrew], *Ha'olam*, January 9, 1920, 12.

44. "Professor Freud on the University" [in Hebrew], *Ha'aretz*, March 29, 1925, 4.

45. "The Travels of Bialik" [in Hebrew], *Haolam*, February 4, 1932, 12.

46. The earliest record of correspondence between Weinreich and Freud I have found is a handwritten note from December 29, 1929, in which Freud writes (implying an earlier correspondence), "If you still need my name for the Presidium, be my guest. I wish you the best success with your enterprise." Sigmund Freud (1929), Library of Congress, *Sigmund Freud Papers: General Correspondence, 1871–1996; Weinreich, Max, 1929, 1931* [Manuscript/Mixed Material], box 43, mss39990. On January 7, 1930, YIVO directors Weinreich and Zalmen Reyzen responded by thanking Freud, acknowledging that publicity about his endorsement would greatly benefit the institution. See Sigmund Freud (1930), Library of Congress, *Sigmund Freud Papers: General Correspondence, 1871–1996; Reisen, Salman, and Max Weinreich, 1930* [Manuscript/Mixed Material]. The YIVO website Timeline, however, dates Freud's presence on the Presidium to August 1925. See "Timeline: 1925," YIVO, accessed July 28, 2023, http://www.milsteinjewisharchives.yivo.org/site/timeline.php?agency=6.

47. Sigmund Freud, "Greetings" [in Yiddish], *Literarishe bleter* 33 (August 16, 1935): 588. Earlier that year, the journal devoted an article to Freud's biography, writing that the Yiddish cultural world was already preparing for his landmark birthday; the article ends with "Freud is, incidentally, a member of the Presidium of YIVO." See "Sigmund Freud's Eightieth Birthday" [in Yiddish], *Literarishe bleter* 20 (May 17, 1935): 316.

48. Y. Sonino, "What Parents and Girls Can Learn from the Glickstein-Reizen Tragedy" [in Yiddish], *Der tog*, December 19, 1921, 3. The Dr. Tannenbaum that the young woman saw may be Samuel A. Tannenbaum (1874–1948), a literary scholar and physician who was among Freud's first American disciples but who broke with Freud in 1922.

49. A. S. Lirik, "Professor Sigmund Freud as 'Murderer'" [in Yiddish], *Haynt*, September 12, 1926, 4; SE 6: 170.

50. SE 6: 170. Amateur psychoanalysis as a tool of aggression was also the subject of

Suppressed Desires: A Freudian Comedy in One Act, a 1915 play by George Cram Cook and Susan Glaspell that satirized the contemporary craze for analyzing dreams; the play had a revival in Jerusalem in 1946. See "At the Play," *Palestine Post*, November 18, 1946, 2.

51. Quoted in Peter Gay, *Freud: A Life for Our Time* (New York: Doubleday, 1988), 640.

52. Lacan, "The Freudian Thing," 109.

53. B. Finkel, "The Latin Quarter from the Inside: The Cradle of All the 'Isms" in America" [in Yiddish], *Di varheyt*, April 28, 1918, 3.

54. "The Ugly End of an Ugly Soul" [in Yiddish], *Forverts*, December 18, 1936, 6.

55. See "To Ask Freud to Come Here," *New York Times*, December 21, 1924, 3; and "Freud Rebuffs Goldwyn," *New York Times*, January 24, 1925, 13. In 1926, *Secrets of the Soul*, a German film about psychoanalysis directed by G. W. Pabst, was released. The producer, Hans Neumann, also approached Freud with the invitation to advise on the project but, after receiving no response, succeeded in enlisting Karl Abraham in that role.

56. "The Person Who Took on His Wife's Name" [in Yiddish], *Dos yidishes tageblat*, October 16, 1917, 2.

57. "Professor Freud Has a Niece in Hunter College; She Is Studying Psychology" [in Yiddish], *Forverts*, April 22, 1938, 10. The only Fuchs in Freud's immediate family I have found is Henny Fuchs Freud, who married his son Oliver in 1923; the family, though, did not immigrate to New York until 1943. Perhaps Shirley was a daughter of Henny's brother, who lived in New York.

58. "Picks 10 'Greatest Jews': Lewisohn Lists Living Leaders, Classing Four as Geniuses," *New York Times*, March 28, 1936, 17.

59. "List of Great Criticized: Some May Not Be Greatest Jews, Rabbi S. S. Wise Holds," *New York Times*, April 6, 1936, 17.

60. "Who Are the Most Famous Jews in the World Today?" [in Yiddish], *Unzer Pinsker leben*, May 13, 1938, 4.

61. Ernest Jones, *The Life and Work of Sigmund Freud*, vol. 3, *1919–1939: The Last Phase* (New York: Basic Books, 1957), 131.

62. "'Wild' Psycho-Analysis" (1910), SE 11: 219–27.

63. YIVO Archive, digital collection (2970/256446) of theater posters, 2023, https://ataleoftwomuseums.yivo.org/exhibits/show/a-day-at-the-museum/item/2970?np=256446.

64. Karolina Szymaniak, "Freud auf Jiddisch in Polen bis 1939," in *Zwischen Hoffnung und Verzweiflung: Psychoanalyse in Polen im polnisch-deutsch-jüdischen Kulturkontext (1900–1939)*, ed. Ewa Kobylińska-Dehe and Paweł Dybel (Giessen, Germany: Psychosocial-Verlag, 2018), 248.

65. Szymaniak, "Freud auf Jiddisch," 245. For more on the teaching of psychoanalysis at YIVO (including a photo of Weinreich with his psychoanalysis class) and on the role of psychoanalysis in Weinreich's career, see Cecile Kuznitz, *YIVO and the Making of Modern Jewish Culture* (New York: Cambridge University Press, 2014), 150–65.

66. Sh. Z. Wulf, *Sigmund Freud: The Inventor of Psychoanalysis* [Zigmund Froyd: der shefer fun psikhoanaliz] (Warsaw: Groschen Bibliotek, 1936), 3, 64. Wulf was the pseudonym of the prolific Shmuel Vulman (1896–1941), who in 1936 alone published, along

with the Freud booklet, other booklets on Zola, the Bundist educator B. Mikhalevich (Izbitzki), Robespierre, *Japan, the Power of the World*, the Boer War, and *The First International with Marx and Bakunin*.

67. Lyudmila Sholokhova, "Groshn-bibliotek Reveals Literary Taste of Polish Jews during Interwar Period," *YIVO yedies* 206 (2010): 19. See also David Mazower and Lyudmila Sholokhova, "The Worker's Library: Groshn-bibliotek Helped Anxious Readers Make Sense of Their Times," *Pakn Treger* 74 (2016). https://www.yiddishbookcenter.org/language-literature-culture/pakn-treger/worker-s-library.

68. Wulf, *Freud*, 10.

69. Kuznitz, *YIVO and the Making*, 5.

70. Kuznitz, *YIVO and the Making*, 5.

71. See Mazower and Sholokhova, "Worker's Library"; and "Benn's Sixpenny Library (Ernest Benn Limited)—Book Series List," 1927–39, https://www.publishinghistory.com/benns-sixpenny-library.html.

72. Sukanta Chaudhuri, *Translation and Understanding* (New Delhi: Oxford University Press, 1999), 14.

73. Dr. M. Greenwald, "Meetings with Sigmund Freud," *Ha'aretz*, September 21, 1941; quoted in *Sefer Buczacz: Memorial Monument to a Sacred Community*, ed. Israel Cohen (Tel Aviv: Am Oved, 1957), 119.

74. See Damrosch, "Scriptworlds," 195–219. I wish to thank Adriana X. Jacobs for drawing my attention to this article.

75. The articles appeared on May 6, 1936, 3, 7; May 7, 1936, 7, 8; May 8, 8; May 9, 3, 11; and May 11, 5, 8, and were collected in Max Weinreich, *Psychoanalysis: Freud and His Approach* [Psikhoanaliz: Froyd un zayn shite] (Vilna: YIVO, 1937).

76. Max Weinreich, "Professor Sigmund Freud, Famous Researcher of Mental Illnesses, Turns Eighty Years Old Today" [in Yiddish], *Forverts*, May 6, 1936, 3.

77. Weinreich, "Professor Sigmund Freud," 3.

78. Dr. A. Gliksman, "Sigmund Freud" [in Yiddish], *Literarishe bleter* 20 (September 19, 1924): 3.

79. Dr. A. Gliksman, "Professor Sigmund Freud I" [in Yiddish], *Literarishe bleter* 17 (August 29, 1924): 2.

80. On the notion of modern Hebrew as an "echo chamber" of traditional sources, whether writers intend these allusions or not, see Robert Alter, *Hebrew and Modernity* (Bloomington: Indiana University Press, 1994), 12, 22. Yiddish might work similarly, primarily through its Hebrew component.

81. Dr. A. Gliksman, "Professor Sigmund Freud II: What Is Psychoanalysis?" [in Yiddish], *Literarishe bleter* 20 (September 19, 1924): 3.

82. Gliksman, "Professor Sigmund Freud II," 3.

83. Dr. A. Gliksman, "Professor Sigmund Freud IV: Mistakes and Obstacles" [in Yiddish], *Literarishe bleter* 35 (January 2, 1925): 2. Gliksman misquotes or misremembers the Rashi on Genesis 24:39, which in fact says that Eliezer had not a son but a daughter, whom he hoped that Abraham would choose for his son.

84. Gliksman, "Professor Sigmund Freud IV," 2.

85. Slavet, *Racial Fever*, 2–7.
86. See, for instance, "Sigmund Freud to Leave Vienna" [in Hebrew], *Davar*, January 30, 1938, 2. A flurry of mistaken reports in March 1938 about Freud's arrest were retracted as the situation was clarified. See "Was Freud Arrested or Not?" [in Hebrew], *Ha'aretz*, March 18, 1938, 1.
87. "To Bring Freud and Neumann to the Land of Israel" [in Hebrew], *Ha'aretz*, March 21 1938, 1. Neumann is probably a reference to Heinrich Neumann, the foremost ear, nose, and throat specialist in Vienna, who died in New York in 1939. Erich Neumann, the Berlin-based Jungian psychologist, escaped to Tel Aviv in 1934.
88. "Dr. Neumann Released; Freud Will Probably Settle in Holland" [in Yiddish], *Forverts*, March 25, 1938, 9.
89. "They Want to Bring Freud to America" [in Yiddish], *Forverts*, March 31, 1938, 9.
90. "Hitler Won't Let Freud Leave" [in Yiddish], *Forverts*, April 2, 1938, 1.
91. "Freud's Son Denies That His Family Has Dutch Relatives" [in Hebrew], *Ha'aretz*, April 3, 1938, 1.
92. "Professor Sigmund Freud in Nazi Hands: The Great Tragedy in the Evening of His Life" [in Yiddish], *Unzer Byalistoker ekspres*, April 6, 1938, 5.
93. "I No Longer Wish to Prolong My Life: Freud's Friends Try to Arrange for Him to Travel to Paris" [in Yiddish], *Unzer ekspres*, May 20, 1938, 4. Freud is quoted in this article as saying that the illnesses and suffering of old age have the advantage of lessening one's fear of death.
94. M. Glickfon, "Evian" [in Hebrew], *Ha'aretz*, July 6, 1928, 2.
95. "Freud Finally Leaves Vienna: On His Way to New York" [in Yiddish], *Forverts*, June 5, 1938, 1.
96. Y. L. Teller, "The Jewish Community of Vienna Now under the Shadow of Hitlerism" [in Yiddish], *Morgn Zhurnal*, March 14, 1938, 3. A very similar story appeared in the *Forverts* the next day, stating that "one of the greatest geniuses of our time is presently living in Vienna, Professor Sigmund Freud. Not far from the completely irreligious Professor Freud reside famous Hasidic Grand Rabbis, who arrived in Vienna during the Great War from various parts of Galicia, which was then a province in the Austro-Hungarian Empire." "What Is Happening among the Jews of Vienna" [in Yiddish], *Forverts*, March 15, 1938, 2. For more on Teller's life as a journalist and poet, see Ken Frieden, "New(s) Poems: Y. L. Teller's *Lider fun der tsayt*(ung)," *AJS Review* 15, no. 2 (1990): 269–90.
97. Teller, "The Jewish Community of Vienna," 3.
98. Ken Frieden, "Teller's First and Last Visits to Sigmund Freud," in *Proceedings of the Tenth World Congress of Jewish Studies* (Jerusalem: World Union of Jewish Studies, 1990), 2:86. Teller's poem was published in *In Zikh*, October 1937, 91–92.
99. Frieden, "New(s) Poems," 276.
100. J. L. Teller, "Jud' Süss Oppenheimer during His First Visit to Sigmund Freud," in *Sing, Stranger: A Century of American Yiddish Poetry—A Historical Anthology*, ed. and trans. Benjamin Harshav, Barbara Harshav, and Kathryn Hellerstein (Stanford, CA: Stanford University Press, 20066), 510–11.

101. J. L. Teller, "Sigmund Freud on His Eighty-Second Birthday," in Harshav, Harshav, and Hellerstein, *Sing, Stranger*, 516.

102. Weinreich, *History of the Yiddish Language*, 193–95.

103. Stefan Zweig, *The World of Yesterday: An Autobiography*, ed. and trans. Harry Zohn (New York: Viking Press, 1943), 292.

104. "Professor Freud in Exile" [in Yiddish], *Haynt*, July 15, 1938, 7.

105. Dr. M. Greenwald, "The Family Tree of Professor Sigmund Freud" [in Hebrew], in *Sefer Buczacz: Memorial Monument to a Sacred Community*, ed. Israel Cohen (Tel Aviv: Am Oved, 1959), 119. Where Greenwald found the family tree remains unspecified.

106. Dr. M. Greenwald, "Meetings with Sigmund Freud" [in Hebrew], *Ha'aretz*, September 21, 1941, 9, 13; reprinted in *Sefer Buczacz*, 119.

107. "Preface to the Hebrew Translation" [of *Introductory Lectures of Psychoanalysis*, 1930], SE 15: 11–12; "Preface to the Hebrew Translation" [of *Totem and Taboo*, 1930], SE 13: xv.

108. Editor's note to Greenwald, "Meetings with Sigmund Freud" [in Hebrew], in *Sefer Buczacz*, 122; emphasis in original.

109. "Stammbaum des Hauses Freud," in *Sefer Buczacz*, 120. The family tree begins with Jesucher and Freide (from where the family name derived), continues to Ester and Josef Freud, Ephraim and Debora Freud, to Salomon (or Shlomo) Freud (after whom Sigmund was named), Jakob, ending with the twig "Prof Dr Siegmund" (*sic*). For more on the origins of the Freud name, bestowed on the family by an Austrian official in 1812, see Dr. M. Strauch, "The Relationship of Sigmund Freud to Judaism" [in Hebrew], *Lamerchav*, July 13, 1956, 8.

110. "In Defense of Freud" [in Hebrew], *Ha'aretz*, October 20, 1938, 3.

111. SE 23: 7.

112. Gay, *Freud: A Life*, 638.

113. Aaron Zeitlin, "Freud the Jew and Moses . . . the Egyptian" [in Hebrew], *Hatzofeh*, April 8, 1939, 6.

114. Shlomo Ben Horin, "Freud on Our Teacher Moses" [in Hebrew], *Davar*, May 5, 1939, 13–14. Freud confesses that he is "totally incompetent to answer" the question of whether Aton and Adonai (and the Syrian god Adonis) are related. But he surely did know that Adonai was a later substitute for the Tetragrammaton, a topic he discussed with Stekel, who believed that names in dreams often stood in for other names that had a similar association of a succession of vowels. See "The Significance of Sequences of Vowels" (1911), SE 12: 341.

115. Benjamin Gutsman, "Freud and His Teachings [*Torato*] on Moses and His Teachings [*Torato*]" [in Hebrew], *Haboker*, June 9, 1939, 3.

116. "Great Jews and Small Jews" [in Yiddish], *Haynt*, May 17, 1939, 3.

117. A. Ginsburg, "Professor Sigmund Freud and Jethro's Daughters" [in Yiddish], *Forverts*, June 17, 1939, 8.

118. A. Almi, "Was Freud a Jew?" [in Yiddish], *Freye Arbeter Shtime*, August 25, 1939, 3.

119. Eliezer Lowenstein, "By Way of Response: On Sigmund Freud's *Moses and Monotheism*" [in Hebrew], *Davar*, August 11, 1939, 7.

120. Benjamin Mintz, "Passing Days" [in Hebrew], *She'arim*, August 4, 1939, 4.

121. Rabbi Dr. Aaron Kaminka, "Freud's War against Moses Our Teacher" [in Hebrew], *Hatzofeh*, August 18, 1939, 7.

122. Jones, *Life and Work*, 3:234.

123. I. N. Steinberg, "The Godless Jew: A Visit to Sigmund Freud" [in Hebrew], *Davar*, January 23, 1939, 2. In the 1930s, Steinberg was the chief exponent of Freeland Territorialism, which sought to procure land for Jewish settlements in many parts of the world. The visit is also described by Meitlis, "Last Days," 20, and in an anonymous report in the Warsaw daily *Haynt*: "Sigmund Freud's Appeal for YIVO" [in Yiddish], *Haynt*, December 23, 1938, 8. Similarly, "A Conversation with Freud in London" [in Yiddish], *Folksblat*, February 5, 1939, 6, reports that Dr. Shtendik, editor in chief of the pedagogical journal *Das kind*, had a long conversation with Freud in which Freud expressed his interest in developments in Polish psychoanalysis. Whether this was the same meeting as the one with Steinberg is unclear.

124. This may be the "learned Jewish historian" Abraham Shalom Yahuda, born in Jerusalem in 1877 to a family of Iraqi heritage, who was professor of medieval Sephardic literature at the University of Madrid beginning in 1914, wrote the book *The Language of the Pentateuch in Its Relation to the Egyptian* (1934), and was residing in London in 1938. Jones, however, mentions not a letter but a visit from Yahuda: in his account, among the visitors who called on Freud early in his London exile was Professor Yahuda, "who begged Freud not to publish his Freud book." Jones, *Life and Work*, 3:234. Yahuda also "published in Hebrew a long review of Freud's book" in which he totally rejected Freud's hypotheses (370). This review, "Sigmund Freud on Moses and His Torah" [in Hebrew], appears in *Ever v'Arav* [in Hebrew and Arabic], ed. Abraham Shalom Yahuda (New York: Shulsinger, 1946), 37–73. There are, however, sufficient candidates for the letter Freud read aloud to the YIVO members; Yahuda was not the only prominent Jew to object to the book, as the newspaper reports demonstrate. Yahuda's visit to Freud is reimagined in the British playwright Terry Johnson's play *Hysteria* (premiered 1993), which dramatizes the last months of Freud's life, focusing on a visit by Salvador Dali but including as well a visit by Yahuda. See also Ilan Benattar, "The Modernity of Tradition: Abraham Shalom Yahuda on Freud's *Moses and Monotheism*" (master's thesis, New York University, 2016).

125. Steinberg, "Godless Jew," 2.

126. SE 17: 248.

127. On the Paper Brigade, see David E. Fishman, *The Book Smugglers: Partisans, Poets, and the Race to Save Jewish Treasures from the Nazis* (Lebanon, NH: ForeEdge, 2017). See also David E. Fishman. "Split Identity: Jewish Scholarship in the Vilna Ghetto," *In geveb*, June 30, 2020, https://ingeveb.org/articles/split-identity.

128. Summary of a lecture delivered by Dr. Daniel Feinstein, "The Myth of Paradise in the Light of Psychoanalysis" [in Yiddish], June 16, 1942, ROS_IE11164754, YIVO Institute for Jewish Research.

129. Summary of a lecture delivered by Dr. Daniel Feinstein, "The Familiar and the Strange (literally, "the Near and the Far"): A Chapter of Anthropology" [in Yiddish], September 13, 1942, ROS_IE11159140, YIVO Institute for Jewish Research. Feinstein also

delivered a lecture that same year on Egyptian monotheism; see summary of a lecture delivered by Dr. Daniel Feinstein, "Egyptian Monotheism and Its Creator," 1942, Box 8, Folder 496, Abraham Sutzkever-Szmerke Kaczerginski Vilna Ghetto Collection, RG 223.1, YIVO Institute for Jewish Research.

Chapter 7

1. Dan Miron, "Between Science and Faith: Sixty Years of the YIVO Institute," *YIVO Annual* 19, ed. Deborah Dash Moore (1990): 14–15.

2. On Weinreich's Yiddishist and psychoanalytic understanding of and engagement with American Jews in the 1940s, see Markus Krah, *American Jewry and the Reinvention of the East-European Past* (Berlin: De Gruyter, 2018), 53–60.

3. On this point, see Young, "Freud and Cultural Translation," 370.

4. Max Weinreich, "Froyd laboratoriye," RG584, folder XIX3390, YIVO Archives.

5. Bettelheim, *Freud and Man's Soul*, 8–9 and throughout.

6. "When Freud appears to be either more abstruse or more dogmatic in English translation than in the original German, to speak about abstract concepts rather than about the reader himself, and about man's mind rather than about his soul, the probable explanation isn't mischievousness or carelessness on the translators' part but a deliberate wish to perceive Freud strictly within the framework of medicine and, possibly, an unconscious tendency to distance themselves from the emotional impact of what Freud tried to convey." Bettelheim, *Freud and Man's Soul*, 32.

7. Bettelheim, *Freud and Man's Soul*, 41.

8. Freud's fear that psychoanalysis would be understood as a Jewish science is recorded primarily in his correspondence, for instance, in a letter to Karl Abraham and another to Ferenczi in which he argued against a Swiss psychiatrist's attempt to explain the differences between Viennese and Swiss psychoanalysis as reflecting a Jewish/Aryan difference: "Certainly there are great differences," Freud wrote, "between the Jewish and the Aryan spirit. . . . But there should not be such a thing as Aryan or Jewish science." Quoted in Yerushalmi, *Freud's Moses*, 43, citing Jones, *Life and Work*, 2:149. See also Fishman, "Split Identity."

9. YIVO changed its name in the move to the United States to Institute for Jewish Research but retained the acronym YIVO.

10. Jonathan Boyarin, "Yiddish Science and the Postmodern," trans. Naomi Seidman, *In geveb*, March 2016, https://ingeveb.org/articles/yiddish-science-and-the-postmodern.

11. The Yiddish literary critic Sh. Charney contrasted YIVO's aspirations to found a "Jewish university" with the Zionist aim to create a university for Jews in "On the Idea of Founding a Jewish University" [in Yiddish], *Di yudishe velt* 2, no. 1 (April 1914): 128; cited in Kuznitz, *YIVO and the Making*, 23.

12. See such forums as the 2016 seminar at the Freud Museum in London, featuring Joseph Berke, Stephen Frosh, Naftali Loewenthal, and Anthony Stadlen on the question of "Is Psychoanalysis a Jewish Science?," November 10, 2017, https://thefreudmuseum.podbean.com/e/is-psychoanalysis-a-jewish-science/.

13. Moisés Kijak, born in Argentina in 1934 to Polish immigrants, is a psychoanalyst

and professor who publishes widely on Yiddish literature as well. His Yiddish book *Freud and Psychoanalysis* [Froyd un di psikhoanaliza] (Buenos Aires: YIVO, 1971), is based on Yiddish lectures delivered at YIVO.

14. Sigmund Freud, "O snovideniiakh" [On Dreams], in *Piatoe prilozhenie k Vestniku psikhologii, kriminal'noi antropologii i gipnotizma*, trans. unknown (St. Petersburg: Brokgauz-Efron, 1904). A year after Brill's 1913 translation of the *Traumdeutung*, M. D. Eder published an English translation of "Über den Traum" with introduction by W. L. Mackenzie (London: Heinemann; New York: Rebman, 1914).

15. SE 14: 33.

16. Hutton, "Freud and the Family Drama," 10.

17. Hutton, "Freud and the Family Drama," 10.

18. Kohn, *Freud et le Yiddish*, 7.

19. Steinberg, "The Godless Jew," 2.

20. Meitlis, "The Last Days," 21.

21. David G. Roskies, "The Emancipation of Yiddish," *Prooftexts* 1 (1981): 28–42.

22. Weiman-Kelman, "Eroto-Philology," 60.

23. Roskies, "Emancipation," 30.

24. Freud's letter goes on to request that Weinreich not ask him to write an introduction, since he had sworn off doing so and others might resent his making an exception. "Instead of an Introduction to the Yiddish Publication" appears in Freud, *Introduction to Psychoanalysis* [Arayfir in psikho-analiz], trans. M. Weinreich (Vilna: YIVO, 1936), n.p.

25. See Paul Roazen, *Helene Deutsch: A Psychoanalyst's Life* (Garden City, NY: Anchor Press, 1985), 3–17. In the chapter "The Center of the Earth," Roazen describes the role of Poland in Deutsch's life and those of other psychoanalysts as a country whose repression from the surface of Europe's maps did not mean that it—like the unconscious—did not exist.

26. Edyta Dembińska and Krzysztof Rutkowski, "The Beginnings of Psychoanalysis in Poland before the First World War," *Psychoanalysis and History* 23, no. 3 (2021): 325.

27. Ewa Kobylińska-Dehe and Paweł Dybel, eds., *Zwischen Hoffnung und Verzweiflung: Psychoanalyse in Polen im polnisch-deutsch-jüdischen Kulturkontext (1900–1939)* (Giessen, Germany: Psychosocial-Verlag, 2018), 9.

28. Paweł Dybel, *Psychoanalysis—the Promised Land? The History of Psychoanalysis in Poland 1900–1989*, part I, *The Sturm und Drang Period: Beginnings of Psychoanalysis in the Polish Lands during the Partitions 1900–1918*, trans. Tomasz Bieroń (Berlin: Peter Lang, 2020), 27.

29. Sigmund Freud, "Letter to Carl G. Jung" (October 17, 1909), in S. Freud, C. G. Jung, W. McGuire, R. Manheim, R. F. C. Hull, and A. McGlashan, *The Freud-Jung Letters: The Correspondence between Sigmund Freud and C. G. Jung* (Princeton, NJ: Princeton University Press, 1974), 253; cited in Dembińska and Rutkowski, "Beginnings of Psychoanalysis," 329n2.

30. Wojtech Tworek makes a case for the ways that Eastern Europe has been occluded by scholars of Hasidism, for instance, in their focus on strictly Jewish frames of reference extracted from the larger geographic and cultural context in which it flourished. See

Wojtech Tworek, "The Eastern European Problem of Hasidic Studies," *Jewish Quarterly Review* 112, no. 2 (2022): 256–59.

31. André Haynal, "On Psychoanalysis in Budapest," in *100 Years of the IPA: The Centenary History of the International Psychoanalytical Association 1910–2010: Evolution and Change*, ed. Peter Loewenberg and Nellie L. Thompson (London: Karnac, 2011), 95. Relating the "silent treatment" given to Ferenczi for his reported psychoanalytic "transgressions" to the *Todschweigen* (death by silence) by which Orthodox Jews punish disobedient children, Arnold William Rachman describes a moment in which he considered speaking up in Ferenczi's defense at a psychoanalytic meeting, but "my Yiddish grandmother's phrase for a sense of helplessness came to me at that moment: '*Es garnisht helfen* [sic]: It is useless!; nothing good will happen." Arnold William Rachman, *Elizabeth Severn: The "Evil Genius" of Psychoanalysis* (New York: Routledge, 2018), 66. Rachman sees Severn as having similarly been given the silent treatment by Freud and his followers for the same sorts of sin.

32. Dybel, *Psychoanalysis—the Promised Land?*, 90.

33. On the "linguistic kaleidoscope" of Hapsburg Vienna, see Amati-Mehler, Argientieri, and Canestri, *Babel of the Unconscious*, 21.

34. Otto F. Kernberg, "Preface," in Amati-Mehler, Argientieri, and Canestri, *Babel of the Unconscious*, xi.

35. Maya Balakirsky Katz, "A Rabbi, a Priest, and a Psychoanalyst: Religion in the Early Psychoanalytic Case History," *Contemporary Jewry* 31, no. 1 (2021): 3–24. The Rashab's travels to Vienna were supported by a follower and relative of the Rashab, Isaiah Berlin, who enabled what Stekel called the rabbi's *Reiseneurose*, the "traveling neurosis" that expressed itself in persistent visits to spas and doctors in faraway locations, which the Rashab (if indeed he is the figure hiding behind Stekel's rabbi) described as voluntary "exile for the purpose of self-refinement or self-purification." For a discussion of the association of *Ostjuden* with mental illness and regeneration, an association that partly was reversed in the later judgment that Eastern European culture was more psychically healthy than the deracinated and neurasthenic German-speaking Jew, see John M. Efron, *Medicine and the German Jews: A History* (New Haven, CT: Yale University Press, 2008), 151–85.

36. Wilhelm Stekel, *Nervöse angstzustände and deren behandlung* (Berlin: Urban and Schwarzenberg, 1908), 161; cited in Balakirsky Katz, "A Rabbi, a Priest, and a Psychoanalyst," 12.

37. Joseph H. Berke, *The Hidden Freud: His Hasidic Roots* (London: Routledge, 2015), 17.

38. See Jessica Benjamin, "Beyond Doer and Done To: An Intersubjective View of Thirdness," *Psychoanalytic Quarterly* 73 (2004), 5–46.

39. Sigmund Freud, "Notes upon a Case of Obsessional Neurosis ('Rat Man') and Process Notes for the Case History," in *The Freud Reader*, ed. Peter Gay (New York: Norton, 1989), 328.

40. Weinreich, *History of the Yiddish Language*, 194.

41. On *Davke*, its history, and its philosophical orientation, see Shlomo Berger, "Interpreting Freud: The Yiddish Philosophical Journal *Davke* Investigates a Jewish Icon," *Science in Context* 20, no. 2 (2007): 303–16.

42. Kijak, *Freud and Psychoanalysis*.

43. Sigmund Freud, *Group Psychology and the Analysis of the Ego* [Di psikhologiye fun di masn un der analiz fun menshlikhn 'ikh'], trans. Sarah Lerman (Warsaw: Yeruchamson Press, 1928). The quote is from an advertisement on the opening flyleaf of the second, 1929 edition, also by Yeruchamson Press.

44. Female pseudonyms were common enough among Yiddish writers and translators—Weinreich himself translated two expressionist dramas by Ernst Toller as Sarah Brenner, including *Masse Mensch* (1920) and *Die Wandlung* (1919).

45. Sigmund Freud, *The Future of an Illusion* [Di tsukunft fun an iluziye], trans. Y. Dodnik (Cleveland, OH: Progressive Printing, 1932).

46. The advertised series also claimed that Weinreich would define all terms, presumably in a glossary. But no glossary is included in the series as it appeared, so perhaps that was intended for the final volume, and the notebook in the Weinreich archive was a draft for that.

47. Freud, *Group Psychology*, trans. Sarah Lerman, back cover.

48. Freud, *Group Psychology*, trans. Sarah Lerman, back cover.

49. The major figures of this intellectual current in the 1920s were the Soviet philosopher V. Yurenets and linguist Valentin Voloshinov, and in German-speaking lands, Siegfried Bernfeld (whose work on education, children, and youth would become important for Weinreich) and Wilhelm Reich.

50. Kenneth B. Moss, *An Unchosen People: Jewish Political Reckoning in Interwar Poland* (Cambridge, MA: Harvard University Press, 2021), 174.

51. Gustaw Bychowski, "Rozmowa z Freudem," *Wiadomosci literackie*, May 10, 1936, 4; cited in Moss, *Unchosen People*, 174.

52. Dr. A. Litvak, *Freud's Teaching: Investigations of the Human Soul and the War against Its Diseases* [Torat Frayd lehakirat nefesh ha'adam ulemilhama neged mahaloteha] (Tel Aviv: Sifriya leshmirat ha'ruah, 1925); the booklet, the first volume of a series, refers to the discoveries of Sigismund Freyd (spelling the family name with two yuds). For the first Hebrew translation of one of Freud's essays, see Yohanan Tversky, "Resistances to Psychoanalysis" [Ha'hitnagduyot lepsikhoanalyza], *Hado'ar*, November 12, 1926, 20–21, and November 19, 1926, 38–39; SE 19: 212–24. *Hado'ar* was a Hebrew periodical, initially daily but then weekly, published in the United States from 1921 to 2005, edited by the Hebraist Menahem Ribalow.

53. Rolnik, *Freud in Zion*, 53. The translator, Yehuda Dwossis (1896–1971) was an educator with a special interest in the Bible. Eran Rolnik writes: "In contrast with the socialist brand of nationalism subscribed to by most of the political elite that had emerged from the labour and agricultural settlements, the Yishuv's teachers held more liberal views."

54. Freud, *Introduction to Psychoanalysis*, 1:75.

55. Freud, *Introduction to Psychoanalysis*, 1:n.p.

56. SE 19: 59.

57. Weinreich, speaking about the disadvantages of relying on the youth autobiographies YIVO had collected, acknowledged that they were incomplete since they excluded "whatever does not wish to be remembered, for whatever reason, is 'forgotten,' that is to say,

repressed in the unconscious" (*dos vos es vilt zikh nit gedenken, tzulib di oder yene taymim, "fargest men," d"h man farshtoyst es in umbavustzayn arayn*). Weinreich, *Path to Our Youth*, 163. A problem similar to the one Weinreich identified in Yiddish exists with the English term "unconscious," which also means "comatose." For a discussion of Weinreich's terminology, see Mordkhe Schaechter, "Max Weinreich's Translation of Freud" [in Yiddish], in *For Max Weinreich on His Seventieth Birthday*, ed. Lucy S. Dawidowicz, Alexander Erlich, Rachel Erlich, and Joshua A. Fishman (The Hague: Mouton Press, 1964), 319–306.

58. Schaechter, "Weinreich's Translation," 314.

59. Schaechter, "Weinreich's Translation," 314.

60. Uriel Weinreich, *Modern English-Yiddish, Yiddish-English Dictionary* (New York: Schocken Books, 1964), 64. See Kijak, *Freud and Psychoanalysis*, 8 and throughout.

61. Weinreich, *History of the Yiddish Language*, 656–57.

62. "Di seksualitet, oder libido, iz posht dos vos yidishe folks-shprakh batseykhent mit der 'yetser hore." See Dr. Tz. Rudy, "Jews in Psychology Today" [in Yiddish], *YIVO Bleter* 1 (1931): 318.

63. SE 15: 224, 223.

64. GW 11: 231.

65. Weinreich, *Path to Our Youth*, 4.

66. Weinreich, "Froyd laboratoriye," n.p. Weinreich is referring to Freud's discussion of objections to the idea that dreams are inevitably wish fulfillments: "Warum muß dieser Sinn aller Evidenz zum Trotze immer wieder in die Formel der Wunscherfüllung gepreßt werden?" GW 11: 226. The *Standard Edition* renders this phrase as "Why must that sense [of the dream], all evidence to the contrary, be invariably pushed into the formula of wish-fulfilment?" SE 15: 221. Dwossis has "letzamtzem atzmo tamid bemitat sdom shel hanoskha al milui hamishala?" (to always force itself into the Bed of Sodom of the formula of wish fulfillment). The Bed of Sodom, a Hebrew variation of the Procrustean Bed, refers to the bed offered guests by the evil, inhospitable Sodomites; if the guests were too tall, they would be cut to size, and if they were too short, stretched to fit. Freud, *Introductory Lectures*, 193.

67. See Max Weinreich, "Letter to Professor Gershon Brownstein" (May 21, 1936), RG 8000, YIVO Archives.

68. GW 11: 185.

69. SE 15: 185.

70. Sigmund Freud, *Introduction to Psychoanalysis*, vol. 3, trans. Max Weinreich (Vilna: YIVO, 1938), 157.

71. As evidence that the word *shabes* played a role in Freud's treatment room (and that he associated it with the "sin" of smoking), we have the American psychiatrist Joseph Wortis's account of Freud's dropping the idiom "Go celebrate a Sabbath with it" into a session, a phrase he understood only in its literal meaning until Freud translated it into English for him: "Put it in your pipe and smoke it." Joseph Wortis, *Fragments of an Analysis with Freud* (New York: Jason Aronson, 1984), 136.

72. Erich Fromm, "Der Sabbath," *Imago* 13 (1927): 223–34. For a discussion of this essay and the psychoanalytic interpretation of Jewish law, see Paul Lerner, "German Jews

between Freud, Marx, and Halakha: Frieda Fromm-Reichmann, Erich Fromm, and the Psychoanalysis of Jewish Ritual in 1920s Heidelberg," *Leo Baeck Institute Year Book* 64 (2019): 219–39, particularly 230–31.

73. Kosofsky Sedgwick, *Touching Feeling*, 8.

74. Philip Rieff, *The Triumph of the Therapeutic: Uses of Faith after Freud* (Chicago: University of Chicago Press, 1987).

Chapter 8

1. Sh. Shariya, "Words and Writers" [in Hebrew], *Haboker*, June 14, 1940, 4. Freud's works were burned by university students in bonfires across Germany on May 10, 1933.

2. Shariya, "Words and Writers," 4.

3. Shariya, "Words and Writers," 4.

4. On the project and the reasons for its academic and popular failure, see Avner Holtman, *Hayim Nahman Bialik: Poet of Hebrew* (New Haven, CT: Yale University Press, 2017), 178–79.

5. Rivka Katzenelsen, "Bringing 'Straying' Sons Home" [in Hebrew], *Ma'ariv*, November 28, 1958, 13.

6. I borrow the term "salvage translation" from the related term "salvage ethnography," as used by Sheila Jelen, on the post-Holocaust Eastern European Jewish ethnography. See Sheila E. Jelen, *Salvage Poetics: Post-Holocaust American Jewish Folk Ethnographies* (Detroit, MI: Wayne State University Press, 2020).

7. Danielle Drori, "Fortresses and Open Cities: Debating Translation and Nation Formation in Early Twentieth Century Hebrew Literature" (PhD diss., New York University, 2018), 21.

8. See Roni Henig, "Stammering Hebrew: Y. H. Brenner's Deferred Beginnings in the Novel *Me-hathala*," *Comparative Literature Studies* 56, no. 2 (2019): 239, where she traces the novelist Y. H. Brenner's "excessive attention to accents, speech impediments, and different forms of talk" as a symptom of the ideological complexities of language revival in which the contradictions inherent in ideological attempts to revive Hebrew as a vernacular are inevitably signaled by dysfluency, artificiality, and muteness.

9. Ernest Jones, "Letter to Strachey" (September 28, 1939), quoted in Riccardo Steiner, "A World Wide International Trade Mark of Genuineness? Some Observations on the History of the English Translation of the Work of Sigmund Freud, Focusing Mainly on His Technical Terms," *International Review of Psycho-Analysis* 14, no. 33 (1987): 43.

10. Ernest Jones, "Letter to Baggs" (December 13, 1939), quoted in Steiner, "World Wide International Trade Mark," 47.

11. Steiner, "World Wide International Trade Mark," 44.

12. Emanuel Berman, "Ferenczi, Rescue, Utopia," *American Imago* 60, no. 4 (2003): 432.

13. On the connection between the "dream" of Zionism ("If you will it, it is not a dream") and psychoanalysis, see Drori, "Fortresses and Open Cities, 224–25.

14. Rolnik, *Freud in Zion*; Guido Liebermann, *The Origins of Psychoanalysis in Israel: The Freudian Movement in Mandatory Palestine 1918–1948* (New York: Israel Academic

Press, 2019); and Rakefet Zalashik, *History of Psychiatry in Palestine and Israel, 1892–1960* (Tel Aviv: ha-Ḳibuts ha-meʾuḥad, 2008).

15. See Rolnik, *Freud in Zion*, 41–43; and Mathew Thomson, "'The Solution to His Own Enigma': Connecting the Life of Montague David Eder (1865–1936), Socialist, Psychoanalyst, Zionist and Modern Saint," *Medical History* 55, no. 1 (2011): 61–84.

16. Dorian Feigenbaum, "Palestine Must Have Sound Nerves," *Jewish Ledger*, December 1924, 15, Israeli State Archive 1576 54/3 2595; cited in Rakefet Zalashik and Nadav Davidovitch, "Professional Identity across the Borders: Refugee Psychiatrists in Palestine, 1933–1945," *Social History of Medicine* 22, no. 3 (2009): 412.

17. Alex Liban and Dodi Goldman, "Freud Comes to Palestine: A Study of Psychoanalysis in a Cultural Context," *International Journal of Psychoanalysis* 81 (2000): 893–906.

18. Liban and Goldman, "Freud Comes to Palestine," 894.

19. Rolnik, *Freud in Zion*, 73.

20. See Rolnik, *Freud in Zion*, 84–85.

21. On the sobriquet "Berliners," see H. Shmuel Erlich, "Letter from Jerusalem," *International Journal of Psychoanalysis* 91 (2010): 1330.

22. Dan G. Hertz, "Pioneers and Psychoanalysis: Beginnings of the Psychoanalytic Movement in Eretz-Israel," *Israel Journal of Psychiatry and Related Sciences* 20, no. 1–2 (1983): 10.

23. As Eitingon put it, "Neither Orthodox Jews nor Arabs are suitable in any way for psychoanalysis," cited in Rolnik, *Freud in Zion*, 143. On the map of the world, see Mary-Kay Wilmers, *The Eitingons: A Twentieth-Century Story* (London: Verso, 2010), 240. Interestingly, Mordechai Brachyahu, translator of *The Interpretation of Dreams* and expositor of Freud's work, had a "huge map of Palestine" hanging on "the wall facing the analytic couch" in his consulting room. Rolnik, who sees this as evidence of Brachyahu's "amalgamation of the individual's mental plight with the Zionist cause," quotes a personal communication with Dr. Itamar Levi on this detail. See Rolnik, *Freud in Zion*, 153.

24. Henrietta Szold, *Max Eitingon: In Memoriam* (Jerusalem: Israel Psycho-Analytic Society, 1950), 44.

25. Anna Freud to Ernest Jones (unpublished letter, March 6, 1934), cited in Riccardo Steiner, *"It Is a New Kind of Diaspora": Explorations in the Sociopolitical and Cultural Context of Psychoanalysis* (London: Karnac Books, 2000), 17.

26. On Freud's March 13, 1938, talk with the Board of the Vienna Society, see Jones, *Life and Work*, 3:221. For the letter to Weinreich, see Willy Aron, "Notes on Sigmund Freud's Ancestry and Jewish Contacts," *YIVO Annual of Jewish Social Science* 11 (1956): 286–95.

27. SE 23: 115.

28. See Daniel Boyarin, "Masada or Yavneh? Gender and the Arts of Jewish Resistance," in *Jews and Other Differences: The New Jewish Cultural Studies*, ed. Jonathan Boyarin and Daniel Boyarin (Minneapolis: University of Minneapolis Press, 1997), 306–29.

29. Sigmund Freud, *Interpretation of Dreams* [Pesher hahalomot], trans. M. Brachyahu (Tel Aviv: Yavneh, 1957).

30. Gay, *Freud: A Life*, 455; and Roy Macleod, "Balfour's Mission to Palestine: Science,

Strategy, and the Inauguration of the Hebrew University in Jerusalem," *Minerva* 46, no. 1 (2008): 53–76.

31. Liebermann, *Origins of Psychoanalysis*, 84.

32. Liebermann, *Origins of Psychoanalysis*, 86.

33. Sigmund Freud, *Group Psychology and the Analysis of the Ego* [Psikhologia shel ha-hamon ve-ha-analiza shel ha-ani], trans. Yehuda Dwossis (Jerusalem: Sifriyat hed ha-hinukh, 1928); Sigmund Freud, *Introductory Lectures on Psychoanalysis* [Shi'urei mevo le-psikhoanalizah], trans. Yehuda Dwossis (Tel Aviv: Shtybel Press 1934–35); and Sigmund Freud, *Totem and Taboo* [Totem ve-tabu], trans. Yehuda Dwossis (Jerusalem: Kiryat sefer, 1939).

34. Sigmund Freud, "Resistances to Psychoanalysis," trans. Yohanan Tversky, *Hadoar*, November 12, 1926, 20–21; and November 19, 1926, 38–39. See also Sigmund Freud, "On War," *Ha-shomer ha-tsair*, no. 7(1940): 8.

35. Anna Freud, *Introduction to the Theory of Psychoanalysis: Edited for Educators* [Mavo le-torat ha-psikho-analizah: ⬛arukh le-mehankhim], trans. Aryeh Ilan (Jerusalem: Histadrut ha-morim le-ivrit be-eretz Israel, 1930).

36. Rolnik, *Freud in Zion*, 178.

37. SE 15: 11.

38. Rolnik cites a personal communication with Ora Rafael for this detail, *Freud in Zion*, 56.

39. Hertz, "Pioneers and Psychoanalysis," 9.

40. Sigmund Freud, "Letter to Yehuda Dwossis" (December 12, 1938), Freud Museum (London).

41. Yehuda Dwossis, "Letter to Sigmund Freud" (November 30, 1938), Freud Museum (London).

42. Elon Gilad, "Fixation, Repression, Consciousness: This Is How Freudian Psychoanalysis Contributed to the Hebrew Language" [in Hebrew], *Ha'aretz Magazine*, October 19, 2022, https://www.haaretz.co.il/magazine/the-edge/mehasafa/2022-10-19/ty-article/.highlight/00000183-ef25-df45-a7eb-efafe9400000?gift=ea843a32b62842f68430f9ddd287e064.

43. Like the clitoris and the "iceberg" of the psyche, what was visible on the surface was only a small part of the story. In a 1935 medical dictionary prepared by Aharon Meir Mazi and edited by the doctor-poet Saul Tshernikhovski, Mazi provided *dagdegan* for the clitoris, a term that already appeared in slightly different form in Nathan Hameati's 1533 Hebrew translation of Avincenna's Arabic *Canon of Medicine* as well as Naftali Herz Tur-Sinai's 1927 German-Hebrew dictionary, as a translation of the slang term *Kitzler* (tickler); to Mazi and Tur-Sinai's *dagdegan*, Tshernikhovski added the synonyms *batar* (also from Arabic) and *hevyonit* (hidden) to *hamdan*. The Committee of the Hebrew Language, which supervised the dictionary, rejected all these terms as improper and unscientific. It wasn't until the "free-wheeling 1960s" that the *dagdegan* had its day in the sun, when poets like Yonah Wallach began including the "rude" word in their works. Gilad Elon, "Word of the Day *Dagdegan*: How Linguists Writhed over a Nice Hebrew Word for Clitoris," December 31, 2013, https://www.haaretz.com/2013-12-31/ty-article/.premium/dagdegan-the-hebrew-

word-for-clitoris/0000017f-db9a-df62-a9ff-dfdf5ecb0000?gift=784bac85140d4572b795
7647c7aa2de8.

44. The phrase does have some parallels and rhymes in such rabbinic terms as *yemey bereshit* (the days of Creation, or primordial times) and *ma'aseh bereshit* (the work of Creation).

45. SE 13: 101.

46. Freud, *Totem and Taboo*, 115.

47. SE 13: 18.

48. Freud, *Totem and Taboo*, 22.

49. SE 13: 101.

50. Freud, *Totem and Taboo*, 116.

51. A. Isserlin, "A Totem Clan Is Created," in Szold, *Max Eitingon: In Memoriam*, 179–83.

52. Dwossis was also raised in Eastern Europe and considered an excellent Hebrew teacher and Bible scholar, but he was less conversant with German, and he was criticized for the gaps in his knowledge of German.

53. Rolnik, *Freud in Zion*, 177–78. Rolnik quotes the committee discussion notes and Tel Aviv mayor Israel Rokach, "Letter to Zvi Woyslawski" (January 29, 1945), Tel Aviv City Archives.

54. GW 4: 192; and Freud, *Psychopathology*, 184.

55. Roland Végső, "The Parapraxis of Translation," *CR: The New Centennial Review* 12, no. 2 (2012): 50.

56. Végső, "Parapraxis of Translation," 55.

57. Freud, *Psychopathology*, 180; SE 6: 170; and GW 4: 188.

58. Freud, *Psychopathology*, 183; Walter Benjamin, "The Task of the Translator," trans. Harry Zohn, in *Illuminations: Essays and Reflections*, ed. Hannah Arendt (New York: Schocken, 1968), 71.

59. Scholem's 1926 letter to Rosenzweig on the Hebrew language, in which he describes the Zionist settlement as "a volcano" and rejects the belief that if a "language has been secularized . . . its apocalyptic thorn has been pulled out," is translated and discussed in William Cutter, "Ghostly Hebrew, Ghastly Speech: Scholem to Rosenzweig, 1926," *Prooftexts* 10, no. 3 (1990): 413–33.

60. Galili Shachar, "The Sacred and the Unfamiliar: Gershom Scholem and the Anxieties of the New Hebrew," *Germanic Review* 83, no. 4 (2008): 301.

61. GW 4: 192.

62. Sigmund Freud, *The Psychopathology of Everyday Life*, trans. A. A. Brill (London: T. Fischer Unwin, 1914), 189.

63. SE 6: 173.

64. I wish to thank Yael Sela for alerting me to the possibility that Freud is reenacting the *Polterabend* ritual.

65. Peter Gay described the marriages of Freud's two oldest daughters in these terms: "Four years [after Mathilde's marriage], in January 1913, Freud's second daughter, Sophie,

also deserted him." Both daughters "followed their own inclinations." See Gay, *Freud: A Life*, 309.

66. Gay, *Freud: A Life*, 309.

67. Sigmund Freud, "Letter to Sándor Ferenczi" (February 7, 1909), in *The Correspondence of Sigmund Freud and Sándor Ferenczi*, vol. 1, *1908–1914*, ed. Eva Brabant, Ernst Falzeder, and Patrizia Giampieri-Deutsch, trans. Peter T. Hoffer (Cambridge, MA: Harvard University Press, 1993), 42–43.

68. Dan Ben-Amos and Jerome R. Mintz, eds. and trans., *In Praise of the Baal Shem Tov: The Earliest Collection of Legends about the Founder of Hasidism* (Bloomington: Indiana University Press, 1970), 19; for a discussion, see Boyarin, *Unheroic Conduct*, 63–66.

69. Michael Schröter and Daniela Haller write that Freud "made inquiries concerning the financial situation of the chosen one and, not to be forgotten, his health and any hereditary diseases in his family background. He quite delicately asked his daughter to permit 'the older people to take circumstances into account that the feelings of the younger ones usually do not consider sufficiently.'" Michael Schröter and Daniela Haller, "Freud as a Father: The Testimony of His Letters to His Five Older Children," *American Imago* 68, no. 1 (2011): 15.

70. The nuclearization of Jewish families and its post-traditional cultural effects are explored in Seidman, *Marriage Plot*.

71. Rey Chow, *Not like a Native Speaker: On Languaging as a Postcolonial Experience* (New York: Columbia University Press, 2014), 63.

72. Chow, *Not like a Native Speaker*, 66.

73. In this case, Freud's melancholic repetition of the act he has denied himself may be complicated by its appropriation across gender lines, which is to say, by Sigmund's relationship with Martha, the mother of the bride whose opportunity to participate in the ritual betrothal of her eldest daughter has been short-circuited by her husband, along with her desire to light Sabbath candles. Freud's blunder, in this case, is a kind of admission to his wife of his affective connection to Jewish rituals, even as it is also a ritual stripped of everything but its internal seed or external shell, a violent motion that accomplishes nothing, a "surface" performance of a social ritual that only calls attention to its emptiness on the modern stage.

74. Benjamin, *Task of the Translator*, 78.

75. Barbara Johnson, *Mother Tongues: Sexuality, Trials, Motherhood, Translation* (Cambridge, MA: Harvard University Press, 2003), 64.

76. "Sigmund Freud Chair Established at Hebrew University," *Jewish Telegraphic Agency*, December 23, 1976.

77. Rafael Moses, "Address of Welcome: Jerusalem Congress," *International Journal of Psychoanalysis* 59 (1978): 3–4.

78. Moses, "Address of Welcome," 4.

79. Paul Schwaber, "Title of Honor: The Psychoanalytic Congress in Jerusalem," *Midstream* 24, no. 2 (1978): 29.

80. For reports on the Congress, see "The International Psychoanalytic Congress Will

Be Held in Jerusalem" [in Hebrew], *Davar*, August 18, 1977, 4; and "Psychiatrists in Jerusalem" [in Hebrew], *Al Hamishmar*, August 25, 1977, 6.

81. On this presentation, see Tova Tsimuki, "The Influence of the Holocaust on the Second Generation" [in Hebrew], *Davar*, August 29, 1977, 9.

82. Schwaber, "Title of Honor," 26.

83. Schwaber, "Title of Honor," 27.

84. Schwaber, "Title of Honor," 26.

85. Valenstein may have been chosen for the honor of reading the paper by virtue of his wife's relationship with Anna Freud. She was Katrina Burlingham, daughter of Dorothy Tiffany Burlingham, Anna's close friend, collaborator, and (rumored) partner in Vienna and London.

86. MacLeod, "Balfour's Mission to Palestine," 68.

87. Schwaber, "Title of Honor," 31.

88. Anna Freud, "Inaugural Lecture for the Sigmund Freud Chair at the Hebrew University, Jerusalem," *International Journal of Psychoanalysis* 59 (1978): 148. This comment has been the subject of much critical attention, including Yerushalmi's citation of this speech on the last page of his own book and interpretation of Anna's words as corroboration for his own views that Sigmund Freud believed psychoanalysis to be a Jewish science: "When your daughter conveyed those words to the congress in Jerusalem, *was she speaking in your name?*" Yerushalmi adds, "Please tell me, Professor. I promise I won't tell anyone." Yerushalmi, *Freud's Moses*, 100.

89. Schwaber, "Title of Honor," 31.

90. Schwaber, "Title of Honor," 31. Schwaber was not alone in his interest in where psychoanalysis might be wedded with Jewish observance and religious feeling; Paul Lerner writes about the psychoanalytic sanitarium (Therapeutikum) directed by Frieda Fromm-Reichmann and Erich Fromm in Heidelberg from 1924 to 1928, which "aimed to combine adherence to Jewish ritual with psychoanalytic practice and radical politics for a group of German Jews who were rethinking their Orthodox backgrounds in the light of new intellectual and political currents and modern sensibilities; he examines two articles by Fromm-Reichmann and Fromm published in *Imago* in 1927 that subjected Jewish rituals (*kashrut* and *shabbat*) to psychoanalytic interpretation. Lerner, "German Jews," 219–38.

91. Schwaber, "Title of Honor," 32.

92. Schwaber, "Title of Honor," 32–33.

93. Shelley Orgell, "Report from the 7th Pre-Congress Conference on Training," *International Journal of Psychoanalysis* 59 (1978): 511. The Pre-Congress, which was the first of its kind, aimed to connect psychoanalytic training programs with each other to compare methods and structure and share strategies.

94. Edward Said, with Christopher Bollas and Jacqueline Rose, *Freud and the Non-European* (London: Verso, 2014), 44–45.

95. Said, *Freud and the Non-European*, 36.

96. Jacqueline Rose, "Response to Edward Said," in Said, *Freud and the Non-European*, 66.

97. Haim Ormian, "With the Edition," in *Writings of Sigmund Freud* [Kitve Zigmund Freud], ed. Dr. H. Ormian, trans. Haim Isaac (Tel Aviv: Dvir Press, 1966), vii.

98. Sigmund Freud, "Selected Essays" [Masot nivharot], in *Writings of Sigmund Freud*, vol. 2, trans. Aryeh Bar (Tel Aviv: Dvir Press, 1966). As the table of contents, which provided the dates of publication for each essay, readily showed, the collection began with Freud's 1908 "Creative Writers and Day-Dreaming" as introduction to the essays that followed, on Moses and Michaelangelo (1927), Jensen's *Gradiva* (1907), the "Three Caskets" motif (1913), Goethe (1917), Leonardo (1910), Dostoevsky (1928), and so on.

99. Zvi Zohar, "Freud's Writings in Hebrew" [Hebrew], *Al Hamishmar*, February 23, 1968, 7.

100. Emanuel Berman, "My Way," *Psychoanalytic Inquiry* 30 (2010): 130.

101. Emanuel Berman, "My Way," 128.

102. Ruth Ginsburg, "A German Gentleman in Hebrew/Yiddish Garb," *Languages of Modern Jewish Cultures: Comparative Perspective*, ed. Joshua L. Miller and Anita Norich (Ann Arbor: University of Michigan Press, 2016), 60.

103. Ginsburg, "A German Gentleman," 60–61.

104. Ginsburg, "A German Gentleman," 61.

105. Said, *Freud and the Non-European*, 46–47.

106. Said, *Freud and the Non-European*, 49.

107. Ruth Ginsburg, "The Cracked Mirror of Translation: Freud's Reflection in Hebrew," in *Sprache, Erkenntnis, und Bedeutung: Deutsch in der jüdischen Wissenskultur*, ed. Susanne Zepp and Arndt Engelhardt (Leipzig: Universitätsverlag, 2015), 155.

Chapter 9

1. Steinberg, "Godless Jew," 2.

2. Weinreich, *Path to Our Youth*. For a description of the context in which Weinreich taught psychoanalysis, see Kuznitz, *YIVO and the Making of Modern Jewish Culture*, 149–54. Page 151 features a photograph of Weinreich with students at a 1936 seminar on psychoanalysis; about forty students are pictured, though some may have been auditors rather than full participants.

3. SE 13: xv.

4. Abigail Gillman, "Freud's Moses and Viennese Jewish Modernism," in *The Jewish World of Sigmund Freud: Essays on Cultural Roots and the Problem of Religious Identity*, ed. Arnold D. Richards (Jefferson, NC: McFarland, 2010), 129, 134.

5. The first lecture Freud gave to his Bnai Brith "brothers," on December 7, 1897, was "On Dream Interpretation." It was his first public presentation on his new ideas. See Hugo Knoepfmacher, "Sigmund Freud and the B'Nai B'Rith," *Journal of the American Psychoanalytic Association* 27 (1979): 442.

6. For a description of the Yale seminar and Weinreich's participation in it, see Barbara Kirshenblatt-Gimblett, "Coming of Age in the Thirties: Max Weinreich, Edward Sapir, and Jewish Social Science," *YIVO Annual* 23, ed. Deborah Dash Moore (1996): 1–105. The phrase "the relativity of cultural values," in "Coming of Age," 11, appears in the course

description, preserved in Box G10 of the Margaret Mead Papers, Manuscript Division, Library of Congress.

7. According to Leila Zenderland, "Participants read John Dewey's *Human Nature and Conduct*, Alfred L. Kroeber's *Anthropology*, Franz Boas's *Mind of Primitive Man*, Clark Wissler's *Man and Culture*, and Robert and Helen Lynd's *Middletown*. They also met a Who's Who of 1930s social science, including the political scientist Harold Lasswell, the economist Frank H. Knight, the criminologist Thorsten Sellin, the anthropologist Bronislaw Malinowski, the psychologist Arnold Gesell, the psychiatrist Harry Stack Sullivan, and the sociologist W. I. Thomas. In Leila Zenderland, "Social Science as a 'Weapon of the Weak': Max Weinreich, the Yiddish Scientific Institute, and the Study of Culture, Personality, and Prejudice," *Isis* 104, no. 4 (December 2013): 751.

8. Weinreich also registered his impatience with the seminar's approach to "religion," responding to the question "In what ways does the religion actually help youth, and in what ways may it be said to be detrimental to them?" with the response: "There is so much of a value judgment in the terms 'help' or 'detriment' that I feel embarrassed by this question." See Kirschenblatt-Gimblett, "Coming of Age," 21. The problem was not only the ham-handed approach to religion, its Protestant bias of the questions, or the predictable misconstruing of Jews through the lens of religion rather than ethnicity ("nationality," to use Weinreich's term). It was that the comparative nature of the seminar, by lining up family structures and religious cultures as if they were parallel phenomena, failed to take into account how these religions or cultures impinged on and even co-construct each other within larger, asymmetrical cultural formations, as was clearly the case with a minority community like Polish Jewry.

9. Kirschenblatt-Gimblett, "Coming of Age," 34–35. The questionnaire and answers are in Box G9, Margaret Mead Papers, Manuscript Division, Library of Congress. These magical formulae were still to be heard in my own childhood in Brooklyn of the 1960s, although more common was one Weinreich did not mention, a Hebrew biblical verse: "Not a dog shall snarl at any of the Israelites, at man or beast—in order that you may know that the Lord makes a distinction between Egypt and Israel [*Ulekhol benai yisrael lo yeheratz kelev leshono*]." Ex 11:7.

10. Weinreich, *Path to Our Youth*, 175.
11. Weinreich, *Path to Our Youth*, 176.
12. Weinreich, *Path to Our Youth*, 176.
13. Weinreich, *Path to Our Youth*, 9.
14. Weinreich, *Path to Our Youth*, 9.

15. While other similar works that emerged from YIVO's Yungfor (*yungnt forshung*, or youth research) tended to describe youth in ideological or collective fashion, Weinreich preferred to speak of the contingent, individual, and unpredictable reasons young people moved from the right to the left, chose Hebraism over Yiddishism, risked their lives in illegal political activity, turned inward and "autistic," craved business success, or devoted their lives to intellectual activity.

16. Jacob Emden, *She'elat Ya'avetz* (Altona, Germany: Aharon Katz, 1738) 1:17.
17. Weinreich, *Path to Our Youth*, 187.

18. Weinreich, *Path to Our Youth*, 173, 194–97.

19. Zenderland, "Social Science"; and Jennifer Young, "Race, Culture, and the Creation of Yiddish Social Science: Max Weinreich's Trip to Tuskegee 1932," in *Choosing Yiddish: New Frontiers of Language and Culture*, ed. Shiri Goren, Hannah S. Pressman, Lara Rabinovitch, et al. (Detroit, MI: Wayne State University Press, 2012), 217–32.

20. John Dollard, "Christmas and Summer Trips," Box G10, Folder 6, Mead Papers; cited in Zenderland, "Social Science," 752.

21. Although Weinreich does not cite Du Bois, Young recognizes the influence of the notion of "double consciousness" in Weinreich's work. See Young, "Race, Culture," 221–22.

22. Jacques Derrida, "Abraham, the Other," trans. Gil Anidjar, Bettina Bergo, Joseph D. Cohen, and Raphael Zagury-Orly, in *Judeities: Questions for Jacques Derrida* (New York: Fordham University Press, 2007), 9.

23. Derrida, "Abraham," 10.

24. Cynthia Baker, *Jew* (New Brunswick, NJ: Rutgers University Press, 2016), 1–15.

25. Baker, *Jew*, 49.

26. On this history and its traumatic reverberations, see Tyler D. Parry and Charlton W. Yingling, "Slave Hounds and Abolition in the Americas," *Past & Present* 246, no. 1 (2020): 69–108.

27. As Jennifer Young points out, Weinreich must have recognized in this discourse a familiar need among Jews "to justify their own presence in Eastern Europe." Young, "Race, Culture," 224.

28. Weinreich, *Path to Our Youth*, 196.

29. Weinreich, *Path to Our Youth*, 197.

30. On the 1942 contest, see Daniel Soyer, "Documenting Immigrant Lives at an Immigrant Institution: YIVO's Autobiography Contest of 1942," *Jewish Social Studies* 5, no. 3 (1999): 218–43.

31. The appendix is taken over largely by an extended quote from Autobiography 237, in which the anonymous writer (a young man) suggests that, in his experience, sex occupies a less-significant feature of Jewish adolescent life than the "more burning issue of the struggle for existence." Perhaps by consequence of this difference, "the whole attitude [of Jewish teenagers toward sex] is free of masquerade and hypocrisy." In the Polish gymnasium, the social scene is filled with drama: The Polish girls flirt and pretend not to understand the boys' salacious jokes, while "dreaming about love with a delicious quiver." But because Jews lack "a feudal chivalric tradition," their love affairs are "hard, practical [*balebatish*]." A boy and girl "go out" for a while, and then they get married. Weinreich, *Path to Our Youth*, 299. On Weinreich's unwillingness to make general pronouncements on the character of Jewish sexuality, despite acknowledging the importance of sexuality, see Weiman-Kelman, "Eroto-Philology," 62. Weiman-Kelman sees the absence of a theory of Jewish sexuality in Weinreich's work as a symptom, among others, of the incompleteness of the Yiddish sexology archive, an incompleteness that invites their own queer "method of eroto-philology" (65).

32. Whether Freud provided a rocking horse for little Hans before or after he developed his horse phobia is of obvious interest. Graf first reported that the rocking horse was a present for Herbert's third birthday in Max Graf, "Reminiscences of Professor Sigmund Freud,"

Psychoanalytic Quarterly 11, no. 4 (1942): 474; but he revised the memory in a 1952 interview with Kurt Eissler, saying that the rocking horse was provided after the conclusion of the case, when Herbert was five. See Jerome C. Wakefield, "Max Graf's 'Reminiscences of Professor Sigmund Freud' Revisited: New Evidence from the Freud Archives," *Psychoanalytic Quarterly* 76 (2007): 167–73.

33. Jay Geller, *On Freud's Jewish Body: Mitigating Circumcisions* (New York: Fordham University Press, 2007), 114.

34. Graf, "Reminiscences," 473.

35. Max Weinreich Papers, RG 584, YIVO Archives.

36. SE 10: 36.

37. Geller, *Freud's Jewish Body*, 112.

38. Boyarin, *Unheroic Conduct*, 239.

39. Boyarin, *Unheroic Conduct*, 234.

40. Boyarin, *Unheroic Conduct*, 232. The assumption that Freud was unaware of or unable to access more positive Jewish approaches to circumcision than those cited in the little Hans footnote may be overstated. In *Moses and Monotheism*, Freud writes that "those who have adopted circumcision are exalted by it, ennobled, as it were, and look down with contempt on the others, who are unclean. Even to this day a Turk will abuse a Christian as 'an uncircumcised dog.'" SE 23: 29–30.

41. Slavet, *Racial Fever*, 115.

42. Weinreich, *Path to Our Youth*, 189.

43. The mother's threat to castrate her son for touching his genitals is particularly striking given that Freud described the couple as "among my closest adherents," who had agreed "in bringing up their first child they would use no more coercion than absolutely necessary for maintaining good behavior." SE 10: 6.

44. Gilles Deleuze and Felix Guattari, *A Thousand Plateaus: Capitalism and Schizophrenia*, trans. Brian Massumi (London: Athlone, 1989), 259.

45. Jones, *Life and Work*, 3:141.

46. Jones, *Life and Work*, 3:308. In a passage that otherwise praises Jones for his fine biography of Freud, Walter Kaufmann writes that Jones is mistaken in attributing the saying to Jewish "ancestral tradition, . . . as if the point were not plainly that the Jew identifies himself with the hunted creature." Walter Kaufmann, *From Shakespeare to Existentialism: Essays on Shakespeare and Goethe; Hegel and Kierkegaard; Nietzsche, Rilke and Freud; Jaspers, Heidegger, and Toynbee* (Princeton, NJ: Princeton University Press, 2020), 329.

47. See Michael J. Burlingham, "The Relationship of Anna Freud and Dorothy Burlingham," *Journal of the American Academy of Psychoanalysis* 19, no. 4 (1991): 612–19. Bob was psychoanalyzed by Anna, and Dorothy by her father. Dorothy was a wealthy heiress, having inherited the Tiffany fortune.

48. Genosko points out that the association of *Wolfehunde* with National Socialism, and as the "visible vehicles of the persecution of Jewish citizens in Austria and elsewhere," was a product of the 1930s (thus, after Anna acquired her dog); it is also true that Van Stephanitz's project of selectively breeding a local population of "coyote-like" dogs to produce a "racially better canine" was under way by the 1920s. See Gary Genosko, "Introduction to

the Transaction Edition," in *Topsy: The Story of a Golden-Haired Chow*, by Princess Marie Bonaparte (New Brunswick, NJ: Transaction, 1994), 3–4.

49. Susan Martha Kahn, "The Extraordinary Life of Rudolphina Menzel," in *Canine Pioneer: The Extraordinary Life of Rudolphina Menzel*, ed. Susan Martha Kahn (Waltham, MA: Brandeis University Press, 2022), 3–81. Kahn writes that Menzel's work as a cynologist paralleled Freud's efforts in the human realm, for instance, in weighing the significance of biological factors in dogs' behavior versus "social environment" (14) or in mapping the five developmental stages of canine life, roughly matching the oral, anal, phallic, latent, and genital stages Freud identified in humans (16).

50. Yerushalmi, *Freud's Moses*, 70. Yerushalmi quotes Sigmund Freud and Arnold Zweig, *Briefwechsel*, ed. Ernst L. Freud (Frankfurt am Main: S. Fischer, 1968), 140. The English translation is in *Letters of Sigmund Freud and Arnold Zweig*, 130.

51. H.D., *Tribute to Freud*, 98.

52. H.D., *Tribute to Freud*, 59.

53. H.D., *Tribute to Freud*, 11.

54. H.D., *Tribute to Freud*, 62.

55. Evidence that Freud considered the household dogs "Freuds" is also in H.D., who writes: "He told me that Yofi's first husband was a black chow and Yofi had one black baby, 'as black as the devil.' It died when it was three-quarters of a year old. Now the new father is lion gold and the Professor hopes that Yofi's children will survive, this time. He said, if there are two puppies, the father's people have one, but if only one, 'it stays a Freud.'" H.D., *Tribute to Freud*, 166.

56. H.D., *Tribute to Freud*, 117.

57. H.D., *Tribute to Freud*, 98.

58. H.D., *Tribute to Freud*, 162. Joseph Wortis, another American who underwent a "didactic analysis" with Freud in 1934, overlapping for a few months with H.D.'s analysis—her hour began at four, his at six—also mentions the dog. Describing his first session, Wortis writes: "I lay on the couch, Freud behind me, his dog sitting quietly on his haunches at the foot of the bed . . . a large dog . . . a big chow I thought it was. . . . I didn't notice exactly." Joseph Wortis, *Fragments of an Analysis with Freud* (New York: Jason Aronson, 1984), 23. In the 1930s, Freud's dogs became nearly as famous as their owner, appearing not only in family photos and home movies but also in newspaper reports and even a *New Yorker* parody by Wolcott Gibbs. The parody, "A Couch of My Own," borrowed liberally from Joseph Wortis's book, making fun not only of Freud's love of dogs but also his deafness, a particular problem with his American patients as his hearing deteriorated. Wolcott Gibbs, "A Couch of My Own: Some Reminiscences Prompted by, and to a Certain Extent Patterned after, Dr. Joseph Wortis's *Fragments of an Analysis with Freud*," *New Yorker*, February 19, 1954, 29.

59. SE 10: 135.

60. Graf, *Reminiscences*, 474.

61. SE 10: 135.

62. On the neologisms Weinreich forged in creating a Yiddish sociological lexicon, see Yudel Mark, "Neologisms in the Work of Max Weinreich" [in Yiddish], in *For Max*

Weinreich on His Seventieth Birthday, ed. Lucy S. Dawidowicz (The Hague: Mouton Press, 1964), 435–12. Among the neologisms Mark discusses (431) are *mitkind* for "sibling" and *dervaksling* for "adolescent," a term so crucial in *The Path to Our Youth*.

63. Zizek, *Absolute Recoil*, 331, referring to Hegel's *The Egyptian Mysteries*.

Epilogue

1. Kathryn R. Barush, *Imaging Pilgrimage: Art as Embodied Pilgrimage* (London: Bloomsbury Publishing: 2021), 63.

2. Barush, *Imaging Pilgrimage*, 58. Barush's note on the "medial shift" refers to C. S. Wood's conception of a certain "transfer of meaning from original building to replicated building to painting building." See C. S. Wood, *Forgery, Replica, Fiction: Temporalities of German Renaissance Art* (Chicago: University of Chicago Press, 2008), 339.

3. Simon Goldhill, *Freud's Couch, Scott's Buttocks, Brontë's Grave* (Chicago: University of Chicago Press, 2011), 113. The kiddush cups, we know, disappeared en route from Vienna to London; the menorah Goldhill missed in the Freud Museum has appeared in museum exhibits of Freud's treasures, for instance, in 1991 in *The Sigmund Freud Antiquities: Fragments from a Buried Past* at the Jewish Museum of New York. On this exhibit, see Suzanne Slesin, "Analyzing Freud's Menorah," *New York Times*, November 28, 1991, C3.

4. Sherry Simon, *Translation Sites: A Field Guide* (Abingdon, Oxon, UK: Routledge, 2019).

5. William Cook, "Analysing Freud's Couch," *The Guardian*, August 21, 2006, https://www.theguardian.com/artanddesign/2006/aug/21/heritage.austria.

6. H.D., *Tribute to Freud*, 116.

7. Goldhill, *Freud's Couch*, 111.

8. Goldhill, *Freud's Couch*, 119.

9. Gaston Bachelard, *The Poetics of Space* (Boston: Beacon Press, 1994), 8.

10. Bachelard, *Poetics of Space*, 18.

11. Kosofsky Sedgwick, *Touching Feeling*, 8.

12. The first mention of Freud's collecting antiquities is in a December 6, 1896, letter to Fliess; Freud's father died on October 23 of that year. See Jones, *Life and Work*, 330. In the preface to the second edition (1909) of *The Interpretation of Dreams*, Freud described his belated realization that the book was occasioned by his father's death, "the most important event, the most poignant loss, of a man's life." SE 4: xxvi. Many decades later, Freud wrote in *Moses and Monotheism* about the connection between the invisible God and a father whose paternity cannot be established by the senses. SE 23: 117.

13. Benjamin, "Unpacking My Library," 67.

Index

Abraham (biblical figure), 164–65, 268, 309n83
Abraham (father of the Besht), 235, 322n68
Abraham, Karl, 108, 180, 193, 217, 286n20, 308n55, 313n8
Acosta, Uriel, 43
Actor-Network-Theory (ANT), 14
Adelman, Howard Zvi, 295n23
Adler, Alfred, 20, 145
adolescents and adolescence, 64, 99–101, 121, 255, 326n31, 328n62. *See also* YIVO autobiography contest; youth
Adonai, 67, 175, 311n114. *See also* God
Adorno, Theodor, 289n65
African-Americans. *See* Black Americans
affect, 5–14, 24, 39, 79, 86–87, 109, 114, 117, 121, 125, 132–33, 137, 166, 188, 212–15, 239, 297n66, 322n73; as theme of International Psychoanalytic Congress, 238
affect theory, 5, 86, 132–33, 238
alienation, 4, 40–41, 52, 64, 68, 80, 94, 119, 144, 168, 191
Alter, Robert, 65–66, 294n13, 309n80
Amati-Mehler, Jacqueline, 119, 303n57, 303n58, 303n59, 303n60, 315n33, 315n34
America. *See* United States of America
Amichai, Yehuda, 78
amnesia and forgetting, 1, 54, 72–73, 96, 131, 183, 191, 194, 202, 233, 235
Am Oved Press, 244
anal-eroticism, 20
animals and animal phobias, 16, 229–30, 248, 250–56, 258, 261, 264–70. *See also* dogs; horses
Anna O., 15, 48–51, 53–56, 58, 84, 112, 156–59, 195, 291n12, 327n46. *See also* Pappenheim, Bertha
Ansell, Charles, 237
antisemitism, 22, 34, 73, 88–89, 124, 152–53, 156, 168–69, 171, 174, 177, 199, 239, 250, 257–64, 267–69, 307n39; as allo-Semitism, 81; internalized, 60, 124, 263
Appiah, Kwame Anthony, 89–92, 102, 298n8
après-coup, 114–16
Apter, Emily, 104
Arabic, 122, 229, 312n124, 320n43
Arabs, 219, 238. *See also* Palestinians

archaeology, 45–48, 60, 80–81, 84, 227, 246, 291n3
archives, 69, 84, 104, 143, 158, 259, 272, 275
Arendt, Hannah, 244
Argentina, 65, 147–49, 186, 198, 242, 307n39, 313n13
Argientieri, Simona, 119, 303n57, 303n58, 303n59, 303n60, 315n34
Aron, Willy, 319n26
Artenstein, Isaac, 295n20
Ashkenormativity, 62. *See also* Jews, Ashkenazic
assimilated and acculturated Jews, 8, 23–35, 43–44, 51, 57–59, 62–63, 72–76, 81–82, 88, 95, 99, 101–3, 127, 167–70, 191, 203, 211, 212, 259–61, 270, 288n51
Asya, M., 143–44
Ater, Moshe, 245–46
Auden, W.H. 1–2, 47
Austria, 19, 31, 166–67, 171, 176, 186, 190, 193, 194, 311n109, 327n48
Aylon, Menahem, 226

Bachelard, Gaston, 40, 182, 279, 289n66
Bakan, David, 117–18, 303n51, 303n52, 303n53
Baker, Cynthia, 257–58
Barthes, Roland, 244
Barush, Kathryn R., 276–77, 329n2
Basile, Elena, 79, 114, 297n66
Bass, Alan, 47
Bass, Jeffrey, 307n39
Begin, Menachem, 240
Belzer, Richard, 91–92, 298n11
Ben-Amos, Dan, 26, 170
Ben Horin, Shlomo, 311n114
Benattar, Ilan, 312n124
Benjamin, Jessica, 196, 315n38
Benjamin, Walter, 3, 29, 232, 280, 281n2, 281n4, 293n37, 321n58
Ben-Yehuda, Eliezer, 121–22

Berger, Shlomo, 315n41
Bergmann, Hugo, 149, 238, 307n42
Bergmann, Martin, 238
Bergner, Elizabeth, 155
Bergson, Henri, 154, 211, 222
Berke, Joseph H., 195, 313n12, 315n37
Berkovski, K., 144, 306n24
Berlin, 18, 74, 108, 155, 193, 217–18, 256, 283n1, 306n18
Berlin, Isaiah, 315n35
Berman, Antoine, 116
Berman, Emanuel, 215, 243, 318n12, 324n100, 324n101
Berman, Lila Corwin, 71, 95, 296n34
Bernfeld, Siegfried, 9, 267, 316n49
Best, Stephen, 71
Bettelheim, Bruno, 105, 107, 184–85, 221, 223, 299n5, 300n11, 313n6
Bialik, Hayim Nahman, 150, 209–10
Bible, 17, 65, 98, 106, 126, 147, 164, 173–80, 210, 227–29, 245–47, 306n30, 325n9; Exodus, 98, 248; Freud's family, 25, 28; Genesis, 65, 180, 204, 309n83; Psalms 54; *Tsenerene* ("Jewish women's Bible"), 52
bilingualism, 17, 35, 38, 47–48, 63, 84, 138, 140, 194; "external" and "internal," 129–30. *See also* multilingualism
Birnbaum, Nathan, 63, 121
Black Americans, 86–103, 258; and dogs, 326n26
Black Lives Matter (BLM), 85–103
Black Panthers (Israel), 240
Bleuler, Eugene, 193
Blum, Leon, 156
Bnai Brith, 18–19, 199, 250, 324n5
bodies, 21, 40, 49, 60, 87, 90, 96, 110, 113–14, 123–24, 190, 209, 289; Anna O.'s, 49; Freud's 28, 236, 278; Jewish, 4, 71, 91, 117, 169, 188, 263; of language, 31, 118, 278; scholar's, 86–87; and translation, 117, 130, 132, 277
Bollas, Christopher, 323n94

Bonaparte, Princess Marie, 266
books as material objects, 2–3, 65, 279–80
Borden, Miriam, 2
Borochov, Ber, 36, 63–64, 100–101, 121
Borrow, George, 17
Bose, Girindrashekar, 93
Bourguignon, André, 107, 301n16, 301n18, 302n46, 302n48
Boyarin, Daniel, 3–5, 44, 93–97, 99, 103, 281n5, 290n79, 298n6, 298n16, 298n17, 319n28, 322n68
Boyarin, Jonah, 97–99, 299n28
Boyarin, Jonathan, 185–86
Boym, Svetlana, 105
Boynton, Robert S., 301n14
Brabant, Eva, 322n67
Brachyahu, Mordechai, 2, 147, 221, 226, 319n23, 319n29
Brandes, Georg, 211, 230
Brazil, 78, 295n21
Brenner, Michael, 52, 292n25, 292n26
Brenner, Sarah (pseudonym of Max Weinreich), 316n44
Breuer, Josef, 46, 48–51, 53–54, 112, 135, 188, 195, 291n14
Brill, Abraham Arden, 56–57, 135, 137, 144–45, 151, 186, 192, 230, 234, 293n39, 299n5; translation of Freud, 56, 192, 230, 233–34, 237; Yiddish accent, 57, 293n39; in the Yiddish press, 151
Bronner, Simon J., 81, 297n71, 297n72
Brown, Jack, 85
Buber, Martin, 154, 222, 230, 292n24
Buck-Morss, Susan, 244
Buczacz, 30, 171–73
Buenos Aires, 119, 145, 148–49, 198, 307n39, 313n13
Bühler, Charlotte, 9
Bukharin, Nikolai, 199
Bulgarian, 30–31, 39
Burlingham, Dorothy Tiffany, 266, 323n85, 327n47

Burlingham, Katrina, 323n85
Burlingham, Michael J., 327n47
Burshtin, Mikhoel, 140–42
Burton, Nylah, 88, 298n7
Bychowski, Gustav, 193, 199

Canada, 134, 148
Canestri, Jorge, 119, 303n58, 303n60
Canetti, Elias, 30–31, 33, 38–40, 66
Caplan, Marc, 100
Carroll, Michael P., 67, 295n21
Carson, Alan, 291n15
Cassirer, Ernst, 198
Castilian, 43
castration, 19, 56–57, 261–64, 327n43
Catholicism, 42, 67, 129, 162–63, 274, 211, 228
Champollion, Jean-François, 48
Chaudhuri, Sukanta, 157–59
children, 69, 74–76, 80, 114–17, 121–27, 134–39, 250–66, 269–70. *See also* adolescents; infants; youth
childhood, 115, 119, 195, 204, 217, 223, 257, 264, 325n8; languages of, 38, 59 119, 122
Chile, 194
Chouraqui, André, 126
Chow, Rey, 236
Christian Science, 151
Christianity, 36, 41–43, 67–68, 73–74, 89, 92–93, 117–18, 128, 130, 167, 188, 211, 234, 268, 281n9, 289n70, 295n23, 303n52, 327n40
circumcision, 4, 28, 56–57, 117, 260–64, 270, 327n40
Cixous, Hélène, 68
class, 20, 27, 101–3, 156–59, 256
closet, "Freud," 1–10, 14, 16, 85–87, 263, 275–80; Jewish, 4–5, 76–77, 91–94, 263, 281n9; queer, 4–5, 281n9
colonialism, 3–4, 17, 38, 88, 92–97, 103, 188, 288. *See also* postcolonialism
compensatory mechanisms, 103, 256, 258–61, 270

component consciousness, in Yiddish, 203
condensation, 111–13, 126, 130
confession, 28, 41–43, 72, 162–63
converts and conversion, 23, 40–43, 49, 62, 67–69, 74–75, 80, 128, 167, 211, 253, 295n23, 296n45. *See also* Crypto-Jews
Cook, George Cram, 308n50
Cook, William, 278
Cotet, Pierre, 116
Crick, Joyce, 59–60
crypto-Jews, 17–25, 27–44, 61, 66–69, 73–75, 91, 94, 289n70, 295n19, 295n20. *See also* converts and conversion
Cuddihy, John Murray, 34–35, 43–44, 59, 108, 206, 288n51
Cutter, William, 321n59
Cwodziński, Antoni, 155
Czech (language), 30–31, 39, 283n1
Czech Republic, 278

da Costa, J.M., 42
Dali, Salvador, 312n124
Damrosch, David, 33, 111, 287n47, 309n74
Davies, Keith, 283n24, 284n4, 304n88
daytshmerish, 100, 188, 205, 227. *See also* Yiddish
Dean, Tim, 281n8
Deleuze, Gilles, 10, 264–65
demons, 144–46
depths, 5–6, 30, 76–77, 80, 84, 177, 221, 257, 279
Derrida, Jacques, 28, 57, 62, 64, 66, 68, 126–27, 257–58, 295n27
Deutsch, Helene, 190, 314n25
Dewey, John, 325n7
Diamond, Elin, 87
diaspora, 32, 36, 94, 96, 98, 156, 240–242, 246; Freudian, 104–106. *See also* doikayt
Dickman, Milton, 134

dictionaries, 197, 202, 320n43
differentiation language, 102–3, 169
Diller, Jerry, 284n1, 284n2
displacement, 79, 111–13, 124, 130, 165, 211, 282n16
Dodnick, Y., 198
dogs, 248–73, 328n49, 328n58; fear of dogs, 252–53, 261, 327n46. *See also* animals; horses
doikayt, 94, 97
Dollard, John, 256, 326n20
Doolittle, Hilda, H.D., 46, 209, 267–68
Douglass, Frederick, 85
dreams, 13–14, 48, 78–79, 82–83, 109–12, 116, 138–39, 204, 206–8, 215–16, 239, 317n66, 318n13; of American Jews, 182–83, 208; Freud's, 54–56; images in, 48, 110; interpretation, 117, 144–48, 182–83, 207–8, 250; of new Hebrew speakers, 122
dream work, 109–10, 113, 147, 182
Drori, Danielle, 211, 318n13
Du Bois, W.E.B., 256, 326n21
Dvir Press, 242–244, 324n97, 324n98
Dwossis, Yehuda, 2, 6–8, 11–12, 174, 206, 214, 224–30, 245, 316n53, 317n66, 321n52
dybbuks, 144, 146

Eder, David, 216, 314n14
education and pedagogy,19, 24, 42, 54, 58, 122, 140, 143, 157, 189, 200, 209, 216–218, 223–224, 283n1, 308n66, 316n49, 316n53, 321n52
Efron, John M., 282n20, 315n35
ego, 27, 43–44, 105, 109, 147, 201, 256, 299n5; alter, 27, 57, 75; Freud's, 147; Jewish, 256, 258,
Egypt, 45, 56, 98, 170, 176, 246, 248, 325n8. *See also* hieroglyphics
Eichler, Lillian, 139, 305n11
Einstein, Albert, 20, 146, 149–50, 154–55, 222, 259, 269

Eissler, Kurt, 296n54, 327n32
Eitingon, Max, 193, 217–20, 222, 229, 319n23, 319n24, 321n51
Elisabeth R., 46
Ellis, Havelock, 145, 284n3
Emden, Jacob, 248, 325n16
Engelman, Edmund, 291n1
English, 30–32, 50–51, 98–99, 101, 105–9, 119–21, 125–28, 134, 138–41, 159, 162, 164, 167, 202–3, 241, 245, 303n58; translation of Freud, 56–57, 59, 74, 105–9, 125–28, 130, 151, 174, 184–86, 221, 223, 230, 233, 299n5, 300n13, 313n6, 313n14, 316n57, 317n71
English press, 88, 92, 137, 153–54, 178
Epstein, Isaac, 225
Ernest Benn's Sixpenny Library, 157
eroto-philology, 79, 326n31
Ernst, Max, 278
Esau, 89, 102, 168–69, 255–56
ethnic minimalism and maximalism, 146, 161
ethnicity, 81, 88, 98, 102, 125, 135, 159, 191, 255–59, 267, 307n39, 325n8. *See also* race
European languages, 15, 30–31, 34, 36–37, 63, 101, 138
evenly suspended attention, 77–78, 118
Everett, Patricia, 293n39
Ezrat Nashim hospital, 216

Falzeder, Ernst, 286n20, 299n3, 322n67
family, 138–39, 153–54, 165–66, 188, 190, 215, 235–36, 249, 251, 257, 259, 265, 308n57, 311n109, 312n124
famous Jews, 11, 149, 153–55, 269–70, 308n58, 308n59
Fanon, Frantz, 4, 90–92, 94–95, 97
Farate, Carlos, 305n5
Fass, Paula, 293n39
father, 23, 31, 32, 37, 40, 49–50, 55, 75, 80, 103, 121, 128, 131, 140, 180, 252–53, 259–61, 264, 279, 298n54, 322n69; God as, 36; Little Hans', 234–37, 250, 259, 269–70; Name of the Father, 84; role in traditional marriage, 234–37. *See also* Freud, Jakob; Graf, Max
father-in-law, 235
Fathy, Safaa, 68, 295n27
Feigenbaum, Dorian, 216
Feinstein, Daniel, 180–81, 312n128, 312n129, 313n129
Feitler, Bruno, 295n21
Felski, Rita, 14, 71, 77, 296n36, 296n37, 296n56, 297n57
femininity and feminization, 4, 57; and Yiddish, 57, 121, 183, 187, 288n58
feminists and feminism, 51, 57, 62, 246, 294n1
Ferry, Barbara, 67, 295n20
fetish, 7–8, 45, 79, 81, 170, 282n16
Fifth Aliyah, 217, 219
Fishman, David E., 312n127, 313n8
Fitzgerald, Michael, 305n3
Fletcher, John, 114
Fliess, Wilhelm, 112, 114, 128, 284n1, 329n12
Floyd, George, 85, 87, 93, 298n17
foreign: accent, 32, 139; languages, 8, 32, 34, 40, 53, 74, 80–83, 101, 116–17, 120, 128–29, 210–12, 225, 236, 247, 273, 288n50, 289n65; sources, 157, 159, 212
Forrester, John, 79, 297n65
Foucault, Michel, 41–42, 71, 163, 244
Freedman, Jonathan, 281n9, 282n9
Freeman, Erika, 283n1
Freiburg, 30, 218
Fremdwörter, 40, 129, 289n65
French, 31, 50–51, 59, 61, 64, 66, 81, 107, 110–11, 113, 115, 119–20, 123, 126, 128–29; translations of Freud, 107, 113–16, 186, 245
Freud, Alexander, 138, 305n10

Freud, Amalie (Nathanson), 18, 57, 283n1
Freud, Anna, 220, 223, 265–66, 278, 282n11, 285n7, 301n21, 301n22, 319n25, 320n35, 323n85, 323n88, 327n47
Freud, Debora, 311n109
Freud, Ernst, 12, 155, 166, 282n15, 328n50
Freud, Jakob, 11, 18, 19, 24–25, 28, 127, 142, 173, 178, 283n1, 295n31, 329n12
Freud, Josef, 311n109
Freud, Marthe (Bernays), 49, 173, 234, 322n73
Freud, Mathilde, 197, 234–36
Freud, Oliver, 308n57
Freud, Shlomo, 277, 286n19, 311n109
Freud, Sigmund: ancestors, 142, 169, 191, 245, 267; antiquity collection, 2, 7, 45, 151, 232, 268, 279, 291n1, 291n2, 329n3; arrest and exile, 104–16, 166–70, 178–79215, 221, 310n86; and dogs, 6, 265–69, 327n46, 328n55; and Einstein, 154–55; as famous Jew, 153–55, 160, 165, 270; as "the Professor," 260, 267–68, 270; atheism of, 43, 290n75; birthdays, 147, 149, 153, 155–56, 160–61, 168, 184, 200, 307n47; conception of translation, 109–17, 130; couch, 267–68, 278–79, 328n58, 329n7, 329n8; death of, 2, 18, 22, 168, 212–15, 310n93; family tree, 159, 165, 171–73, 277, 311n105, 311n109; household, 166, 171–72, 196, 232–37, 268; Jewish appearance, 93, 153, 159, 167; Jewish background, 5, 9–11, 13, 15, 26, 61, 70–71, 85–103, 143, 160–61, 164, 249, 266–72, 283n1, 284n1, 284n2; knowledge of Hebrew, 6, 8, 18, 22, 28, 30, 57, 66, 176, 267, 272; knowledge of Yiddish, 6, 8, 18–25, 30, 33, 57, 59, 66, 187, 272; name, 22, 134, 143, 176, 197, 286n19; topographical model of the psyche, 15, 38, 45–48, 61; and Weinreich, 7, 16, 131, 133, 187, 220, 249–51, 260, 269, 307n46, 319n26; winning the Goethe prize, 153; and YIVO, 18, 20, 131, 150, 171, 220, 307n46, 307n47, 308n65, 312n123, 313n124; youth, 75, 290n76

Freud, Sigmund, Works:
"Analysis of a Case of Childhood Phobia" (Little Hans), 260–265, 270
Beyond the Pleasure Principle, 245, 287n36
Complete Correspondence of Sigmund Freud, 286n20
Complete Letters of Sigmund Freud to Wilhelm Fliess, 302n33
Complete Psychological Works of Sigmund Freud, 300n8
The Ego and the Id, 108, 299n5
"Family Romances," 69, 235
Future of an Illusion, 198
Group Psychology, 2, 198–201, 206, 223–24, 226–27
"Instead of a Preface" to the Yiddish translation of *Introductory Lectures*, 6, 11, 132–33
Interpretation of Dreams, 48, 54, 78, 82, 110, 116, 118, 138, 144–47, 186, 221, 239, 245, 250, 306n30, 314n14, 319n23, 319n29
Introductory Lectures on Psychoanalysis, 6–7, 133, 189, 200, 243, 304n88, 314n24
Jokes and Their Relation, 18, 24, 76, 188
Letters of Sigmund Freud, 282n15, 328n50
Moses and Monotheism, 69–72, 78, 83–84, 96, 174–78, 220, 224, 230, 238, 242, 245–49, 295n31, 312n24, 327n40, 329n12

"Mourning and Melancholy," 237
"On Dream Interpretation," 324n8
"On Dreams," 186, 314n14
"Preface to the Hebrew Translation" of *Introductory Lectures*, 6, 133, 214, 223–24
"Preface to the Hebrew Translation" of *Totem and Taboo*, 6–7, 11–13, 133, 214, 223–25, 249
Psychopathology of Everyday Life, 72–76, 113, 123–27, 133, 164, 214, 230–33, 290n77, 321n54, 321n55, 321n58
Standard Edition, 6, 9, 18, 105–7, 111, 115, 125, 128, 184, 201, 204, 212–14, 223, 226, 234, 245, 299n5, 300n7, 300n8, 313n5; as "salvage translation," 212–15
Totem and Taboo, 2, 6–7, 12–13, 16, 171, 223–30, 245, 249
"The Uncanny," 179–80, 245, 247, 285n9
"Why War?" 155, 223
See also Hebrew translations of Freud; Yiddish translations of Freud
Freud craze, 140–42, 148
Freudian Lullaby Contest, 134, 139–40, 143
Freud Museum, London, 241–42, 276–79, 283n24, 284n1, 313n12, 329n3
Freud Museum, Příbor, 278
Freud Museum, Vienna, 278
Freudo-Marxism, 199, 316n49
Frieden, Ken, 55–56, 82, 110
Fromm, Erich, 207, 317n72, 318n72, 323n90
Fromm-Reichmann, Frieda, 318n72, 323n90
Frosh, Stephen, 313n12
Fuchs, Shirley, 154, 308n57

Galicia, 52, 175
Gallop, Jane, 128

games, 10, 57; "Jew, Not a Jew" (SNL), 23–26, 28–29, 286n27; "Jew or Not a Jew" (Hey Alma), 61–62, 294n1, "Jewish geography," 62, 294n2
Gamwell, Lynn, 45, 284n1, 291n1, 291n2, 291n3
Garner, Eric, 87
Gay, Peter, 151, 222, 234, 308n51, 315n39, 321n65
Geller, Jay, 3, 262
gender, 117, 262, 302n49, 303n50, 304n80, 304n85, 319n28
Genosko, Gary, 266, 327n48
geology, 35, 45, 65
German, 15, 24–25, 30–34, 43, 50–53, 61–63, 66, 74, 81, 105–10, 116, 120, 123–34, 138, 141, 147, 163, 169, 184, 187–93, 197–99, 201–3, 206–11, 231–33, 247; critical edition of Freud's work, 106, 184; as a Jewish language, 81, 294n5; Viennese, 8; and Yiddish, 32–34, 36, 51–57, 59, 61–63, 66, 100–1, 120–21, 130–33, 187–95, 200–208, 227, 283n1, 292n21, 292n30, 293n39;
German literature, 42, 65, 73, 141
Germany, 32, 142, 166–67, 176, 183, 199, 209, 212, 219, 234, 266, 316n39, 317n72, 318n1
Gesell, Arnold, 325n7
Gillman, Abigail, 250, 292n29
Gilman, Sander L., 3–4, 51, 57, 92, 96–97, 102, 106, 281n7, 292n21
Ginsburg, Ruth, 245–47, 306n30, 324n102, 324n103, 324n104
Glaspell, Susan, 308n50
Gliksman, Avrom, 141–42, 161–65, 184, 200, 305n16, 306n16, 309n83
glossaries, 84, 184, 201, 222, 225, 243, 316n46
Glossary Committee, 107–8, 301n20
Glossary of Psychoanalytic Terms (Jones), 184

God, 36–37, 53, 55, 137, 145, 170, 175, 177, 220, 232, 253. *See also* Adonai
Goldfaden, Abraham, 136
Goldhill, Simon, 277–79, 329n3
Goldwyn, Samuel, 153
Gordon, Yehuda Leib, 41, 63, 289n68
Gottesman, Itzik, 2
Graf, Herbert, 260–62, 270, 326n32, 327n34, 328n60. *See also* little Hans
Graf, Max, 260–61, 269–70, 326n32, 327n32
Graf, Olga Hönig, 260
grandfathers, 170–71, 276–77, 286n19, 311n109
Grasina, Ana Alexandra G., 305n5
Greek, 45, 48, 106, 108, 185, 229
Greenberger, David, 134
Greenwald, Dr. M, 171, 173, 311n105
Groshn-bibliotek, 156–57, 160, 309n67
Grubrich-Simitis, Ilse, 300n7
Guattari, Felix, 10, 264–65
Guralnik, Orna, 92
Gutsman, Benjamin, 175

Haifa, 65, 210, 218
Hake, Sabine, 47
Hale, Nathan G., 293n39
Hameati, Nathan, 320n43
Hammerschlag, Samuel, 25
Handelman, Susan, 118
Harshav, Benjamin, 138
Hartevelt Kobrin, Nancy, 42–43, 290n76
Hasidism, 19, 24, 52–53, 141–42, 146, 167, 169, 195, 235, 310n96, 314n30. *See also* Jewish mysticism
Haskalah, 11, 41, 63, 188
H.D. *See* Doolittle, Hilda
Hebrew, 31–32, 41, 53, 62–67, 74, 98, 106, 119–20, 130, 138, 169, 171, 175–80, 184, 188–89, 275, 288n58, 294n5, 294n13, 309n80, 320n43, 321n59; as acrolect, 37, 129, 138, 163–64, 168; as Jewish language, 11, 127–29, 294n5; as language of liturgy, 51, 55, 67, 246; component of Yiddish, 36, 120–21, 163–64, 195, 206, 226; Freud's knowledge of, 6, 8, 18, 22, 28, 30, 57, 66, 176, 267, 272; in Freud's work, 13, 14, 18, 54–55, 82–83, 123–27, 133, 206, 304n79; inscription in family Bible, 25, 28, 272; and masculinity, 38, 52, 288n58; names, 7, 22–23, 117, 229, 266–67; new speakers of, 121–23, 219; philology, 83; psychoanalytic terms in, 202, 222–26, 243; rabbinic, 37, 123, 223–226, 230; revival of, 7, 11–12, 121–22, 129, 212, 226, 230, 232, 318n8; script, 7, 12, 16, 18, 19, 30, 33, 98, 189, 227, 284n3, 287n47
Hebrew College (Baltimore), 261
Hebrew College (Boston), 209
Hebrew Language Academy, 222, 243
Hebrew literature, 209–212, 312n124, 318n8, 320n43
Hebrew press, 143–53, 161, 165–71, 174–75, 177–80, 316n52
Hebrew translations of Freud, 2, 5–16, 44, 72, 80, 83, 123, 133, 171, 174, 200–6, 210–17, 221–36, 242–47, 249, 277, 306n30, 311n107, 316n52
Beyond the Pleasure Principle, 245
Group Psychology, 200, 223–24, 226–27
Interpretation of Dreams (1959), 2, 146–47, 221, 306n30, 319n23
Interpretation of Dreams (2007), 245, 306n30
Introduction to Psychoanalysis (1934), 6, 206, 223
Introduction to Psychoanalysis (1965), 243
Moses and Monotheism (Freud's desire that Dwossis translate), 174, 224
Moses and Monotheism (1978), 245
Moses and Monotheism (2009), 245–47

Psychopathology of Everyday Life, 72–75, 214, 230–34
"Resistances to Psychoanalysis," 200, 223
Three Essays on the Theory of Sexuality, 226
The Uncanny, 245, 247
Writings of Sigmund Freud, 242
Hebrew University, 149–50, 178, 222, 237–39, 313n11
Heine, Heinrich, 211, 290n75
Heller-Roazen, Daniel, 39–40, 288n54
Hellerstein, Kathryn, 282n17
Henig, Roni, 212, 318n8
Herzl, Theodor, 54, 72, 93, 95, 103, 211, 216, 239, 241
Heschel, Abraham Joshua, 69
Hewett, Russell, 291n15
Hey Alma, 61–62, 294n1
heymish, 8, 19, 159, 179
hieroglyphics, 48, 60, 110–11, 119, 246, 287n47
Hoffer, Peter T., 322n67
Hoffman, Eva, 32
Hogarth Press, 300n7, 301n24
Hollitscher, Robert, 234–35
Holocaust, 7–8, 32, 67, 88, 90, 98, 183, 192, 202, 238, 241, 281n9, 298n9, 298n17, 323n81
Holy Land, 150, 171, 209, 216–17, 222, 229, 241. *See also* Israel; Palestine
home, 1, 8, 17, 29, 33, 27, 41, 64, 66, 101, 131, 141, 178, 182, 190, 204, 209, 211, 216, 222, 237, 239, 241, 244, 246, 254, 278; Freud's, 25, 153, 176, 232–36, 278
homecoming, 211, 237, 244–45
homeland, 173, 176, 183, 187, 210, 215, 241, 245
homosexuality, 4, 235, 249
horses, 252, 256, 260–65, 269–70, 326n32
Hungary, 113, 190, 192–93, 250

Hutton, Christopher, 187, 293n42
hysteria, 42, 46–49, 124, 186, 188, 291n14, 291n15, 301n24, 312n124

Ibsen, Henrik, 162
id, 44, 105, 108, 119, 201, 206, 299n5, 301n20,
Imago, 161, 207, 225
incest, 140, 180, 207, 228–29, 234
India, 93, 238, 250
infants, 114, 119, 136–37, 253, 264. *See also* children
Inquisition, 41–43, 66, 68, 71, 295n23
interiority, 33, 36–37, 40–41, 43, 63, 69, 81, 197, 221, 257
International Psychoanalytic Association, 193–94, 237–38
International Psychoanalytic Congress (Jerusalem), 237–40, 322n80, 323n88
Isaac, Haim, 230, 243
Israel and Israelis, 36, 38, 93, 175, 177, 182, 209, 212, 215–16, 219, 221–22, 237–42, 248. *See also* Palestine; Palestinians
Israel Psychoanalytic Society, 229, 243
Italian, 50, 186, 245
Italian Jews, 62

Jacobs, Adriana X., 309n74
Jakobson, Roman, 26, 113, 283n25
Janet, Pierre, 135, 305n3
jargon, 15, 50–51, 55–57, 59, 138, 187, 189, 195. *See also* Yiddish
Jelen, Sheila E., 318n6
Jerusalem, 2, 210, 213–14, 216, 218–21, 224, 237–38, 241–42, 308n50, 312n124, 323n88
Jesus, 2, 144, 147, 174, 213
Jewish Agency, 166, 242
Jewish American literature, 70
Jewish authenticity, 11, 37, 41, 64, 81, 97, 284n2
Jewish jokes, 24, 26–27, 43, 57–61,

63–64, 81, 84, 284n2; about the Baroness at her confinement, 58–61, 64, 80–81, 84, 110, 121; about the Galician Jew on a train, 26–27, 57–58; about the two Jews in a train station in Galicia, 76, 80

Jewish languages, 11–16, 21–22, 24–26, 30–37, 62–67, 81–84, 123–24, 127, 129–30, 146–47, 176, 189, 206–7, 294n5; as denigrated, 52, 53, 56, 100, 187; and insult, 123–27, 131, 137–38, 140, 169, 197; and intimacy, 15, 19, 26, 37–40, 64, 81, 88, 197; as layered or stratified, 15, 35, 38, 59, 62, 127, 133, 232; diasporic, 98. *See also* Hebrew; Jewish multilingualism; languages of modern Jewish psyche; Yiddish

Jewish law, 317n72, 322n73

Jewish mothers, 253, 264

Jewish multilingualism, 31, 35–36, 49, 57, 63, 81, 119, 129, 226

Jewish mysticism, 19–20, 40, 117–18, 145, 165, 285n17, 303n53

Jewish National Library, 149, 238

Jewish peddlers, 252, 267

Jewish press, 145, 150, 154–56, 161, 166, 171, 176, 178, 200. *See also* Hebrew press; Yiddish press

Jewish pride, 19, 102, 159, 188, 259, 270

Jewish psychoanalysts, 214, 219–20

Jewish religion and rituals, 117, 224–25, 246, 258, 284n1, 318n72, 322n73, 323n90

Jewish Renaissance, 52, 292n25

Jewish sexuality, 183, 205, 260, 326n31

Jewish Studies, 3, 10, 24, 28, 29, 45, 57, 76, 80, 84, 94–96, 103, 107, 117, 206, 272, 294n4, 310n98

Jewish tradition, 19, 103, 117, 145–46, 207, 224, 245–46, 250, 258, 301n21

Jewish visibility, 4, 23–27, 91, 93

Jewish whiteness, 88–102

Jewish women, 52, 59

Jews, American, 88–103, 99, 182–83, 202, 313n2, 313n5; Ashkenazic, 15, 19, 30, 42, 62, 89, 99, 138, 170, 188, 288n58, 304n79; Galician, 27, 57–58, 82, 283n1; German, 24, 27, 30–34, 43, 52, 63, 69, 74, 133, 165, 167, 175, 211, 282n20, 294n13, 315n35, 317n72, 323n90; Italian, 62, Mizrahi and Sephardic, 30, 42–43, 62, 68, 170, 240 290n76, 312n124; of color, 62, 88, 98, 294n2; Polish, 27, 57, 101, 141, 286n31. *See also* assimilated Jews; Israel and Israelis; *Ostjuden*

Johnson, Barbara, 237

Johnson, Matthew, 51, 292n29

Johnson, Terry, 312n124

Johnston, Ruth D., 282n9

jokes, 24, 26–27, 29, 34, 57–61, 64, 76–77, 80–82, 84, 134–35, 142–43, 228, 286n31, 288n51. *See also* Jewish jokes

Jokl, Katherine, 301n21

Jones, Ernest, 108, 212–14, 219–20, 265–66, 283n1, 284n3, 285n18, 291n12, 291n14, 301n20, 301n21, 312n124, 319n25, 319n26, 327n46

Jonte-Pace, Diane, 18–19, 284n6, 285n9

Jung, Carl, 135, 145, 152, 192, 244, 286n20

Kafka, Franz, 29–30, 32, 40, 70, 289n65

Kahn, Susan Martha, 328n49

Kaminka, Aaron, 177

Kandiyoti, Dalia, 67–68, 295n22, 295n24

Karo, Jacob, 228

Katharina, 48, 109

Katz, Maya Balakirsky, 194–95, 315n35

Katzenelsen, Rivka, 318n5

Kaufmann, Walter, 327n46

kibbutz, 217

Kijak, Moisés, 186, 196, 202, 313n13

Kilcher, Andreas, 40, 289n65

Kirshenblatt-Gimblett, Barbara, 324n6
kinship, 68, 80, 82, 128, 140, 179, 188, 192; with Freud, 171, 214
Kirzane, Jessica, 100, 103, 299n29
Knight, Frank H., 325n7
Knoepfmacher, Hugo, 324n5
Kobrin, Nancy Hartevelt, 42
Kohn, Max, 66, 81
Kollek, Teddy, 237
Krah, Markus, 313n2
Krapf, Eduardo, 119, 303n60
Kraus, Karl, 8, 134, 282n20
Krauss, F. S., 20–21
Kristeva, Julia, 282n16
Kroeber, Alfred L., 325n7
Krüll, Marianne, 283n1
Kurtz, Aaron, 85
Kuspit, Donald, 46, 291n3, 291n5
Kuznitz, Cecile, 157, 294n4, 308n65, 313n11, 324n2

Lacan, Jacques, 10, 40, 76, 79–80, 84, 104–7, 111, 113, 131, 152, 220–21
Ladino, 30–31
language loss, 8, 49, 63, 69, 84, 119, 121, 212
languages of modern Jewish psyche, 30–45, 65–66, 80, 129–30
Latin, 73, 105, 108, 128, 163, 185, 223, 245, 257, 291
Latour, Bruno, 14
Langer, Marie, 149
Laplanche, Jean, 107, 113–17, 133, 302n32, 302n49
Lecercle, Jean-Jacque, 120, 123
Leftwich, Joseph, 178
Legevulam series, 210–11, 244
lehavdil loshn. *See* differentiation language
Lensing, Leo A., 283n20
Lerman, Sarah, 2, 159, 198–99, 201–2, 206, 223, 227, 316n43
Lerner, Paul, 317n72, 323n90
Levi, Itamar, 319n23

Levi, Primo, 62, 86
Lewisohn, Lewis, 154
Liban, Alex, 217
Lilienblum, Leib Moshe, 41
Lipszyc, Adam, 55, 82, 293n37
Liska, Vivian, 294n13
Lispector, Clarice, 78
literary critics and criticism, 71, 78, 201, 211, 307n48, 313n11
literature, 30, 34, 38, 43–44, 68; psychoanalysis as, 106–7; as source for psychoanalysis, 43, 46, 164–65, 290n77
Litt, Solomon, 288n51
little Hans, 4, 250, 260–70, 326n32, 327n40. *See also* Graf, Herbert
Loentz, Elizabeth, 52, 290n72, 292n30
London, 12, 18, 166, 170, 174, 214, 219–20, 224, 276–78, 283n24, 312n123, 312n124, 313n12
Lowenstein, Rudolf, 193
lullabies, 134–40, 305n5
Lynd, Helen, 325n7

Macleod, Roy, 319n30
Magnes, Judah, 149, 238
Mahony, Patrick J., 109, 118–19, 123, 126, 130, 300n11
Maimon, Solomon, 211
mameloshn, 37, 57, 59, 63–64, 84
Mandelshtam, Osip, 65
Manheim, Ralph, 283n1, 289n63
Mann, Barbara E., 281n4
Marcus, Sharon, 71, 296n35, 296n38
Marinelli, Lydia, 57, 138, 305n10
Mark, Yudel, 328n62, 329n62
Marks, Elaine, 68
marriage, 49, 195, 204–5, 234–36, 260, 288n58, 321n65
Marx, Karl, 6, 77, 230, 269
Marxism, 71, 112, 199, 288n51, 309n66, 318n72
Massumi, Brian, 133

materiality, 5, 7, 9, 16, 71, 111, 114–18, 124, 178, 279
maternal instinct, 265
maternal language, 31, 37–38, 65, 121, 173. *See also* mameloshn; mother tongue
maternal rage, 137
mauscheln, 51, 58, 292n21
Mayer, Andreas, 57, 138, 305n10
Mazi, Aharon Meir, 320n43
Mazower, David, 156, 309n67, 309n71
McClintock, Anne, 128, 304n85
McLeod, Roy, 239
medicine, 42, 105–6, 109–10, 125, 143, 156, 162, 185, 192, 209, 216, 222, 291n15, 301n25, 313n6, 315n35, 320n43
Meitlis, Jacob, 178, 312n123
Memmi, Albert, 17, 38
memory, 1, 43, 49, 65, 73, 112, 122, 128, 190, 236, 250, 298n9, 326n32. *See also* amnesia and forgetting
Mendelssohn, Moses, 211
Mental illness, 50, 143–45, 151, 160, 291n15, 315n35
Merkin, Daphne, 300n10
Michaux, Henri, 289n66
midrash, 118, 204, 230
Mintz, Benjamin, 177, 312n120
Mintz, Jerome R., 322n68
Miron, Dan, 182, 279
mistranslation, 111–12, 140, 243
Moscow Psychoanalytic Institute, 193, 218
Moses (biblical character), 69–70, 72, 78, 83, 96, 171, 173–78, 220, 223–24, 237–38, 245–47, 249, 295n31, 312n124, 327n40
Moses, Rafael, 237, 239
Moss, Kenneth B., 199
Mossad Bialik, 156
mother, 19, 23, 30–32, 37, 40, 56, 58, 114, 119–22, 128–29, 134–36, 261, 264. *See also* maternal instinct; maternal rage
mother tongue, 31, 34–35, 38, 57, 63, 66, 119–22, 244–45, 287n45, 288n52, 294n5. *See also* maternal language
mourning, 234, 236
multilingualism, 31, 35–36, 47–49, 63, 84, 129–30, 138, 140, 194, 303n60; and wordplay, 117, 122–23. *See also* bilingualism
museums, 275, 278–79, 329n3. *See also* Freud Museum, London; Freud Museum, Příbor; Freud Museum, Vienna

Nadler, Steven, 244
Nakhmen of Bratslav, 37
narcissism, 175–76, 215, 225, 259
Nathan, Debbie, 67, 295n20
Nazism, 69, 101, 148, 166–68, 180–81, 211, 214, 217, 221
Négritude, 97
Neulander, Judith, 295n20
Neumann, Erich, 310n87
Neumann, Hans, 308n55
Neumann, Heinrich, 310n87
New York, 120, 134, 140, 143–44, 147, 151–53, 166–67, 192–93, 198, 308n57, 310n87
Nida, Eugene A., 302n45
Nietzsche, Friedrich, 77, 86–87
non-Jews, 11, 19, 21, 27, 34, 37, 55, 61–62, 95–97, 102–3, 130, 153, 163, 234, 242, 253–69; children or boys, 130, 169, 262; and dogs, 253–56, 266–69; languages of, 33, 37, 66, 81, 124, 129, 185, 209–11, 253; literature, 34, 42–43, 164; neighborhoods, 34, 36, 253
non-Jewish press, 153, 166
Norich, Anita, 7–8, 282n17, 282n18, 324n102
nostalgia, 63, 104, 105, 212

Oedipus, 16, 134–35, 140, 157, 201, 217, 235, 251, 253, 260–66, 269
Opatoshu, David, 100, 103
Oppenheim, David Ernst, 20, 285n14
Oppenheimer, Jud' Süss (Joseph), 167–68, 310n100
Orgell, Shelley, 240–41, 323n93
Ormian, Haim, 243
Ornston, Darius Gray, 107, 111, 300n5, 300n7, 300n11, 301n16, 301n17, 301n31
Orthodox Jews, 1, 8, 92, 103, 148, 218, 219, 222, 289n70, 315n31, 319n23, 323n90
Orthodox Jewish press, 170, 177–78
Ostjuden, 44, 93, 195, 272, 315n35. *See also* Galician
Our Lady of Victory shrine, 276–77

Paglia, Camille, 244
Palestine, 65, 147, 149, 166, 177, 193, 210, 216–20, 222, 230, 266. *See also* Israel
Palestine Psychoanalytic Society, 193, 218–19, 222
Palestinians, 241–2, 246, 294n5
Pappenheim, Bertha, 15, 42, 48, 50–53, 163, 195, 290n72, 291n12, 292n23, 292n29, 292n30. *See also* Anna O.
parapraxis, 75, 105, 163, 226, 296n54; translation as, 231
Paris, 31, 38, 141, 166, 170, 193, 217
Paris Psychoanalytic Society, 193
Parker, Andrew, 112, 115, 301n15, 302n41
Parry, Benita, 4, 281n5
Parry, Tyler D., 326n26
Pascoe, Emily, 294n1
Paul, 220–21
Pellegrini, Ann, 3, 117, 302n49
Penguin translation, 61, 301n25
Perec, Georges, 64
Perlman, Samuel, 209–14, 230, 244, 246

Pessoa, Fernando, 41, 289n70
phatic function of language, 13, 26, 283n25
Phillips, Adam, 106–7, 245
philology and philologists, 36, 54–55, 79–80, 82–83
pilgrimage, 16, 276–77, 279, 329n2
Plotkin, Mariano Ben, 148
Poe, Edgar Allan, 7, 71–72, 162
Poland, 32, 36, 141–42, 147–48, 156, 190–92, 199, 244, 250, 257, 306n18
Pollin-Galay, Hannah, 32
Polterabend, 234, 236, 321n64
Portnoy, Eddy, 91–92, 298n11
postcolonialism, 3, 97
Prague, 39, 283n1, 287n38
Priver, Gabriel, 140
Probyn, Elspeth, 86, 298n3, 298n4
projection, 4, 58, 107, 168, 171, 180, 195, 215, 286
Proust, Marcel, 29, 106, 281n9, 282n9
psyche, 2, 13, 31, 40, 80, 83, 109, 124, 128, 130, 145, 200; Jewish, 38, 65, 123, 127, 169, 255, 272; stratified, 15, 38, 44–48, 61, 78–81, 112, 162, 246, 288n54; translations of, 105, 110–17, 162; as translator, 110–17, 128, 133;
psychoanalysis: in Buenos Aires, 119, 145, 148–49, 198, 307n39, 313n13; flight from Nazism, 104, 220; global dispersion of, 183, 186–87, 190–93, 219, 221, 250; in Israel, 193, 229, 237–47, 310n87; Jewish influence on, 18, 22, 24, 117–18, 146, 227, 247, 284n3; as a Jewish science, 4, 16, 22, 25, 125, 146, 185, 222, 240–41, 243, 260, 313n8, 313n12, 323n88; of Jewish sources, 161–62, 228, 245; in Palestine, 122–23, 193, 215–19, 222, 225, 319n23; in Poland, 141–42, 190–92, 244–45, 306n18, 314n28; resistance to, 9, 159–61, 204; as scan-

dalous, 151–53; as translation, 15, 48, 109–12, 126, 207, 212, 215
psychoanalysts, 8, 9, 10, 47, 76–78, 83, 92, 93, 104, 106, 113, 122, 125, 134–35, 137, 151, 186–87, 192–96, 214–19, 222, 224–26, 238–42, 268, 307n39, 313n13, 314n25, 315n35, 315n36; multilingual, 31, 38, 119–22, 194–96, 225; refugee, 104–6, 148–49, 214–22
Psychoanalytic Quarterly, 216, 302n38, 303n60, 304n77, 315n38, 327n32
public lectures on psychoanalysis, 141–43, 180, 201; by Bychowski, 200; by Feinstein, 180–81; by Anna Freud, 239, 241, 323n88; by Sigmund Freud, 184, 220, 250, 324n5; by Gliksman, 141–43, 161, 305n16; by Lacan, 104, 299n1; by Laplanche, 115; by Kijak, 186, 198, 313n13; by Rabinowitz, 148; by Said, 241–42
Putnam, James, 299n5

queer theory, 3–5, 79, 297n66, 326n31

rabbinic Hebrew, 37, 52–53, 222–28, 321n44
rabbinic hermeneutics, 40, 118, 122, 145, 164–65, 268
rabbinic Judaism, 52, 138, 170–71, 180, 204, 220, 228, 230, 231, 236, 245, 255, 262
rabbis, 118, 123, 164–65, 171, 177, 194–95, 204, 308n59, 312n121, 315n35, 315n36
Rabbi Yohanan, 187, 220–21
Rabinowitz, Paulina, 148
race, 4, 72, 85–103, 181
Rachman, Arnold William, 315n31
racial thinking, 89, 94–97, 103, 165
racism, 93, 95–97, 99, 102–3, 299n30
Rashab. *See* Schenierson, Sholem Dov
Rat Man. *See* Lanzer, Ernst

Ravitsh, Melekh, 141–42, 162, 306n17
Reik, Theodor, 26–27, 57, 59, 80, 82, 283n1, 286n31, 286n32, 297n69, 297n70
repression, 31, 47, 71, 73, 87, 92, 96, 114, 119, 121 128, 135, 140, 168, 190, 192, 194, 212, 218, 230, 235, 316n57; as political, 118, 242, 314n25; of Jewishnessness, 72–75, 119, 168, 184, 187, 285n9. *See also* return of the repressed
rescue fantasies, 215
Resling Press, 244
retranslations, 112, 115, 124, 126, 243
return of the repressed, 47, 92, 168, 183, 192, 295n31; antisemitism, 87–88, 168
Ricoeur, Paul, 297n57
Rieff, Philip, 208
Riviere, Joan, 108, 299n5, 300n5, 301n20, 301n22
Rivkin, Ellis, 295n23
Roazen, Paul, 75, 190, 314n25
Roback, A. A., 18–25, 143–44, 146, 284n3, 285n10, 285n11, 285n12, 285n13, 285n16, 285n17, 285n18, 286n18, 286n19, 304n88, 306n22 *Jewish Influence on Modern Thought*, 18–19, 22, 24, 117, 146, 227, 247, 284n3, 285n10, 304n88, 306n27; Yiddish dedication of, 24–25
Roback-Freud correspondence, 22–23, 61, 198
Robert, Marthe, 283n1, 295n31
Rolland, Romain, 284n3, 290n75
Rolnik, Eran, 216–17, 223–24, 304n77, 306n28, 306n29, 307n40, 307n41, 318n14, 319n15, 319n19, 319n20, 319n23, 320n36, 320n38, 321n53
Rose, Jacqueline, 242, 244, 323n94, 323n96
Rosetta Stone, 47–48, 51, 246
Roskies, David, 188–89

Rosten, Leo, 60, 293n43, 294n49
Roth, Cecil, 67–68
Roth, Philip, 70
Roth, Samuel, 152–53
Rothberg, Michael, 298n9
Rozenblit, Martha, 290n76
Rudy, Tz., 204, 317n62
Russia, 148, 186, 191, 193, 218
Russian, 64, 120, 122, 186, 193, 199
Ruth, Alysha, 294n2

Sabbath, 162, 206–7, 304n79, 323n90, 317n71, 322n73,
Said, Edward, 242, 246
Saketopoulou, Avgi, 117, 302n49
Samacher, Robert, 119, 121, 287n41, 303n61, 303n67
Sapir, Edward, 250, 324n6
Scanlan, Patrick, 174
Schaechter, Mordkhe, 79, 202
Schalit, Ilja, 218
Schliemann, Heinrich, 45
Schmalhausen, Ivan, 135
Schneierson, Sholem Dov, 1194–96, 315n35
Schreier, Benjamin, 70, 95
Schröter, Michael, 322n69
Schulz, Miram, 100–101, 299n31, 299n32, 299n33, 299n34, 299n35
Schwaber, Paul, 239–40, 242, 323n90, 323n91, 323n92
scriptworlds, 33, 111, 160, 287n47, 309n74
Sedgwick, Eve Kosofsky, 4, 77, 207, 281n6, 282n10
Segal, Hanna, 244
Segalovitz, Yael, 77–78, 297n58, 297n62, 297n63
Segel, Benjamin Wolf, 285n13
Seidman, Naomi, 288n58, 292n42, 305n15, 322n70
sex, 4, 24, 41–42, 48, 52, 72–73, 75, 79–80, 128, 135, 137, 140–43, 152–

53, 156, 163, 191, 204–5, 233–35, 262, 269, 293n39, 302n49, 305n15; Jewish, 4, 92, 141, 183, 189, 204–7, 217, 264, 326n31
sexology, 79, 189, 326n31
sexual aggression and assault, 27, 29, 47, 57, 59, 114–14, 151, 197
sexual difference, 4, 288n58
sexuality, 4, 20, 79–80, 113–14, 117, 193; childhood, 137; Jewish, 20, 183, 260, 326n31; translations of, 204
Sellin, Thorsten, 325n7
Severn, Elizabeth, 315n31
Shaked, Gershon, 70
Shakespeare, William, 50, 164, 290n77
shame, 12, 58, 64, 87, 98, 129, 183, 189–90, 215; about being Jewish, 12, 22, 91, 183, 189, 307n39; scholar's, 86–87
Shandler, Jeffrey, 294n4
Shapiro, Claire I., 136
Shapiro, Susan E., 285n9
Sharpe, Michael, 291n15
Shaw, Bernard, 284n3
Shin Shalom, 72–75, 177, 296n40, 296n42, 296n48
Sholokova, Lyudmila, 156
Shorter, Edward, 291n15
Sigmund Freud Chair, 222, 237–239, 323n88
sign system, 110, 113
Silberstein, Eduard, 43
Simmel, Ernst, 217–18
Simon, Sherry, 278, 329n4
Skolnik, Jonathan, 42
Slavet, Eliza, 29, 95–96, 263
Slavic languages, 36, 39, 101, 120–21, 188
Slesin, Suzanne, 329n3
Slezkine, Yuri, 129
Słonimski, Antoni, 101
Smiliansky, Anna, 218
smoking, 207, 317n71

social sciences, 105, 107, 141, 324n6, 325n7
socialism, 2, 63, 199, 216, 218–19, 316n53
Soviet Union, 62, 148, 156, 190, 192, 199, 316n49
Soyer, Daniel, 326n30
Spinoza, Baruch, 43, 162–63, 244, 289n70, 290n70, 290n75
Spitz, Ellen Handler, 291n1
Spitzweg, Carl, 3, 281n2
St. Petersburg, 65
Stadlen, Anthony, 313n12
Stanislawski, Michael, 289n68
Steinberg, Isaac Nachman, 178–79, 248, 312n123, 312n125, 314n19, 324n1
Steiner, George, 31, 33, 35, 63, 213–14, 287n40, 287n48, 288n53, 291n13, 318n10, 318n11
Stekel, Wilhelm, 145, 194–96, 311n114, 315n35
Stephanitz, Van, 327n48
Stone, Jon, 291n15
Strachey, Alix, 108, 282n11, 300n8, 301n21, 301n22
Strachey, James, 55, 58, 105–8, 111–12, 114, 163, 184–85, 201, 300n5, 300n7, 300n8, 300n13, 301n20, 301n21
Suchoff, David Bruce, 289n65
superego, 108, 119, 127
surface reading, 2, 5–7, 13, 15, 18–19, 71, 84, 94, 296n35, 296n38
surfaces, 2, 5, 7, 13, 15, 18–19, 24, 30, 33, 35, 37, 61–84, 121–22
Switzerland, 142, 218
Szasz, Thomas, 282n20
Szold, Henrietta, 219–21, 319n24, 321n51
Szymaniak, Karolina, 155, 308n64, 308n65

Taber, Charles R., 302n45

Taiana, Cecilia, 148–49
talking cure, 50, 53, 118–19, 159, 163–64, 259
Talmud, 18, 65, 77, 118, 201, 221, 224, 228, 231, 255, 283n1
Tannenbaum, Samuel A., 151, 307n48
Tausk, Marius, 296n54
Tausk, Victor, 74–76, 80, 128, 296n51, 296n53, 296n54
Taylor, Breonna, 85, 87, 93, 298n17
Teller, Yehuda Leyb (Judd), 167–69, 310n96, 310n97, 310n100, 311n101
Tenenbaum, Adam, 226
Tel Aviv, 2, 193, 209, 210, 218, 221, 243, 307n47, 310n87, 321n53
Teresa of Avila, 41
Thomson, Mathew, 319n15
Toller, Ernst, 316n44
Torquemada, 43
Totemism, 227–30
Trachtenberg, Barry, 288n56
transference, 11, 80, 109, 112–14, 117, 180, 194–97, 245, 266, 268, 291n14
translation: and affect, 11–14, 79, 114–17, 125, 132–33, 211–15, 242; as assimilation, 104–6, 185, 213, 221; as betrayal, 14, 128, 215; of dead languages, 111; as displacement, 79, 11–13, 124, 131, 211, 231, 277; as encounter with the foreign, 82–83, 116–19, 247; of enigmatic messages, 39, 83, 111, 114–17, 127, 194, 273; Freud's conception of, 15m 109–17, 130; improper or abnormal, 113, 120, 122, 124, 231; interlingual, 113, 122, 123; intersemiotic, 113, 123; as intimate entanglement, 14–16, 79–80, 269; intralingual, 113, 122; and Jewish linguistic conceptions, 117–19, 122–23; Laplanche's conception of, 107, 113–17, 124, 126, 133; and loss, 107, 199, 206, 211, 215; as the movement of sacred relics, 277–78; as recovery,

106–8, 184, 212, 235–36; as rescue and salvage, 16, 211–15, 221, 318n6; and temporality, 112–17, 125
trauma, 8, 41–43, 46–49, 67, 78, 112, 115, 119, 125, 135, 189–90, 254–58, 264, 326; Holocaust, 238, 241
Trunk, Y.Y., 141
Tshernikhovski, Saul, 320n43
Turkow, Jonas, 155
Turner, Victor, 244
Tversky, Yohanan, 223
Tyson, Alan, 125, 230, 233–34, 237, 282n11, 300n8

uncanny, 18–19, 39, 160, 179–80, 232, 247, 285n9
unconscious, 16, 29, 43, 72–73, 77, 87, 92, 105–7, 114, 128, 136, 143, 148, 151, 157, 160, 162–65, 168, 190, 193, 203, 215, 216, 223, 225, 232–34, 237, 262, 278–79, 302n44, 302n49, 306n34, 314n25, 315n33, 315n34, 317n57; and antisemitism, 262, 284n2; as cellar, 136, 182–83, 208, 279; as closet, 278–79; and Hebrew, 122–23; Hebrew translation of, 226; Jewishness, 43, 250–61; and language, 114, 193–94, 303n60; proto-Freudian conceptions of, 43, 45–46, 164, 290n77; and translation, 14, 39, 79, 114–16, 126, 147, 223, 231, 313n6; and Yiddish, 38, 40, 66, 84, 182–83, 187–190; Yiddish translation of, 162, 201–2, 316n57
United States of America, 98, 100, 104, 151–53, 157, 166, 219, 229, 258, 293n39, 299n3
US Immigration Act, 125

Valenstein, 239, 323n85
Végső, Roland, 231, 321n55
Velikhovsky, Immanuel, 122, 304n71, 304n72

Vermorel, Henri, 290n75
Vienna, 8–9, 74, 104–5, 131–32, 144–45, 166–67, 173, 176, 209–10, 266–67, 276–78, 283n1, 290n76, 291n1, 310n87, 310n96
Vienna Psychoanalytic Society, 190, 218, 220, 260
Viennese Jews, 48–49, 119, 266
Vilna, 16, 143, 182, 184, 189, 256, 259, 269; ghetto, 180–81, 312n129
Voloshinov, Valentin, 316n49

Wagner, Richard, 34, 288n50
Wakefield, Jerome C., 327n32
Wallach, Yonah, 320n43
Warhol, Andy, 278
Warlow, Charles, 291n15
Warsaw, 3, 65, 101, 142, 147, 150, 151, 155, 161, 166, 170, 175, 192–93, 198–99, 245
weddings, 233–236. *See also* marriage
Weiman-Kelman, Zohar, 8, 79, 297n67, 304n89, 314n22, 326n31
Weininger, Otto, 262
Weinreich, Max, 12, 187, 189, 199–200, 204, 223, 227, 279, 308n65, 316n44, 316n49; and American Jews, 182–83, 202, 261; antisemitic attack on, 257; as authorized translator of Freud, 16, 184, 192, 198, 200, 224; as expositor of Freud, 160–1, 198, 324n2 ; as founder and leader of YIVO, 182–83, 250; and Freud, 7, 16, 131, 187, 220, 249–51, 259–60, 307n46, 319n26; Freud notebook, 84, 183–86, 316n46, 317n66; *History of the Yiddish Language*, 102, 202–3; non-native Yiddish, 64, 121; *Path to Our Youth*, 3, 102, 202,205, 250–60, 270; and race theory, 99–103, 256–58, 326n21, 326n27; translation choices, 202–8, 243, 272, 316n57, 328n62; Yale Seminar, 251–56, 324n6, 325n7,

325n8, 325n9; youth research, 13, 16, 198, 252–72, 325n15, 326n31. See also Yiddish translations of Freud, *Introduction to Psychoanalysis*; YIVO
Weinreich, Uriel, 197, 202, 317n60
Weiser, Kalman, 63
Wells, Richard, 284n1, 291n1, 291n2, 291n3
Wetherall, Margaret, 132
Whiteread, Rachel, 278
Wilde, Oscar, 278
Wise, Rabbi Stephen, 154
Wissenschaft, 86, 145, 185, 249
Wissenschaft des Judentum, 185, 289n65
Wissler, Clark, 325n7
Wolf-Man, 104
Wolfson, Louis, 120–22, 303n62, 303n63, 303n64
Wollstonecraft, Mary, 51–52, 292n23
Woolf, Leonard and Virginia, 152, 301n21
Wortis, Joseph, 317n71, 328n58
Woyslawski, Zvi, 72, 214, 226, 230, 232, 236–37, 245
Wulf, Sh. Z., 156–57, 159, 308n66, 309n68
Wulff, Moshe, 193, 202, 218

Yahuda, Abraham Shalom, 312n124
Yale Seminar on Culture and Personality, 250–56, 324n6
Yavneh, 187, 220–21
Yavneh Press, 221
Yehuda Leib Teller, Yehuda Leib, 166–68
Yerushalmi, Yosef Hayim, 6–7, 24–26, 28, 71, 282n14, 282n15, 283n1, 284n1, 284n2, 286n22, 286n23, 286n24, 295n31, 323n88, 328n50
Yeshiva, 187, 230–31, 235
yetzer, 204–5
Yiddish, 5–8, 10–15, 18–26, 30–40, 44, 51–66, 79–84, 97–103, 119–22, 129–31, 137–42, 173–75, 182–208, 224–27, 258, 270–72, 283n1, 284n1, 284n2; accent, 32, 57, 139, 292n21; as "bedrock" of the Jewish psyche, 40, 81, 272–273; Blackness in, 97–99, 299n28; "component consciousness," 203–4; components of, 36, 101, 121, 138, 141, 163–64, 206, 309n80; as deformed or grotesque, 11, 15, 53, 130, 188; eruption of, 34–35, 58, 63, 108, 127, 129; femininity, 57, 119, 121, 183, 187, 288n58; German component of, 36, 101, 121, 203, 227; as preserving German history, 193; Hebrew component of, 36, 120–21, 163–64, 195, 206, 226, 309n80; high culture, 44, 139, 143, 147, 155, 157, 162, 163, 197, 249; ideologies about, 11–15, 30, 35, 38, 45, 57, 61, 63, 67, 69, 72, 100, 121, 129, 157, 173, 186–89, 196, 249, 325n15; insult, 27, 120, 123–24, 126–27, 131, 133, 137–38, 169, 197, 257, 262–63; ; interiority, 33, 36–37, 40, 63, 81, 83, 197; intimacy, 8, 15, 19, 31, 36–37, 40, 58, 64, 81, 87, 119, 197, 284n2; as *Jargon*, 11, 15, 37, 50–59, 100, 138, 187–88, 195, 287n38; as language of science, 179–181, 185–87; association with the left, 100; lowness, 35–38, 44, 121, 129, 155, 183; as *mame-loshn*, 64, 294n6, 294n9, 299n31; neologisms, 205, 272, 328n62; philology, 36, 189, 288n56, 299n31; proverbs, 20, 53, 285n13; proximity to German, 187–88, 202, 227; psychoanalytic terms in, 36, 101, 120–21, 162, 188, 203, 204, 316n57; Slavic component of, 36, 101, 120–21, 188, 203
Yiddish Language Conference, 294n6
Yiddish literature, 18, 20, 44, 52, 100, 138, 141, 164–65, 221, 231, 156–57, 164, 186, 284n3

Yiddish press, 143–44, 146–47, 149–154, 161–62, 165–66, 180, 306n32
Yiddishism and Yiddishists, 7, 12, 38, 97, 100, 103, 156–57, 173, 178, 188–90, 199, 203, 273
Yiddishland, 155, 192
yidishkayt, 93–94, 97, 99–101, 103, 257–58, 263, 272–73, 299n31
Yiddish Studies, 36, 98, 100, 294n4
Yiddish translations of Freud, 2, 9, 10, 13, 84, 127, 131, 141, 161, 184 192, 197–98, 201, 206, 226
  Future of an Illusion, 198
  Group Psychology, 2, 159, 198–201, 223, 226–27, 316n33, 316n34
  Introduction to Psychoanalysis, 6,7, 133, 189, 200, 207–8, 243, 304n88, 314n24
yidishe visnshaft, 179, 181, 185, 187
Yildiz, Yasemin, 32, 287n45, 288n52, 294n5
YIVO, 131, 155, 157, 180–89, 202; chapters, 18, 148, 178–80, 198, 269; and Hebrew University, 185–86, 313n11; and "Jewish science," 16, 178–79, 183–85, 248–50, 270; Presidium, 20, 150–51, 172, 200, 269, 284n3, 307n46, 307n47; psychoanalysis at, 192, 199, 249, 308n65, 313n13, 324n2; and *Wissenschaft des Judentum*, 185–86; youth research, 250–59, 316n57, 325n15. *See also* YIVO press; youth autobiographies
YIVO press, 131, 184

Yofi, 7, 267–68, 328n55
Yom Kippur, 27, 29, 287n35, 301n21
Young, Jennifer, 256, 326n19
Young, Robert, 109, 256, 301n24, 301n25, 326n21, 326n27
youth, 30–31, 99, 102, 198, 204–5, 250–52, 254, 259–60, 299n35, 299n36, 299n37, 317n57, 317n65, 325n8, 325n11, 325n12, 325n13, 325n14. *See also* adolescence
youth autobiographies, 254–55, 259–60, 316n57, 326n31. *See also* YIVO
youth movements, 64, 199, 217, 255
Yovel, Yirmiyahu, 41, 289n70
Yurenets, V., 316n49

Zangwill, Israel, 146
Zaretzky, Eli, 191
Zeitlin, Aaron, 174, 311n113
Zenderland, Leila, 256, 325n7, 326n19, 326n20
Zhitlowsky, Chaim, 157
Zion, 136, 219, 222, 307n41, 316n53, 319n15, 319n23, 320n38, 321n53
Zionists and Zionism, 98, 148–50, 166, 170–71, 212, 216, 218–21, 232, 240–41, 266, 305n16, 313n11, 318n13, 319n23
Zivin, Erin Graff, 68, 295n26
Žižek, Slavoj, 82–83, 273
Zweig, Arnold, 6, 219, 267, 282n15, 328n50
Zweig, Stefan, 170, 311n103

STANFORD STUDIES IN JEWISH HISTORY AND CULTURE

David Biale and Sarah Abrevaya Stein, Editors

This series features novel approaches to examining the Jewish past in the form of innovative work that brings the field into productive dialogue with the newest scholarly concepts and methods. Open to a range of disciplinary and interdisciplinary approaches, from history to cultural studies, this series publishes exceptional scholarship, balanced by an accessible tone that illustrates histories of difference and addresses issues of current urgency. Books in this list push the boundaries of Jewish Studies and speak compellingly to a wide audience of scholars and students.

Immanuel Etkes, *The Invention of a Tradition: The Messianic Zionism of the Gaon of Vilna*

2024

Viola Alianov-Rautenberg, *No Longer Ladies and Gentlemen: Gender and the German-Jewish Migration to Mandatory Palestine*

2024

Susan Rubin Suleiman, *Daughter of History: Traces of an Immigrant Girlhood*

2023

Sandra Fox, *The Jews of Summer: Summer Camp and Jewish Culture in Postwar America*

2023

David Biale, *Jewish Culture Between Canon and Heresy*

2023

Alan Verskin, *Diary of a Black Jewish Messiah: The Sixteenth-Century Journey of David Reubeni through Africa, the Middle East, and Europe*

2023

Aomar Boum, Illustrated by Nadjib Berber, *Undesirables: A Holocaust Journey to North Africa*

2023

Dina Porat, *Nakam: The Holocaust Survivors Who Sought Full-Scale Revenge*

2023

Christian Bailey, *German Jews in Love: A History*

2023

Matthias B. Lehmann, *The Baron: Maurice de Hirsch and the Jewish Nineteenth Century*

2022

Liora R. Halperin, *The Oldest Guard: Forging the Zionist Settler Past*

2021

Samuel J. Spinner, *Jewish Primitivism*
2021

Sonia Gollance, *It Could Lead to Dancing: Mixed-Sex Dancing and Jewish Modernity*
2021

Julia Elsky, *Writing Occupation: Jewish Émigré Voices in Wartime France*
2020

Alma Rachel Heckman, *The Sultan's Communists: Moroccan Jews and the Politics of Belonging*
2020

Golan Y. Moskowitz, *Wild Visionary: Maurice Sendak in Queer Jewish Context*
2020

Devi Mays, *Forging Ties, Forging Passports: Migration and the Modern Sephardi Diaspora*
2020

Clémence Boulouque, *Another Modernity: Elia Benamozegh's Jewish Universalism*
2020

Dalia Kandiyoti, *The Converso's Return: Conversion and Sephardi History in Contemporary Literature and Culture*
2020

Natan M. Meir, *Stepchildren of the Shtetl: The Destitute, Disabled, and Mad of Jewish Eastern Europe, 1800–1939*
2020

Marc Volovici, *German as a Jewish Problem: The Language Politics of Jewish Nationalism*
2020

Dina Danon, *The Jews of Ottoman Izmir: A Modern History*
2019

Omri Asscher, *Reading Israel, Reading America: The Politics of Translation between Jews*
2019

For a complete listing of titles in this series, visit the
Stanford University Press website, www.sup.org.

The authorized representative in the EU for product safety and compliance is:
Mare Nostrum Group
B.V Doelen 72
4831 GR Breda
The Netherlands

www.ingramcontent.com/pod-product-compliance
Lightning Source LLC
Chambersburg PA
CBHW030604230426
43661CB00053B/1835